BIG FELLOW, LONG FELLOW

A JOINT BIOGRAPHY OF COLLINS AND DE VALERA

BIG FELLOW, LONG FELLOW

A JOINT BIOGRAPHY OF COLLINS AND DE VALERA

T. RYLE DWYER

St. Martin's Press
New York

BIG FELLOW, LONG FELLOW
Copyright © 1998 by T. Ryle Dwyer

St. Martin's Press, Scholarly and Reference Division,
175 Fifth Avenue, New York, N.Y. 10010

First published in the United States of America in 1998

Printed in Ireland

ISBN: 0-312-21919-9

Library of Congress Cataloging-in-Publication Data

Dwyer, T. Ryle.
Big fellow, long fellow : a joint biography of Collins and de
Valera / T. Ryle Dwyer.
p. cm.
Includes bibliographical references and index.
ISBN 0-312-21919-9
1. Collins, Michael, 1890-1922. 2. Ireland—History—Civil War.
1922-1923—Biography. 3. Ireland—Politics and government—20th
century. 4. Revolutionaries—Ireland—Biography. 5. Presidents—
Ireland—Biography. 6. De Valera, Eamon, 1882-1975. I. Title.
DA965.C6D97 1999
941.5082'2'092—dc21

[B]   98-34378
                                                            CIP

To Harry

CONTENTS

PREFACE

My interest in Irish history developed quite by chance at university in the United States in 1966. While taking a course on European history between the world wars at the University of North Texas, I chose to write a term paper on the Irish Civil War. I had grown up in Ireland from the age of four and received all my primary and secondary schooling in Tralee, but I was intrigued to learn that the partition question had essentially nothing to do with the Treaty split between Eamon de Valera and Michael Collins that was largely blamed for the ensuing Civil War.

As this was not a period of history that was covered in Irish schools in either the 1950s or the early 1960s, I became fascinated with the subject and later wrote a Master's thesis on the Treaty negotiations, and a doctoral dissertation on relations between the United States and Ireland during the Second World War. This book draws heavily on research going back over thirty years. I have already written both a short and a full-length biography of de Valera, as well as two detailed studies of his quest for national independence, and two monographs on Collins: *Michael Collins: 'The Man Who Won the War'*, and *Michael Collins and the Treaty*.

During the course of the ongoing research I corresponded with a number of people who appear in these pages, including de Valera, Robert Barton, Seán Mac Eoin, Ernest Blythe, Geoffrey Shakespeare, and Tom Barry. I would like to acknowledge the help of the late Liam Collins who trusted me with his trunk of papers of Michael Collins, even though someone to whom he had previously loaned diaries had never returned them.

My only agenda is to tell the story as fairly and as dispassionately as I can. On all sides people succeeded and made mistakes, even though partisans of de Valera and Collins have tended to paint the period in black and white terms, whereas in reality there were many shades of grey. It was for long assumed that the two men worked closely together and trusted each other implicitly until the Treaty split, but their differences really went back much earlier.

This is a study of the parallel lives of de Valera and Collins with emphasis on how their careers intermingled and finally diverged. Their differences undoubtedly became a major factor in the split that led to the Civil War and cast a shadow over Irish politics not just for decades, but arguably for most of the century.

TRD

Tralee,
September 1998

1

An Unwanted and a Cherished Child

Eamon de Valera was an unlikely Irish hero, much less the virtual personification of nationalist Ireland. Born in New York city on 14 October 1882, he was the son of an Irish immigrant mother, Catherine Coll, and, according to her, a Spanish father, Vivion de Valera.

Considerable mystery surrounds Vivion de Valera. According to Eamon — or Edward as he was christened and called until his adult years — his parents were married in New York in 1881, but there is apparently no mention of the marriage in the church records. Shortly after Eamon was born, Vivion moved west for health reasons and died two years later in Denver. If he died of tuberculosis, the mystery surrounding him would be understandable, because Irish people tended to view the disease as a kind of social plague. If spoken about at all, it was in terms of being as bad as some fatal venereal disease.

When Eamon was two years old his mother sent him to Ireland with her brother to be reared by her own family near the village of Bruree, County Limerick, while she remained in the United States. Eamon never forgot his first morning in the Coll family home — a one-roomed thatched cottage, housing himself, his grandmother, two uncles and an aunt. He woke up to find the house deserted. The family was moving to a new slate-roofed, three-roomed labourer's cottage nearby and nobody had bothered to ensure the child would not be frightened waking up alone in a strange, deserted house.

It has long been believed that a person's character is shaped as a child. Like any child, de Valera would have first looked to his parents for security. Never having known his father, he would have become especially dependent on his mother, and his subsequent separation from her would undoubtedly have had a profound effect on him. She remained in the United States, and the uncle who brought him to Bruree soon returned to America, to be followed shortly afterwards by Eamon's teenage aunt, Hannie, to whom he had become attached. Thus the people to whom de Valera looked first for security during those formative years were in America, and it was hardly surprising that he would look first to the United States for help or security throughout his life.

His mother visited Bruree briefly in 1887, before returning to the United States, leaving the boy to be reared by her mother, Elizabeth, and her brother, Pat. Eamon's mother was planning to remarry and he pleaded with her to take him back, but she refused. One can only imagine the scarring consequences of being rejected by his mother, especially when the rejection fuelled speculation about his legitimacy.

Before emigrating Catherine Coll worked as a domestic servant in a large house owned by the Atkinson family, and there was considerable local speculation that she had become pregnant by Thomas Atkinson, the randy son of the owner. It was rumoured that the Atkinsons paid for her to go to America to conceal the pregnancy. It would have been understandable for an Irish emigrant to send home an illegitimate child to be reared by her family, and even to leave the child in Ireland after she married; but it was something else for a former widow not to reclaim a legitimate child after she had remarried, and especially after she had started a second family.

De Valera always maintained that his mother emigrated two years before he was born. If this was true, Tom Atkinson could not have been his father, but no biographer has yet found evidence of his mother's arrival in the United States. Possibly nobody ever looked for this evidence, because in the last analysis it is of little historical importance. Whether de Valera was illegitimate or not is not nearly as important as the rumours that he was illegitimate, because those rumours clearly bothered him.

When he began at the local national school at the age of five, he was registered as Edward Coll. This may have been the first sign of a certain sensitivity that de Valera would later betray about his foreign background. Maybe his touchiness was the result of conditioning brought on by the attitude of his grandmother or uncle, or just the reaction of a little boy trying to fit into a society in which he probably felt rejected.

He would later recall being irritated that his uncle was known locally as 'the Dane Coll', which was one of those family nicknames transferred from father to son. De Valera's grandfather, Patrick Coll, used to lead prayers in the local church and as a result he was given the nickname, 'the Dean', which was pronounced locally as 'the Dane', much to the subsequent embarrassment of his grandson, who thought the nickname had something to do with the Norse invaders who had plundered Ireland a millennium before.

Saddled with supporting his elderly mother and young nephew, Pat Coll was a rather frustrated individual. He could not afford to get married and seemed to take out his frustration by being severe on the boy. He disapproved of him playing games, which he considered were a waste of time. De Valera was expected to perform various duties.

'From my earliest days I participated in every operation that takes place on a farm,' he later recalled. 'Until I was sixteen years of age, there was no farm work, from the spancelling of a goat to the milking of a cow, that I had not to deal with. I cleaned out the cowhouses. I followed the tumbler rake. I took my place on top of the rick. I took my place on the cart and filled the float of hay. I took milk to the creamery. I harnessed the donkey, the jennet, and the horse.'

He never learned to plough, because the Colls had only a half-acre of land. It was not even enough to support the three or four cows owned by his uncle. As a result they used what de Valera called 'the long farm' — the grass margins by the roadside. This was against the law, so he was given the task of keeping watch for the police. If he saw them approaching he would just pretend to be driving the cattle from one field to another.

While on 'the long farm', de Valera relieved the boredom by reading books about the French Revolution, Scottish mythology, and Abbé MacGeoghegan's *History of Ireland*. He did not study history at school, so he knew little about Irish history. He later credited the local parish priest, Father Eugene Sheehy, with introducing him to nationalist politics, though he could not have been very impressed with the early introduction, because it was some years before he showed any interest in the nationalist renaissance taking place at the time.

De Valera's aunt, Hannie, returned from the United States for a short period to nurse her ailing mother before the latter's death in 1895. Hannie then returned to the United States, leaving de Valera to undertake much of the housekeeping and the preparation of his uncle's meals. As a result the boy's school attendance suffered. Clearly disillusioned with life in Bruree, he wrote to Hannie in January 1896, pleading with her to intercede with his mother to allow him to return to America, but his efforts were in vain.

He did manage to persuade his uncle, however, to allow him to attend the Christian Brothers' secondary school in Charleville, some seven miles from home. He frequently made the long journey to and from school on foot. He won a three-year scholarship worth £20 a year for his results in the junior grade examination of 1898. This allowed him to continue his education at a boarding school. Although he was rejected by the two boarding schools in Limerick, a local priest managed to get him accepted into Blackrock College in the Dublin suburbs.

Why was he rejected? Was it because of the rumours of his illegitimacy? The £20 a year did not quite cover his full costs at Blackrock College and it was rumoured locally that the Atkinson family made up the difference. Another possibility is that the Holy Ghost Fathers who ran the school waived the remainder of the fee. Whatever the case, they indignantly ignored a request from Pat Coll for £5 out of the scholarship for himself.

Blackrock College had a strict routine. Boys rose at six o'clock in the morning and had a full schedule of prayer, class, study, and recreation outlined for each day. Discipline was strict and they were obliged to remain silent going to class and during meals, as well as during study periods. Among de Valera's classmates were the future Roman Catholic Cardinal and Primate of Ireland, John D'Alton, and the famous Gaelic poet, Pádraic Ó Conaire.

De Valera initially had difficulty fitting into his new class midway through secondary school, especially when he had to adjust to a very different environment. It would have been quite normal for a fifteen-year-old boy to have been homesick on going away to school for the first time, but he was delighted to get away. On his first night, he later recalled, he lay in bed thanking God for his deliverance from Bruree. He just could not understand the sobbing homesickness of the boy in the next bed.

Boys brought up in the stable atmosphere of warm family surroundings were naturally homesick and sought compensation by forming new friendships, but de Valera, having been reared in cold, loveless surroundings, had no pressing need for camaraderie. He would not become particularly friendly with anyone during his first year. 'He had,' according to one of his teachers, 'a certain dignity of manner, a gentleness of disposition, a capability of adapting himself to circumstances, or perhaps I should rather say, of utilising those circumstances that served his purpose.'

Despite initial misgivings, de Valera fitted into his new surroundings relatively quickly. In the school examinations before Christmas he was placed sixth in a class of eighteen, which was headed by John D'Alton, who later remembered de Valera as 'a good, very serious student, good at Mathematics but not outstanding otherwise'. Ironically, in addition to finishing at the top of his class in arithmetic, de Valera also finished first in religious instruction, leaving the future cardinal in his wake.

It would have been natural for de Valera to look forward to going home for the Christmas break, but he asked to remain at the school instead. He later said his memories of his first Christmas at Blackrock were his most vivid recollection of his years there. It was obvious that he had begun to look on the college as a kind of home. For a time he would seriously consider entering the priesthood with the Holy Ghost Fathers. In later life he liked to return to the college for the midnight services at Christmas, and he repeatedly made his home in the Blackrock area. He even chose to move into a nursing home there when he retired from public life over seventy years later.

Blackrock College was a good school and de Valera was one of its star pupils. In the public examinations at the end of his first year, the college won more prizes and scholarships than any other school in the country. Three classmates won gold medals for finishing first in Ireland in specific subjects. Although de Valera was not among the gold medalists, his accumulated marks in the various subjects were the highest in his class, so he had the distinction of being Student of the Year. As such he was appointed reader of prayers in the church, study hall and dormitory, and he was the main reader in the dining-room during retreats. But he later recounted that he was haunted in his new role with memories of that dreaded nickname, 'the Dane Coll'. His disquiet was probably as much a reflection of his unhappy childhood as of his unease about his own background.

During his second year at Blackrock, de Valera became friendly with a new boy, Frank Hughes, who brought him home to Kiltimagh, County Mayo, for Christmas 1899. They were to cement a lifelong friendship in which each would act as best man at the other's wedding and stand as godfather to the other's first child.

After finishing secondary school at the turn of the century, de Valera still had one year of his scholarship from Charleville remaining, so he enrolled at University College, Blackrock, an extension of the secondary school. Opportunities for third-level education were quite limited for Roman Catholics at the time, since Trinity College Dublin was almost exclusively Protestant and the Royal University of Ireland — the alternative prior to the founding of the National University of Ireland in 1908 — was strictly an examining body. The various Catholic colleges scattered throughout the country prepared students for examinations conducted by the Royal University.

Blackrock College was handicapped in that none of its teachers was involved in either setting or marking examination papers. De Valera thought students at other colleges, whose professors helped to set the examination papers, had an unfair advantage, because their professors inevitably made sure the material relating to the examination questions was thoroughly covered in their classes. Although he felt unfairly handicapped in the competitive examination system, he still received second class honours in his first arts examination. As a result, he got a three-year scholarship from the Royal University.

While studying for his degree he was particularly active in the college's debating society, where he displayed a distinctly conservative outlook. He contended, for instance, that 'the old monastic form' of distributing 'charity to the poor was preferable to the modern state social services'. In view of the excesses of the French Revolution, he argued, constitutional monarchy was preferable to republicanism, and he even expressed reservations about democracy. 'There is,' he wrote, 'no rule so tyrannical as that of them all.'

His conservatism was further apparent in his attitude to the Gaelic renaissance that was sweeping intellectual circles at the time. Although it seemed to herald a new era, de Valera was slow to show any interest. He shied away from involvement in things Gaelic, despite the presence at Blackrock of enthusiasts like Ó Conaire and Michael Cusack, one of the driving forces of the Gaelic Athletic Association (GAA), who was a teacher there. Maybe his reticence had something to do with his love of rugby, which was condemned as a foreign game by the rather xenophobic Gaelic enthusiasts.

During his second year of university study there was a noticeable softening of his conservatism. In presenting a paper to the debating society on the question of establishing a national university — one of the more hotly debated issues of the period — he candidly admitted having modified some of his views in the course of researching the lengthy paper.

'Is it that the problem is too hard for English statesmen to solve?' he asked on that night in February 1903. 'They pretend they can legislate for us better than we could for ourselves. And yet if we had but a free Parliament in College Green for the space of one single hour, this vexing question would be put to rest for ever. It seems, indeed, that Englishmen, even the most liberal amongst them, with one or two notable exceptions, have never been able to understand the needs of Ireland properly.' Here were set the seeds which later blossomed into his ardent nationalism.

In autumn of that year he got a job as a mathematics teacher at Rockwell College, run by the Holy Ghost Fathers just outside Cashel, County Tipperary. After five years in Dublin he was returning south as a young man on the verge of his twenty-first birthday, free for the first time in his life from the confines of home and the restrictive atmosphere of student life at Blackrock. He enjoyed his new-found freedom and often referred to his two years at Rockwell College as the happiest period of his life.

Earning a regular salary for the first time, he was able to socialise in a way that he had never been able to afford before, even if the opportunities had presented themselves. He enjoyed the social life, and became particularly active in the local rugby club, which boasted two members of Ireland's Triple Crown winning side of three years earlier. Playing in the demanding position of full back on the first team, which reached the final of the Munster Senior Cup, de Valera was rated good enough to be considered for a place on the provincial team. Yet, as often happens, he would be better remembered for a ball he dropped than for any of his accomplishments on the field.

In 1903 de Valera was literally tall, dark, and handsome. With his sallow complexion and distinctive features, he was fancied by many of the local girls, especially the daughter of the owner of the hotel frequented by the rugby players, but he shied away from her. He was deliberately avoiding amorous entanglements because he still harboured notions of entering the priesthood.

He got on well with both the clerical and lay teaching staff at Rockwell and it was one of his teaching colleagues who first contracted his name to

'Dev'. He was liked by his pupils, partly because he was not a very demanding taskmaster. He was apparently so enthusiastic about his subjects that he expected the students to be likewise and failed to notice those who were indifferent.

In the midst of his duties at Rockwell coupled with his new-found freedom, his own studies suffered. At the end of the school year he returned to spend three months at Blackrock College, cramming for his final arts examination at the Royal University. As he awaited the results he went on a religious retreat to determine for once and for all whether he had a vocation for the priesthood. When he tried to talk about it to one of the Jesuit priests giving the retreat, the priest was more interested in other matters.

'But what about my vocation?' de Valera asked impatiently.

'Oh! your vocation,' the priest replied. 'You have what is known as an incipient vocation.'

'If that is all I have after all those years,' de Valera said, 'it is time I forgot about it.'

He graduated from the Royal University with only a pass degree, which was a great disappointment to him. He returned to Rockwell for another year before deciding to move back to Dublin, where he hoped to continue his studies. It was a hasty, ill-considered decision. He had considerable difficulty finding a new job; at one point, in desperation, he crossed the Irish Sea for an interview in Liverpool before eventually obtaining a temporary post at Belvedere College, Dublin. In the following years he depended on a series of temporary and part-time teaching positions at various colleges around the city.

For most of the first three years following his return to Dublin he lived within the confines of Blackrock College, which was unprecedented because he was neither enrolled as a student nor working as a member of the staff. He played rugby with the seconds team, which reached a cup final in 1908. Some people were never to forget his role in that game. Fancying himself as a place-kicker, he insisted on taking all the penalty kicks, which he duly missed, with the result that he was blamed for losing the game. In later years some people would remember the game as a manifestation of a trait to hog the limelight without regard to the cost to his own team.

In late 1908 de Valera finally moved out of Blackrock College, and his love of rugby was gradually replaced by a developing passion to learn Gaelic. His initial motivation was professional or mercenary. He had ambitions of lecturing at the National University, which was about to be set up. As Gaelic was likely to be made an entrance requirement, he decided to join the Gaelic League and soon became enthralled with the language. He changed his first name to its Gaelic equivalent, Éamon, and even sought to Gaelicise his Spanish surname by spelling it Bhailéra for a time.

One of his instructors was a primary-school teacher, Sinéad Flanagan. She was already in her thirties and it has been suggested de Valera became infatuated with her because, as his first woman teacher, she provided the mother-figure he had always lacked. Whatever the case, he followed her to Tourmakeady, County Mayo, where she was teaching at the Irish summer school, and a romance blossomed. They were married on 8 January 1910. Although they quickly started a family, he was never much of a family man, which was hardly surprising in view of his own family background. He became so involved in other matters that he had little time for his family. In the coming years he would be preoccupied with the Gaelic League, then the Irish Volunteers, and later with politics.

He was elected to the executive committee of his branch of the Gaelic League in 1910, and he was a branch delegate at the organisation's national convention the following summer. At that convention he ran for election to the national executive, but was unsuccessful. His reaction to his defeat betrayed a certain immaturity as well as a degree of vanity. He thought he had failed to win one of the fifty seats on the national executive because Sinn Féin, the radical nationalist political party, had somehow orchestrated the whole election as if it was just out to defeat him, rather than elect its own people. Actually it was not Sinn Féin at all but the more militant Irish Republican Brotherhood (IRB), a secret, oath-bound society dedicated to the establishment of an Irish republic, which had sought to orchestrate the election, as part of its policy of gaining control of all nationalist organisations by secretly permeating their executive bodies with IRB members.

The Gaelic League professed to be non-political and its president, Douglas Hyde, strove to keep the organisation out of party politics, but it was nevertheless highly politicised, with deep internal divisions. Conservatives like Hyde tended to support the more moderate nationalistic aims of the Irish Parliamentary Party (IPP), while so-called progressives like Thomas Ashe publicly identified with Sinn Féin and secretly worked for the IRB.

In 1912 de Valera was appointed a part-time temporary professor of mathematics at St Patrick's College, Maynooth, where courses were confined to the Roman Catholic clergy and students for the priesthood. While there he extended his already wide contacts with priests, many of whom were destined to become influential figures, both in Ireland and abroad. The college president, Daniel Mannix, who offered de Valera the teaching post, soon emigrated and became the Cardinal Primate of Australia, while another member of the staff, Joseph MacRory, was to become the Cardinal Primate of Ireland towards the end of the following decade. Such contacts were to prove very useful to de Valera during his subsequent political career.

Meanwhile the divisions within the Gaelic League came to a head at the organisation's national convention in Galway in July 1913. Hyde denounced

Ashe and five of his comrades as 'disrupters' and tried to purge them from the leadership of the organisation by calling for their defeat and seeking to limit the size of the national executive to twenty-five members. Ashe countered by proposing a thirty-five-strong executive, while de Valera, who was generally regarded as being in neither camp, played the role of peace-maker by successfully suggesting the two sides split the difference and agree to a thirty-member executive. In the subsequent election, five of the six whom Hyde had tried to purge lost their seats. Only Ashe hung on. It looked like Hyde had routed his critics, but behind the scenes he had really lost out, because almost two-thirds of the new executive were secretly backed by the IRB, which effectively took control of the Gaelic League. Following his own election defeat, de Valera's involvement waned and he began to focus his energies elsewhere.

One of his branch colleagues in the Gaelic League had been Eoin MacNeill, who had been responsible for calling the meeting at the Rotunda at which the organisation was established in 1893. Now, twenty years later, writing in the Gaelic League's official organ, *An Claidheamh Soluis*, he called for the formation of a nationalist force to counteract the influence of the Ulster Volunteer Force (UVF), set up in the north-east of the island to resist the introduction of Home Rule. A public meeting was arranged for 25 November 1913 at the Rotunda.

Believing the British government would not implement Home Rule unless there was also a show of force from Irish nationalists to counter the UVF, de Valera attended the Rotunda meeting and enlisted in the Irish Volunteer Force which was established that night. The gathering was made up largely of members of the Gaelic League, GAA, Sinn Féin and the IRB. Though de Valera was comparatively unknown outside Gaelic League circles, he rose quickly within the ranks of the Irish Volunteers. When a new company was set up in the Donnybrook area of Dublin, he was elected captain, and he took charge of his men during the landing of arms at Howth the following summer.

Bolstered by the morale-building success of the Howth gunrunning, the Irish Volunteers expanded rapidly, especially after John Redmond, the leader of the IPP, threw his political weight behind the force. The Home Rule Bill for Ireland was duly passed at Westminster, but in deference to the threat posed by the UVF, its implementation was postponed until after the First World War, which began in August 1914.

When Redmond called on the Irish Volunteers to come to the defence of the British empire, the force split, with the overwhelming majority supporting his call. Had Home Rule been implemented at the time, de Valera later said, he would probably have joined those who went to fight for the rights of small nations. But, under the circumstances, with Westminster vacillating in the face of unionist intransigence, he felt the Irish Volunteers would eventually be needed at home to insist on the implementation of Home Rule.

A meeting of the Donnybrook company of the Irish Volunteers was held on 28 September 1914 to discuss the situation created by Redmond's call to arms. Unwilling to heed the call, de Valera walked out of the meeting and was joined by a majority of his men. 'You will need us before you get Home Rule,' was his departing cry.

Although a majority of the company walked out, it was hardly right to say they followed de Valera. Most of those men would probably not have joined in the first place if they had not been carried away by the enthusiasm which greeted the formation of the force. They had obviously joined without considering the ultimate implications of their actions. Now they seized on the opportunity to extricate themselves by leaving with de Valera, but when he then tried to reorganise the company, only seven of the men were interested.

As one of the few remaining officers, de Valera found himself in a more prominent position when the Irish Volunteers began to reorganise, largely at the instigation of the IRB, which planned to stage a rebellion in the hope of establishing an independent Irish republic while Britain was preoccupied with fighting the Great War. Although de Valera was unaware of these plans at the time, he enthusiastically involved himself in the reorganisation and quickly came to the notice of the leadership.

———

Michael Collins was born, the youngest of eight children, on the night of 16 October 1890 near the tiny County Cork hamlet of Sam's Cross, where his father had a sixty-acre farm. 'Well do I remember the night,' his sister Helena wrote some eighty years later. She was seven years old at the time. 'Mother came round to the three youngest Pat (6), Katie (4) and myself, to see us safely landed in bed. Next morning we were thrilled to hear we had a baby brother found under the proverbial head of cabbage.'

It was a background that contrasted greatly with that of de Valera. 'We were a very happy family even though we lived under very primitive conditions in the old house, where we *all* were born,' Helena Collins recalled. Michael had a very normal childhood, though being the youngest of such a large family he tended to be rather spoiled.

Michael John Collins, his father, was somewhat aloof from his children. His wife Mary Anne looked after their needs, but he had a particular fondness for his namesake. He would frequently bring Michael on his rounds of the farm. At other times the boy's older sisters were charged with looking after him — a duty they relished. 'We thought he had been invented for our own special edification,' his sister, Johanna, or Hannie as she was called, would recall many years later.

In addition to the eight children it was a home in which there were always a number of aunts and uncles to be found. Michael's father was born in 1815, the youngest of six boys. He lived throughout his life at Woodfield, the farm where he was born. He was believed to have been the sixth generation of the family born there. In 1875, at the age of fifty-nine, he married his god-daughter, Mary Anne O'Brien.

It was a made match. Michael John was living with his three older bachelor brothers and they needed a housekeeper. Mary Anne was twenty-three at the time. She was the eldest daughter of a family of ten. Her father, James O'Brien from Sam's Cross, was killed in an accident in which her mother was seriously injured. As a result Mary Anne and her older brother, Danny, had to take responsibility for the large family at an early age, and she became like a second mother to the younger members of her family. Hence after she married, the Collins home was like a second home to Mary Anne's younger brothers and sisters.

The family usually gathered in the kitchen at night. This was the age before rural electricity, radio, or television, so they had to make their own entertainment. Discussions would invariably take on a patriotic slant, with nationalistic songs or poems figuring prominently. Mary Anne's brother, Danny, would sing rebel ballads, and her mother, Johanna O'Brien, who lived until 1916, would tell of seeing victims of the Great Famine dying by the roadside a half a century earlier. West Cork was, in fact, one of the areas most severely hit by the Famine.

Such stories would have formed some of Michael's earliest memories. At the age of four he began his formal education at Lisavaird National School. 'The boys were on one side and the girls on the other side of a semi-detached building,' Helena recalled. 'Both heads were strict disciplinarians. Miss Ellen Collins, a [first] cousin of ours, was head of the Girls' School and Mr Denis Lyons of the Boys'. We had no intercourse with each other; we might have been miles apart.'

People would later remember that Michael Collins took a particular delight in listening to old people reminiscing. 'Great age held something for me that was awesome,' he told an American journalist. 'I was much fonder of old people in the darkness than of young people in the daylight.'

The attachment to old people undoubtedly had something to do with his early memories of the family gatherings in the dimly lit kitchen and the fact that his father was already seventy-five years old when Michael was born. He never forgot an incident that happened when he was with his father on the farm one day. They were out in the fields and his father was standing on a stone wall, from which he dislodged a stone accidentally.

Michael remembered looking at the stone as it came towards him, but he figured that it would not hurt him because his father had dislodged it and the boy obviously revered his father.

'Would you believe it?' his father would say. 'There he was, barefooted, and the stone rolling down on him, and him never so much as looking at it! And when I got the thing off his foot and asked him why he had stood there and let it hit him, what do you think he replied? He told me "'Twas you who sent it down!"'

In December 1896, when Michael was six, his father had a heart attack from which he never fully recovered. He lingered on for a couple of months, but never went out again. 'Our darling Papa died on 7 March 1897,' Helena recalled. 'Mamma called us all at about 10 p.m. and we all got round the bed. Papa, who was quite conscious, spoke: "Mind that child," he said, pointing to Michael. "He'll be a great man yet, and will do great things for Ireland."' He added that 'Nellie', his pet name for Helena, 'will be a nun'.

One can easily imagine the kind of influence that such an incident would have on a child, especially at such an impressionable age. Helena duly entered a Sisters of Mercy convent and spent the rest of her life as a nun.

In view of her own family background in helping to bring up her own brothers and sisters, Mary Anne Collins was probably better prepared than most other people to cope with the trials of being widowed with a young family. At eighteen, Johnny Collins was the oldest of the boys, and he took over the running of the farm.

The headmaster, Denis Lyons, who was a member of the IRB, had a great influence on Michael's developing sense of nationalism. Lyons and the local blacksmith, James Santry, whose forge was across the road from the school, regaled young Collins with stories of past Irish rebellions. In his mid-twenties Michael would recall their formative influence.

'In Denis Lyons and James Santry I had my first tutors capable of — because of their personalities alone — infusing into me a pride of the Irish as a race,' he wrote to a cousin. 'Other men may have helped me along the searching path to a political goal, I may have worked hard myself in the long search, nevertheless, Denis Lyons and James Santry remain to me as my first stalwarts. In Denis Lyons, especially his manner, although seemingly hiding what meant most to him, had this pride of Irishness which has always meant most to me.'

When Lyons and Santry talked of the events of the nineteenth century, the Great Famine, the Young Ireland rebellion, and the trauma of the 1870s and 1880s, they were talking about times through which Michael's father and uncles had lived. His paternal grandparents went back well into the eighteenth century. Indeed one of his father's brothers had been old enough to remember the rebellion of 1798. Michael's paternal grandmother's brother, Teigh O'Sullivan, had been a professor of Greek at the University of Louvain and had acted as an emissary for Wolfe Tone, who was regarded as the father of Irish republicanism. It was therefore understandable that young Michael should show a great interest in the history of the past century.

Lyons detected 'a certain restlessness in temperament'. He described the boy as 'exceptionally intelligent in observation and at figures'. In one school report he noted that Michael was 'a good reader' and added that he 'displays more than a normal interest in things appertaining to the welfare of his country. A youthful, but nevertheless striking, interest in politics.'

The way in which Michael was developing could be seen in some of his early writing, even before he was a teenager. In one school essay he described the IPP as 'chains around Irish necks'. His early political idol was Arthur Griffith. 'In Arthur Griffith there is a mighty force afoot in Ireland,' Collins wrote in 1902. 'He has none of the wildness of some I could name. Instead there is an abundance of wisdom and an awareness of things which ARE Ireland.'

After finishing Lisavaird National School, Michael went on to school in Clonakilty to prepare for the civil service entrance examination. During the school-week he lived with his eldest sister, Margaret O'Driscoll. Her husband owned a local newspaper, and Michael helped out with the reporting, usually on hurling or football matches. While there he learned to type.

During those early days his best friend was Jack Hurley, whose sister married Michael's brother, Johnny, and so established an in-law relationship with the Collins family. The two boys were inseparable and often stayed the night at each other's home.

Collins went to London to take up a job with the Post Office Savings Bank in July 1906. There was little prospect for him in west Cork, and emigration was natural for an ambitious boy of his age. His sister Hannie was already in the civil service in London, and they lived together at 5 Netherwood Place, West Kensington. 'I had Irish friends in London before I arrived, and in the intervening years I had made many more friends among Irish residents in London,' he recalled later. 'For the most part we lived lives apart. We chose to consider ourselves outposts of our nation.'

One of those friends was his boyhood pal, Jack Hurley, who had emigrated some months earlier. Hurley's presence undoubtedly eased the transition to life in London, but Collins retained a rather romantic view of Ireland. 'I stand for an Irish civilisation based on the people and embodying and maintaining the things — their habits, ways of thought, customs — that make them different — the sort of life I was brought up in,' he wrote. As a result he and his friends never really integrated into British society, and never wanted to. 'We were proud of isolation,' he said, 'and we maintained it to the end.'

'Once,' he explained some years later, 'a crowd of us were going along the Shepherd's Bush Road when out of a lane came a chap with a donkey — just the sort of donkey and just the sort of cart they have at home. He came out quite suddenly and abruptly and we all cheered him. Nobody who has not been an exile will understand me, but I stand for that.'

During the nine and a half formative years Collins spent in London he took a very active part in the Irish life of the city. He helped raise money when Arthur Griffith's new party, Sinn Féin, ran a candidate in a parliamentary by-election in North Leitrim in early 1908. The candidate, C. J. Dolan, who had resigned his own seat in order to recontest it on a Sinn Féin ticket, was defeated. Party supporters tried to put the gloss of moral victory on what was really a devastating defeat from which the party did not recover for many years.

Collins remained active in the party for some time and prepared a number of formal talks for party meetings. Two that were especially memorable concerned 'The Political Role of the Catholic Church in Ireland' and his assessment of 'The Irish Famine of 1847'. Like many young Irishmen, he went through an anti-clerical phase during his adolescent years, and his paper on the Catholic Church raised some eyebrows when he called for the extermination of the clergy.

His paper on the Famine was equally volatile. He blamed the British for deliberately orchestrating the Great Famine 'to get rid of the surplus Irish by some means, fair or foul'. He also complained that Queen Victoria had only contributed £5 to famine relief. In fact, she personally donated £500, which was probably the largest single subscription made by anybody, but Collins and all too many of his fellow countrymen swallowed the old canard. 'We may forgive and forget many things,' Collins added sarcastically, 'but it would pass even Irish ingratitude to forget this £5.'

He talked about following the example of revolutionaries who gained a national parliament for Finland after murdering the Russian Governor-General, Nicholai Bobrikov, in 1904. The murder had consequences that were like a 'fairy tale', according to Collins. The Russian Tsar, fearing revolution, agreed to free elections and the establishment of a national parliament in Finland, based on proportional representation and universal adult suffrage. Women were given the vote for the first time in Europe. Even though that freedom did not last long, the fact that it happened at all was enough to encourage Collins.

'As a rule I hate morals and hate moralists still more,' Collins exclaimed in another prepared speech. He warmly approved of the actions of the Irish rebels who assassinated the Chief Secretary and his Under-Secretary in the Phoenix Park in 1882 and he condemned 'the foolish Irish apologists' who were critical of them. 'I do not defend the murder simply as such,' he continued. 'I merely applaud it on the ground of expedience.' The Finns had helped themselves by aligning with Russian revolutionaries. 'May not we also find it beneficial to allow our best to be helped by the English revolutionists?' Collins asked.

During 1907 and 1908 he attended evening classes at King's College, London. Many of the essays that he wrote there have survived and they give an insight into his adolescent thinking. Presence of mind was probably the single characteristic which most distinguished him under pressure in the coming years, and as a teenager he actually wrote an essay on the subject at King's College. Quick thinking was 'one of the most valuable qualities as well as one of the least common', he wrote. 'To know what to do at a crisis we must, if we have an opportunity to, learn up thoroughly the matter before-hand, and by practising this in trivial things we will beget a habit of ready resource in untried or un-foreseen circumstances.'

'History and tradition are rich in instances demonstrating the value of presence of mind,' Collins continued. 'All great commanders have been famed for their coolness in the hour of danger, which perhaps contributed more largely to their success than their actual courage. . . . Real valour consists not in being insensible to danger, but in being prompt to confront and disarm it.' His own illustrious career was a testament to the validity of his youthful assessment.

Collins was particularly active in the GAA in London. He enjoyed playing hurling with the Geraldines Club. He usually played at either wing back or centrefield. Opponents remembered him as an effective though not very polished player. He had a particularly short temper which often got the better of him, and he was a very poor loser. He liked to have things his own way, which did not endear him to many of his contemporaries. He faced keen competition when, at the age of seventeen, he made a successful bid for the post of secretary of the Geraldines Club.

The club minutes, which have been preserved in the National Library, show him to have been a committed and enthusiastic member, with an intense nationalistic outlook. He insisted that the club purchase all jerseys and medals from Dublin firms, and he demonstrated his commitment by getting the club to drop the practice of paying the expenses of the club's delegates to GAA conventions. But, of course, he expected the same kind of dedication from others.

He was a stickler when it came to club finances. In his first formal report, he complained that the treasurer had misappropriated some of the club's money for a time. As a result the club nearly lost its playing pitch. 'Eventually,' Collins continued, 'we got him to disgorge', which has a rather painful connotation to it. Collins persuaded the meeting to expel the individual 'as an undesirable and untrustworthy member'.

His initial secretary's report betrayed all the brashness and candid realism that were so much a part of his character. 'Our internal troubles were saddening,' he explained, 'but our efforts in football and hurling were perfectly heartbreaking. In no single contest have our colours been crowned with success. In hurling we haven't even the consolation of a creditable performance.'

While club secretary Collins vociferously supported the ban on members of the GAA taking part in 'foreign games' like rugby or soccer, even though many young Irishmen in England were anxious to play soccer. He also resented Irish athletes competing for the United Kingdom in international events. He took exception in 1913, for example, when the controlling body of the London GAA reinstated four Irishmen who had competed on the United Kingdom's team at the Olympic Games in 1912. As far as he was concerned, sport was both a recreation and a political weapon.

Ever since Ireland became a part of the United Kingdom in 1801 Irish people had tended to look to London for leadership in political, economic, and recreational matters, but Collins believed the GAA, founded in 1884, had begun to reverse this trend by reminding Irish people of their separate nationality. 'It provided and restored national games as an alternative to the slavish adoption of English sport,' he contended. The most significant development of all was the foundation of the Gaelic League in 1893. 'It checked the peaceful penetration and once and for all turned the minds of the Irish people back to their own country,' Collins wrote. 'It did more than any other movement to restore the national pride, honour, and self-respect.'

Both of Michael's parents were native Gaelic speakers, but they associated the Irish language with the economic backwardness of Gaeltacht areas, so they spoke only English to their children. They spoke Irish to each other when they did not wish the children to understand them. Michael started to learn Gaelic on a number of occasions after leaving home but other events inevitably dominated his time.

He was busy with his work, his study, and his political and sporting activities. He was particularly friendly with fellow Cork immigrants like Jack Hurley and Joe O'Reilly, whom he met in London. Hurley was still his closest friend. 'We think the same way in Irish matters,' Collins wrote. 'At worst he is a boon companion, at best there is no one else I would have as a friend.'

Unlike most of his contemporaries, Collins reportedly showed little interest in the opposite sex at this stage of his life. 'The society of girls had apparently no attraction for him,' according to Piaras Béaslaí. 'He preferred the company of young men, and never paid any attention to the girls belonging to the [Gaelic League] Branch, not even to the sisters and friends of his male companions.' Béaslaí, the only biographer of Collins who could claim to have been more than a passing acquaintance, noted that 'the usual philanderings and flirtations of young men of his age had little interest or attraction for him, though he sometimes amused himself by chaffing his young friends over their weaknesses in that direction'.

Maybe this teasing of friends prompted him to cover up a relationship that he had been conducting across the water with Susan Killeen, a girl he had met in London. His frequent correspondence with her in Dublin certainly bespoke an affectionate relationship, but it would be many years before the letters of that discreet relationship would come to light. In the interim the image of Mick the misogynist would take root.

Some people — who never knew Collins — would later suggest that he may have been homosexual. It was all pure speculation, based largely on the portraits of his earlier biographers, Béaslaí and Frank O'Connor, though neither author ever suggested it.

O'Connor relied heavily on Joe O'Reilly for his portrait, which showed Collins as a contradictory conglomeration of various characteristics — a buoyant, warm-hearted, fun-loving individual with a thoughtful, generous nature, but also a thoughtless, selfish, ill-mannered bully. While other young men went looking for sex, he was more inclined to go looking for 'a piece of ear'. He would burst into a room, jump on a colleague and wrestle him to the floor, and then begin biting the unfortunate friend's ear until the other fellow surrendered, often with blood streaming from his ear. It was certainly the portrait of a rather strange fellow. Yet as a working young man, deeply involved in furthering his education and very active in sport and politics, it would not have been surprising if Collins was in no hurry to form an amorous attachment. After all, his father was nearly sixty years old when he married, and Michael would not be that age until 1950.

Through his involvement in the GAA he met Sam Maguire, a fellow Corkman working for the Post Office. It was Maguire who persuaded Collins to join the IRB in 1909. Ever since the Sinn Féin defeat in the Leitrim by-election, Collins had been losing faith in the non-violence approach advocated by the party. He began to believe that only physical force would provide the solution to the Irish question.

Collins concluded that lack of organisation 'was chiefly responsible for the failure of several risings' in the past, and it was as an organiser that he would make his name in the coming years. 'A force organised on practical lines and headed by realists,' he wrote, 'would be of great consequence. Whereas a force organised on theoretical lines and headed by idealists would, I think, be a very doubtful factor.' His own organisational ability was recognised with his appointment as treasure of the south of England district of the IRB.

In 1910 Collins quit the Post Office Savings Bank to work for a stockbroker, but after the outbreak of the Great War in 1914 he moved back into the civil service to work as a labour exchange clerk in Whitehall. He did not want to fight in the British army, but neither did he want 'the murky honour of being a conscientious objector', so he considered emigrating to the United States. For some time his brother, Patrick, who was already in America, had been encouraging Michael to cross the Atlantic. It was apparently with that ultimate aim in mind that Michael had secured a job in London with an American firm, the Guarantee Trust Company of New York, in July 1913.

Having worked in England for so long, Collins became liable to conscription in early 1916. In order to avoid the draft he returned to Ireland, where the IRB was planning a rebellion, using the Irish Volunteer Force in which Collins had been enrolled by his friend Jack Hurley in April 1914. On handing in his notice he told his employers he was going 'to join up'. They naturally assumed he was joining the British army to fight on the continent, but he was going home to fight the British in Ireland.

His sister Hannie later said she tried to persuade him to have nothing to do with the planned rising. 'They'll let you down, Michael,' she warned. 'They'll let you down.' But, of course, he was not deterred. He left London for Ireland on 15 January 1916.

2

Easter Rebellion

In March 1915 de Valera was promoted to the rank of commandant in the Irish Volunteers. As he was not in the IRB, which secretly controlled the Volunteers and usually ensured the appointment of its own members to top posts, his promotion was a testimony to his organisational ability. Before informing him of the promotion, however, the IRB leader, Patrick Pearse, satisfied himself about de Valera's likely attitude to the planned uprising. Posing a supposedly hypothetical question, Pearse asked how de Valera would react in the event that the leadership of the Volunteers decided to stage a rebellion. De Valera replied he would follow orders. This was good enough for Pearse, who promptly informed him of his promotion.

Two days later de Valera was invited to a meeting chaired by Pearse at which plans for a rising in September 1915 were discussed. The plans called for the seizure of the centre of Dublin, which the Volunteers would then try to hold. Various battalions were assigned to defend the city against Crown forces stationed in the different barracks on the outskirts. As commandant of the 3rd Battalion, de Valera was to repel troops from Beggar's Bush Barracks.

Although the rising was postponed for several months, his ultimate role remained the same, and he familiarised himself thoroughly with the south-east section of the city that he had been assigned to defend. His enthusiasm was rewarded with his appointment as adjutant of the Dublin Brigade under Thomas MacDonagh. In his new post de Valera soon realised that some of his subordinates knew more about what was going on than himself. He complained to MacDonagh, who explained that those men were members of the IRB. They were privy to secrets he could not be told unless he was prepared to take the organisation's oath of secrecy.

De Valera hesitated. Not only was he uneasy because the Catholic Church disapproved of secret societies, but he was also afraid that IRB membership might compromise his position within the Volunteers. What would he do, for instance, in the event of conflicting orders from his superiors in the IRB and Irish Volunteers? Assured by MacDonagh that

there would be no real conflict of interest because the IRB secretly controlled the Volunteers, de Valera took the oath, but made it clear from the
outset that he would not attend IRB meetings. In short, he would keep its
secrets but had no intention of being an IRB activist.

———————

Meanwhile Collins was very active within the IRB. He was assigned as an
aide to Joseph Mary Plunkett, the chief military strategist of the rebellion. A
slender, pale, sickly young man with absolutely no military experience,
what Plunkett knew about military strategy had been gleaned from books or
from his own fertile imagination. He was a poet with a romantic vision and
a desperate need to leave his mark on a world in which he was not destined
to stay very long. He was already dying of tuberculosis.

While looking for a job in Dublin, Collins got a temporary part-time
position as a financial adviser to Plunkett's sister, Geraldine, who still lived
with her parents at Larkfield in Kimmage. Some fifty of the London-Irish
Volunteers were staying on their grounds, making up what Pearse would
call a standing army.

At night many of the men would gather at Constance Markievicz's home
on the north side of the city, in Surrey House. It was not a mansion as the
name suggested, but a small red-brick building in a row of suburban houses
at 49B Surrey Road, Raheny.

'Crowds used to gather into it at night,' Frank Kelly recalled. 'We had
tea in the kitchen; a long table with Madame cutting up slices of brack
about an inch thick, and handing them around. The bread was eaten as
quick as she could cut it. She had lovely furniture and splendid pictures. We
used to go into the sitting-room and someone would sit at the piano and
there would be great singing and cheering and rough amusements. She had
lifted her lovely drawing-room carpet but left the pictures on the walls and
on the bare boards there was stamping of feet.'

Kelly remembered Collins there one night reciting Robert Emmet's
speech from the dock at the top of his voice. Emmet had tried to stage a
rebellion in 1803 but the whole thing went disastrously awry. He was arrested and tried but entered no defence, with the result that the jury convicted
him without even retiring to consider a verdict. When Emmet was asked if
he had anything to say before the judge passed sentence, he responded with
a long eloquent speech from the dock.

'I have but one request to make at my departure from this world: it is the
charity of its silence,' Emmet said. One can easily imagine Collins as he
delivered the famous concluding words of the speech with gusto: 'Let me

rest in obscurity and peace, and my tomb remain uninscribed and my memory in oblivion until other men can do justice to my character. When my country takes her place among the nations of the earth, then and not till then, let my epitaph be written.'

As Easter approached Collins was particularly busy. He rushed about Larkfield and was unusually irritable, according to Joe Good, one of those who had returned from London around the same time. The London-Irish Volunteers were frequently called 'the refugees' or Count George Plunkett's 'lambs'. Collins arrived one day while they were in high spirits, making grenades. 'Mick spoke roughly to one of the "lambs" who was slotting screws, suggesting he was not working hard enough, and passed generally abusive remarks,' Good recalled. 'I suggested Mick should show us how to work faster, put a three-cornered file in his hand and gave him a bolt-head to slot. He proceeded to show us how and a crowd gathered about him. Of course the file slipped on the round bolt-head.'

'Do you think this way might be right, Mick?' Good asked, having already put half a dozen bolts in a vice. He then ran a hacksaw across the bolts and slotted the six at once. 'The "lambs" roared with laughter and Mick, swearing at us, went up the stairs to George Plunkett, followed by a gibing chorus of "The birds of the air fell a sighing and a sobbing when they heard of the death of poor Mick Collins . . ."'

The story of the Easter Rebellion has already been told so often that there is no need to go into detail here. De Valera had little to do with overall policy, which was decided by IRB leaders like Pearse, MacDonagh, and Thomas Clarke. The operation was timed to begin on Easter Sunday, when the combined forces of the Irish Volunteers and Irish Citizen Army would seize Dublin as well as other selected areas and set up a provisional government. Germany had promised arms, and these were to be landed at Fenit, near Tralee, that day.

De Valera had only learned on the Wednesday that the rising was to begin on Sunday. But the plans were thrown awry by a sequence of unforeseen events.

Eoin MacNeill, chief of staff of the Volunteers, learned of the plans on the Thursday and threatened to call the whole thing off, but IRB leaders persuaded him to wait; they convinced him that the British intended to round up the Volunteers and they explained that Roger Casement had made arrangements for German help. On Saturday, however, came news that Casement had been arrested near Tralee and the arms ship had been scuttled. The game was up as far as MacNeill was concerned. He ordered that the rising be called off and, to ensure his order reached all units, he inserted a notice in the *Sunday Independent* announcing the cancellation of all manoeuvres planned for the weekend.

De Valera had already said goodbye to his wife and four children on Good Friday. 'I know you will not think it was selfish or callous indifference or senseless optimism that made me so calm when I was about to offer up you and the children as a sacrifice,' he wrote to his wife in recalling the moment afterwards. 'When I stooped over to give you that parting kiss you would know that though I gave it as lightly as if we were to meet again in the morning it was simply to save you, to give you some sixteen hours of respite; for in my heart I believed it was the last kiss I would give you on earth.'

'We'll be all right,' he told one of his captains, Joseph O'Connor, next day. 'It's the women who will suffer. The worst they can do to us is kill us, but the women will have to remain behind to rear the children.'

De Valera briefed his officers in detail that Saturday night. 'He was able to tell each company captain where he would enter on to his area and what he would find to his advantage or disadvantage when he got there,' O'Connor noted afterwards. 'He was able to discuss every detail, even to the places where it would be possible to procure an alternative water supply, where we could find tools for such things as loopholing walls and making communications.'

O'Connor said he could not remember a query that de Valera could not answer. Of course that was on Saturday night; everything changed when de Valera ended up with only about a quarter of the men he expected to have under his command when the rising began.

He was perplexed when he read the notice in the *Sunday Independent* over MacNeill's name, cancelling all operations for the weekend. Shortly afterwards he received a handwritten order from MacNeill confirming the cancellation, which was subsequently confirmed by MacDonagh, but the latter advised him to expect further orders.

The six main IRB leaders met along with James Connolly, the labour organiser, and decided to reset the date of the rebellion for the following morning, thereby catching not only the British but also most of the Volunteers by surprise. The whole operation was reset at such short notice that there was confusion in the ranks.

On the eve of the rising William J. Brennan-Whitmore was assigned to help Joseph Mary Plunkett and arrived at a nursing home in Mountjoy Square to find him being assisted by Collins, whom Plunkett introduced as his aide-de-camp. 'I can't say that, at that time, I was much impressed with Collins,' Brennan-Whitmore later wrote. 'He appeared to be silent to the point of surliness, and he gave my hand a bone-creaking squeeze without saying a single word.'

The two of them helped Plunkett from the nursing home and brought him to the Metropole Hotel, where he had a suite. Collins helped Plunkett to dress again next morning and then went out to Kimmage to join the London contingent. Dressed in his staff captain's uniform, Collins looked smart, especially in comparison to the others, clad in ill-fitting military outfits which were an assortment of different shades of green that were anything but uniform. He was not impressed with them and flushed with anger when they — irritated by his smug air of self-importance — retaliated by sniggering at his appearance.

Around eleven o'clock the contingent boarded a tram for the city centre at Harold's Cross; they were a rather motley bunch, some with bandoleers, rifles, and pistols, and others with pickaxes, sledgehammers and shovels. A woman passenger was upset at being prodded by the rifle of one heavily laden man who insisted on sitting down beside her without removing any of his equipment. 'Fifty-seven two-penny fares, and don't stop until we reach O'Connell Bridge,' the officer told the conductor as he handed over the exact money. One of the Volunteers sat down with his rifle casually pointed at the head of the driver, who ignored the pleas of passengers wishing to alight as he raced by their stops on the way to the city centre.

There was an air of farce about the proceedings as the men formed up outside Liberty Hall. It was hard to believe that the stout, scholarly Pearse was a revolutionary leader. He was flabby from a sedentary life and spoke slowly, with a carefully measured cadence, as he struggled to overcome a habitual stutter. He was about to take his place at the head of the group when he was embarrassed by one of his sisters.

'Come home, Patrick, and leave all this foolishness!' she pleaded. Pearse blushed with embarrassment, and the men around him shuffled nervously.

'Form Four,' the pot-bellied Connolly shouted. With his bandy legs, he began the proceedings as he ordered the men to march off, giving Pearse the excuse to brush past his sister to the head of the group marching off towards Sackville (now O'Connell) Street.

Plunkett, Connolly and Pearse formed the first line, with more than three hundred men marching four abreast behind them. Brennan-Whitmore was on the extreme left of the first full line, with Collins on his immediate inside. It was a holiday and the streets were relatively quiet. Onlookers, used to such parades, did not realise anything unusual was happening until the men reached the General Post Office (GPO) and Connolly gave the order to charge the building.

The staff and customers were ordered out unceremoniously. Some left reluctantly, muttering in resentment as they were hustled out the door. Lieutenant Chambers of the Royal Fusiliers was sending a telegram to his wife when the men charged in, and Plunkett ordered that he be taken prisoner. Collins went into a telephone booth and yanked out the flex, which he used to tie up the unfortunate officer, whom he lifted bodily and dumped in the telephone booth with a laugh.

'Please don't shoot me,' pleaded Constable Dunphy of the Dublin Metropolitan Police as he was taken prisoner. 'I done no harm.'

'We don't shoot prisoners,' replied Collins, who told two Volunteers to bring the man upstairs and lock him in a room. Connolly ordered that the ground floor windows be knocked out, and Collins took a boyish delight in smashing the glass as he laughed boisterously. Pearse went outside and, before a small, indifferent group, proclaimed the Irish Republic 'in the name of God and of the dead generations'.

Inside the men continued with their task of fortifying the building for the expected counterattack. Collins and Brennan-Whitmore were detailed to ensure all windows were properly barricaded.

Their only real engagement with the enemy on the first day was when a company of British Lancers rode down Sackville Street in formation on horseback, apparently hoping that their intimidating appearance would frighten the rebels. It was an absurd gesture. When the firing began three of the horsemen and two of their horses were shot dead and another man fell mortally wounded, while the remainder bolted for safety.

The second day was largely one of anticipation as the rebels waited for the British to attack, while an orgy of looting was taking place outside in Sackville Street. Realising that the police would not dare enter the street, people from the nearby slums broke display windows and helped themselves to whatever they desired in the shops. Pearse went out to the foot of Nelson's Pillar in front of the GPO and denounced the looters as 'hangers-on of the British Army'.

———————

De Valera was to defend the south-eastern approaches to the city, but only around 120 men showed up instead of the 500 expected, so he had to improvise. According to Plunkett's plan, de Valera was supposed to occupy sixteen different locations in the Ringsend area. These included the canal works, a railway station, a two-mile stretch of railway line, signal cabins, the gas works, a granary, a railway locomotive shop, several mills, and Boland's Bakery.

He planned to set up his headquarters in the Grand Canal Dispensary. At about 12.10 he and some of his men scaled the wall of Boland's Bakery and rushed across the garden of the dispensary. De Valera was waving his sword as he crossed the garden and the doctor's wife, alone in the dispensary, became terrified.

'You have five minutes to pack your valuables and leave the premises ma'am,' de Valera announced. The woman became hysterical and raced from room to room screaming uncontrollably. De Valera clearly did not know what to do next. 'You'd better handle this,' he said to an aide and hurried back across the back wall.

His men had little difficulty in occupying the bakery and de Valera established his headquarters there instead. Their biggest problem was convincing the bakers that they were serious when they ordered them from the premises. There were thousands of loaves of bread baking at the time and they agreed to allow a few bakers remain.

De Valera's men were reportedly impressed by his humanitarianism. On the Monday he also dismantled part of the gas works for fear that people would be hurt in their homes by explosions. In the process he plunged much of the city into darkness, but he reasoned that this would prevent the British forces from using city trams. He also demonstrated a concern for the animals in the dogs and cats pound in Grand Canal Street, and ensured the horses in the grounds of the bakery were looked after.

On Tuesday morning de Valera called a parade and announced that all the boys under eighteen had to go home. Two of them — fifteen-year-old Willie Fitzgerald and sixteen-year-old Richard Perle — refused to leave and had to be chased away, but they kept returning and were eventually allowed to remain.

Little happened throughout that day as de Valera continued to race around burning up energy without any clear picture of what he wished to do. 'Ceaselessly he moved among the men along the railway seeing that sentries were posted and were on alert,' his authorised biographers, Longford and O'Neill, noted. 'He gave orders to the company officers to keep the men occupied so as to divert their minds from fear.'

'As he strode among his men, his mind was working on possible schemes which might help in the event of an attack,' they added. At one point he suggested using a railway engine to launch a surprise attack on the British troops approaching from Kingstown, but he had no one who could drive an engine. He also suggested that the men use the signal wires along the tracks in order to make trip wires to delay the enemy if they decided to come along the tracks, but it was of little consequence because no attack ever came from that quarter.

In the distance they could hear shooting in the direction of St Stephen's Green. At one point de Valera brought twelve men together and told them that he would lead them to the area to help out the garrison in the College of Surgeons. The men were provided with ammunition and rations and he set off along the railway line in the direction of Westland Row railway station, while the others followed after him. But they had not gone very far before de Valera returned, calling the whole thing off. 'It's all off,' he told them. 'The fact is I don't feel justified in leading an attack with only twelve men.' He did not feel that he could take the risk. 'In God's name therefore, we'll go back and stand by our own area.'

He carefully prepared what appeared to be important operations but then he would suddenly cancel them. A striking feature of all the accounts of his part in the rebellion is the paucity of detail about what he actually did other than run around and change his mind.

'In one of their positions a sniper gave the Volunteers much trouble,' according to David T. Dwane, de Valera's first biographer. 'All attempts to locate him having failed, a message was sent to de Valera, who quickly arrived on the scene. With the aid of glasses he soon detected a soldier hidden in the ivy near a chimney stack, from which point a dangerous fire was directed on the Volunteer position. De Valera pointed him out to two of his men, and giving a hand himself, the sniper was not heard of again.'

According to his authorised biographers, de Valera sent word to the officers at the nearby Sir Patrick Dun's Hospital that a British cadet, G. F. Mackay, who had been taken prisoner the first day, would be shot if the British placed snipers at the hospital. He assured the cadet, however, that this was just a bluff as he had no intention of carrying out the threat.

The incident on which much of his reputation as a leader and tactician rested was a piece of intelligent anticipation. Realising that Boland's Bakery would not stand up to a bombardment by heavy artillery, he came up with an idea to deflect attention from the building by having a rebel flag mounted on the tower of a disused distillery building some 300 metres away. This was to give the impression that the distillery was occupied by Volunteers. The Crown forces fell for the ruse and began shelling the distillery. De Valera was so delighted that he reportedly ran up and down the nearby railway line, cheering like a schoolboy.

The men were spread out to defend the various bridges in his sector: those at Ringsend, Grand Canal Street, and Lower Mount Street. It was the last-mentioned that would see the greatest action. Two men, Michael Malone and James Grace, were placed in No. 25 Northumberland Road overlooking Mount Street Bridge. Others defending Clanwilliam House also joined in the defence of the bridge. Malone went to complain about the lack of fire power, and de Valera personally gave him a Mauser pistol and some 400 rounds of ammunition.

Malone and Grace were to inflict some of the heaviest casualties on the British on the Wednesday when they tried to enter the city via Mount Street Bridge. Seventeen men kept a whole battalion at bay for several hours. They inflicted the heaviest casualties of all on the British forces. They killed or wounded a total of 234 officers and men, which was about half of the total British casualties for the week. De Valera was the commandant credited with this, but he never made any serious attempt to help or relieve the men. Those at his battalion headquarters merely waited for the British to turn their attention to Boland's Bakery, but that attack never came.

De Valera was running around so much and had not slept since the rebellion began, with the result that 'by Friday he presented a very worn and tired-out appearance', according to one of his men. Efforts to persuade him to get some sleep proved futile. 'I can't trust the men,' he said. 'They'll leave their posts or fall asleep if I don't watch.'

He was eventually prevailed upon to get some sleep one night, but he obviously had a nightmare. 'His eyes wild, he sat bolt upright and in an awful voice, bawled: "Set fire to the railway! Set fire to the railway!"'

Meanwhile at the GPO, Wednesday had dawned with no sign of the expected British assault, but as the morning progressed there were sounds of shelling when the gunship *Helga* opened up on Liberty Hall. The men had not expected the shelling. Connolly, a dedicated Marxist, had predicted the forces of British capitalism would be so anxious to avoid damaging property that they would not use artillery on expensive buildings but storm them with troops instead.

There were rumours that the British were preparing to attack the GPO with gas, so one of the men who had some chemical training was assigned to prepare an antidote. He put together a concoction and distributed it throughout the building in buckets.

'What the hell good will that do?' Collins asked him.

'None,' the man conceded, and that put an end to the idiotic scheme.

Collins was much too practical to waste time on such matters. 'All through this week he gave me the impression that he was in a post that was too minor for a man of his temperament,' wrote Joe Good. He was singled out as 'the most active and efficient officer in the place' by Desmond FitzGerald, who had been placed in charge of the GPO canteen.

Having been ordered to economise rigidly in order to ensure that the food supply would last for three weeks, FitzGerald irritated many of the men by providing only meagre portions, but Collins was not about to put up with petty restrictions. He came in one morning with some men who had been working hard on demolishing walls and building barricades. He told FitzGerald the men were to be fed properly, even if that meant they took all the remaining food. 'I did not attempt to argue with them,' FitzGerald related. 'The men sat down openly rejoicing that I had been crushed. Apparently some of them had already been the victims of my rigid economy.'

The weather on Thursday was glorious, with a slight breeze from the east blowing over the putrefying carcasses of the two dead horses outside on the street. Having knocked out all the glass in the windows of the GPO, the men had to endure the nauseating stench while the interminable waiting for an assault continued. The British never did attack as Plunkett and Connolly had anticipated; instead they began shelling Sackville Street with heavy artillery placed a short distance away in Rutland (now Parnell) Square.

Connolly led some men out of the GPO on a raid but he was wounded in the process. Meanwhile Pearse was busy preparing an address that he delivered to all the available men in the main hall of the GPO that evening. Although it was supposedly a pep talk for the troops, it was really an address to posterity over the heads of the gathered men to whom he referred in the third person throughout. 'Let me, who have led them into this, speak in my own name, and in my fellow commandants' names, and in the name of Ireland present and to come, their praise, and ask those who come after them to remember them,' he said. 'They have held out for four days against the might of the British Empire. They have established Ireland's right to be called a Republic, and they have established this government's right to sit at the peace table at the end of the European war.'

Collins had little time for Pearse, an impractical dreamer, politically inexperienced, and militarily naive. Pearse was obsessed with mystical visions of a blood sacrifice. Writing in December 1915, he described the first sixteen months of the Great War as 'the most glorious' period in European history. 'Heroism has come back to the earth,' he wrote. 'The old heart of the earth needed to be warmed with the red wine of the battle-fields. Such august homage was never before offered to God as this, the homage of millions of lives gladly given for love of country.' A medium-sized man with a handsome face, except for a pronounced cast in his right eye which usually prompted him to ensure that his photograph was taken in profile to conceal his cock-eyed appearance, Pearse had a messianic complex.

Some months on Collins would be quite critical of the way the rebellion was conducted in general and of the leadership of Pearse in particular. This was hardly surprising, given his earlier quoted views on the need to have the Irish forces organised on practical grounds and headed by realists and his belief that a force organised on theoretical lines and headed by idealists would be 'a very doubtful factor'. Time proved him right, in his own mind anyway. 'I do not think the Rising week was an appropriate time for the issue of memoranda couched in poetic phrase, nor of actions worked out in similar fashion,' he wrote. 'It had the air of a Greek tragedy about it, the illusion being more or less completed with the issue of the before mentioned memoranda. Of Pearse and Connolly I admire the latter the most.'

While Connolly shared Pearse's enthusiasm for the rebellion, he had a saner view of the horror of war. He thought that anyone like Pearse who believed the battlefields had to be warmed with blood was 'a blithering idiot'. 'Connolly was a realist, Pearse the direct opposite,' according to Collins. 'There was an air of earthy directness about Connolly. It impressed me. I would have followed him through hell had such action been necessary. But I honestly doubt very much if I would have followed Pearse — not without some thought anyway.'

Collins also thought highly of two of the other leaders, Clarke and Seán MacDermott. Not being soldiers, they went into and remained in the GPO as excited spectators rather than participants. 'Both were built on the best foundations,' according to Collins, who was especially impressed by MacDermott. 'Wherever he walked there went with him all the shades of the great Irishmen of the past. He was God given. He was humble in the knowledge of his own greatness and in the task which he had chosen to do. He did not seek glory as a personal investment but as a National investment.'

In writing to friends about the rebellion, it was particularly noticeable that Collins ignored the fifth and only other member of the military council in the GPO, Joseph Mary Plunkett. Possibly his reticence was out of a sense of loyalty to the man for whom he had been an aide. Plunkett, like Pearse, was a poet with an overdeveloped sense of the dramatic. His jewellery — a bangle on a wrist and a large antique ring on one of his fingers — seemed incongruous with military masculinity. In addition, he was physically weak and tired very easily. Just three weeks earlier he had had an operation for the glandular tuberculosis that was obviously killing him, with the result that he spent a great deal of time resting in the GPO.

'On the whole I think the Rising was bungled terribly costing many a good life,' Collins explained. 'It seemed at first to be well organised, but afterwards became subjected to panic decisions and a great lack of very essential organisation and co-operation.'

On Friday, the fifth day of the rebellion, the British began firing incendiary shells at the GPO. Collins and a large detail of men held the fire at bay for as long as possible, putting barriers of sand across doorways and flooding the floors with water, but this was only a delaying measure. The fire gradually took hold, and Collins and Joe O'Reilly worked hard in combating it. At one point the Big Fellow's trousers caught fire and O'Reilly 'put it out by hosing Mick down', Good recalled. Collins was furious, much to the amusement of his colleagues.

Pearse called all the available men together to deliver another of his addresses in the main hall. 'If we have accomplished no more than we have accomplished, I am satisfied,' he told them. As the fire in the GPO went totally out of control, it was decided to move the headquarters to a factory on Great Britain Street, but Pearse took the decision without making any enquiries about the positioning of enemy forces in the area. The O'Rahilly and some men went to make preparations. They had only just left when one of the Volunteers told Pearse that Great Britain Street had been solidly in the hands of the Crown forces since Thursday.

'Stop The O'Rahilly,' Pearse shouted. 'He's gone into Moore Street with some men.'

Collins darted out the door and ran up Henry Place but was too late. The O'Rahilly had already been cut down. Collins and those who followed him took refuge in the terraced cottages lining Moore Street, where they were joined by the other survivors of the headquarters staff. Pearse had led them from the burning building with his sword drawn and held aloft in a heroic gesture, symbolic of his own impracticality.

Some food was brought from the GPO, as Pearse had insisted that every man carry provisions. One or two of the men tried to cook rashers and tea with little success. 'Mick Collins was one of these,' Good recalled. 'He would listen to no one, but fastidiously cut himself bacon, cleaned a very dirty pan, and placed it on a small fire. He was warned not to put on more fuel but persisted. Then a sniper hit the chimney, and his pan was full of soot. Mick was absolutely furious — and his language was choice.'

On Saturday morning Pearse decided to look for surrender terms. When the British insisted on an unconditional surrender, he decided to concede, though some of the Kimmage contingent wanted to fight on. Clarke tried to convince them it was futile but failed, as did Plunkett.

'If you fight on,' Collins pleaded, 'you'll do nothing but seal the death warrants for all our leaders.'

'Sure, they'll all be shot anyway,' someone replied. In desperation, Collins asked MacDermott to talk to them.

'Now what is it you fellows intend to do?' MacDermott asked them. He listened patiently to their arguments and then tried to persuade them to surrender, mentioning some civilians shot that morning.

'We're hopelessly beaten,' MacDermott said. 'The thing you must do, all of you, is survive, come back, carry on the work so nobly begun this week. Those of us who are shot can die happy if we know you'll be living on to finish what we started.'

They then ate what was left of their rations and said the rosary, some holding a rifle in one hand and a rosary beads in the other.

Collins marched out with the headquarters staff into Sackville Street and turned left up towards the Parnell monument where they downed arms and surrendered. They were joined by men from the Four Courts and then marched up to the green in front of the Rotunda Hospital, where they were herded together, surrounded by a ring of soldiers with bayonets at the ready.

The officer in charge of the Crown forces was Captain Lee Wilson, a florid-faced, thick-lipped individual, who behaved as if he had a little too much to drink. He roared at his own men and issued contradictory orders while rushing from one prisoner to another, shouting that he was going to have them shot. He singled Clarke out for particularly harsh treatment. 'That old bastard is the Commander-in-Chief. He keeps a tobacco shop across the street. Nice general for your fucking army.' He had Clarke stripped naked and prodded him mercilessly, while nurses looked on from the windows of the Rotunda. Collins watched in indignation. Four years later he would take particular delight in having Wilson killed in revenge for what he did that day.

On Sunday morning the prisoners were marched through the streets to Richmond Barracks. W. E. Wylie, who was put in charge of the guard, feared that there would be trouble as people tried to rescue the rebels. But his fears proved groundless. 'I might have saved myself the trouble,' Wylie wrote, 'for instead of cheering the prisoners, all of the old women and men in the streets cursed them. The prisoners needed more protection from the crowd than the soldiers did.'

The rebels were pelted with rotten fruit and vegetables by Dublin people, who blamed them for the week's destruction in which more innocent civilians perished than combatants on either side; 262 civilians were reported killed, while the Crown forces suffered 141 dead, and the rebels 62, among them Collins's friend, Jack Hurley.

'Do you think they'll let us go?' a Volunteer asked as they were being walked through the hostile crowd of onlookers.

'Bejasus, I hope not,' replied Jim Ryan.

'The citizens of Dublin would have torn us to pieces,' Piaras Béaslaí wrote later.

The prisoners were taken to the gymnasium at Richmond Barracks, where police detectives circulated among them, picking out known activists for special treatment. These were Irishmen singling out other Irishmen for trial and in some cases, execution.

Collins had been in Dublin for only three months, and so he was not known to the detectives. He ended up among a group of 489 prisoners who were marched to the North Wall and shipped directly to Britain, herded together in a cattle boat. 'Well it was a good fight, Mick,' a colleague said as they were going down the quays. 'What do you mean a good fight?' he snapped in reply. 'We lost, didn't we?'

Meanwhile de Valera was so cut off that news of the surrender did not reach him until Sunday. Elizabeth O'Farrell, a member of Cumann na mBan, the women's auxiliary of the Irish Volunteers, brought the surrender order, but de Valera refused to accept it, because it had not been countersigned by his own commanding officer, Thomas MacDonagh. She therefore went off to get his signature.

As they waited for her to return, de Valera discussed the situation with his vice-commandant, Joseph O'Connor, and, realising that the shooting around the city had stopped, they concluded that the surrender message had indeed been genuine. 'He then instructed me to mobilise the men and be prepared to march down from the position to the point of surrender, stating that he himself would, under cover of a white flag, inform the British that we had been ordered to surrender,' O'Connor recalled.

De Valera was naturally afraid for the lives of himself and his men. He had heard stories of surrendering soldiers being shot at the battlefront in France, and he feared the Volunteers might be summarily killed. He gave his Browning automatic pistol to the British cadet they had been holding prisoner and asked him to give it to his oldest son, Vivion, some day. He then accompanied the cadet to Sir Patrick Dun's Hospital.

Dr Myles Keogh witnessed the events at the hospital as de Valera and the cadet approached.

'Hello,' cried de Valera.

'Who are you?' an officer asked.

'I am de Valera!'

'And I am a prisoner,' Cadet Mackay shouted.

De Valera then surrendered to the British military. 'You may shoot me, but my men must be unmolested when surrendering,' he said, according to Desmond Ryan. Thus de Valera surrendered before his men. It was O'Connor who led them out a short time later.

'I marched from Boland's Bakery into Great Clarence Street, thence to Grand Canal Street and into Grattan Street where we saw the Commandant and the British officers,' O'Connor wrote. 'I passed over command of the Battalion to the Commandant. He ordered the ground arms.' They were then marched off, four abreast, to the Royal Dublin Society's showgrounds at Ballsbridge.

Flanked by two British officers, de Valera was at the head of his men. He bitterly resented local people coming out with cups of tea for the British soldiers. He blamed the people of Dublin for the failure of the rebellion because they had not helped. 'If only the people had come out with knives and forks,' he is reputed to have remarked to his prisoner shortly before surrendering.

De Valera later contended that what he had actually said was that the people should have fought 'though armed with hay forks only'. Against

British rifles and heavy artillery, 'hay forks' would have been about as useful as knives and forks anyway. It was an idiotic remark at best, but it did betray his tendency to blame others for the failings of the rebels themselves. Pearse and some of the other leaders realised from the outset that the rebellion was likely doomed, but they believed their ultimate goals would be realised by others in the long run if they made a blood sacrifice at this time. They were right, but de Valera would only realise this later. He was one of those who had believed the rebellion might actually succeed in establishing an independent Irish republic, right then and there.

After two days in Ballsbridge, de Valera and the others were marched under a heavily armed guard across the city to Richmond Barracks. On the way they were also jeered by onlookers. The people of Dublin clearly resented the rebellion, but the British authorities made the mistake of over-reacting, and in the process antagonised the Irish people.

The British rounded up Irish nationalists indiscriminately and jailed them without trial. Many of those people had absolutely nothing to do with the rebellion; they were, in fact, critical of it as a foolhardy venture. 'Those wholesale arrests, dictated by panic, were a huge blunder from the British point of view,' Piaras Béaslaí wrote. 'They helped to convert many to sympathy with us; they provided a fresh grievance and a standing subject for agitation, and by bringing representative men from all parts of Ireland together in the intimacy of an internment camp they helped to strengthen our nucleus of future organisation, and to secure greater unity of thought and effort.'

The summary executions of the principal leaders and other rebels also did much to win sympathy for those who had fought in the rebellion. Pearse, Clarke, and MacDonagh were shot by firing-squads in the early hours of de Valera's first morning at Richmond Barracks. He was sharing a cell with Count Plunkett, Seán T. O'Kelly, and others. In the following days eleven others were executed in Dublin as well as one in Cork.

Sinéad de Valera went to the office of the American consul general in Dublin to get the United States government to plead for her husband's life, on the grounds that he was an American citizen. It was only then that anybody bothered to get a copy of his birth certificate and learned that he had been actually been registered as George de Valera but subsequently christened Edward. He was asked about his American background when he was brought before the military court on 8 May, along with Thomas Ashe and four others. Among those who testified at the trial was the former prisoner, a Cadet Mackay, who confirmed de Valera had been in command. He added that he himself had been well treated as a prisoner in Boland's Bakery.

Afterwards de Valera was taken to Kilmainham Jail to await his fate. He expected the worst. From his cell he wrote a melodramatic note to Jack

Ryan, a friend from his rugby-playing days at Rockwell. 'Just a line to say I played my last match last week and lost,' he wrote. 'Tomorrow I am to be shot — so pray for me — an old sport who unselfishly played the game.'

As he expected, de Valera was sentenced to death, but the executions had been causing so much revulsion among the Irish public that the British government called for a cessation. His sentence was duly changed to penal servitude for life, along with that of Thomas Ashe and around ninety others. He, Ashe, and Thomas Hunter were the only commandants to survive the Easter Rebellion and the resulting executions. They were deported to English jails along with other survivors the following week.

3

Doing Time

The wholesale arrests and the fifteen executions that followed in the next two weeks were a terrible blunder on Britain's part because they generated enormous compassion which turned to sympathy for the rebels. In death Pearse became a national hero and his mystical rhetoric coloured the perception of what he had tried to do.

Henceforth the rebellion would be seen in terms of a kind of religious experience. The executed were referred to as 'martyrs' and it was said that the executions 'helped to convert' the Irish people to the separatist cause. The rebellion itself would become known as the Easter Rising, and in the process Pearse's accomplishment would be symbolically equated with the greatest of all of Christ's miracles.

Upon arrival in Holyhead, Collins and the other prisoners found two trains waiting for them on either side of a railway platform. One went to Knutsford, and the other, which Collins boarded, to Stafford, where he and 288 other rebels were marched from the railway station to Stafford Military Detention Barracks. At one point on the way a couple of bystanders tried to attack one of the prisoners, but was driven off by a burly English sergeant. 'Get back you bastards,' he shouted at the assailants. 'These men fought for their country, you won't.'

For three weeks the prisoners were kept in solitary confinement and only allowed out for short periods to walk in single file around a courtyard in total silence. They had no news of the outside world. In the monotony of this daily routine, each man got to know his cell intimately: the stone floor, the thirty-five panes of glass and the black, iron door. They had a slate to write on, a pencil, a bedboard, a stool, a table, a can, a bowl, a glass, and endless time to think. They could hear the noise of the town in the distance.

'It was for the most part an unpremeditated solitary confinement,' Desmond Ryan recalled. 'Our khaki guardians came round to give us mugs and mattresses and to examine the cells; it took them the best part of a week to adjust themselves completely to the invasion.'

'What caused the riots?' the British soldiers kept asking.

'We heard early that we must shine tins, until we could see our faces therein, must fold our blankets along certain lines, keep our cells as clean as pins, listen to what the staff had to say to us, preserve the strictest military discipline with silence, not whistle or sing, not attempt to communicate with other prisoners, not to look out the windows under penalties of bread and water and an appearance before the commandant,' Ryan explained.

After two weeks they were allowed to write home, and Collins wrote to Hannie in London. 'Positively you have no idea of what it's like — the dreadful monotony — the heart-scalding eternal brooding on all sorts of things, thoughts of friends dead and living — especially those recently dead — but above all the time — the horror of the way in which it refuses to pass.' He asked her to send him some novels and a French grammar that had been at the flat before he left London. He found it very hard to concentrate and Oscar Wilde's 'Ballad of Reading Gaol' kept running through his mind.

He also had plenty of time to think about 'our little "shemozzle"', as he called the rebellion in a letter to his friend Susan Killeen on 25 May. 'If our performance will only teach the housekeepers of Dublin to have more grub in reserve for the future it will surely not have been in vain.' This was his idea of being funny. 'But seriously,' he added, 'I'm afraid there must have been a lot of hardship and misery which must continue for many a day and which all our sympathy cannot soften.'

'Life here has not been so ghastly since communications from the outer world have been allowed, and since we've been allowed reading matter and write letters,' he continued. 'I saw poor Pearse's last letter in the *Daily Mail* this day and it didn't make me exactly prayerful.'

As the restrictions were relaxed, the authorities became very benign. 'Conditions have improved wonderfully during the last week,' Collins explained in another letter to Susan Killeen four days later.

'We had the life of Riley,' Joe Sweeney wrote afterwards. They revived their spirits with impromptu football games in the courtyard, using a makeshift ball of brown paper and rags wrapped with twine.

'A frenzied mass of swearing, struggling, perspiring men rolled and fought over the ball in the middle of the yard,' Desmond Ryan recalled. 'From the din a tall, wiry, dark haired man emerged and his Cork accent dominated the battle for a moment. He went under and rose and whooped and swore with tremendous vibrations of his accent and then disappeared again.'

'That's Mick Collins,' someone said.

On 28 June 1916 Collins and more than a hundred others were transferred from Stafford to an internment camp at Frongoch, near Bala in north Wales. He seemed as if he might even have had some regrets about leaving Stafford, because henceforth he would be limited to one letter a week. He was certainly in a reflective mood on the eve of his transfer.

'One gets plenty of time to think here and my thoughts are often self-accusing goodness knows. I can't tell how small I feel sometimes. 'Tis all very fine for the writers to talk about the sublime thought which enters into people when they are faced by death — once, when I was in a pretty tight corner, what struck me was, how much nicer I might have been to the people who had a regard for me.'

Collins enjoyed the train journey through what he described as 'a most engaging country'. At Frongoch they joined internees from Knutsford and other detention centres, and numbers swelled to more than 1,800 men. The camp, which had until recently housed German prisoners of war, was divided into two barbed wire compounds, separated by a road. Collins, internee No. 1320, was put in the north camp; this consisted of a series of thirty-five wooden huts, which were sixty foot long and sixteen foot wide and only ten foot high in the centre. Each hut housed thirty internees, so conditions were very cramped.

'It's situated most picturesquely on rising ground amid pretty Welsh hills,' Collins wrote shortly after his arrival in the camp. 'Up to the present it hasn't presented any good points to me, for it rained all the time.' As a result the grass pathways between the huts quickly turned into 'a mass of slippery shifting mud'. The huts were cold and drafty even during the summer, which gave rise to anxiety among the men as to what conditions would be like later in the year. 'I cheer them all up by asking them — what'll they do when the winter comes?' By then he would actually welcome the conditions in the north camp, but that is getting ahead of the story.

The internees were given the control and management of the camp within the barbed wire. Collins readily adapted himself to the conditions and made the most of his internment. 'He was full of fun and mischief,' remembered Batt O'Connor. 'Wherever he was, there were always ructions and sham fights going on. Mock battles took place between the men of his hut and the adjoining one. We had a football field and whenever there was a game he was sure to be in it. He was all energy and gaiety.' Each night the men were locked up at 7.30. Between then and lights out at 9.45 they were free to read or play cards. 'They were listening all the time to talk and plans about the continuance of the war as soon as we got home,' according to Batt O'Connor. Many of the men had their own musical instruments, and they frequently staged their own concerts and sing-songs.

Each day finished with rebel songs and recitations. Collins had a poor singing voice; so his party-piece was a forceful rendition of the poem, 'The Fighting Race', by J. I. C. Clarke. It was about three Irishmen — Kelly, Burke, and Shea — who died on the battleship *Maine* at the start of the Spanish-American war. Collins would deliver the lines of all five verses with an infectious enthusiasm that made up for his inability to recite properly.

There was plenty of time to think about what had gone wrong during Easter Week. Collins realised the strategy was faulty; it had been foolish to confront the might of Britain head on by concentrating their forces in one area. Henceforth he would learn from the mistake, but he did not believe in dwelling in the past. His attitude was best summarised in an autograph book entry he made in Frongoch. 'Let us be judged by what we attempted rather than what we achieved,' he wrote.

Each morning the men rose at 6.15. After breakfast, about a quarter of them were assigned to various fatigue groups to clear out fireplaces, sweep buildings, empty garbage, prepare meals, tend a vegetable garden, etc. Those not on fatigue duty would normally go to a playing field until eleven o'clock, when all the internees gathered for inspection. The commandant inspected everything in company with internee officers. The blankets on the bunks had to be folded precisely and placed on the bedboards so that they were in a straight line from one end of the room to the other, and the commandant at times used his stick to determine whether the line between any two beds was exactly straight.

The camp commandant, Colonel F. A. Heygate-Lambert, whom the internees nicknamed 'Buckshot', was a cranky, fussy individual with a lisp, always looking for something or other to complain about. 'It's hard to imagine anything in the shape of a man being more like a tyrannical old woman than the commandant in charge of this place,' Collins complained. 'The practice of confining to cells for trivial things is a thing which the commandant glories in.'

Following inspection the men were free to do much as they pleased within the camp. They played football, engaged in athletic contests, and set up classes to teach Irish, French, German, Spanish, shorthand, telegraphy, and various military skills. They drilled regularly and conducted military lectures, using manuals smuggled into the camp.

'We set up our own university there, both educational and revolutionary,' Sweeney recalled, 'and from that camp came the hard core of the subsequent guerrilla war in Ireland.' Frongoch was indeed a veritable training camp for the rebels, who acquired skills and made contacts that would prove invaluable afterwards.

'They could not have come to a better school,' O'Connor wrote. 'They were thrown entirely in the company of men to whom national freedom and the old Irish traditions were the highest things in life.'

Collins and the solicitor Henry Dixon, then in his seventies, were prime movers in organising an IRB cell within the camp, and one of their recruits was Richard Mulcahy. Others in the camp who would work closely with Collins in future years included Joe O'Reilly, Seán Hales, Gearóid O'Sullivan, J. J. 'Ginger' O'Connell, Seán Ó Muirthile, Michael Brennan, Michael Staines, Terence MacSwiney, Tomás MacCurtain, and Thomas Gay.

Those were only a few of the very valuable contacts he cemented at Frongoch.

People from the camp were to be found in the forefront of Irish life throughout much of the next half-century, especially in the army and police, as well as in the political arena, among them a future Governor-General of the Irish Free State in Domhnall Ó Buachalla, and a future President of the Republic of Ireland in Seán T. O'Kelly, as well as future cabinet ministers in Mulcahy, O'Kelly, Oscar Traynor, Tom Derrig, Jim Ryan, and Gerry Boland.

Of course, not all of them liked Collins personally. Many found him childish and overbearing. It was here that he earned the nickname, 'the Big Fellow'. He was not quite six foot tall and had a rather wiry, athletic build together with a youthful appearance that belied his twenty-six years, so the nickname had nothing to do with his physical characteristics. It would later become a term of affection, but it did not have its origins in affection; rather, it was a sarcastic reflection of Collins's exaggerated sense of his own importance.

Many colleagues were repulsed by his bullying tactics and his inability to concede gracefully. Being highly competitive, he hated to lose at anything. 'In the camp, if he didn't win all the jumps, he'd break up the match,' Gerry Boland recalled. When Collins had a good hand playing cards, he would concentrate intensely and would resent interruptions, but when the cards were running against him, he would renege, look into the hands of the men beside him, upset the deck and even jump on the likely winner and wrestle him to the floor. He was fond of wrestling, or looking for 'a piece of ear', but these wrestling bouts often ended up in real fights. He was not only a bad loser but also a bad winner. Having forced someone into submission, he would crow with delight in a high-spirited show of exuberance that more than a few found irritating.

Morale was comparatively good considering the circumstances under which many of the men were interned. All of those with whom Collins had been sent to Stafford had taken part in the rebellion, but he was surprised to learn that many of the men in Frongoch played no part in the fighting. 'By my own count,' he wrote, 'at least a quarter of the men in the north camp know very little about the Rising. One man, a former labourer of my acquaintance, said that he was just forced off the street in the roundup. His only crime appears to be that he was walking the street.'

When Prime Minister Herbert H. Asquith visited Dublin in May following the executions, he talked to some of the people being held at Richmond Barracks. 'They were mostly from remote areas of the country and none had taken any part in the Dublin Rising,' he wrote to his wife. He therefore instructed the military to comb out the prisoners properly and 'only send to England those against whom there was a real case'. By then, however, more than 1,900 prisoners had already been deported, so the

British government set up a committee to examine the case against each of those being held. All of the internees were brought, in turn, before the committee in London, and a considerable number were freed.

Collins went before the committee in early July. He spent overnight in a prison waiting for the interview. 'This morning I was able to see through the open pane of my window the convicts at exercise,' he wrote. 'It was the most revolting thing I have ever seen. Each convict seems to have cultivated a ghastly expression to match the colour of his turf-ash-grey garb. Broad arrows everywhere. As the men walked round and round the ring, those wretched arrows simply danced before the eyes. That awful convict dress is one horror we're saved at any rate.'

Jim Ryan, who had been in the GPO during the rebellion, was released, but Collins was returned to Frongoch, where the internees held a sports meeting on 8 August. Collins won the 100 yards dash. As he breezed past the leader, he grinned gleefully. 'Ah, you whore,' he said, 'you can't run!' Collins described it as 'a great day'. There was high tea afterwards for the prize winners. 'It consisted of such stuff as tinned pears, jam and pudding,' he wrote to the recently released Ryan. 'We gorged ourselves and ended up with a concert.'

His victory was mentioned in the House of Commons, much to his own annoyance, because the person who raised it cited his winning time as evidence that the men were being properly fed at the camp, but this had nothing to do with camp food, as far as Collins was concerned.

'Actually there isn't a solitary man here of no matter how slender an appetite who could live on the official rations,' Collins wrote. 'There are two or three committees supplying us with additional vegetables and sometimes apples and cocoa.' It was also possible to buy extra food, but most of the men had little money. They could avail of parole to work at a nearby quarry for five and a half pence an hour, but on 1 September the camp commandant announced he was deducting three pence an hour for their upkeep, and they promptly downed tools and refused to do further work. Hence the meals at the camp were important.

There were three meals each day. Both breakfast and the evening meal consisted of eight ounces of bread and almost a pint of tea, and the midday dinner did not show much more imagination. 'With the exception of Friday when we get uneatable herrings, the food never varies,' Collins wrote. 'Frozen meat, quite frequently bad, and dried beans, are the staple diets. The potato ration is so small that one hardly notices it.'

In mid-August, after some 600 men had been released, those remaining in the north camp were transferred to the south camp, and the north camp was retained as a punishment centre. Collins's own reaction to the move was rather mixed. 'Most of us do not appreciate the change as much as we ought to,' he wrote. 'But there are many consolations all the same.'

The south camp contained a disused distillery in which an abandoned granary building was converted into five large dormitories, with between 150 and 250 beds in each. The beds consisted of three boards on a frame, four inches off the floor, and each man had two blankets. The low, nine-foot-high ceiling contributed to the claustrophobic atmosphere in the large rooms with so many men crammed together and confined from 7.30 at night until 6.15 the following morning. Long before morning the air would become quite foul, no doubt aggravated by the renowned flatulent qualities of the men's daily diet of beans.

'In some unfavoured spots, breathing is almost difficult in the mornings,' Collins wrote. Luckily his bunk was beside a window and he did not suffer so much in that respect, but when it rained he could get wet as he could not close the window. To make matters worse, the place was infested with rats ever since it was a granary. 'Had a most exciting experience myself the other night,' he explained in one letter. 'Woke up to find a rat between my blankets — didn't catch the blighter either.'

Although he detested rats, he had an easier time adapting himself to the conditions than many of the men, especially those married with families. He did not have to worry about a wife or children and, in any case, most of his friends were interned with him, with the result that he was never really lonely, as were many others. 'It is pitiable to see those who have given way to imprisonment now enforcing on themselves the extra burden of loneliness,' he wrote. It was easier for him, a bachelor, to take a more philosophical outlook.

'I'm here and that's the thing that matters,' he wrote. 'Prating about home, friends and so on doesn't alter the fact that this is Frongoch, an internment camp, and that I'm a member of the camp. There's only one thing to do while the situation is as it is — make what I can of it.'

There was, of course, strict censorship at the camp, but Collins set the groundwork for his future intelligence work by establishing secret channels of communication with the outside. Letters were smuggled out in various ways. Sometimes guards were bribed to post them outside the camp. Another favourite method was to have someone being released take letters out in old envelopes as if they were letters that had already been censored on entering the camp. The camp staff never bothered to inspect the contents. The freed man would then simply transfer the contents to another envelope and post it. Another method was to place letters in the wrapping of sandwiches being prepared for men being released. Messages and letters were smuggled into the camp, on the other hand, by visitors. In addition, a man who worked in the censor's office used to remove mail for Collins before the censor could read it. In this way a two-way system of communication was established with the outside.

Collins initially viewed the smuggling as just a contest between the guards and internees. 'The game of smuggling and communication is one for which there is no definite end,' he wrote. 'It gives some spice to the usual mono-tony. In its present form it could go on for ever. Daily the British grow more weary of attempting counteractions to it. As one of them remarked, "If you were bloody Jerries we'd know what to do. But you're not."'

Although the smuggling may have started as a kind of game, it soon proved invaluable for propaganda purposes as the camp was gradually whit-tled down to the hard core of activists. Collins found a new spice to life with the need to avoid detection, as he was eligible for conscription because he had been living in Britain when the Great War began.

On 3 September Hugh Thornton, one of the internees, was informed that, because he had been living in Britain at the outbreak of the war, he was being drafted into the British army. All told, some sixty internees were in the same category. Before the rebellion they had been known as 'refugees' in Dublin and the name stuck.

When the authorities came looking for Thornton two days later, he refused to identify himself. All the internees were forced to turn out in the yard and line up in two straight rows, but the guards were unable to recog-nise Thornton. The camp adjutant ordered the roll be called. As each man's name was read out he was to answer, 'Here, Sir', and then march in front of the adjutant to the end of the yard and re-form in numerical order. These instructions were cheerfully obeyed by the prisoners. By the time Thornton answered to No. 1454, the camp authorities were irate.

'You have hitherto conducted the camp in an excellent manner, but this incident this morning was the worst exhibition of insubordination which I have met so far, and I cannot overlook it,' the commandant told the assembled men. As a punishment, he suspended all letters, newspapers, and visits for a week.

This 'harsh and unjust punishment' was resented by the internees, according to Collins. Many of them did not know Thornton. Michael Staines, their leader, could not have identified him 'even if he had wished to', the prisoners contended.

'Obviously everybody could not have known the particular man,' Collins wrote to Hannie. 'It is not very just to attempt to make prisoners identify a fellow prisoner,' he added. 'On the same day another man was sentenced to cell with bread and water for forgetting to say "sir" to an officer.'

Another dispute came to a head on 9 September when internees refused to clear rubbish from the huts of guards. Until the start of the month this work had been contracted to an outside company, but the camp command-ant decided to save money by using internees. When they balked, he ordered that those who refused to carry out the assigned duties be sent to the north camp and deprived of letters, newspapers, smoking material, and visits as a punishment. Each day thereafter eight more men were transferred after they refused to do the work.

Although the men had difficulty communicating with the outside, Collins was still very much on top of things, as was evident from a letter that he wrote to Jim Ryan on 2 October 1916. 'Most of my letters have been meeting with accidents,' he wrote. 'Things go on in much the same way here, but there have been some interesting happenings lately, which the Censor's Department forbids us to speak about. Even so the Dublin Corporation meeting tomorrow will give you some idea.'

This was obviously a reference to the refuse strike. Notwithstanding the many 'accidents', the men had managed to smuggle out detailed reports of the refuse strike to Alfie Byrne of Dublin Corporation, who proceeded to publicise the whole affair at a meeting on 4 October. They also smuggled details to Tim Healy, nationalist member of parliament, who raised the matter in the House of Commons. As a result the refuse strike received extensive coverage, especially in the Irish-American press.

The camp authorities relented on 21 October and reinstated the men's privileges. They then moved all the internees to the north camp, where the pathways again quickly turned to mud as a result of some heavy autumn rains. In spite of the mud, however, Collins welcomed the move back. 'Nothing could be as bad as the horrible stuffiness of the other place,' he wrote to Hannie. 'On the whole, I think the huts are better . . . In any case they're more desirable and there's a fire. There are only 29 in each now and we have a nice crowd in ours.' Some of them enjoyed reading like Collins, and they shared their books and magazines. 'Between us we haven't a bad library,' he explained.

Hugh Thornton, the 'refugee' discovered in September, had been sentenced to two years at hard labour for evading conscription, with the result that while Collins was very active in the camp, he had to remain inconspicuous and, in order to avoid detection, he never acted as a formal spokesman.

They were slow about identifying themselves, much to the annoyance of guards. 'Why the fuck don't ye holler out when I call yer fucking names!' exclaimed the Welsh sergeant major.

'For Christ's sake,' another exasperated guard pleaded, 'answer to the name you go by, if you don't know your real name.'

The men naturally took delight in upsetting the guards. One morning while a count was being conducted, an internee started coughing, and the officer of the guard shouted at him to stop, whereupon all the internees began coughing.

In early November the camp authorities tricked one of the refugees, Fintan Murphy, into identifying himself by announcing that he should pick up a package, and they tried to single out Michael Murphy by saying he was to be released as his wife was ill, but that ruse failed because Michael Murphy was not married. The commandant then tried to find him by using the same tactic used to uncover Thornton, but this time 342 men refused to answer to their names. As a punishment they were moved back to the south camp, and their privileges were withdrawn. Most of the 204 men who answered the roll-call on that occasion did so by agreement in order to keep the two camps open and thereby maintain their contact with the outside world. Fifteen of the hut leaders were court-martialled.

'The court may understand this better if I put it this way,' Richard Mulcahy explained in his defence. 'If a German interned among English soldiers by the Germans were wanted for the German Army what would be thought of those English soldiers if they gave the man up and informed on him to the German authorities? There are men here who fought in the insurrection; many are here who did not; but most of them now are very sympathetic with those who did.'

A number of the refugees felt badly about others suffering to protect them. They considered giving themselves up, but Collins — who was generally recognised as the leader of the refugees — would not hear of it. 'Mick burst into the meeting and sat down,' Joe O'Reilly recalled. 'When he heard their proposition he told them to do nothing of the kind but sit tight, and not to mind the cowards.'

The Easter Rebellion had taught him that Ireland was not capable of beating the British militarily, but in Frongoch he learned it was possible to beat them by wearing down their patience. 'Sit down — refuse to budge — you have the British beaten,' he wrote to a friend. 'For a time they'll raise war — in the end they'll despair.'

He was right. The authorities soon tired of trying to uncover the refugees. But that was not all. With the war on the continent grinding to a virtual stalemate, and the British feeling heavily dependent on American goodwill, the whole internee problem was becoming an embarrassment not only in Ireland but also in the United States.

As a result of Alfie Byrne's agitation on the men's behalf, Sir Charles Cameron, a retired medical officer of Dublin Corporation, visited Frongoch on 7 December along with a doctor nominated by the Home Office. The internees tried to project an image of deprivation by dressing in their worst clothes. They also complained bitterly about their food, which was actually upgraded for the occasion. 'Is there anything which you get enough of?' Cameron asked.

'Oh yes,' replied Collins, 'we get enough salt.'

Collins was clearly encouraged by the visit. 'This state of affairs can't last much longer,' he wrote next day. 'While many of the men are looking forward dismally to the prospect of spending Christmas here, I would not be surprised to find myself at home for that event.'

On 21 December the men were summoned to the dining hall and told they were being released. The officer on duty said, however, that he needed their names and addresses.

'It's no use,' cried Collins. 'You'll get no names and no addresses from us.'

The officer explained that he had no further interest in Michael Murphy, and did not 'give a damn' who was who, but they would have to help him if they wanted to get home by Christmas. 'I will have to telegraph the name and address of every prisoner to the Home Office and Dublin Castle before he leaves the camp,' he said. 'It will be an all-night job for me unless you help. I will not be able to get through on time.'

Collins and Brennan-Whitmore talked to the officer and agreed to draw up the list themselves, which solved the officer's problem. The men were then taken to Holyhead, where Collins got a boat to Kingstown (now Dún Laoghaire), arriving back in time for Christmas, a free and wiser man.

After his release Collins went home to Clonakilty for a brief holiday, but it was not the best of homecomings. His maternal grandmother had just died. 'Poor old grandmother was dead when I came home, and then that brother of mine and his wife were both very unwell.' The political scene, too, disturbed him. 'From the national point of view,' he wrote to Hannie, 'I'm not too impressed with the people here. Too damn careful and cautious. A few old men aren't too bad but most of the young ones are the limit. The little bit of material prosperity has ruined them.'

After a brief stay he returned to Dublin and applied for a job as secretary of the Irish National Aid and Volunteers' Dependants' Fund, an amalgamation of two charitable organisations established following the Easter Rebellion to help rebel prisoners and their families. One had been set up by Dublin Corporation and the other by Tom Clarke's widow, Kathleen, who used gold left over from what Clan na Gael had provided to finance the rebellion. Collins did not realise that some friends from Frongoch pulled strings to get him the job. 'We worked like hell, though we were careful to keep any knowledge from him of what we were doing,' one of them recalled. 'Mick would have taken a very sour view of our part in the affair.'

Collins realised that there was resistance to his appointment. 'I was regarded with a certain amount of suspicion,' he wrote to a friend. 'I was young and would therefore be almost certain to be irresponsible to the importance of the position.' He thought his involvement in the rebellion was frowned upon by the committee, especially the ladies. 'In the end,' he wrote, 'chiefly by good fortune the job became mine.'

In his new position he was in contact with a wide spectrum of people sympathetic to the separatist movement. Kathleen Clarke provided him with the names of IRB contacts throughout the country. As his work was of a charitable nature, he was able to travel widely without rousing the slightest suspicion. With the recognised leaders still in jail, he became particularly influential in rebuilding the IRB. He took an active part and, in his own words, 'had a great time' supporting Count Plunkett's campaign for a vacant parliamentary seat in Roscommon in the February 1917 by-election.

From the outset Collins was optimistic. 'Consider the situation,' he wrote on 19 January. 'It is ripe for whatever one may wish.' He believed the Irish Parliamentary Party and the Crown authorities were now 'in a corner, driven there by what they have done and by the will of the people'.

'The crowds were splendid,' he wrote to Hannie. 'It was really pleasing to see so many old lads coming out in the snow and voting for Plunkett with the greatest enthusiasm. Practically all the very old people were solid for us and on the other end the young ones.' Plunkett won the seat, and in the process provided a tremendous boost for the separatist movement.

The work of reorganising the IRB took up a lot of Collins's time because there was so much to be done. 'It is only since being released that I'm feeling to the full all that we have lost in the way of men and workers,' he noted. As a result he was 'kept going from morning till night and usually into the next morning'. He was suspicious of some of the people who were offering help. 'I haven't the prevailing belief in the many conversions to our cause,' he wrote. Indeed, he found that he 'incurred a good deal of unpopularity through telling people so'.

The separatist movement at this time consisted of a number of different organisations, each with its own leader. Arthur Griffith was the head of Sinn Féin, Count Plunkett of the Liberty League, Eoin MacNeill was still nominally the head of the Irish Volunteers, and Thomas Ashe had been elected head of the IRB. In addition, there was Eamon de Valera, the elected spokesman of the prisoners in Lewes Jail. He had nominally been a member of the IRB, but had never been really active in the organisation.

De Valera owed his prominence to two facts: first, the men fighting under his command had inflicted the heaviest casualties on the British during the Easter Rising, and second, he was not closely identified with any of the various organisations. It was also later suggested that he was the only commandant to survive the executions and was the last commandant to surrender, but neither of those statements was true. Thomas Ashe and Thomas Hunter also survived the executions, while Ashe was the last to surrender and had been arguably the most effective commandant of the rising, seeing that the men under his command actually had victories over the Crown forces, whereas de Valera's men had been defeated at Mount Street Bridge after putting up a stout resistance.

De Valera was in Dartmoor Jail one morning when, noticing MacNeill coming down a stairs, he called the other rebel prisoners to attention to salute their chief of staff. Even though MacNeill had nothing to do with the planning of the rebellion, indeed had tried to call it off and took no part in it, he was still sentenced to life in prison by the British. Many of the men despised MacNeill but in the circumstances they complied with the order, which cast de Valera in the role of a healing force among the prisoners. This was probably more responsible than anything else for de Valera's subsequent election as spokesman for the prisoners.

The prisoners in the jail were held under much more stringent conditions than the internees at Frongoch. De Valera had to wear prison clothes and he was given the number 'q95' at Dartmoor. Silence was rigorously imposed and they were only allowed one letter a month. The tougher conditions, coupled with the fact that the Irish prisoners had little chance of associating with each other, meant that life in Dartmoor was vastly different from that which some of the men later said they 'enjoyed' at Frongoch.

'Labour, as labour, we rather welcome for its own sake and as an employment, be it digging, carting manure, carrying sacks of coke on our back, or scrubbing our halls,' de Valera wrote.

On one occasion he was caught throwing food to a colleague in another cell and the two of them were punished for breaking prison discipline. He went on hunger strike to protest and was transferred to the infirmary and then to Maidstone Prison, where he remained only a short time before being sent to Lewes, where the bulk of the Irish prisoners were brought together. The conditions there were much more relaxed and they were allowed to talk freely during the exercise period. De Valera was elected spokesman by the Irish prisoners over Ashe, who was seen as one of the IRB manipulators. De Valera, on the other hand, was regarded as a moderate who was more likely to unify the prisoners.

Robert Brennan, who was a fellow prisoner at the time and a lifelong supporter afterwards, noted later that de Valera was a very good listener. He actually encouraged debate; yet in the end he would insist on having his own way. 'You can talk about this as much as you like, the more the better and from every angle,' he would say. 'In the last analysis, if you don't agree with me, then I quit. You must get someone else to do it.'

His own abortive hunger strike had turned him against the tactic. 'You may be tempted to Hunger Strike,' he argued. 'As a body do not attempt it whilst the war lasts unless you were assured from outside that the death of two or three of you would help the cause.' Even at this early stage he obviously understood the value of propaganda, and it was mainly as a propagandist rather than as a soldier that he would distinguish himself as a leader.

From the outside the prisoners heard word of Count Plunkett's election to Westminster and his refusal to take his seat. De Valera had shared a cell with him in Richmond Barracks only months earlier while awaiting trial, but he was sceptical about people associated with the rebellion entering politics. 'It is a question whether it is good tactics (or strategy if you will) to provoke a contest in which *defeat* may well mean *ruin,*' he wrote. 'We should abstain *officially* from taking sides in these contests and no candidates should in future be *officially* recognised as standing in our interests or as representing our ideals.'

Collins managed to set up secret communications with Ashe through visitors smuggling messages into the jail. In April Collins came up with a plan to nominate one of the Lewes prisoners, Joe McGuinness from the Longford area, for a forthcoming by-election in the county. His aim was to dramatise the issue of the prisoners by asking the people to elect McGuinness as a means of demonstrating public support for the release of all the prisoners who took part in the rebellion. Although the response from de Valera and some IRB prisoners had been pretty critical, Collins was not about to be deterred.

'If you only knew of the long fights I've had with A. G[riffith] and some of his pals before I could gain the present point,' Collins wrote to Ashe. He had only with difficulty persuaded Sinn Féin not to put up a candidate in order not to split the separatist vote. Although Griffith had played no part in the Easter Rising, it was nevertheless widely identified with his party in the public mind, because Sinn Féin had been in the vanguard of the separatist movement for more than a decade.

'This Sinn Féin stunt is bloody balderdash!' Collins declared. 'We want a Republic.'

Griffith stared at him and Collins became uneasy. 'Of course,' he said, 'I don't know much about Sinn Féin.'

'Evidently not, Mr Collins, or you wouldn't talk like you do,' Griffith replied.

Collins knew well what Sinn Féin stood for. As a boy he had admired Griffith and had been active in the party during his early years in London. While he no longer shared Griffith's more moderate views, he still thought enough of him to try to excuse his rash remark.

A stubborn, opinionated politician with a resolute determination, Griffith was a fanatic in his own right, but he was unselfish in his dedication to the separatist cause. He wanted full independence for Ireland, but he was not a republican. Instead, he advocated an Anglo-Irish dual monarchy on Austro-Hungarian lines, as he believed it could be achieved by non-violent means. Hence he agreed not to put up a Sinn Féin candidate against McGuinness so that the release of all the remaining prisoners who had taken part in the rebellion could be made an election issue.

While Collins probably still had a sneaking admiration for the Sinn Féin leader, he possibly felt that he had to play this down because of Griffith's failure to support the rebellion. 'Some of us have been having fierce rows with him,' Collins wrote to Ashe. 'In view of this it is rather disgusting to be "chalked up" as a follower of his.' The Big Fellow did not want Ashe to think he was going soft because of his willingness to deal with Griffith, or even Eoin MacNeill who was in Lewes with Ashe. 'For God's sake,' Collins wrote, 'don't think that Master A. G. is going to turn us into eighty-two'ites. Another thing, you ask about Eoin — well we did not approach him and by the Lord neither shall we.'

The remark about 'eighty-two'ites' was clearly a reference to the so-called Kilmainham Treaty that Parnell made with the authorities while in jail in 1882. It is not clear why he was referring to MacNeill — possibly Ashe had asked if they had considered running him as a candidate for Westminster — but Collins's response ruled out having any truck with the man who had tried to call off the rebellion. The Big Fellow tended to express his views with a harshness that was often unattractive. He was described later as 'the very incarnation of out-and-out physical force republicanism' by Desmond Ryan.

Although Ashe liked the idea of running McGuinness, de Valera objected because a by-election was likely to be closely contested. De Valera argued that the movement's morale would be irreparably damaged by defeat at the polls. While in prison he drew up guidelines that provide an insight into his cautious approach. 'Never allow yourselves to be beaten,' he wrote. 'Having started a fight see that you win. Act then with caution. Carefully size up the consequences of a projected action. If you feel that *in the long run* you can be beaten then *don't begin*.' He persuaded McGuinness to decline the invitation to stand in the by-election.

But Collins was not about to stand for such timidity. Ignoring the instructions from Lewes Jail, he had McGuinness's name put forward anyway, much to the annoyance of IRB prisoners like Seán McGarry and Con Collins, who had sided with de Valera against Ashe on the issue.

'You can tell Con Collins, Seán McGarry and any other highbrows that I have been getting all their scathing messages, and am not a little annoyed, or at least was, but one gets so used to being called bad names and being misunderstood,' Collins wrote to Ashe. The Big Fellow's judgment was vindicated when McGuinness was elected in early May on the slogan: 'Put him in to get him out.'

The victory helped to increase pressure on the Lloyd George government to release the remaining prisoners. Although de Valera had been slow to appreciate the changes in Ireland during his absence, he was a better judge of the international political scene. After the United States entered the war in April 1917 with the avowed aim of making the world 'safe for democracy', American pressure on the British was increased to force them to do something about the Irish question. Lloyd George announced plans for a convention in which people representing all shades of Irish opinion would be charged with drawing up a constitution for Ireland. Astutely perceiving that the British government might try to curry favour with public opinion by making the magnanimous gesture of releasing the remaining Irish prisoners, de Valera advocated a prison strike in order to deprive Britain 'of any credit she may hope to gain from the release'.

The prisoners began their campaign on 28 May by demanding prisoner-of-war status and refusing to do prison work. When they were confined to their cells as punishment, they set about destroying the furnishings. De Valera and some other Irish prisoners were transferred to Maidstone, where he treated the prison governor with insolence and proceeded to wreck his cell.

Exaggerated accounts of what was happening in the prison were published in the press, and a public meeting was called in Dublin for 10 June to 'protest against the treatment of the men in Lewes Jail'. Although the meeting was banned by the military authorities, a crowd of some two to three thousand gathered in Beresford Place in the early evening. They were addressed by Cathal Brugha, a veteran of the rebellion. He was arrested by Inspector John Mills of the Dublin Metropolitan Police, and a riot ensued. As the inspector was leading Brugha to a nearby police station, he was hit over the head with a hurley and died of his injuries some hours later in Jervis Street Hospital. The father of three teenage children, he was a native of County Westmeath.

Against such a backdrop the British received little credit for their magnanimity when they released the prisoners a week later. It seemed Lloyd George was simply trying to make a virtue out of necessity. All were freed on 18 June. On the mail-boat home that night it was significant that de Valera's first act was to turn to the United States by drawing up an appeal to President Woodrow Wilson and the American Congress. After signing it himself, the first person he asked to sign was Eoin MacNeill. It was also signed by twenty-four others, including Austin Stack, Desmond FitzGerald, Sean MacEntee, and Fionan Lynch.

Noting that Wilson had written that the United States was fighting 'for the liberty, self-government and undictated development of all peoples', they called for the Americans to act in Ireland's case. 'We ask of the Government of the United States of America, and the Governments of the free peoples of the world, to take immediate measures to inform themselves accurately and on the spot about the extent of liberty or attempted repression which we may encounter.' The document was inserted into the US Congressional record and a facsimile of the original was published in the *Gaelic American* newspaper.

It was little over a year since the prisoners had been deported in disgrace, despised and dispirited, but they arrived back in Dublin to a tumultuous welcome next day. At around 4 a.m. there were some three thousand people waiting at the North Wall for the boat, but it docked at Kingstown. The men lined up and de Valera gave the order to march off to an awaiting train.

By the time the train reached Dublin the crowd had moved from the North Wall to Westland Row railway station and the entire length of the platform was thronged with young men and women carrying and waving tricolours. De Valera and the other leaders refused to make any comment about their prison treatment. Some of the men also refused, saying they were under orders that all statements should come through de Valera.

Collins, who helped organise the welcoming reception, was a model of efficiency in his capacity as secretary of the Irish National Aid and Volunteers' Dependants' Fund. He had worked out the travel costs of all the released prisoners from Dublin to their homes, but his rather abrupt, businesslike manner was a little too officious for some.

Robert Brennan, one of those released from Lewes, had already noticed the pale, fast-moving, energetic young man darting here and there. He was all business. He frequently dispensed with formalities like shaking hands or even saying good morning. He came over and, without bothering to introduce himself, told Brennan to look after those returning to Wexford.

'He had a roll of notes in one hand and silver in the other,' Brennan recalled. 'He said that the fares to Enniscorthy amounted to so much, and I found out later the sum was correct to a penny. He added that he was giving me five shillings, in addition, for each man, to cover incidental expenses. As he handed me the money, he looked into my eyes as if appraising me. With a quick smile, he shook my hand and turned to someone else.'

'Who is he?' Brennan asked.

'Michael Collins,' a friend replied.

'I don't like him,' said Brennan.

4

Reorganising

Having been deported in disgrace little over a year earlier, de Valera returned the hero of the hour as he was by now generally recognised as leader of the men of Easter Week. But he returned to a separatist movement that was distinctly fragmented. While the press erroneously depicted it as being under the control of Sinn Féin, Count Plunkett had actually been establishing a rival political organisation, the Liberty League, and the IRB was reorganising quietly in the background.

A by-election was called for East Clare in July and de Valera was invited to contest the seat against the Irish Parliamentary Party. From the outset he acted as a unifying influence by insisting that Eoin MacNeill accompany him when he made his first appearance on an election platform. Some, like Collins, wanted to have nothing to do with MacNeill, but de Valera brushed aside their objections. 'The clergy are with MacNeill and they are a powerful force,' he explained. By associating himself with MacNeill, de Valera acquired a reputation as a moderate as well as a unifying influence. MacNeill was in fact representative of a majority of those arrested after the rebellion. Most had not taken part in the fighting, and with someone like him at the forefront they would not feel like second-class supporters.

Adopting the approach of a seasoned politician, de Valera remained suitably vague during the campaign. He was opposed to the Irish Convention because of the necessity of not surrendering the rights of the majority to the unionists in Ulster. He was convinced that it was just a British ruse to depict the Irish as being unwilling to agree among themselves. The Convention was inevitably going to fail to reach an agreement, because the northern unionists were so opposed to Home Rule that there was no chance they would agree to an independent Ireland. De Valera therefore endorsed the idea of appealing to the postwar Peace Conference instead. But he relied most heavily during the campaign on an emotional appeal associating himself with the ideals of the executed leaders of the Easter Rebellion. He even suggested the possibility of resorting to arms again in order to demonstrate his own commitment to those ideals, but he was careful not to commit himself to any specific course. 'To assert it in arms, were there a fair chance of military success,' he said, 'I would consider a sacred duty.'

'We want an Irish Republic,' he explained, 'because if Ireland had her freedom, it is, I believe, the most likely form of government.' But he nevertheless emphasised he was not a doctrinaire republican. He was not firmly committed to any form of government. 'So long as it was an Irish government,' he said, 'I would not put a word against it.'

He was elected by a comfortable margin of more than two to one, following which he threw himself into the reorganisation of the separatist movement, travelling around the country. If Ireland was even to obtain a hearing at the postwar Peace Conference, he realised the country would first need to assert its own nationhood, and he suggested it would be as a republic that the country would have the best chance of enlisting the sympathetic support of influential republics like the United States and France. 'To be heard at the Peace Conference,' he told a Dublin gathering on 12 July 1917, 'Ireland must first claim absolute independence.'

The next by-election was in Kilkenny, where he went to campaign for W. T. Cosgrave, who stood on behalf of Sinn Féin. They were fighting England first with ballots, de Valera told a rally in Kilkenny on 5 August. If that failed, they would fight with rifles. Cosgrave duly won election to Westminster. It was the fourth by-election victory in a row for the separatists associated with the Easter Rebellion, and the British authorities began to react.

Sinn Féin's policy remained vague, but de Valera refuted charges that the party had no policy. Like a good chess player, he had no intention of telegraphing his intention in advance. He admitted there was no guarantee that the appeal to the postwar Peace Conference would be successful. 'We will give it a chance,' he said, 'and we will have a far better chance of getting our freedom from the Peace Conference than in going begging and letting English statesmen fool us.'

While de Valera travelled about the country to political rallies in Limerick, Cootehill, Dublin, and Waterford, Collins concentrated on the Longford, Roscommon, and Leitrim area. He was a young man and he had taken a particular fancy to Helen Kiernan, one of four daughters who were helping their brother Larry to run their family hotel, the Greville Arms, in Granard, County Longford. The other Kiernan sisters also had boyfriends in the movement. Harry Boland was in love with Helen's sister Kitty, and Thomas Ashe was courting her sister Maud.

Ashe was arrested in August and charged with making a seditious speech in Ballinalee, County Longford, where Collins had shared the platform with him. For some weeks he had been observed travelling to organisational meetings with Ashe, and he visited him in custody at the Curragh detention centre. Collins also attended his court martial a fortnight later.

'The whole business was extremely entertaining, almost as good as a "Gilbert and Sullivan skit trial by jury"', Collins wrote to Ashe's sister immediately afterwards. 'The President of the Court was obviously biased against Tom, and, although the charge is very trivial, and the witnesses contradicted each other, it is quite likely that Tom will be sentenced.'

Ashe was duly convicted and sentenced to a prison term. He demanded prisoner-of-war status and when this was refused, he went on hunger strike. The authorities decided to feed him forcibly and he died on 25 September 1917 as a result of injuries received in the process. His death was to have a tremendous impact on public opinion, especially young people.

Collins was particularly upset. 'I grieve perhaps as no one else grieves,' he wrote. Dressed in the uniform of a vice-commandant, he delivered the graveside address, which was stirring in its simplicity. 'Nothing additional remains to be said,' he declared, following the sounding of the last post and the firing of a volley of shots. 'That volley which we have just heard is the only speech which it is proper to make over the grave of a dead Fenian.'

On 8 October Collins went back to speak in Ballinalee. The local police had warned that since the speech for which Ashe had been arrested had been made there, 'speeches of a strong seditious nature' could be expected, especially if Collins and Darrell Figgis attended, as advertised. They were likely 'to use fairly strong language and make the occasion a somewhat dramatic one,' the local police warned.

'In the circumstances,' Collins noted, 'I came out on the strong side.' Joe McGuinness, who preceded him on the platform, referred to the recent by-election victories and predicted that Sinn Féin 'will win all seats that will become vacant in Ireland'. Collins then delivered the main speech on Ashe and denounced the local police for lying at his court martial. 'Thomas Ashe is not dead,' he declared. 'His spirit is still with us.' Although Collins predicted that they would not have any difficulty in putting Ireland's case before the Peace Conference if they organised properly, he still thought the British would not concede anything unless compelled to do so. 'You will not get anything from the British Government,' he said, 'unless you approach them with a bullock's tail in one hand and a landlord's head in the other.'

All went well, as far as Collins was concerned, except, he wrote, that there was 'a bit of unpleasantness with a policeman who was taking notes'. The man was confronted for those notes and thought it best to surrender them, and there was no further problem.

As a result of Ashe's death, the IRB had no recognised leader of its own, so the organisation threw its full support behind de Valera when the various separatist organisations came together to unite under the Sinn Féin banner at the party's Ard Fheis (national convention) on 25 October 1917. The three main contenders for the leadership of the party were Griffith, the existing president of Sinn Féin, Count Plunkett, and de Valera. The big difference between de Valera and Griffith was over the most advantageous form of government for Ireland. As has been mentioned, Griffith had been advocating the establishment of a dual monarchy between Britain and Ireland on Austro-Hungarian lines for over a decade. A few days before the Ard Fheis was due to begin, however, de Valera managed to persuade him to accept a compromise formula, whereby Sinn Féin would pledge itself to securing a republic and once it had been achieved, the Irish people would then freely choose their own form of government by referendum. De Valera also prevailed upon Griffith to withdraw from the race for the presidency of Sinn Féin and propose him instead. At the last moment Plunkett also withdrew, so de Valera was elected unanimously.

He then delivered a presidential address that had something for moderates and militants alike. They were not irrevocably committed to securing a republic. 'This is not the time for discussion of the best forms of government,' he said. 'But we are all united on this — that we want complete and absolute independence. Get that and we will agree to differ afterwards. We do not wish to bind the people to any form of government.' Yet he continued in contradictory terms, as he declared that it was 'necessary to be united under the flag for which we are going to fight for our freedom, the flag of the Irish Republic. We have nailed that flag to the mast; we shall never lower it.'

Nobody seemed bothered by the contradictions, as he was hailed as a born leader. Everybody was supposedly following him, though none of them could have been sure exactly where he was going. On the one hand he was outlining a political path, but in the same speech he also talked in the most militant terms of forcing Britain to resort to the sword. 'England pretends it is not by the naked sword, but by the good will of the people of the country that she is here,' de Valera told the Ard Fheis. 'We will draw the naked sword to make her bare her own naked sword, to drag the hypo-critical mask off her face, and to show her to the world for what she is, the accursed oppressor of nations.'

Griffith was elected vice-president along with Father Michael O'Flanagan, while Darrell Figgis and Austin Stack were elected joint honorary secretary. Collins had campaigned enthusiastically for de Valera, and gave members of the IRB a list of twenty-four people to be supported for the party executive, for which he was standing himself. Most of those on his list were defeated, and to add insult to injury, MacNeill headed the poll with 888 votes, while Collins and his IRB colleague, Ernest Blythe, tied for the last two places with 340 votes each.

The following day the Irish Volunteers held a separate convention at which de Valera was elected president. Consequently, he was the head of the most important political and military wings of the separatist movement. This time Collins, who again enthusiastically supported de Valera, was appointed director of organisation, which was the influential position from which Patrick Pearse had essentially taken over the Volunteers less than two years earlier. A twenty-six-man executive was established, with a small 'resident executive' to oversee the day-to-day running of the Volunteers. Cathal Brugha was put in charge of the resident executive.

Following the two conventions, de Valera toured the country as a paid national organiser for Sinn Féin. Calling on the people to repudiate the so-called Irish Convention then sitting, he held out the hope that President Woodrow Wilson's announced war aims would lead to Irish freedom. With the Allies supposedly fighting for the rights of small nations, de Valera challenged them to name those countries concerned. Once earnest proof had been given that Ireland would be included among those nations, he promised that half a million Irishmen would be prepared to help the Allies. 'Then they will find,' he said, 'that these half a million men will be ready to defend their own land, and ready to give a helping hand to the oppressed.'

He was deliberately linking the Irish question with the most emotional international issue of the day — the First World War. The Volunteers were struggling for the principle of self-determination, he explained, so if Wilson was sincere, then the Volunteers and the Americans were 'genuine "associates" in this war'. De Valera aimed to depict the Irish cause in a favourable light for the Americans because, he believed, if Britain ignored Ireland's right to self-determination after the war, it would be possible to call on the 'great bulk of the Irish in the States' to use their 'weighty influence' to put pressure on the British.

'If President Wilson is honest, he will easily pardon us for not trusting him with an implicit faith,' the new Sinn Féin leader candidly explained. 'If he is a hypocrite, if he is a meet partner for those who began this world war with altruistic professions of liberty and freedom, then the sooner America and the sooner mankind knows it the better.' He emphasised, however, that he was not pronouncing any judgment on Wilson. The Irish case would be the test to 'prove to the world the sincerity or hypocrisy of the Allies and President Wilson when they declared that they were fighting for the self-determination of nations'.

Despite de Valera's strenuous efforts to bolster Sinn Féin, the party lost three consecutive by-elections to IPP candidates in early 1918. The first defeat was in South Armagh, where the unionist community apparently supported the IPP candidate to the obvious fury of de Valera, who afterwards described the unionists as 'a rock on the road' to Irish freedom. 'We must if necessary blast it out of our path,' he added rather recklessly. Within three weeks of his inflammatory remarks, Sinn Féin suffered two further defeats — one in Waterford and the other in East Tyrone, where unionists were again blamed for supporting the IPP candidate.

Meanwhile the arrangement with Brugha at the head of the resident executive committee of the Volunteers was not working out. Things were too loose, so it was decided to elect a chief of staff. Brugha was quite content to leave it to the younger men to pick their own chief. Seven members of the resident executive met at the headquarters of the printers' union at 35 Lower Gardiner Street to select a chief of staff in March 1918. Those attending were Collins, Richard Mulcahy, Dick McKee, Gearóid O'Sullivan, Diarmuid O'Hegarty, Rory O'Connor, and Seán McMahon. Even those closest to Collins were 'wary of entrusting him with anything like complete control', according to Mulcahy. They clearly had doubts about his volatile temperament, and they looked to Mulcahy instead.

'We agreed among ourselves that I would become chief of staff,' Mulcahy wrote. He was a very different character from Collins. A self-composed and impassive individual, he never sought to impress people with the kind of bombast that the Big Fellow used. He could sit patiently and listen or wait, while Collins always had to be on the move. But, in spite of the differences, they still got on very well together, partly because Mulcahy was sure enough of himself not to be upset by what others might have considered meddling. He recognised the tremendous organisational talents of Collins and was prepared to give them full rein without the kind of jealousy that was to mar the Big Fellow's relations with others.

In addition to being director of organisation, Collins was now also appointed adjutant general, which meant that he was in charge of training and discipline. He therefore travelled about the country reorganising the force and speaking to various meetings, in spite of being under police surveillance. Speaking in Ballinamuck, County Longford, on 3 March, he said he wished that 'Longford and every county in Ireland was like Clare today, that every little village in it was occupied by military with artillery, armoured cars and machine guns'. It was not that he wanted every place occupied, but that if more places were, it would be easier to seize arms. He told the Volunteers at the meeting 'not to take old swords or shot guns' from their friends or neighbours. 'What they wanted was rifles, and they knew where to get them,' he said, according to a police report.

Charles Collins, the local county inspector of the Royal Irish Constabulary (RIC), concluded that the Big Fellow's 'language was seditious, and intended to cause disaffection'. It seemed 'to be a direct incentive to rob the Police of their rifles', the inspector reported, and he warned that if Collins was not restrained soon, there would be 'serious mischief'. The decision to arrest him on a charge of inciting people to steal arms was taken within a matter of days, on 11 March, but before he was arrested he would be in trouble for another speech, this time at a public meeting held in the town square of Skibbereen, County Cork, on 31 March.

During the address Collins denounced a recent court case in which a local man, Bernie O'Driscoll, was sentenced to jail for a seditious speech threatening retaliation if Ernest Blythe died while on hunger strike in Cork Jail. 'If the words of Bernie O'Driscoll's mean inciting to crime then I say in the presence of the Police who are here making mental and other notes that I tender the very same advice, that I stand where Bernie stood. That too is the advice I give to the Volunteers,' Collins said, according to one police report.

'Bernie cheered "Up the Germans" in the court-house,' Collins continued. 'You would think the Germans heard that cheer of Bernie's, for on the very same day they the Germans captured 1,500 British.'

If anything happened to O'Driscoll, another policeman reported Collins as saying, 'I hope every Volunteer will know what to do.' If anybody doubted what was meant, the Big Fellow's friend Gearóid O'Sullivan left little room for doubt when he spoke next. He referred to the police as the principal enemy and advised that nobody should speak to them.

'The British threatened to torture the Commanders of German submarines they captured, but the Germans retorted that if they did, they (the Germans) would kill five British officers for every one of them they illtreated,' O'Sullivan was reported as saying. 'This had the desired effect, and I now declare that if anything serious happens to Bernie O'Driscoll (who is on hunger strike in Cork Gaol) then we too can make similar reprisals and the volunteers here know when and how to do it.'

Two days later Collins was arrested by the Dublin Metropolitan Police (DMP) as he emerged from his office on Bachelor's Walk, Dublin. He resisted strenuously and a crowd gathered and began cheering and jeering before he was taken away. He appeared in a Longford court next day. According to the police report, he 'was very abusive and insulting'. He refused to recognise the court, and when he was bound over to a further hearing in July, he refused to give bail, so he was removed to Sligo Jail.

'Before me therefore is the prospect of a prolonged holiday and of course July will only be the real commencement of it,' he wrote to Hannie. He had 'hardly anyone to talk to' in Sligo, so he did a good deal of reading and study, especially Irish history. He also tried to follow the political crisis that was brewing as the British government mulled over the possibility of introducing conscription in Ireland. Sinn Féin no longer seemed in such a strong position after the loss of the three by-elections, but the proposal to introduce conscription played right into Sinn Féin's hands.

'I'm very anxious to know what Lloyd George has done about conscription for this country,' Collins wrote on 10 April. 'If he goes for it — well he's ended.' In fact, the British government had already introduced a bill the previous day to enable it to extend conscription to Ireland. The bill was rushed through parliament, and members of the IPP walked out of Westminster in protest, which was tantamount to endorsing the abstentionist policy that Sinn Féin had been following all along. Collins quickly appreciated the implications of what was happening. 'The conscription proposals are to my liking as I think they will end well for Ireland,' he wrote.

This was another major turning-point for the independence movement. De Valera played the major role in dramatising the conscription threat in the coming days. The lord mayor of Dublin, Laurence O'Neill, invited representatives of various shades of nationalist opinion to the Mansion House for a conference on what to do about conscription on 18 April 1918. A standing committee was established, with de Valera and Griffith representing Sinn Féin, while John Dillon and Joe Devlin represented the IPP. There was also the mayor, three labour representatives and two independent members of parliament, William O'Brien and Tim Healy. The uniformity of opinion bringing such a diverse group of Irishmen together was evidence of the unpopularity of conscription.

During the Mansion House deliberations de Valera stood out. 'His transparent sincerity, his gentleness and equability captured the hearts of us all,' according to O'Brien, who described the Sinn Féin leader's obstinacy as 'sometimes trying', but it nevertheless 'became tolerable enough, when, 'with a boyish smile', de Valera would say: 'You will bear with me, won't you? You know I am an old schoolmaster.'

De Valera's influence was evident with the adoption of a declaration bearing the indelible imprint of separatist thinking. Basing the case against conscription on 'Ireland's separate and distinct nationhood' and the principle that governments 'derive their just power from the consent of the governed', the conference denied 'the right of the British government, or any external authority, to impose compulsory service in Ireland against the clearly expressed will of the Irish people'.

At de Valera's suggestion the conference sought the support of the Roman Catholic hierarchy, which responded by virtually sanctifying the campaign against conscription. The hierarchy publicly called for a special mass to be celebrated the following Sunday 'in every church in Ireland to avert the scourge of conscription with which Ireland is now threatened'. It also asked the people to subscribe to an anti-conscription pledge drafted by de Valera.

While Collins was in jail, Brugha put together an assassination team and went to London with the aim of shooting members of the British cabinet. There were eleven men engaged in the operation, who staked out cabinet ministers and watched their habits with the intention of assassinating them once the order was given. At one point during their preparations Brugha and two colleagues, each armed with a revolver, were signed into Westminster as guests of Larry Ginnell. They sat in the visitors' gallery of the House of Commons. But the assassination plans were never implemented, because the British never introduced conscription.

Collins, who had nothing to do with Brugha's scheme, realised the conscription controversy afforded a tremendous opportunity for Sinn Féin to exploit public resentment. Two Longford businessmen put up bail for him, and he was released on 22 April.

'Some local Sinn Féiners were not pleased, when he gave bail,' according to the RIC. But there were about sixty supporters waiting to welcome him outside the Greville Arms Hotel in Granard when he arrived there by car. There was a fair in progress in the town and a 'considerable crowd collected', according to the police. The gathering waved tricolours and sang the 'Soldier's Song'. Charles Collins, the local head of the RIC, observed that the decision to post bail 'may be taken as an indication the resistance to conscription will not be merely passive'.

Meanwhile de Valera sought to enlist American support by giving his first formal newspaper interview to a correspondent of the *Christian Science Monitor*. If Britain was really fighting for the principles enunciated by President Wilson, he contended, 'she could apply them without trouble and without delay' in Ireland's case. Under the circumstances he was not prepared to take the chance that the Irish people would be fairly treated, if they dropped their opposition to conscription.

'Ireland cannot afford to gamble,' he said. 'Great powers strong enough to enforce their contracts can safely enter a combination, knowing their strength is a guarantee that the contract will not be violated and that what they stipulated for will not be denied them when success is achieved.' A small nation like Ireland, however, would have no such guarantee.

De Valera also prepared a draft text for a formal appeal to the United States on behalf of the Mansion House Conference. While it was being circulated among the other members of the conference, he learned from Collins that the authorities planned to arrest the whole Sinn Féin leadership. Joe Kavanagh, a police detective, gave Thomas Gay, a public librarian, a list of those to be arrested that night, 18 May. Gay, a former colleague in Frongoch, passed the list on to Collins, who had already received a warning from a different source. Two days earlier a friend had been tipped off by another detective, Ned Broy, though he had not been able to mention any specific names at the time.

It so happened that the Sinn Féin executive was meeting that night at its headquarters in 6 Harcourt Street. Darrell Figgis, one of the joint national secretaries, arrived to find people busy spiriting away papers in preparation for a raid. There was some discussion at the meeting as to the best course of action.

'It seemed to us that our arrests could not but stiffen the nation's resistance,' Figgis wrote later. 'The shock would startle and arouse the country.' Having lost three consecutive by-elections, the Sinn Féin leaders concluded that they could stop the rot and virtually ensure the victory of Arthur

Griffith in a forthcoming by-election in East Cavan by allowing the Crown authorities to arrest them. 'There would be many others to take our places,' Figgis noted.

Collins had no intention of allowing himself to be taken. After the meeting he went to warn Seán McGarry, the president of the IRB, but his home was already in the process of being raided. Collins joined the curious onlookers as McGarry was taken away. He then spent the night in McGarry's home, as it was unlikely to be raided again that night.

Though Collins evaded the authorities, much of the Sinn Féin leadership was rounded up that night in the so-called 'German Plot' arrests. No convincing evidence of a plot was ever produced. Joseph Dowling, one of those that Roger Casement had recruited for his Irish Brigade, was sent to Ireland by the Germans in April 1918, to make contact with Sinn Féin, but he was arrested on an island off the Galway coast before he could make contact. In view of de Valera's speeches emphasising that Sinn Féin would accept help wherever it could get it, he would undoubtedly have given Dowling a hearing, but there was no evidence of any plot involving Sinn Féin. As a result most Irish people assumed that the whole thing was just a ruse for Britain to take Sinn Féin leaders out of circulation in order to pave the way for conscription. The Germans were trying to make contact with Sinn Féin, but people like de Valera, Griffith, Plunkett, McGuinness, Cosgrave, and MacNeill were certainly not involved with the Germans at the time. Indeed none of them were ever charged with any offence, yet they were held in jail for the next nine months. In the circumstances Sinn Féin was able to make enormous political capital out of the arrests.

An edited version of de Valera's appeal to the United States was published in pamphlet form. It ended in mid-sentence, as if he had been arrested with pen in hand while actually drafting the document. By arresting only members of Sinn Féin, the British inevitably gave the impression they thought the party was primarily responsible for organising the widespread opposition to conscription and, as a result, Sinn Féin profited most from the popular backlash generated by the issue.

With the country in uproar, the British dared not use the new authority to introduce conscription. Popular feelings were so strong in Ireland that the Westminster government announced on 3 June that conscription would be postponed until October, at least. As the IPP had been unable to prevent the passage of the bill in the first place, Sinn Féin was given the credit for forcing the government to back down, and the jailed Griffith ended the series of Sinn Féin by-election defeats by easily winning in Cavan less than three weeks later.

The popular urge to fight conscription was a great impetus to enlistment in the Volunteers. Although there was a decline in the membership following the easing of the crisis, many new recruits had still been gained.

An even more far-reaching consequence of the crisis was the vacuum left at the top of the movement by the arrest of moderates like de Valera, Griffith, and MacNeill, who had been exerting a restraining influence. They had designated replacements within the party but those people lacked the stature to keep militants like Collins and Cathal Brugha in line. The militants suddenly had more influence than ever, and they were gradually able to exert a kind of ascendancy of their own. Collins soon gained effective control of both the IRB and Sinn Féin itself. He became 'the real master' of the Sinn Féin executive, according to Figgis, who described him as 'a man of ruthless purpose and furious energy, knowing clearly what he wanted and prepared to trample down everybody to get it'.

On 5 July 1918 the British government banned all public gatherings such as political rallies and even football matches without a police permit. Sinn Féin set about defying the ban. The GAA held football and hurling matches throughout the country in open defiance on 4 August and again on Assumption Thursday, eleven days later. In all Sinn Féin held some 1,800 public rallies throughout the country in mass defiance of the government.

The incitement case against Collins for his speeches in March had been moved from Longford to Derry on 17 July, but he did not bother to show. A bench warrant was issued for his arrest, but it was never executed and indeed the authorities decided not to proceed with it for some unexplained reason. Of course, by then the police in Cork were looking to arrest Collins for his seditious remarks in Skibbereen following the jailing of Bernie O'Driscoll.

With so many prominent members of the movement locked up, Collins set about organising a network to smuggle letters in and out of jail. Calling on his own experience from Frongoch, he enlisted the help of certain guards, while visitors to the prisons often carried messages for him.

He concentrated on organisational matters within the Volunteers and was largely contemptuous of politicians. Although he was a member of the Sinn Féin executive, he felt it lacked direction. Executive meetings were poorly attended, and the discussions 'lacked any great force', according to him. He was particularly critical of Sinn Féin vice-president, Father Michael O'Flanagan, for 'hobnobbing' with Crown officials, or the 'enemy', as Collins saw it. With de Valera and Griffith in jail, O'Flanagan was nominally in charge of Sinn Féin, and he presided at meetings of the executive. Collins still had little time for the clergy, and even less for that political priest and the people around him. They did too much talking and not enough work, as far as Collins was concerned.

As a member of the party's executive Collins was more involved in establishing clubs at the grass-roots level and also in arranging meetings to select candidates to stand for the party in the next general election. He was chosen himself to stand in the constituency of South Cork.

His radical views were best represented in an article written for *An t-Óglach* by Ernest Blythe, the man whose hunger strike in March had led to so much commotion in Skibbereen. He was a northern Protestant who had adopted the nationalist cause with all the zeal of the radical convert. 'We must recognise,' Blythe wrote, 'that anyone, civilian or soldier, who assists directly or by convenience in this crime against us, merits no more consideration than a wild beast, and should be killed without mercy or hesitation as opportunity offers.' As director of organisation, Collins was deeply involved with the publication of *An t-Óglach*. He wrote the column, 'Notes on Organisation', and also directed and distributed the publication personally. He was so taken with Blythe's article that he asked for more of the same from him.

Collins wanted things done immediately, with no excuses. 'Have you got it?' he would ask. 'If you haven't got it, don't mind the excuses, but go and get it.'

'There are one hundred copies of the September number of *An t-Óglach* allotted to your brigade, so the amount due is 16/8, please forward this sum without delay,' he wrote to Michael de Lacy in Limerick on 31 August 1918. 'By attending to this at once you will greatly facilitate matters.' In the next ten days he impatiently sent two more reminders, and when he still had not received the money after a fortnight, he despatched a demand. 'I do not request,' Collins wrote. 'I insist.'

When Ernie O'Malley met him in his office at Bachelor's Walk, he found Collins pacing up and down impatiently. 'He jerked his head to a chair to indicate I should sit,' O'Malley noted. He took a chair which he tilted back against the wall. It was an awkward gesture, not an indication of relaxation, because Collins was not relaxed. Instead he projected an image of frustrated restraint with energy exuding in his rapid gestures. A lock of hair would fall down over his forehead, and he would toss it back with a vigorous twist of his head. His tilted chair was an unconscious display of arrogance. This was the Big Fellow showing off. At one point Collins mentioned a recent raid in which Inspector Bruton of the DMP found empty packing cases and ammunition wrappers. 'This looks as if there were brains behind it,' he quoted the inspector as supposedly having said. 'I bet it's that fellow from Mountjoy Street.' At the time Collins was living in the Munster Hotel at 44 Mountjoy Street. He was trying to impress O'Malley, and, of course, he was trying too hard. His display of raw vanity had the opposite effect. O'Malley formed an instinctive dislike that he was never quite able to overcome.

Probably the best insight into the thinking of Collins around this time can be gleaned from his correspondence with Austin Stack, while the latter was in jail. Stack had been closely associated with Ashe, a fellow Kerryman, and this probably prompted Collins to hold Stack in extremely high regard, although they could hardly have known each other very well at the time. Collins wrote to him in effusive terms, for instance informing him of happenings on the outside and seeking his advice. 'I was very glad to get your letter, especially the personal note which I appreciated,' Collins wrote to him on 29 August. 'Without insincerity I can say that I do appreciate it more from yourself than from anyone I know.' It was ironic that they would become the bitterest of political enemies in the days ahead.

The signing of the armistice ending the Great War was warmly welcomed throughout much of the world, especially in the victorious countries. There were several days of celebrations in Dublin, but there were some very ugly incidents from the second night on. These incidents were probably sparked by people who had had too much to drink, but Collins seemed to take a vicarious delight in writing about attacks made on soldiers.

'As a result of various encounters there were 125 cases of wounded soldiers treated at Dublin Hospitals that night,' he wrote to Stack. 'Before morning three soldiers and one officer had ceased to need any attention and one other died the following day. A policeman too was in a precarious condition up to a few days ago when I ceased to take any further interest in him. He was unlikely to recover.'

The British Prime Minister, David Lloyd George, called a general election for December 1918. Sinn Féin put up candidates throughout Ireland. With so many leaders still in jail as a result of the German Plot, Collins played a large part in the campaign. Together with Harry Boland and Diarmuid O'Hegarty, he was primarily responsible for the selection of Sinn Féin candidates, and they resorted to the tried and trusted formula that had proved so successful in the McGuinness campaign in May 1917. Most of the nominated members of the party were in prison. Such was the extent of the backstage management of the party's campaign that many of the candidates did not even know their names were being put forward. Some only learned when prison authorities informed them that they had been elected to parliament.

Collins also tried to highlight the divisions within the IPP. Tim Healy, who had been in parliament since before the Parnell split in which he had played a major role, had recently resigned his seat in protest over the government's policy in Ireland, together with the IPP's failure to take a proper stand for Irish rights. Boland and Collins therefore asked him to come out publicly in favour of the call for self-determination for Ireland. This would, of course, have had the effect of saying that Sinn Féin had been right all along. Healy would undoubtedly have been glad to get involved with Sinn Féin had they been prepared to invite him to play a major role, but he felt the brains of the party were in jail and he was not really impressed by either Boland or Collins. He was dismissive of the two of them in a rather cryptic comment. 'As scavengers of corruption, splendid, as builders and framers of policy, nowhere,' he wrote.

The whole election process was a propaganda exercise in which Collins played a very active — though he would have had some believe a somewhat reluctant — part. He indicated that he would have preferred to have been able to devote more time to preparations to spring Stack from Belfast Jail, to which he had been recently transferred. 'Damn these elections,' he exclaimed in a letter to Stack in the midst of the campaign. His own election address to the voters of Cork was brief and to the point: 'You are requested by your votes, to assert before the nations of the world that Ireland's claim is to the status of an independent nation, and that we shall be satisfied with nothing less than our full claim — that in fact, any scheme of government which does not confer upon the people of Ireland the supreme, absolute and final control of all this country, external as well as internal, is a mockery and will not be accepted.'

Any remaining doubts about the tide of opinion sweeping Ireland since the Easter Rebellion were dispelled by the Sinn Féin landslide in the general election of 14 December. Sinn Féin enjoyed a magnificent victory at the polls, winning seventy-three seats against twenty-six for the Unionist Party and only six for the once powerful IPP. Its leader, John Dillon, was trounced in East Mayo by de Valera, who received almost twice Dillon's support. De Valera's name was also put forward in East Clare, where he was un-opposed, and in West Belfast, where he was defeated by Joe Devlin. It was a case of organisational brilliance of which there are few parallels. Sinn Féin had asked for a clear mandate, indicating in its election manifesto that its successful candidates would not sit at Westminster but would establish a sovereign, republican assembly in Ireland instead. It now had that mandate.

Meanwhile in jail de Valera still hoped President Wilson would stand by his lofty wartime pronouncements. The American President had continued to speak in idealistic terms during the final year of the war. '"Self-determination" is not a mere phrase,' Wilson had declared in February 1918. 'It is an imperative principle of action, which statesmen will henceforth ignore at their peril.'

'If America holds to the principles enunciated by her President during the war she will have a noble place in the history of nations,' de Valera wrote to his mother from Lincoln Jail on 28 November 1918. He believed those Wilsonian principles could be 'the basis of true statecraft — a firm basis that will bear the stress of time — but will the President be able to get them accepted by others whose entry into the war was on motives less unselfish? . . . What an achievement should he succeed in getting established a common law for nations — resting on the will of the nations — making national duels as rare as duels between individual persons are at present; if that be truly his aim, may God steady his hand.'

Shortly after the election Collins and three colleagues went over to Britain in the hope of explaining the Irish situation to Wilson, who arrived in London on a short visit on 26 December. They stayed at the home of Moya Llewlyn Davies, whom Collins had known during his emigrant days when she was Moya O'Connor. But the trip was futile, because the American President was unwilling to meet them. Collins was so annoyed that he suggested kidnapping Wilson to make him listen. 'If necessary,' he said, 'we can buccaneer him.' Fortunately nobody took the suggestion too seriously, but the proposal provided an insight into why some of his colleagues thought he was inclined to allow his enthusiasm to get the better of his judgment.

Having failed to meet him in London, Collins suggested on 3 January 1919 that Dublin Corporation pass a resolution to grant the freedom of the city to President Wilson. The lord mayor of Dublin duly invited the American President to receive the honour, but nothing came of this either, because Wilson pleaded that he was too busy to visit Ireland.

On 5 January Collins presided at a Volunteer meeting in Kilnadur, near Dunmanway, County Cork, of the senior officers from the six west Cork battalions in Bandon, Clonakilty, Dunmanway, Skibbereen, Bantry, and Castletownbere. It was at that meeting that it was decided to form the Cork No. 3 Brigade of the Irish Volunteers, which ironically was the brigade that was behind the ambush in which Collins would lose his life little over three and a half years later. Two of the men elected at this meeting — the new brigade commandant, Tom Hales, and the adjutant, Liam Deasy — would be the two main men behind the fateful ambush.

The Dunmanway meeting had initially been planned for Clonakilty, but it was proscribed by the local authorities. The police had made plans to arrest Collins in Clonakilty for his Skibbereen speech the previous March. They then planned to arrest him at the Dunmanway meeting, but they reported that the meeting was warned that the police were coming and broke up before they could get there. Though the RIC report depicted the gathering as scurrying off in all directions, using byroads and running across fields, they were actually a day late.

Collins was still in Dunmanway, but he evaded capture and returned to Dublin for a meeting of those members of Sinn Féin who had recently been elected to Westminster. Twenty-four of the victorious candidates met on 7 January to consider their next move, most of their colleagues still being in jail. At the outset they took the following oath:

> I hereby pledge myself to work for the establishment of an independent Irish Republic; that I will accept nothing less than complete separation from England in settlement of Ireland's

claims; and that I will abstain from attending the English Parliament.

The meeting proceeded to discuss arrangements to set up the promised national assembly, Dáil Éireann. Collins wrote that he was 'very much against' this while so many elected representatives were in jail. It was significant that he was not present in the Mansion House on 21 January when Dáil Éireann formally met for the first time and ratified the establishment of the Irish Republic that had been proclaimed in 1916. He felt he had better things to do. He was later accused of being behind an ambush that day at Soloheadbeg, County Tipperary, in which two policemen were killed while escorting a consignment of explosives to a quarry. As national organiser of the Irish Volunteers, Collins was blamed for this attack, but it was really a local operation.

Feeling that 'the Volunteers were in great danger of becoming merely a political adjunct to the Sinn Féin organisation,' some local Volunteers led by Seán Treacy and Dan Breen decided to force the pace. 'We had enough of being pushed around and getting our men imprisoned while we remained inactive,' Breen later wrote. 'It was high time that we did a bit of pushing.' They shot the two policemen in cold blood with no apparent remorse. 'Our only regret was that the escort had consisted of only two Peelers instead of six,' Breen wrote. 'If there had to be dead Peelers at all, six would have created a better impression than a mere two.'

'It is said that if Tipperary leads, all Ireland is sure to follow,' the parish priest declared from the pulpit in nearby Tipperary town, 'but God help Ireland if it follows in this trail of blood.' Collins had no involvement in the ambush, but General Sir Nevil Macready, later head of the British forces in Ireland, wrote that the action bore 'the first fruits of a policy of which Michael Collins was the prime mover if not the originator'. The Big Fellow was certainly anxious to resume the armed struggle with Britain, and *An t-Óglacht* actually mentioned that 'a state of war exists with Britain'. In time the Soloheadbeg ambush would be seen as the start of the Anglo-Irish war. It was ironic, therefore, that Collins was not even in the country when it began. He was in England personally supervising final arrangements to spring de Valera, Seán McGarry, and Seán Milroy from Lincoln Jail.

As it became apparent that the British were not about to release those held without trial over the supposed German Plot, de Valera set about escaping. He regularly acted as a server at mass for the prison chaplain, and one day he managed to make an impression of the chaplain's master-key. He then got Milroy to draw a Christmas card, showing McGarry, the president of the IRB, holding a large key which he was trying to fit into a small keyhole, with a caption: 'Xmas 1917 can't get in.' Beneath was another drawing of McGarry looking through a large keyhole above the caption: 'Xmas 1918 can't get out.' Inside the card there was a note supposedly passing on best wishes from de Valera in Gaelic. In fact, the message explained that the key on the card was an exact drawing of the master-key, and the large keyhole provided a cross-section of the key's dimensions. There was a note to the effect, 'Field will translate.' Field was a code-name for Collins. It was a clever card which fooled not only the prison censor, but also McGarry's wife. It became necessary to get a separate message out to Collins explaining that the details of the key were on the Christmas card.

De Valera had hoped to be out in time for the opening of the Dáil on 21 January, but there were a number of delays. The first two keys smuggled into the jail did not work, so a suitable blank key was delivered, along with cutting material to enable the prisoners to fashion a key inside the prison. Collins supervised the escape arrangements on the outside. He arranged to collect de Valera, McGarry, and Milroy outside the jail and spirit them to hiding-places in England, where they would wait until he could arrange their safe passage back to Ireland.

The night of 3 February was chosen for the escape attempt. While Paddy O'Donoghue waited in a taxi, Collins and Harry Boland approached the jail from a nearby field and gave a prearranged signal with a flashlight — three staccato flashes — indicating everything was ready. Milroy responded in the jail by setting light to a whole box of matches at his cell window. Collins tried to open a side-gate with one of the keys he had made, but it jammed. With characteristic impetuosity, he tried to force it, only to have the head of the key snap off in the lock. By this time he could hear de Valera and the others approaching the other side of the gate. 'Dev,' he exclaimed, 'the key's broken in the lock!'

Fortunately de Valera managed to knock the broken piece out with his own key. The three prisoners then emerged, to the immense relief of those outside. Collins gave de Valera a jubilant thump on the shoulder, and they all made for the taxi, which took them to the city centre. Collins and Boland got off there and took a train to London, while the three escapees changed cars and set off for the Manchester area, where they went into hiding.

With the success of the escape Collins was hoping for a military confrontation with the British. 'As for us on the outside,' he wrote to Stack upon his return to Dublin, 'all ordinary peaceful means are ended and we shall be taking the only alternative actions in a short while now.'

The independence movement was entering a new phase. Collins had played a major role in the reorganisation that would now allow the movement to take up the armed struggle from where it had been left off in 1916. A determined, opinionated young man, he was capable of making fast decisions with all the confidence of youth, but his determination was blended with an arrogance that often made him intolerant of views differing from his own. In his desire for action he often failed to realise the significance of symbolic events such as the Proclamation of the Republic by Pearse, or the establishment of Dáil Éireann, or even the importance which de Valera placed on keeping people like MacNeill within the movement. The Big Fellow would not have been able to unify Sinn Féin in 1917, as de Valera had done.

In early 1919 Collins took over as director of intelligence of the Irish Volunteers. It was in this area that he made his greatest mark.

For centuries the British were renowned for their secret services. In the Great War just ended, British intelligence had functioned magnificently, breaking German codes and using the information to steer the United States into the war against Germany. During the Second World War, Britain would again break the German codes, but in between those two wars British intelligence suffered at the hands of Collins, who made their people look like bungling amateurs, for a time at any rate.

As director of organisation, Collins had put together an escape network that was later emulated by Britain's MI9 in the Second World War. Éamonn Duggan was appointed the first director of intelligence for the Volunteers, but he never built up much of an organisation. It was merely an adjunct of his legal practice, and he had only one man working for him. Collins, on the other hand, set up a far-reaching network, incorporating intelligence gathering, counter-intelligence, and matters relating to prison escapes and smuggling, both arms and people. He was the brains behind the whole network and his industry was phenomenal. He retained personal control over work similar to that done by three different intelligence agencies in Britain, MI5, MI6, and MI9.

An intelligence office was set up at 3 Crow Street over the print shop of J. F. Fowler, with Liam Tobin in charge. A tall, gaunt man with a cynical expression, he was a fairly inconspicuous individual. Unlike Collins, who bounded from place to place, Tobin moved listlessly, walking with his arms hanging straight by his sides, but his appearance was deceptive. Tom Cullen and Frank Thornton were Tobin's principal lieutenants. A staff was built up with people like Frank Saurin, Joe Guilfoyle, Joe Dolan, and Charlie Dalton. Dalton recalled his first day on the job.

'I was given the daily papers to look through,' he wrote. 'I was told to cut out any paragraphs referring to the personnel of the Royal Irish Constabulary, or military, such as transfers, their movement socially, attendance at wedding receptions, garden parties, etc. These I pasted on a card which were sent to the Director of Intelligence for his perusal and instructions. Photographs and other data which were or might be of interest were cut out and put away. We often gathered useful information of the movements of important enemy personages in this manner, whom we traced also by a study of *Who's Who*, from which we learned the names of their connections and clubs. By intercepting their correspondence we were able to get a clue to their movements outside their strongholds.'

With the help of his intelligence people, Collins, who as a rule did not visit the office in Crow Street, set about demoralising the police. At the time there were two separate police forces in Ireland — the Royal Irish Constabulary and the Dublin Metropolitan Police. The latter, which functioned only in the Dublin area, was divided into seven divisions, lettered A through G. Divisions A, B, C, and D were uniformed police dealing with different sections of the city, while E and F dealt with the outskirts, and G was an overall division of plain-clothes detectives dealing with all types of crime, not just political crimes.

The intelligence staff's initial task was to gather as much information as possible about the police, especially G Division. Information such as where they lived and the names of members of their families would prove invaluable to Collins in the coming months. His agents were a whole range of people, with no one too humble to be of use. 'We compiled a list of friendly persons in the public service, railways, mail boats, and hotels,' Charlie Dalton explained. 'I was sent constantly to interview stewards, reporters, waiters, and hotel porters to verify the movements of enemy agents.' Maids in guest-houses and hotels, porters, bartenders, sailors, railwaymen, postmen, sorters, telephone and telegraph operators, warders, and ordinary policemen all played an important part, and Collins had the splendid ability of making each feel important, even though he rarely, if ever, thanked them for what they were doing. 'Why should I thank people for doing their part?' he would ask. 'Isn't Ireland their country as well as mine?'

When Collins gave Thomas Gay £5 for Detective Sergeant Kavanagh for supplying the names of those about to be arrested in connection with the so-called German Plot, there was something contemptuous about the gesture. Gay recognised this and returned the money to Collins a few days later.

'You didn't give him the money!' Collins exclaimed.

'No.'

'You didn't think he'd take it?'

'No.'

'A bloody queer G man!'

It was, of course, early days yet and Collins was still very raw. In his contempt for the police force, it had not initially occurred to him that there could be patriotic Irishmen in the police as in any other walk of life. But, unlike others in the movement, he soon learned this lesson and turned it to the advantage of the cause.

At the heart of his intelligence-gathering network were his police spies. The first to be recruited were the two G men, Joe Kavanagh and Ned Broy, who had warned about impending arrests at the time of the German Plot. Kavanagh — a short, dapper, sixty-year-old Dubliner with a waxed moustache — had taken part in identifying leaders of the Easter Rising at Richmond Barracks, and had obviously come to regret his role. He was now secretly committed to Sinn Féin, though he did not have long to live. He died of a heart attack in 1920, by which time he had been of invaluable service to Collins.

Broy, on the other hand, was only in his mid-twenties. A rather stooped individual with a broad face, he was a native of County Kildare and worked as an official typist at G Division's headquarters in Great Brunswick (now Pearse) Street. He thought of himself strictly as an Irishman and had been looking for somebody within Sinn Féin who could make proper use of important information which he was prepared to pass on. Then one day in January 1919 he was asked to see Collins. 'Immediately I met him,' Broy later explained, 'I knew he was the man who could beat the British and I decided to work for him from then on.' As a confidential typist Broy was in a particularly sensitive position. When he typed any report of interest to Collins, he simply inserted an extra carbon and made an additional copy. He then passed these on at weekly meetings that he and Kavanagh had with Collins at the home of Thomas Gay.

Collins had a fairly clear vision of what he wished to do and how he wished to do it. He wanted a military confrontation with the British, but not a conventional war.

'If we were to stand up against the powerful military organisation arrayed against us,' Collins later explained, 'something more was necessary than a guerrilla war in which small bands of our warriors, aided by their know-ledge of the country, attacked the larger forces of the enemy and reduced their numbers. England could always reinforce her army. She could replace every soldier that she lost.'

'But,' he added, 'there were others indispensable for her purposes which were not so easily replaced. To paralyse the British machine it was necessary to strike at individuals. Without her spies England was helpless. It was only by means of their accumulated and accumulating knowledge that the British machine could operate.' He basically considered the DMP and RIC as spies. Detectives from G Division had, after all, segregated the leaders from the rank and file at Richmond Barracks after the Easter Rising, and the British had relied on the RIC to select those who were deported from other parts of the country in the aftermath of the rebellion. 'Without their police through-out the country, how could they find the men they "wanted"?' he asked.

The British administration was dependent on such people and would be virtually blind without them. Thus Collins determined that the first step should be to undermine the political detectives in G Division of the DMP. He antici-pated that once the detectives were neutralised or eliminated, the British would inevitably react blindly and in the process hit innocent Irish people and thereby drive the great mass of the people into the arms of the republicans.

Collins recognised de Valera's leadership qualities and looked to him to lead the renewed struggle. After all, in his presidential address at the Sinn Féin Ard Fheis in October 1917 de Valera had promised to 'draw the naked sword' in order to make the British do likewise, if more peaceful methods failed. But when de Valera was spirited back to Ireland after a fortnight in hiding in Britain, he had no intention of renewing the armed struggle, at least not for the time being. He thought Ireland's best chance of success still lay in enlisting American help in view of President Woodrow Wilson's eloquent pro-nouncements. Collins tried but failed to persuade de Valera to stay at home and direct the forthcoming struggle. 'You know what it is to argue with Dev,' Collins told a friend. 'He says he thought it out while in prison, and he feels that the one place where he can be useful to Ireland is in America.'

Despite his incarceration for almost nine months on trumped-up charges, de Valera gave the distinct impression of being comparatively moderate. From his hiding-place in Dublin, for example, he endorsed Irish-American efforts to enlist President Wilson's help in Paris. Although some people were already saying the American President would not look for justice for Ireland, de Valera called for patience. 'Pronounce no opinion on President Wilson,' he advised. 'It is premature, for he and his friends will bear our country in mind at the crucial hour.'

Collins made arrangements through his shipping contacts for the journey to the United States, and de Valera returned to Britain, where he was to be smuggled on board an American-bound ship. But while he was waiting the British government suddenly released all the German Plot prisoners in early March. De Valera was therefore free to return to Ireland with the others without being apprehended. His impending return was announced with the following statement to the press:

> President de Valera will arrive in Ireland on Wednesday evening next, the 26th inst., and the Executive of Dáil Éireann will offer him a national welcome. It is expected that the home-coming of de Valera will be an occasion of national rejoicing, and full arrangement will be made for marshalling the procession. The Lord Mayor of Dublin will receive him at the gates of the city, and will escort him to the Mansion House, where he will deliver a message to the Irish people. All organisations and bands wishing to participate in the demonstration should apply to 6 Harcourt Street, on Monday the 24th inst., up to 6 p.m.
>
> H. Boland
> T. Kelly, Honorary Secretaries.

As these were the kind of arrangements normally reserved for royalty, Dublin Castle banned the reception, and the Sinn Féin executive held an emergency meeting. Arthur Griffith presided at what was for him and Darrell Figgis their first meeting since their arrest the previous May. Cathal Brugha had complained privately to Figgis some days earlier that Collins and his IRB colleagues had essentially taken over the movement from within while the others were in jail. 'He told me that he had seen what had been passing, but that he had been powerless to change events,' Figgis wrote. 'It was at this meeting I saw for the first time the personal hostility between him and Michael Collins.'

When the executive met to discuss what to do about Dublin Castle's ban on the planned reception, members were to witness an amazing display of contemptuous arrogance. Figgis asked to see the record of the executive meeting authorising the honorary secretaries to announce the plans to welcome de Valera, but he was told that the issue had never come up. 'I therefore asked Alderman Tom Kelly on what authority he, as one of the signatories, had attached his name as secretary, and he answered with characteristic bluntness that, in point of fact, he had never seen the announcement, and had not known of it, till he read it in the press.'

There followed a 'tangled discussion' before Collins rose. Characteristically sweeping aside all pretences, he said that the announcement had been written by him, and that the decision to make it had been made, not by Sinn Féin, though declared in its name, but by 'the proper body, the Irish Volunteers'. Figgis wrote, 'He spoke with much vehemence and emphasis, saying that the sooner fighting was forced and a general state of disorder created through the country (his words in this connection are too well printed on my memory ever to be forgotten), the better it would be for the country. Ireland was likely to get more out of a state of general disorder than from a continuance of the situation as it then stood. The proper people to take decisions of that kind were ready to face the British military, and were resolved to force the issue. And they were not to be deterred by weaklings and cowards. For himself he accepted full responsibility for the announcement, and he told the meeting with forceful candour that he held them in no opinion at all, that, in fact, they were only summoned to confirm what the proper people had decided.'

'He had always a truculent manner, but in such situations he was certainly candour itself,' Figgis continued. 'As I looked on him while he spoke, for all the hostility between us, I found something refreshing and admirable in his contempt of us all. His brow was gathered in a thunderous frown, and his chin thrust forward, while he emphasised his points on the back of a chair with heavy strokes of his hand.'

Although Figgis may have been impressed at the way Collins had 'manipulated' the organisation, Arthur Griffith certainly was not. He had no intention of meekly succumbing to such an arrogant display. Tapping the table in front of him with a pencil, Griffith emphasised that the decision was one to be taken by the meeting, and by no other body.

'For two hours the debate raged fiercely,' according to Figgis. Going ahead with the announced plans would undoubtedly lead to trouble, while abandoning them could have disastrous implications for the morale of the whole movement. Parallels were drawn with the disastrous consequences of Daniel O'Connell's decision to accede to the British ban on the monster meeting at Clontarf over seventy years earlier. The argument was only resolved by deciding to consult de Valera, who duly requested that the welcoming demonstrations be cancelled rather than risk a confrontation in which lives might be lost. He was sure matters of much greater principle would arise in future. 'We who have waited, know how to wait,' he advised the executive. 'Many a heavy fish is caught even with a fine line if the angler is patient.'

Thus the Big Fellow's plans to provoke an early confrontation with the British were frustrated and he was obviously disappointed. 'It is very bad,' he wrote to Stack. 'The chief actor was very firm on the withdrawal, as indeed was Cathal. I used my influence the other way, and was in a practical minority of one. It may be that all arguments were sound, but it seems to me that they have put up a challenge which strikes at the fundamentals of our policy and our attitude.'

The systems being set up by Collins soon began to bear fruit when he masterminded a sensational prison break before the end of March. On the 16th he had helped to spring Robert Barton from Mountjoy Jail. He had escaped after cutting through a window bar with a hacksaw blade provided by Collins. A rope was thrown over the perimeter wall on a given signal from Barton, who used it to pull over a rope-ladder that was held from the other side. He then scaled the wall and was taken immediately to Batt O'Connor's home, where Collins was waiting. 'That's only the beginning,' Collins declared triumphantly.

Barton's escape was like a trial run for a more ambitious break set for the afternoon of 29 March. The plan was to spring Pádraic Fleming and Piaras Béaslaí and whoever else could get out with them. Volunteers, led by Rory O'Connor, threw a rope over the wall with a rope-ladder attached, as they had done in the case of Barton's escape. Some prisoners overpowered the guards within the yard while the others scaled the wall. The whole thing went off better than anyone had hoped, and twenty Volunteers escaped. After observing the escape, Joe O'Reilly cycled furiously to the Wicklow Hotel, where Collins was waiting impatiently.

'Is Fleming out?' he asked.

'The whole jail is out.'

'What! How many?'

'About twenty when I came away.'

Every so often as Collins sat in his office at Cullenswood House in Ranelagh that evening, he would put down his pen and burst out laughing. They had brought off a major coup, which boosted party morale and more than offset whatever damage had been done by the cancellation of the welcoming demonstration for de Valera.

—————————

When the Dáil met on 1 April 1919 de Valera was elected Príomh-Aire (Prime Minister), and he then proceeded to name a cabinet which included Griffith, Plunkett, MacNeill, Collins, Brugha, and Constance Markievicz. The cabinet was representative of the various factions within Sinn Féin.

With the Peace Conference deliberating in Paris, de Valera adopted a statesmanlike approach. He noted there were signs that France was demanding vindictive terms from the Germans, who would inevitably seek their own revenge in the not too distant future, just as the French had done as a result of the treaty ending the Franco-Prussian War in 1871. 'We must try to save France from herself,' he said. 'If there is a peace imposed on Germany now, there will be a desire for revenge on the part of the German people later on.' In fact, he said, 'another war of revenge must surely follow'. He was astutely predicting the outbreak of the Second World War twenty years in advance.

He appointed Collins as Minister for Finance and had plans for him to raise money for the movement by issuing bonds. 'It is obvious that the work of our Government cannot be carried out without funds,' de Valera told the Dáil. 'The Minister for Finance is accordingly preparing a prospectus which will shortly be published for the issue of a loan of £1 million sterling — £500,000 to be offered to the public for immediate subscription.'

Collins's own main goal was to strike at the police forces in order to eliminate the most effective detectives. His audacity seemed to know no bounds. Around midnight on the night of 7 April, he entered the G Division headquarters and had Broy lock him into the documents room, where he spent several hours going through the files, including his own. He later bragged, with characteristic vanity, that his file mentioned he came from 'a brainy' family. The report, dated 31 December 1916, was written by the distinct inspector of the RIC in Bandon. He noted that Collins 'belongs to a family [of] "brainy" people who are disloyal and of advanced Sinn Féin sympathies'. His file included police reports on his involvement in the Longford by-election of 1917 and some of his more controversial speeches, especially the addresses in Ballinamuck and

Skibbereen for which the authorities had wished to prosecute him. Overall, these files gave him an invaluable perspective on what the G Division knew and on its most active detectives.

Although Collins had no sleep, he was in fine form next day when Sinn Féin held a special Ard Fheis at the Mansion House. De Valera performed a balancing act in accommodating both militants and moderates. He sought to keep militants like Collins in check both by getting the Ard Fheis to give the standing committee of Sinn Féin a strong voice in policy matters and by debarring members of the cabinet — other than himself and Griffith — from membership of the committee. He undoubtedly had Collins in mind when he explained the standing committee's consultative role. He said, for example, that if a minister decided that the Irish people should no longer pay income tax to the Crown, the proposal would need the approval of the standing committee, or it would be dropped.

Collins had been arguing in favour of such a scheme within the cabinet, but he had come up against the resolute obstinacy of Brugha. De Valera, as was his wont, had assumed an aloof position in the dispute, but his remarks at the Ard Fheis certainly leaned towards Brugha's more cautious position on this issue. Collins was busy lobbying for the election of his friend and IRB colleague, Harry Boland, as one of the joint national secretaries of Sinn Féin. When it was all over and Boland had won, Collins seemed quite pleased with himself.

'As I left the great hall, the Convention over, I was suddenly stopped by a strange sight,' Darrell Figgis wrote. 'Behind one of the statues with which it was surrounded stood Michael Collins and Harry Boland. Their arms were about one another, their heads bowed on one another's shoulders, and they were shaking with laughter. They did not see me. Their thoughts were with their triumph.'

Figgis, whose position Boland had taken, was obviously taking his defeat badly. He had no way of knowing what Collins was thinking at the time, but it was obvious that while he was a sore loser himself, the Big Fellow was, as ever, a bad winner. He made no effort to placate the vanquished and in the process he made more and more personal enemies. But as a young man in a hurry, he hardly even noticed, which should not have been surprising, because he was now operating at a breakneck pace in at least three different spheres. Within Sinn Féin he was trying to position IRB colleagues, while in his ministerial capacity he was charged with organising the loan, and as director of both organisation and intelligence in the Volunteers, he was preparing for a war with Britain.

On the night after the Ard Fheis, the detectives of the DMP were given a very public warning. Volunteers raided the home of Detective Sergeant Halley, and they held up Detective Constable O'Brien in the street, and bound and gagged him. Neither man was hurt, but it was a warning to their

colleagues that the Volunteers could and would strike at them in the streets
and in their homes.

Addressing the Dáil next day, 10 April, de Valera advocated moral rather
than armed resistance. 'We shall conduct ourselves with all needful forbearance,' he declared. While Collins was anxious to kill those police who did
not heed the warnings to lay off, de Valera called for the ostracism of all
policemen, whom he accused of 'brutal treason', because they were acting
as 'the main instruments' in keeping the Irish people in subjection. 'They
are spies in our midst,' he added, echoing the sentiments of Collins. 'They
are the eyes and ears of the enemy.'

While in jail de Valera had plenty of time to formulate his own policies,
and he now quickly realised that the chances of securing help from the Paris
Peace Conference were extremely slim. Nevertheless he still believed that
the movement's best hope lay in exploiting the international situation, by
enlisting the support of the United States for Irish independence in view of
the war aims pronounced by President Wilson. He would have preferred to
have had Wilson's help, but failing this, he was quite prepared to go over the
President's head and appeal directly to the American people.

Although de Valera had travelled comparatively little since his uncle brought
him to Ireland when he was only two years old, he had a good grasp of the
international situation. His observations in the Dáil on the international
scene would stand the test of time and be confirmed by subsequent history.
He declared a readiness to support the American President in implementing the
lofty ideals enunciated in his famous fourteen points. 'As far as we are concerned,' he said, 'we will back him up if he wishes to establish a League of
Nations in which equality and right amongst nations is the foundation stone.'

'If we want a Covenant to be really lasting it must be based on the principles which occupied 10 of the 14 points of President Wilson — the right
of every nation to self-determination. We take up these principles because
they are right, and we take them up particularly because the acceptance of
these principles will mean that the long fight for Irish liberty is at an end.'

'What we seek is the reign of law based upon the consent of the
governed and sustained by the organised opinion of mankind,' President
Wilson had declared at George Washington's tomb on 4 July 1918. Next
day Lloyd George affirmed that Britain was fighting for the same thing, and
the Irish would later try to hold them to their words.

De Valera chose Collins to propose the Dáil motion to secure approval
for the government's policy. The motion, which was seconded by W. T.
Cosgrave, read:

> The elected Parliament and Government of the Irish Republic
> pledge the active support of the Irish nation in translating into
> deed the principles enunciated by the President of the US
> at Washington's Tomb on 4 July 1918, and whole-heartedly

accepted. We are eager and ready to enter a World League of Nations based on equality of right, in which the guarantees exchanged neither recognise nor imply a difference between big nations and small, between those that are powerful and those that are weak. We are willing to accept all the duties, responsibilities and burdens which inclusion in such a League implies.

The overall occasion afforded enormous publicity for the Dáil, and Collins — despite his dislike of formal occasions — sensed something momentous about the proceedings. 'The week which has passed has been a busy one for us — perhaps it has been an historical one for very often we are actors in events that have very much more meaning and consequence than we realise,' he wrote on 13 April to his sister Helena in England. 'Last week did, I feel, mark the inception of something new. The elected representatives of the people have definitely turned their backs on the old order and the developments are sure to be interesting. Generally the situation is working out to the satisfaction of Ireland — that is in foreign countries. At home we go from success to success in our own guerrilla way.'

'It is a most interesting thing to watch from day to day the downfall of the stern Government regime,' he added. 'Not indeed that it is ended, not even that it won't flash forth occasionally again, but the impotence of the military governors is gradually taking them into a position which is almost chaotic. Certain it is that we are fast reaching the breaking-point.'

'Whether we achieve our object or whether we fail gloriously,' he believed, 'a mark has been made that can never be effaced.' He was rather melodramatic about his own appointment as Minister for Finance which, he told his sister, would 'simply ensure the hanging that was only probable had we remained merely members of the Dáil'.

Although de Valera portrayed a moderate internationalist outlook in his public speeches, he privately expressed antipathy towards conventional politics in conversations with people like Collins and Richard Mulcahy, the Volunteers' chief of staff. 'You're a young man going into politics,' he told Mulcahy. 'I'll give you two pieces of advice, study economics and read The Prince.' That book was, of course, Machiavelli's classic study of political duplicity. Mulcahy would later come to appreciate the advice, at least as a key to understanding de Valera, who was playing a crafty game of his own. He went along with the militants by talking tough, but when it came to acting, he came down on the side of relative moderation.

In the following weeks Collins became somewhat exasperated with de Valera's style of government. Once de Valera made up his mind on any matter he was very difficult to shift, though he was usually prepared to allow others make futile efforts to dissuade him on some point or other. Sitting through such arguments required as much patience of other cabinet members, and this kind of patience was not one of the Big Fellow's strong points. As Minister for Finance Collins had to organise funds and he did so with characteristic thoroughness. He drafted a prospectus for the National Loan, but became rather irritated at de Valera's habit of mulling over every word as if weighing it on some notional scale of history before agreeing to it. Collins wished to include a Dáil pledge to honour Fenian bonds floated in 1866, but de Valera compelled him to drop this from the prospectus. De Valera also agonised over the wording of the Irish submission to the Paris Peace Conference. 'The damned Peace Conference will be over before he's satisfied,' Collins grumbled in frustration.

The terms of the Versailles Treaty were presented to the Germans and published in the first week in April, although it would not be signed until the end of June. An Irish-American delegation tried unsuccessfully to secure a hearing for a delegation from the Dáil, but President Wilson had no intention of going out on a limb for Ireland, notwithstanding his own words about fighting for the self-determination of small nations. 'When I gave utterance to these words I said them without the knowledge that nationalities existed which are coming to us every day,' Wilson explained some weeks later. 'You do not know and cannot appreciate the anxieties I have experienced as a result of those many millions having their hopes raised by what I have said.' He privately acknowledged that Ireland was 'the outstanding case of a small nationality', but there were much bigger issues at stake and he did not think he could afford to antagonise his British allies by pressing the Irish case.

As there was no chance of getting a meaningful hearing in Paris without the help of the American President, Collins thought that agonising over the text of the submission to the Peace Conference was a waste of time. The three-man Irish-American delegation visited Ireland in early May. The Dáil held a special public session for them at the Mansion House on 9 May, where they witnessed some dramatic developments in which Collins essentially upstaged everyone.

'A few of us had a very interesting experience,' he wrote to Stack a couple of days later. During the morning of the 9th Broy telephoned to warn that the Dáil would be raided that afternoon in an effort to capture Collins and a couple of others. As the telephone service of the day was notoriously insecure, Broy gave the warning to Béaslaí in French. 'We'll have our lunch first,' Collins replied rather nonchalantly when Béaslaí passed on the warning. The Big Fellow was obviously enjoying the prospect of becoming the centre of attention. He sent Joe O'Reilly to fetch his uniform.

'About five o'clock the enemy came along with three motor lorries, [a] small armoured car, machine guns, probably 200 or 250 troops,' Collins wrote. 'They surrounded the building with great attention to every military detail. They entered the Mansion House and searched it with great care and thoroughness but they got nobody inside. The wanted ones codded them again.' Collins, Robert Barton, and Ted Kelly had slipped out a back window and hid in an adjoining building. When the military left they returned, only this time Collins was dressed in his Volunteer's uniform. It was a show of bravado that went down well with most of the gathering, though some felt that the Big Fellow was showing off again.

'By this time everybody should know that it is by naked force that England holds this country,' Collins wrote with obvious satisfaction. 'Our American friends got an exhibition of the truth while they were here.'

Tim Healy, the old parliamentarian, happened to be in the vicinity and saw the raid in progress. 'Nothing that the wit of man could devise equalled the Mansion House raid of the military in folly,' he wrote. 'Every damn fool seems to be in the employment of the British Government in Ireland.'

Collins was growing more impatient for a fight. He encouraged local units of the Volunteers to raid police barracks for arms. This, in addition to affording an opportunity of acquiring much-needed weapons, had the advantage of acting as a kind of training operation for the Volunteers. It soon led to the withdrawal of the RIC from isolated areas and the abandonment of literally hundreds of police barracks throughout the country.

Desmond Ryan recalled an incident at Cullenswood House one day when Collins picked up an old copy of *An Claidheamh Soluis* in which Pearse had extolled the virtues of armed conflict. 'We must accustom ourselves to the thought of arms, to the sight of arms, to the use of arms,' Collins read aloud with enthusiasm. 'We may make mistakes in the beginning and shoot the wrong people, but bloodshed is a cleansing and sanctifying thing, and the nation which regards it as the final horror has lost its manhood. There are things more horrible than bloodshed; and slavery is one of them.' With that Collins slapped down the paper and walked out. No matter what he thought of Pearse himself, Collins liked those sentiments. 'When you ask me for ammunition for guns which have never fired a shot in this fight, my answer is a simple one,' he wrote to a brigade commander on 17 May 1919. 'Fire shots at some useful target or get the hell out of it.'

The same day he complained bitterly to Austin Stack about Sinn Féin politicians making things 'intolerable' for militants like himself. 'The policy now seems to be to squeeze out anyone who is tainted with strong fighting ideas, or should I say the utility of fighting.' He was particularly critical of the party's executive committee, which he described as 'a Standing Committee of malcontents' who were 'inclined to be ever less militant and more political and theoretical'. In short, they were talkers and thinkers, rather than men of action, and he was a man of action. 'We have too many of the bargaining type already,' Collins grumbled. 'I am not sure that our movement or part of it at any rate is alive to the developing situation.'

Describing himself as 'only an onlooker' at the executive committee meetings, he complained that the moderates were in control. When Harry

Boland went to the United States to make preparations for de Valera's forth-coming tour, the party replaced him as national secretary with Hanna Sheehy-Skeffington. She was a sister of Father Eugene Sheehy, the parish priest in Bruree, and the wife of a pacifist murdered during the Easter Rising. Collins was appalled. Not only had Boland been replaced by a woman, but the party went on to announce that his replacement was necessary because he was out of the country. With this announcement, Collins fumed, 'our people give away in a moment what the Detective Division had been unable to find out in five weeks'.

He clearly felt there was a lot of hostility towards himself and his militant views. There were 'rumours, whisperings, suggestions of differences between certain people', he wrote. All of this he described as 'rather pitiful and disheartening'. It belied the national unity of which de Valera boasted and it tended towards confusion about the best way of achieving the nation-al aims. 'At the moment,' Collins exclaimed, 'I'm awfully fed up.'

'Things are not going very smoothly,' he was still writing three weeks later. 'All sorts of miserable little undercurrents are working and the effect is anything but good.' Nevertheless, he would soon have a freer hand once de Valera set out for the United States at the start of June.

5

Going Separate Ways

Although he tried to persuade de Valera not to go to the United States, Collins nevertheless arranged through his Liverpool contacts to have him smuggled to America. De Valera left Ireland for the United States on 1 June 1919. His first stop was Britain, where he stowed away on the SS *Lapland*, which was bound from Liverpool to New York. He was seasick for most of the eight-day voyage, holed up in a tiny cabin.

The main aims of the visit were to secure American recognition of the Irish Republic and to collect money. There had also been word of a growing split among Irish-Americans and de Valera, the great conciliator, hoped to resolve that dispute. On the one hand, the leadership of the Friends of Irish Freedom were merely calling for recognition of Ireland's right to self-determination, while their critics were insisting that the call should be for recognition of the Irish Republic as a legitimate government. Daniel Cohalan, a judge on the New York State Supreme Court and widely recognised as the effective leader of the Friends of Irish Freedom, felt that calling just for recognition of the right to self-determination offered the best opportunity for success, because the United States had supposedly fought in the First World War for the rights of small countries to have self-determination. Once that right was recognised in Ireland's case, then recognition of the Irish Republic became a logical step, because Sinn Féin had won the overwhelming majority of Irish seats in the 1918 general election.

Cohalan's main backer was John Devoy, the editor of the *Gaelic American* newspaper and effective leader of the IRB's sister organisation, Clan na Gael. Their main critics were the editor of the Philadelphia-based *Irish Press* newspaper, Joseph McGarrity, and the IRB's emissary, Patrick McCartan; Harry Boland sided with these.

In Ireland de Valera had repeatedly emphasised the self-determination approach. In March when the Irish Self-Determination League was founded in England, for instance, he had called publicly for the organisation's 'moral and financial support in influencing public opinion on behalf of Ireland's claim to self-determination'. McCartan tried to explain the intricacies of the dispute to de Valera on his arrival in New York.

'I had just told him Cohalan had tried to reduce our claim for recognition to a claim for self-determination,' McCartan wrote.

'Self-determination,' de Valera interrupted, 'is a very good policy.'

He initially hoped to persuade Woodrow Wilson to recognise the Irish Republic and he felt the best way to do that was to exploit the President's eloquent pronouncements about democracy and self-determination. He realised American officials would be reluctant to recognise the Irish Republic for fear of offending their wartime ally, Britain, and believed that using the President's own words afforded the best chance of enlisting sufficient popular support to embarrass the American President into helping Ireland.

De Valera therefore insisted on playing up the self-determination theme in a press statement that was prepared on his arrival in the United States. In this he was referred to as 'President of the Irish Republic', but McCartan and McGarrity objected. He had been elected Príomh-Aire of Dáil Éireann, which was something different. From the American standpoint, however, the title Príomh-Aire meant nothing, so the Irish-Americans were anxious to describe him as President. De Valera resolved the matter with his own wording: 'From to-day I am in America as the official head of the Republic established by the will of the Irish people in accordance with the principle of Self-Determination,' he declared. Everyone was satisfied with that description.

From the outset de Valera saw his role in the United States as a propagandist, and he quickly realised that the title of President of the Irish Republic was a much more impressive title in the eyes of Americans. He therefore essentially changed his title without consulting or even informing colleagues at home. 'I wonder what Griffith will say when he reads that I came out in the press as President of the Republic?' de Valera remarked in New York. It has been suggested that de Valera was also afraid that the IRB might take exception, because that organisation had traditionally considered its leader to be President of the Irish Republic. Collins, who was rapidly establishing himself as the real driving force of the IRB, did not seem to have any reservations.

He was delighted with the welcome de Valera received on the other side of the Atlantic. His only criticism was that de Valera and Boland talked too much about their respective trips, which risked exposing those who had helped them. 'You should not be so communicative over there,' Collins wrote to Boland. 'Other people may want to go in the same manner.' He actually referred quite matter-of-factly to de Valera as 'the President' in a letter to his IRB colleague Stack on 20 July 1919. 'The President is getting tremendous receptions and the press in its entirety has thrown itself open to Irish propaganda,' Collins wrote.

De Valera told his first press conference in New York on 23 June that he aimed to arouse public opinion in order to exert pressure on President Wilson. He intended to do this by injecting the Irish question into the controversy over the Versailles Treaty, which was already building in the United States, where there was uneasiness over the covenant of the League of Nations, which had been incorporated into the treaty. He told the press conference:

> We shall fight for a real democratic League of Nations, not the present unholy alliance which does not fulfil the purposes for which the democracies of the world went to war. I am going to ask the American people to give us a real League of Nations, one that will include Ireland.
>
> I well recognise President Wilson's difficulties in Paris. I am sure that if he is sincere, nothing will please him more than being pushed from behind by the people, for this pressure will show him that the people of America want the United States' government to recognise the Republic of Ireland.
>
> This is the reason I am eager to spread propaganda in official circles in America. My appeal is to the people. I know that if they can be aroused government action will follow. That is why I intend visiting your large cities and talking directly to the people.

The Versailles Treaty was formally signed five days later as de Valera was about to set out for a hectic speaking tour. Next day, 29 June, he delivered his first public address to a gathering of some 50,000 people in the Fenway Park baseball stadium in Boston, and the day after that he spoke to the Massachusetts state legislature. This was followed by a speech to some 30,000 people in Manchester, New Hampshire, before he returned to speak to an overflowing crowd of 17,000 people at Madison Square Gardens, New York. The crowd was reportedly the biggest ever crammed into the arena, because the local police force — with its strong Irish presence — had permitted people to fill the isles in blatant contravention of safety regulations. On 13 July de Valera addressed some 25,000 people at Soldier Field, Chicago. Next he met the Chicago City Council, before setting out for San Francisco, where the Ancient Order of Hibernians was holding its convention. Following a brief stay in the San Francisco Bay area, he visited Montana, where he addressed the state legislature, before returning to New York.

In little more than three weeks he had travelled from the Atlantic to the Pacific seaboard and back again. This, of course, was before the era of air travel. He made seventeen major public addresses to an estimated total of half a million people, in addition to numerous short talks at smaller functions. In the process he received enormous publicity in New York, Boston, Chicago, and San Francisco, where he was given prominent front-page coverage with banner headlines in the major newspapers, and inside pages devoted exclusively to activities surrounding his visit. Normally Irish affairs would get little more than an occasional short paragraph on an inside page in those newspapers, with the result that de Valera's visit unquestionably put Irish affairs into the media spotlight.

The enthusiasm of the gatherings helped to obscure his failings as a public speaker. He tended to read his speeches in a dull, halting manner but, as voice amplification was still rather primitive, this failing was of little consequence at the large gatherings. Even though he had been preceded by much better orators on the platform in Fenway Park, the *Boston Herald* reported that de Valera was nevertheless effective on the rostrum because he exuded the outstanding qualities of 'passionate sincerity' and 'utmost simplicity' — two characteristics that 'burn their way into the consciousness of everyone who sees and hears him'.

De Valera repeatedly denounced the Versailles Treaty, but he did so as supporter rather than as critic of Wilsonian ideals. In the light of subsequent historical developments, his comments could be characterised as particularly astute political forecasts. He complained in Boston, for instance, that the treaty was 'a mere mockery' that would lead to twenty wars instead of the one it had nominally ended. Unless the United States was willing to take 'responsibility for the world to which her traditions entitle her', he predicted mankind would be in for 'a period of misery for which history has no parallel'.

'The present opportunity is never likely to occur again,' de Valera argued. 'The idea of a unity of nations recognising a common law and a common right ending wars among nations is today a possibility if America will do what the people of the world look forward to, and expect her to do.' He wanted the Americans to use their influence to get the treaty revised so that the League of Nations could be based on the principle of national equality, which, he contended, was the only basis on which the organisation would be likely to succeed.

The treaty had many defects, as far as de Valera was concerned. While in Dublin he had warned of the futility of expecting a lasting peace, if vindictive terms were imposed on Germany. But while he was in the United States he adopted a positive approach. If he were an American, he said in Chicago, he would have felt obliged to serve in the United States army during the recent war, in view of the country's avowed motives in entering the conflict. 'I hold,' he said, 'that those of us who were fighting England were in reality fighting for the very principles for which the Americans fought.'

When asked by a member of the Chicago City Council why members of Sinn Féin had not fought in the war, de Valera explained that, firstly, they did not think they were strong enough to ensure that their aim of securing freedom for small nations would be respected in Ireland's case, and secondly, they were afraid that Britain would use their participation to undermine the Irish struggle for independence. 'If we had gone in,' he said, 'England would have made it appear we were in as England's partners and therefore content with England's occupation.'

De Valera was careful to present his case in terms that both appeared consistent with America's war aims and at the same time offset what seemed like the betrayal of those aims at Versailles. He took particular exception to Article X of the covenant of the League of Nations, which was part of the Versailles Treaty. It committed members of the league 'to respect and preserve as against external aggression the territorial integrity of fellow members'. The clause was objectionable because it could be used by imperial nations to preserve the international status quo. If the United States subscribed to the covenant, he argued, Americans would be placing their seal of approval on Britain's title to all her imperial possessions, including Ireland.

Before signing the Versailles Treaty, therefore, he suggested that the United States could eliminate the obnoxious implications of Article X by insisting that the imperial powers should 'surrender their colonies and possessions as mandatories of the League'. De Valera complained so much about the covenant that he was popularly believed to be opposed to the League of Nations, whereas he actually favoured the concept and also approved of Article X *per se*. 'If you are going to have a League of Nations, you must have some article in it like Article X, but it must be based on just conditions at the start,' he stated in San Francisco.

'Article X is the whole essence of the League,' de Valera told a Denver gathering. 'It is the preserving clause. If you preserve the conditions under which you start, then start right. It is wrong to preserve wrong: this is why we are against the League of Nations.' The big objection, therefore, was the way the league was being founded. The Irish people were going to be dragged into the organisation as part of the United Kingdom, with the result that Article X could henceforth be used by the British to deny independence to Ireland. In short, the real problem was not the covenant, but Ireland's lack of recognition, and he was exploiting the controversy in an attempt to secure diplomatic recognition.

'A new "Holy Alliance" cannot save democracy,' de Valera declared in Boston. 'A just League of Nations, founded on the only basis on which it can be just — the equality of right among nations, small no less than great — can.' He added that 'America can see to it that such a League is set up and set up now. She is strong enough to do so, and it is her right, in consequence of the explicit terms on which she entered the war.' He said that a new covenant could be formed in Washington just as easily as Paris. 'Now is the time to frame it,' he said. 'It is not enough for you to destroy, you must build.'

De Valera was speaking like a supporter of Woodrow Wilson. Indeed he wrote privately that his strategy was to let Wilson 'know that if he goes for his 14 points as they were and a true League of Nations, Irishmen and men and women of Irish blood will be behind him'. Yet when he was in Madison Square Gardens, the mere mention of Wilson's name provoked a cacophony of disapproval as the Irish-American crowd jeered, booed and hissed for some three minutes. The reaction was so strong that it prompted a banner front-page headline in the *Chicago Daily Tribune*.

De Valera therefore soft-peddled his Wilsonian views before the gathering in Soldier Field, Chicago, a few days later. That gathering had already passed a resolution declaring that it was 'unalterably opposed' to the covenant. As that stand had been taken on 'purely American grounds', he said that he, 'as a stranger and as a guest here, could not presume to interfere'. Yet that did not prevent him from interfering elsewhere.

To the horror of Wilson's Irish-American critics, de Valera's addresses frequently bore the indelible imprint of Wilson's brand of internationalism. In San Francisco the following week, for example, he told a gathering at City Hall that he was looking to the American people 'to make the world safe for democracy'. 'You can do it even now,' he said. 'If America is deter-mined to champion the cause of democracy in the world, that cause will triumph. If America leads the way towards true democracy, the democracy of England even, and of France and of Spain and every country in the world will follow your lead.' 'You are the only people that can lead,' he emphasised, 'and if you lead, democracy will triumph and the world will indeed be safe for democracy.'

When de Valera stated at his initial American press conference that he wanted 'a real League of Nations, one that will include Ireland', he seemed to imply that his real objection to the covenant was that Ireland was not being assured of a place as a separate nation within the organisation, rather than that there was anything wrong with such an organisation, as many Americans believed. Prominent Irish-Americans like John Devoy and Judge Daniel Cohalan were bitterly opposed to the idea of the United States joining the League of Nations, and they naturally resented de Valera saying that they would approve of the idea, if only Ireland were accorded member-ship. Cohalan warned that joining the league would involve abandoning America's traditional policy of avoiding 'permanent, entangling alliances with any countries of the Old World'. He therefore used the Friends of Irish Freedom to organise Irish-Americans to lobby against the league.

Faced with growing opposition, President Wilson set out on a whistle-stop tour of the United States to drum up popular support for America to ratify the Versailles Treaty and join the League of Nations. During the tour he said that Irish fears about Article X were groundless, because it would not apply to struggles of liberation. In fact, he implied that the covenant would actually strengthen Ireland's position by allowing the United States to press the Irish case for self-determination at the council of the league under the provisions of Article XI, which, he said, stipulated that 'every matter which is likely to affect the peace of the world is everybody's business'. 'In other words,' Wilson explained, 'at present we have to mind our own business. Under the Covenant of the League of Nations we can mind other people's business, and anything that affects the peace of the world, whether we are parties to it or not, can, by our delegates, be brought to the attention of mankind.'

De Valera promptly countered those arguments by issuing statements contending that fears concerning Article X were not baseless, because it would commit members of the League of Nations 'to respect and preserve' the territorial integrity of other member states 'against external aggression'. Thus, if the United States ratified the treaty without first recognising the Irish Republic, Americans would be obliged to cut off support to Irish rebels because Ireland would be legally regarded as part of the United Kingdom. To make matters worse, if some foreign power intervened militarily on Ireland's behalf — as France had helped the American colonies in their struggle for independence — the United States and other members of the league would be obliged to help Britain under the terms of Article X.

'There is scarcely a single instance of where a revolution from within, alone and without external aid, was ever successful,' de Valera continued. Once the United States ratified the covenant, he warned, 'England will insist on America acting in the letter and spirit of that declaration. Disguise it as we may, the new Covenant is simply a new Holy Alliance. . . . Unless America makes an explicit reservation in the case of Ireland, the ratification of the Covenant by America will mean that England can hold that America has inferentially decided against Ireland, has admitted England's claim to Ireland as part of her possessions, the integrity of which America must evermore lend her assistance in maintaining.'

Although he did not openly question Wilson's sincerity in suggesting that the United States would support Ireland's claim to self-determination at the League of Nations, de Valera did contend that support would be too late because Britain would kill any discussion of the matter by insisting that Irish affairs were an internal British matter. As a result the proposed use of Article XI would be like trying to recover a horse after it was stolen, rather than trying to prevent the theft in the first place. 'It is before the signing of the Covenant that those who are in sympathy with Ireland, those who do not want to be unjust to Ireland, must act, not afterwards,' de Valera argued. 'Instead of relying on Article XI to undo the wrong of Article X, why not set up Article X in such a form that there will be no wrong to be undone?'

Having secured enormous publicity by contradicting Wilson's remarks about Articles X and XI, de Valera set out to emulate the American President with a whistle-stop tour of his own. He began in Philadelphia on 1 October 1919 and criss-crossed the country to California, with the aim of returning to the east coast via the Deep South. Throughout his tour he stressed that he was just looking for the United States to recognise Irish independence before ratifying the Versailles Treaty. 'If the Irish Republic is recognised,' he told a banquet in Philadelphia on the first night of his tour, 'the Covenant will be acceptable.'

Although it was not generally known at the time, Wilson was gravely ill. He had suffered a stroke three weeks into his nationwide tour and he had to return to Washington, where he suffered a second and much more serious attack. As his lay incapacitated, the controversy over ratification of the Versailles Treaty in the United States Senate came to a head. Wilson was unwilling to allow any amendments or reservations to the covenant, so when the Senate adopted fourteen specific reservations, Wilson's supporters joined with his isolationist critics to defeat the treaty on 26 November 1919.

On hearing the news in southern California, de Valera cancelled the remainder of his tour and returned to New York. He had secured neither recognition nor an American commitment to support Ireland's case at the League of Nations, but he had at least contributed towards the rejection of the covenant, although the significance of his contribution and that of the Irish-Americans was greatly exaggerated at the time.

The prospect of American membership of the League of Nations had suffered a serious setback, but Wilson's supporters worked hard to get the treaty reconsidered. It was brought before the Senate again in March 1920, when two further reservations were adopted. One of those actually referred to Ireland:

> In consenting to the ratification of the Treaty with Germany, the United States adheres to the principle of self-determination and the resolution of sympathy with the expectations of the Irish people for a government of their own choice, adopted by the Senate on 6 June 1919, and declares that when such government is attained by Ireland, a consummation it is hoped is at hand, it should promptly be admitted as a member of the League of Nations.

The reservation, which was passed by thirty-eight votes to thirty-six, would have virtually committed the United States to support Irish membership of the League of Nations. As a result de Valera was ecstatic. He sent Griffith an open telegram describing the resolution as a victory for Ireland. 'Our mission has been successful,' he wrote. 'The principle of self-determination has been formally adopted in an international instrument. Ireland has been given her place amongst the nations by the greatest nation of them all.' The reservation was 'what I had been always wishing for, and it finally came beyond expectations,' de Valera continued. But his jubilation was indicative of his inexperience in American politics. He did not recognise that the reservation was only passed in order to make the reservations to the treaty so unpalatable that Wilson would be sure to instruct his supporters to kill the treaty itself. Sixteen of the senators who voted for the Irish reservation turned around and voted against the treaty two days later, when Wilson's supporters again joined with his die-hard critics to block ratification of the treaty. As a result the United States never did join the League of Nations.

Meanwhile in Ireland Collins was involved in different areas. As Minister for Finance he was responsible for the bond drive to collect money for the movement. As head of intelligence he was involved in the struggle with the police. Within months of de Valera's departure to the United States, Collins would begin a campaign to systematically wipe out the most effective police in order to render Dublin Castle both blind and deaf, and by the end of the year the authorities there would be moving to retaliate. At the same time as director of organisation of the Volunteers. Collins was building up the movement for the coming confrontation with the Crown forces.

While Collins was preparing the bond prospectus for publication, he received word from the United States that de Valera had come to appreciate the merits of agreeing to honour Fenian bonds of half a century earlier, thereby making a direct connection with the Fenian movement. Collins proceeded to write to de Valera rather tactlessly that 'it was worth going to America to be converted to that idea'.

The remark was a mere passing comment, but to someone like de Valera, for whom every written word was carefully calculated, the whole thing was pregnant with significance. 'What did you mean it was worth going to America to be "converted" to the idea of paying the Fenian bonds?' he asked indignantly. 'Surely I never opposed acknowledging that as a National debt. You must mean something else. What is it?'

'I meant about the Fenian Bonds, that it was worth going to America to be converted to my idea,' Collins replied. 'Honestly I did not think the fact that I was practically forced to delete a certain paragraph from the prospectus looked much in favour of the idea. For God's sake, Dev, don't start an argument about its being from the prospectus only, etc. Don't please. It's quite all right.'

Before de Valera went to the United States, the Friends of Irish Freedom had launched a Victory Fund to collect $1million, a quarter of which was earmarked for Ireland. He was convinced he could collect much more by selling Irish republican bonds, but he felt Irish-American leaders adopted obstructionist tactics. They were opposed to any interference with the Victory Fund, which was due to be wound up in August 1919. This really did not matter because de Valera would not have been ready to launch the bond drive by then in any event, but he contended afterwards that Cohalan dragged his feet. The judge pointed out that the sale of such bonds would be illegal unless the United States recognised the Irish Republic first. As a trained lawyer on the bench of the New York State Supreme Court, he knew what he was talking about — selling such bonds would have been a violation of the federal 'blue sky' laws. De Valera, with no training in Irish much less American legal matters, was certainly presumptuous in pitting his own judgment against someone like Cohalan, but then the Irish leader's correspondence with Collins showed that he was clearly touchy about having his judgment questioned on the bond issue.

It took some six months to figure out a way around the American laws to get the scheme off the ground. Collins, on the other hand, was in the happier position of not having to bother with legal niceties when he formally launched the National Loan in Ireland at a meeting of the Sinn Féin executive in the Mansion House on 21 August 1919. Griffith presided and there were delegates from throughout the country. Collins told the meeting that the $1.25 million being sought in the United States had been upped to $5 million. The prospectus, which was issued over the names of de Valera and Collins, explained that 'the proceeds of this loan will be used for propagating the Irish Case all over the World, for establishing in Foreign Countries Consular Services, to promote Irish Trade and Commerce, for fostering Irish Industries, and, generally for National Purposes as directed by Dáil Éireann'.

The British proscribed the loan and ordered that no newspaper should carry any loan advertisements. Newspapers that tried to defy this ban were promptly suppressed and copies of offending editions seized. The suppressions, of course, had the effect of actually advertising the loan. Indeed, it was almost as if the whole editions had been published with nothing but advertisements promoting the loan. In addition, people selling the bonds or even speaking publicly about the scheme were arrested. By 11 September 1919 Collins was writing to Donal Hales in Italy of 'the usual daily round — raids and counter raids, and repression'. The British were gradually being sucked into the confrontation that Collins had been seeking for months.

The prospectus had been published for more than a fortnight when de Valera wrote to complain that he had only just noticed that it contained a promise to pay interest on the bonds from the date of purchase. 'It should be of course from the date of recognition and evacuation,' he wrote. 'I hope you have not made that mistake in your proposed issue in Ireland. The debt accumulated interest might be a very serious handicap later. We must look to the future.'

'I was fully aware at the time of the liability we were incurring, and deliberately drafted the particular paragraph accordingly,' Collins replied. 'We are
responsible for an accumulated interest, at a rate of six per cent per annum,
from varying dates during the period 1864–1867. This was in my mind
when we were going over the original draft prospectus. You remember I
talked a good deal of "continuity of responsibility". I am sorry to be always
fighting with you on these matters.' By then, of course, de Valera realised that
it was already too late to do anything about the bonds on sale in Ireland. 'I
am sorry it is so, but I suppose it is too late now to change it,' he wrote. 'It
must not be so in any foreign subscriptions. It will not be so in America.'

When the Dáil cabinet discussed the situation on 10 October, however, it
agreed with Collins. 'We are, I think, definitely committed to this liability.
You will, I am sure, agree that, having in mind all this, it is not possible to
alter the conditions of the Loan,' Collins wrote to de Valera on 14 October.

'The enemy's chief offensive here at the moment is directed against the
loan,' he continued. The more the Crown authorities tried to interfere with
his efforts to promote the National Loan, however, the more determined he
became to ensure its success, despite mounting promotional problems. 'We
are having extreme difficulties in advertising as far as newspapers are concerned,' he noted. It was illegal for the press to carry advertisements for the
loan, and *The Cork Examiner* and some twenty-one local newspapers were
suppressed between 17 September and 7 October for carrying such ads.

Of course, he was impatient with those newspapers which were not prepared to risk suppression by defying the law. 'The *Independent* is particularly
objectionable and hostile — in its own cowardly and sneaking way,' he
wrote to Donal Hales. 'It has not the courage to express its hostility openly,
but does so with carefully conceived innuendo. We will meet that position
too in due time.'

A novel way of promoting the campaign was found. John McDonagh, a
brother of one of the executed leaders of 1916, made a short film clip of
Collins and Diarmuid O'Hegarty sitting at a table outside Pearse's old
school, St Enda's, signing bonds to Pearse's mother, Clarke's widow, and
Connolly's daughter. Armed Volunteers then raided cinemas throughout the
country and ordered projectionists to run the brief clip. They would then
hightail it with the film before the police or military could be called. Until
then the name of Michael Collins was largely unknown outside separatist
circles, but the film projected his name before the public as never before
and, as the Crown forces concentrated on suppressing the loan, his reputation grew to the point where he became the most wanted man in the
country. 'That film of yourself and Hegarty selling Bonds brought tears to
me eyes,' Harry Boland wrote from the United States. 'Gee Boy! You are
some movie actor. Nobody could resist buying a Bond and we having such a
handsome Minister for Finance.'

Once the loan programme was under way in Ireland, de Valera asked Collins to come to the United States to help arrange things in America, but Collins declined, because he believed his place was at home. He realised that America afforded enormous opportunities for both propaganda and financial assistance, but he was convinced that all this would only happen if the right atmosphere were generated by actual events in Ireland. 'Our hope is here and must be here,' he wrote. 'The job will be to prevent eyes turning to Paris or New York as a substitute for London.' In short, they should not make the mistake of concentrating on efforts to secure international recognition because, in the last analysis, they could only win by wearing down the British government.

Instead of going to the United States himself, Collins sent one of the trustees of the Dáil, James O'Mara, who took over the organisation of a bond-certificate drive. With the help of Cohalan, the law was circumvented by selling certificates entitling purchasers to buy bonds of a similar value once the Irish Republic was recognised. As Cohalan had strong ties to the Republican Party, de Valera had the scheme vetted also by a lawyer with strong ties to the Democratic Party. He happened to be the future President, Franklin D. Roosevelt, who had recently retired from the Wilson administration.

In the spring of 1919 de Valera restrained the Big Fellow's desire for a military campaign by ensuring that the political wing of the movement had a big say in policy, but shortly after de Valera went to the United States, Collins was authorised to kill one of the DMP detectives who had refused to be cowed by the Volunteers.

Many policemen were resigning because of their social ostracisation. Those who were nearing retirement after spending the bulk of their working lives in the police force were too old to find other employment. They stayed on, but most kept their heads down and ignored all political activities, though there were some who were not terrorised by the Volunteers.

'I'm not letting any young scuts tell me how to do my duty,' Detective Sergeant Patrick Smith declared. He had arrested Piaras Béaslaí for making a seditious speech and found some incriminating documents on him. Collins and Harry Boland tried to induce Smith not to produce those documents in court but the detective ignored them, with the result that Béaslaí was sentenced to two years in jail, instead of the two months he might have otherwise expected. Collins was authorised by Richard Mulcahy as chief of staff of the Volunteers and Cathal Brugha as Minister for Defence to eliminate Smith, who was shot and mortally wounded outside his Drumcondra home on the night of 30 July 1919. He had been warned on a number of occasions 'to lay off Republicans or he would be shot', one of those who took part in the assassination later explained.

Although he had authorised the shooting of Smith, Brugha tried to strengthen the political restraints on the military wing introduced by de Valera. On 20 August he proposed in the Dáil that the next convention of the Volunteers should be asked to swear allegiance to Dáil Éireann.

As things stood the Volunteers were an autonomous organisation. De Valera was president of both the Volunteers and Sinn Féin as well as Príomh-Aire of the Dáil, so there was already a considerable amount of overlapping, but Brugha and many others were deeply suspicious of Collins and the IRB. During the summer Collins had taken over as president of the supreme council of the IRB and as such he could claim to be a successor to Pearse as president of the Irish Republic. To remove any doubt about the Dáil being the supreme organ of the new state, Brugha suggested that all Volunteers should take the following oath:

> I . . . do solemnly swear (or affirm) that I do not and shall not yield a voluntary support to any pretended Government, author- ity or power within Ireland hostile and inimical thereto, and I do further swear (or affirm) that to the best of my knowledge and ability I will support and defend the Irish Republic and the Government of the Irish Republic, which is Dáil Éireann, against all enemies, foreign and domestic, and I will bear true faith and allegiance to the same, and that I take this obligation freely without any mental reservation or purpose of evasion, so help me God.

Collins and some of his IRB colleagues had been arguing that an oath to the Republic should be enough, rather than an oath to the Dáil, but Griffith supported Brugha strongly, and this was enough to carry the day. The Dáil passed Brugha's proposal on a division. Thus the soldiers of the movement were required to pledge their allegiance to the politicians. 'The Volunteer affair is now fixed,' Collins wrote to de Valera on 25 August.

But within a matter of days the supremacy of the politicians was effectively undermined by the British. In early September Detective Sergeant Patrick Smith finally succumbed to the bullet wounds suffered in the attack outside his Drumcondra home five weeks earlier. Dublin Castle's reaction was to ban Sinn Féin. It was an ill-conceived act that played directly into the hands of Collins, who would henceforth have little difficulty in outmanoeuvring Sinn Féin moderates and implementing a more militant policy. The checks that de Valera had placed on the militants were wiped out by the banning of the political wing of the movement, which prompted the head of the British civil service, Sir Warren Fisher, to conclude that the Castle regime was 'almost woodenly stupid and quite devoid of imagination'.

'Imagine the result on public opinion in Great Britain of a similar act by the executive towards a political party (or the women's suffrage movement)!' Fisher wrote in near disbelief after he had been sent to investigate the Irish situation a few months later. Dublin Castle had not only banned Sinn Féin but also proscribed Dáil Éireann, Cumann na mBan, and the Gaelic League.

The DMP raided Sinn Féin headquarters at 6 Harcourt Street on 12 September 1919. Collins was in his finance office upstairs as the raiding party burst into the building. 'It was only by almost a miracle I was not landed,' he wrote next day. 'It so happened the particular detective who came into the room where I was did not know me, which gave me an opportunity of eluding him.'

The detective asked Collins about some documents he was carrying. 'What have they got to do with you?' Collins snapped. 'A nice job you've got, spying on your countrymen.' The detective was apparently so taken aback by the confident show of insolence that he made no effort to prevent Collins going upstairs to the caretaker's living quarters on the top floor. There, Collins climbed out the skylight and hid on the roof of the nearby Ivanhoe Hotel. Two prominent members of Sinn Féin were arrested in the building, Ernest Blythe and Pádraig O'Keeffe, the party's general secretary.

One of the policemen involved in the raid was Detective Constable Daniel Hoey, a particular thorn in the side of the Volunteers going back to before 1916. He was shot and killed that night just around the corner from his headquarters by the same men who had gunned down Smith in July.

The following week Collins was formally authorised to set up 'the Squad', a permanent full-time active service unit under his personal direction, to undertake the assassination of detectives who persisted in political work against the movement, as well as any 'spies' who helped them. It was basically the counter-intelligence arm of the Big Fellow's network. It began with the five men who had taken part in the killings of Smith and Hoey, along with two others. It was soon extended to twelve, who were sometimes irreverently known as 'the Twelve Apostles', and the name stuck even after more were included.

Detectives and their would-be touts were warned to desist from political work, or they would be shot. Collins noted that 'spies are not so ready to step into the shoes of their departed confederates as are soldiers to fill up the front line in honourable battle. And even when the new spy stepped into the shoes of the old one, he could not step into the old one's knowledge.'

'We struck at individuals and by so doing we cut their lines of communication and we shook their morale,' he explained afterwards.

Mick McDonnell, a colleague from Frongoch days, was the first head of the Squad, which included his brother-in-law, Tom Keogh, and other inmates from Frongoch, like Bill Stapleton and Jim Slattery. They were never intended as a bodyguard for Collins, as has been suggested. Instead they were a full-time assassination team, made up of clerks, tradesmen, and general workers, who were paid £4–10 a week.

Initially the Squad's meeting-place was in Oriel House, but it soon moved to a builders' yard near Dublin Castle. There was a sign over the main gate, 'Geo. Moreland Cabinet Maker'. Vinny Byrne was a master carpenter and did carpentry work in the yard while not engaged in Squad business, but most prospective customers who ventured into the yard were discouraged by outrageously long delivery dates.

Before ordering the Squad to kill any detective, the consequences were carefully considered. 'Collins would always work out how the public would react to the shooting of a "G" man first,' Ned Broy noted. 'And then he'd hang back for a while before he'd have another one shot. He tried to warn them off first without killing them.'

Usually one of his intelligence people would accompany the Squad to identify the target. 'We'd go out in pairs, walk up to the target and do it, and then split,' Byrne recalled 'You wouldn't be nervous while you'd be waiting to plug him, but you'd imagine that everyone was looking into your face. On a typical job we'd use about eight, including the back-up. Nobody got in our way. One of us would knock him over with the first shot, and the other would knock him off with a shot to the head.'

The Crown authorities naturally retaliated, but the more they reacted, the more they played into the hands of Collins. 'The repressions have been of benefit to us,' Collins wrote to de Valera on 10 October 1919.

Collins opened new offices at 76 Harcourt Street, and this time certain precautions were taken to ensure an escape route for himself and a hiding-place for important papers. Batt O'Connor built a small secret closet into a wall to store documents. 'I also provided a means of escape for Collins,' O'Connor wrote. 'We had an alarm bell on the top landing, so that, when the caretaker saw the enemy coming, he could ring the alarm bell outside the room where Collins worked. I had also provided a light ladder on the top landing, hanging on two hooks, so that he could immediately get this through a skylight. On the outside of the skylight we had bolts, so that it could be bolted from the outside after the ladder had been pulled up after him.'

Collins was told that the owner of the Standard Hotel two doors away was sympathetic, but he was more interested in the porter. 'It is not the friendship of the proprietor I want, but the friendship of the boots.' Collins said. The porter, or boots as they were called at the time, was approached and he promised to leave the skylight on the roof permanently unbolted.

Of course, Collins was much too busy to be personally involved in all of the attempts. He was occupied on other matters like the National Loan, building up his intelligence network, and springing Austin Stack from jail.

He took a particularly active interest in supervising arrangements for the escape of Stack. For more than a year he had been planning to spring him, first from Dundalk Jail and then Belfast Jail, but on each occasion Stack was moved before arrangements could be finalised. Now he was in Strangeways Jail in Manchester. Collins actually visited Stack in the prison to discuss plans for the escape, which was finally set for 25 October 1919. Some twenty men were posted outside the jail, under Rory O'Connor.

Basically the same technique was used as in the mass escape from Mountjoy the previous March. Piaras Béaslaí had been involved in that escape, but had been recaptured by Detective Sergeants Smith and Wharton, and he was again involved in this break, in which Stack, himself, and four others managed to escape. They were taken to safe houses in the Manchester and Liverpool area while Collins personally crossed the Irish Sea to make arrangements for their return to Dublin.

The more the notoriety of Collins grew, the more willing some people were to work for him, and the fact that he was president of the supreme council of the IRB probably helped in recruiting spies. A person in his position in a secret society was someone they could trust. Joe Kavanagh and Ned Broy introduced a new detective, Jim McNamara, who was administrative assistant to the assistant police commissioner in Dublin Castle. The son of a policeman, McNamara was a charming individual, and he joined Kavanagh and Broy in their weekly meetings with Collins in Thomas Gay's home.

In September Collins learned that a Sergeant Jerry Maher of the RIC in Naas might be sympathetic. When an emissary approached Maher about working for Collins, his eyes immediately lit up. 'You're the man I've been waiting for,' Maher replied. He was working as a clerk for the district inspector of the RIC, and he was able to feed Collins with information about various circulars from headquarters, as well as current codes being used. At times in the coming months Collins would have dispatches decoded and circulated to brigade intelligence officers before some of the RIC inspectors had decoded their own messages.

Collins had at least two other sources for police codes. Maurice McCarthy, an RIC sergeant stationed in Belfast, was one, and the other was a cousin of his own working in Dublin Castle. The cousin, Nancy O'Brien, had spent some years working in the post office in London and was brought to Dublin as a cipher clerk to decode messages. She was selected, she was told, because the Castle authorities wanted someone they could trust since Collins was getting some messages even before the British officers for whom they were intended. She, of course, promptly went to Collins. 'Well, Christ!' Collins exclaimed. 'What a bloody intelligence service they have.'

Sergeant Thomas J. McElligott had sought to organise a representative body within the RIC in 1918 but was soon dismissed from the police because of his Sinn Féin sympathies. He secretly went to work for Collins as a kind of police union organiser. Ostensibly he was trying to improve the pay and conditions of the RIC, but, in fact, he was engaged in black propaganda, trying to undermine the morale of the force by sowing seeds of discord.

When the police went on strike in London, Collins sent McElligott there to make some useful contacts. At strike headquarters he met a man using the name of Jameson, who was posing as a Marxist sympathiser but was actually a Secret Service agent. Shortly afterwards he turned up in Dublin and very nearly entrapped Collins, but this is getting ahead of the story.

The ready comradeship between Collins and his military colleagues was particularly striking. Liam Deasy visited Dublin on 14 October 1919, with instructions to go to Vaughan's Hotel, where he met Collins; also there were Gearóid O'Sullivan, Seán Ó Muirthile, Peadar Clancy, Diarmuid O'Hegarty, Dick McKee, Liam Tobin, and Frank Thornton. 'My recollection,' he wrote, 'is of a very informal meeting where GHQ staff were constantly coming and going, and it was a surprise to me to see how nonchalantly they seemed to accept the constant risk that was theirs.'

Next day Deasy was introduced to Brugha and Mulcahy by Collins at Lalor's on Upper Ormond Quay. 'It was quite clear to me that these men were anticipating an early development of hostilities on the part of the enemy,' Deasy wrote. Plans were being made to transfer the allegiance of the Volunteers to Dáil Éireann at a convention called for December, and Deasy was informed that they were changing the name of the Volunteers to the Irish Republican Army (IRA).

While deeply involved in intelligence, fund-raising, and arranging escape plans, Collins also became involved with Dan Breen in a plot to assassinate the Lord-Lieutenant, Lord French. This, of course, was something he had obviously been thinking about ever since he was a teenager when he advocated emulating the Finns in the assassination of the Russian Governor-General Nicholai Bobrikov in 1904. It was Breen and three colleagues who had killed the two RIC men escorting the explosive consignment at Soloheadbeg in January. They had since come to Dublin looking for more meaningful action. 'We felt bigger game was needed,' Breen wrote.

Collins shared their impatience, but he had no intention of getting involved in a numbers game. He believed in striking at individuals who were providing useful service to the British. The person with the highest profile in this regard was Lord French, a symbol of Britain's domination as well as Lloyd George's most influential adviser on Irish matters at the time. Brugha and Mulcahy agreed, so Collins ordered members of the Squad to join with the four Tipperarymen in a plan to assassinate the viceroy.

'For three long months we watched, planned and waited,' according to Breen. 'Mick Collins was with us on the first occasion that we lay in ambush.' He had learned that French was returning from England through Dún Laoghaire that night and the ambush was set up at the junction of Suffolk and Trinity Streets. They waited until dawn but the viceroy never showed. Nothing happened either on a number of other occasions because French — mindful of the need for extreme caution — repeatedly altered his route at the last moment.

In the interim Collins was in his new finance office in 76 Harcourt Street when it was raided on 8 November. The staff managed to get the important papers into the secret closet, while he headed for the skylight with an attaché case, but his escape route and procedures were not nearly as carefully planned as they should have been. For one thing, Collins did not lift the ladder behind him and he obviously forgot to bolt the skylight from the outside. To make matters worse, he found that while the skylight of the Standard Hotel was unlocked as arranged, it was directly above a stairwell, which meant that he had to make a dangerous jump across to the landing.

'Just as I got through the hotel skylight I saw a khaki helmet appear out of the skylight of No. 76,' he told colleagues that evening. 'I flung my bag across, commended myself to Providence, and jumped.' Although he hurt himself a little in the process, he was in great spirits afterwards as he recounted what happened to Batt O'Connor, Joe O'Reilly, and Piaras Béaslaí, who had just arrived back in Dublin that day following his escape from Strangeways. The Big Fellow was in his element — he too had just made his own daring escape.

Three members of the Dáil were arrested in the raid, along with three members of the Volunteers' headquarters staff, but the police failed to find the secret closet. One of the uniformed policemen ordered to search the building was Constable David Neligan, who had no intention of trying to find anything. 'I went upstairs and counted the roses on the wall paper until the raid was over,' he later explained.

'They got no document of importance, so that the only disorganisation is through the seizure of the staff,' Collins wrote. 'The enemy is certainly very keen at the moment in preventing the Dáil loan being a success, so that it becomes a more pressing duty than ever that every supporter of the Republic should increase his efforts.'

The latest raid on his office was probably in response to an attack the previous day on Detective Sergeant Wharton, who — along with the ill-fated Patrick Smith — had arrested Béaslaí earlier in the year. On the eve of Béaslaí's return, Wharton was shot and seriously wounded by a member of the Squad as he walked by St Stephen's Green. Although he survived, his injuries forced him to resign from the police force, but he was luckier than his fellow Kerryman, Detective Sergeant Johnny Barton, who investigated the Wharton shooting. He was shot near the G Division headquarters during the evening rush hour on 30 November 1919. 'What did I do?' he moaned repeatedly as he lay dying. He had been in G Division only two months.

While it was believed that Collins moved about in disguise, highly armed and well-protected, he usually went alone, unarmed and undisguised, on a bicycle. Some of the detectives knew him, but he had so terrorised the G Division that they were afraid to apprehend him, lest the faceless people supposedly protecting him would come to his rescue, or take revenge on the detectives or their families at some later date. Attacking members of anyone's family would have been out of character for Collins, but his enemies were not to know this. They knew only of his ruthless reputation, and he exploited it to the full.

One can imagine the scene as Collins recognised a detective on a tram. He would sit down next to him, ask about specific members of the detective's family, or colleagues in the DMP, and — before alighting — would assure the detective it would be safe for him to get off the tram, at some later stop.

One day in the street Batt O'Connor became uneasy at the way two DMP men looked at Collins. They seemed to recognise him, but he was unperturbed.

'Even if they recognised me,' Collins said, 'they would be afraid to report they saw me.' Anyway, if they did report, it would take the DMP an hour to muster the necessary force to seize him. 'And, of course,' he added, 'all the time I would wait here until they were ready to come along!'

He never stayed in any one place very long; he had difficulty sitting still. He always had something to do, somebody to see, or somewhere to go. Though always on the go, he never thought of himself as being 'on the run'. Wanted men frequently developed a habit of venturing forth only with care. Before leaving a building they would sneak a furtive glance to make sure there were no police around, whereas Collins had contempt for such practices. He just bounded out a door in a carefree, self-confident manner without betraying the slightest indication he was trying to evade anybody. 'I do not allow myself to feel I am on the run,' he explained. 'That is my safeguard. It prevents me from acting in a manner likely to arouse suspicion.'

When the police started looking for him in May 1919, he moved from the Munster Hotel, but in the autumn he felt safe enough to move back again. By acting as he did he gave the distinct impression of not being afraid of the detectives; they were left to ponder whether he was crazy or just very well protected. In either case he was not someone to mess with.

Faced with the demise of the DMP's most active detectives, Lord French set up a three-man committee to consider what to do about the deteriorating intelligence situation from the British point of view. The three were the acting inspector general of the RIC, the assistant under-secretary at Dublin Castle, and a resident magistrate named Alan Bell. Bell, a former RIC man, was particularly close to French and had a great deal of investigative experience going back to the troubles of the 1880s.

The committee reported on 7 December 1919 that 'an organised conspiracy of murder, outrage and intimidation has existed for some time past' with the aim of undermining the police forces. Even though the first killing of policemen had taken place in Tipperary, the committee concluded that 'Dublin City is the storm centre and mainspring of it all'. To remedy the situation it was proposed that the Sinn Féin movement should be infiltrated with spies and some selected leaders should be assassinated. 'We are inclined to think that the shooting of a few would-be assassins would have an excellent effect,' the committee reported. 'Up to the present they have escaped with impunity. We think that this should be tried as soon as possible.'

The same day Collins returned to the Munster Hotel to find a police raid in progress. The DMP were looking for him, but he mingled outside with spectators in the street. He knew that Detective Inspector Bruton was aware he lived there, and he apparently blamed him for the raid. The Squad were ordered to kill Bruton, though this was easier ordered than done.

Bruton ventured out of Dublin Castle only under armed escort, and he took the precaution of not developing any routine. Soon the attempt to kill him began to take on the aspects of a farce as Squad members lurked near a Castle entrance. 'Misters! They're not here today,' a newsboy shouted one day. That was enough. If the boy could twig them, it was time to move to other matters. In any event the finger of suspicion was soon transferred from Bruton to a spy who had wormed his way close to Collins.

H. H. Quinlisk from Wexford had been one of the prisoners of war recruited by Roger Casement for his Irish Brigade in Germany. With credentials like that, Quinlisk was easily accepted in Sinn Féin quarters, especially after Robert Brennan introduced him to Seán Ó Muirthile, the secretary of the supreme council of the IRB. Quinlisk, or Quinn as he called himself, cut a dashing figure and was quite a man for the ladies. 'He was always immaculately dressed and one would have said that with his good looks, his self-assurance and general bonhomie, he would have got anywhere,' according to Brennan. 'He liked to give the impression that he was in on all of Mick Collins's secrets.'

As a result of his enlistment in the Irish Brigade, he had been denied back-pay for the period of his imprisonment in Germany. Collins helped him out financially, and Quinlisk stayed for a time at the Munster Hotel, but he wanted more. On 11 November 1919 he wrote to the under-secretary at

Dublin Castle, mentioning his background and offering to furnish information. 'I was the man who assisted Casement in Germany and since coming home I have been connected with Sinn Féin,' he wrote. 'I have decided to tell all I know of that organisation and my information would be of use to the authorities. The scoundrel Michael Collins has treated me scurvily and I now am going to wash my hands of the whole business.'

He was brought to G Division headquarters to make a statement, which Broy typed up; then, of course, he furnished a copy to Collins. But Quinlisk had taken the precaution of telling Collins that he had gone to the DMP merely to get a passport so he could emigrate to the United States. He said the police put pressure on him to inform on Collins, offering money and promising to make arrangements for him to get his wartime back-pay. He told Collins that he was merely pretending to go along with the police.

Following the raid on the Munster Hotel, Collins found it necessary to move, though he did return there weekly. The owner, Myra McCarthy, an aunt of Fionán Lynch, continued to do his laundry for him. For the next nineteen months, until the truce in the Anglo-Irish war in July 1921, he moved about, never staying in any one place for very long. 'Living in such turmoil,' he wrote to Hannie, 'it's not all that easy to be clear on all matters at all times.' Yet he maintained a very regular daily routine.

After his office at 76 Harcourt Street was raided in November, he opened a new finance office at 22 Henry Street. Like his other offices, it was on a busy thoroughfare with a lot of passing traffic, so that the comings and goings of strangers would not attract attention, as they would if the offices had been place in some quiet, out-of-the-way location. The Henry Street office survived for about eighteen months. He also had another finance office at 22 Mary Street and he set up a new intelligence office at 5 Mespil Road. He kept papers in the home of Eileen McGrane at 21 Dawson Street, and had gold hidden in a house owned by Batt O'Connor at 3 St Andrew's Terrace, and also in O'Connor's home at 1 Brendan's Road, Donnybrook.

In the morning he would go to his intelligence office in Mespil Road. This routine was known only to his secretary Susan Mason, Liam Tobin, Joe O'Reilly, and a couple of other people. He did not meet people there. Afterwards he would cycle over to his finance office in Mary Street, and he would have lunch at either Batt O'Connor's home in Donnybrook or Pádraig O'Keeffe's wife's restaurant in Camden Street. He would meet people in either of those two places or in one of the many 'joints' that he used about the city.

There was a whole cluster of these on the north side of the city around the Rutland (now Parnell) Square area. 'Joint No. 1' was Vaughan's Hotel at 29 Rutland Square. It was a kind of clearing-house for him. People visiting from outside Dublin wishing to meet him for the first time would go to

Vaughan's, where the porter, Christy Harte, was usually able to pass on a message to him. 'Joint No. 2' was Liam Devlin's pub at 69 Parnell Street on the south side of the square. Here Collins met a more select group of people, like members of the Dublin Brigade, while he met warders from Mountjoy Jail in Jim Kirwin's bar on the same street. Other 'joints' around the square included No. 4, the old headquarters of the Irish Volunteers; No. 20, Banba Hall; No. 41, the Irish National Foresters Hall; and No. 46, the Keating Branch of the Gaelic League. Nearby were other joints, Barry's Hotel on Great Denmark Street and Fleming's Hotel in Gardiner Row. He met railwaymen carrying despatches to and from Belfast at Phil Sheerin's Coolevin Dairies in Amiens Street, police contacts in the Bannon brothers' pub in Upper Abbey Street, and sailors with news from Britain in Foley Street at Pat Shanahan's bar, which was also the haunt of Dan Breen and the Soloheadbeg gang.

They and the Squad finally caught up with Lord French on 19 December 1919. He had gone to his country residence in Roscommon, and Collins sent a man there to report when the Lord-Lieutenant left for Dublin. An ambush was then prepared at Ashtown Cross, not far from the Vice-Regal Lodge in the Phoenix Park, Dublin. The attempt was bungled, however, and the only fatality was one of the ambushers who was apparently caught in crossfire.

After his escape French was highly critical of G Division. 'Our Secret Service is simply non-existent,' he complained. 'What masquerades for such a service is nothing but a delusion and a snare. The DMP are absolutely demoralised and the RIC will be in the same case very soon if we do not quickly set our house in order.'

Detective Inspector W. C. Forbes Redmond was brought from Belfast as assistant commissioner to reorganise G Division, and he brought along a number of his own people to work under cover. Not knowing Dublin, he had to have someone as a guide to the city, so he naturally used his administrative assistant, Jim McNamara. Redmond set about capturing Collins, and he came quite close with the help of a Secret Service agent who wormed his way into Collins's confidence.

The agent was John Charles Byrne, alias Jameson, the supposed Marxist whom T. J. McElligott had met at the police strike headquarters in London. He had come to Dublin with a letter of introduction from Art O'Brien, the Sinn Féin representative in Britain. Posing as a revolutionary anxious to undermine the British system, Byrne offered to supply weapons, and arrangements were made for him to meet Collins, Mulcahy, and Rory O'Connor at the Home Farm Produce Shop in Camden Street. They met again the following day at the Ranelagh home of Jennie Wyse Power, a member of the Sinn Féin executive. 'What he was delaying about that prevented him getting us caught with him, at least on the second of these occasions, I don't know,' Mulcahy later remarked. Byrne, however, did make arrangements to have Collins arrested at a third meeting at the home of Batt O'Connor on 16 January 1920.

Redmond had one of his own undercover men watching O'Connor's house, but that man did not know Collins; by a stroke of good luck Liam Tobin, who also happened to be at the house, left with Byrne, and the lookout — assuming that Tobin was Collins — intercepted Redmond on Morehampton Road as he approached with a lorry-load of troops to raid O'Connor's house. The raid was promptly called off, but Redmond had brought McNamara with him, and also used him as a guide that night when he decided to keep O'Connor's house under personal observation.

By next day Collins had been briefed. He was due to have dinner again at O'Connor's house, but he gave it a skip. When Redmond and the police arrived, there was no one in the house, other than O'Connor's wife and children. He left, promising not to bother her again, a prophetic promise as it turned out.

Redmond had already made a fatal mistake when a detective had come to him with a grievance over some of his changes in G Division and he dismissed the complaint with some disparaging comments about G Division as a whole. 'You are a bright lot!' Redmond reportedly said. 'Not one of you has been able to get on to Collins's track for a month, and here is a man only two days in Dublin and has already seen him.' The disgruntled detective duly mentioned this to Broy, who promptly informed Collins. Given this information from McNamara, the spotlight of suspicion was immediately cast on Byrne. He not only had arrived from London recently but had also had a meeting with Collins at Batt O'Connor's house.

Tobin had disliked Byrne from the outset, but had problems convincing Collins, who liked the unusual visitor. The thirty-four-year-old Byrne was clearly an adventurer. Small with a very muscular build, he had a series of tattoos on his arms and hands. There were Japanese women, snakes, flowers, and a bird. He had a snake ring tattooed on the third finger of his right hand and two rings tattooed on his left hand. He also had a strange fascination for birds, which he kept in cages in his hotel room.

Collins wrote to Art O'Brien in London on 20 January that he had grounds for suspecting Jameson, as he called him, because he was in touch with the head of intelligence in Scotland Yard. 'I have absolutely certain information that the man who came from London met and spoke to me, and reported that I was growing a moustache to Basil Thompson,' he wrote.

Collins and Tobin decided to lay a trap for Byrne, by leading him to believe that important documents were being stored in the home of a former lord mayor of Dublin, J. J. Farrell of 9 Iona Road. The Castle authorities had no grounds for suspecting him, because he had no sympathy whatever for Sinn Féin. The greatest moment of his life had been when he received King

Edward VII on a visit to Dublin. Collins's men kept an eye on Farrell's house, and had a great laugh when the police raided it and forced the former mayor to stand outside in his night attire. 'You are raiding your friends,' Farrell protested. 'Do you know I received the King? I had twenty minutes conversation with him.'

Of course the raid looked particularly bad for Byrne, and he promptly left the country. On the night of 20 January Collins was tipped off that Redmond planned a raid that night on Cullenswood House, where Collins had a basement office and Mulcahy had a top-floor flat with his wife. Tom Cullen and Frank Thornton roused Mulcahy from his bed, and he spent the remainder of the night with a friend a short distance away. Redmond was becoming a real thorn, and Collins gave the Squad orders to eliminate him. 'If we don't get that man, he'll get us and soon,' Collins warned the Squad.

Redmond made a soft target, because he underestimated his opponents. Nattily dressed in civilian clothes, topped off by a bowler hat, he looked more like a stockbroker than a policeman. He stayed at the Standard Hotel in Harcourt Street and walked to work at Dublin Castle and back without an escort, though he did take the precaution of wearing a bullet-proof vest. The following evening the Squad got their chance as Redmond returned to his hotel. 'We knew he had a bullet-proof waistcoat,' Joe Dolan later explained with a childish giggle. 'So we shot him in the head.'

Following Redmond's death, his own undercover detectives pulled out and returned to Belfast, and thereafter G Division 'ceased to affect the situation', according to British military intelligence.

Stunned by Redmond's killing, Dublin Castle offered £10,000 rewards for information leading to the arrest and conviction of the person responsible for his death. This was probably where the story about a big reward for Collins's arrest originated. He was the one who had given the order to kill Redmond. Rewards of £5,000 had already been offered in connection with the deaths of the three DMP detectives, Smith, Hoey, and Barton, and these rewards were now doubled. As Collins had ordered all four killings, there was a handsome accumulative reward for the evidence to convict him, though the authorities never officially offered a reward for his capture.

The British gradually began to fight back. On 24 February 1920 a curfew was introduced from midnight until five o'clock in the morning. 'Last night,' Collins wrote next day, 'the city of Dublin was like a city of the dead. It is the English way of restoring peace to this country.' In the following weeks he would complain of growing repression. 'By night the streets of Dublin are like streets of a beleaguered city — no one abroad save the military forces of the enemy fully equipped for all the purposes and usages of war.'

The British were infiltrating undercover people into Ireland, and their established agents made desperate efforts to entrap Collins. Quinlisk, who had lost touch with Collins following the raid on the Munster Hotel, began making determined efforts to contact him. By now, however, Collins had firm evidence of his treachery — having got his hands on Quinlisk's actual letter offering his services to Dublin Castle. But Collins did not ask the Squad to take out the spy immediately. Instead he tried to use him as bait to get at Detective Superintendent Brien of the DMP. The Squad had been trying to kill him for some time, but Brien rarely moved outside the walls of Dublin Castle.

Seán Ó Muirthile was assigned to keep Quinlisk busy, while one of the Squad telephoned the Castle to say that Quinlisk had vital information and would meet Brien outside the offices of the *Evening Mail*, just outside the Castle, at a certain time. Brien turned up, but something spooked him before the Squad could get a shot at him. He darted back into the cover of Dublin Castle. Collins learned afterwards that Brien had twigged he was being set up and blamed Quinlisk, who explained that he had been detained all night by Ó Muirthile. 'You're in the soup,' Collins told Ó Muirthile with a laugh.

Quinlisk should have had the good sense to quit at that point, but he persisted in his efforts to see Collins. So a trap was set. He was told that Collins was out of town and would meet him that night at Wren's Hotel in Cork city. Liam Archer, one of Collins's agents at the GPO, intercepted a coded message to the district inspector of the RIC at Union Quay, Cork. 'Tonight at midnight surround Wren's Hotel, Wintrop Street, Cork,' the message read when decoded. 'Collins and others will be there. Expect shooting as he is a dangerous man and heavily armed.'

'tAnnam an Diabhal,' Collins exclaimed with a laugh on reading the message. 'They'll play *síghle caoch* with the place.'

The RIC duly raided the hotel and, of course, found nothing. Quinlisk stayed in Cork searching for Collins. On the night of 18 February he was met by some members of the IRA, who, promising to take him to Collins, took him outside the city, shot him dead and pinned a note to his body — 'Spies Beware'.

District Inspector MacDonagh of the RIC had made the mistake of looking for Collins in Cork, and he was gunned down on the street in the city three weeks later. No evidence was ever produced to suggest Collins had called for the attempt on his life. But even if the IRA in Cork had done so without directions from Dublin, the ultimate message to the police was still the same — looking for Collins could have fatal consequences.

Around this time Byrne, alias Jameson, returned from England with a suitcase of revolvers. Tobin took the guns and pretended to leave them in a business premises on Bachelor's Walk, which he said was an arms dump for the IRA. When the premises was raided that night, Collins was finally convinced of Byrne's duplicity. Members of the Squad called for Byrne at the Granville Hotel on Sackville Street on the afternoon of 2 March on the pretext of taking him to Collins's hideout, but they brought him to the grounds of a lunatic asylum in Glasnevin instead. Realising what was about to happen, he tried to bluff about his friendship with Collins and Tobin, but the Squad members knew better. They asked him if he wished to pray.

'No,' he replied.

'We are only doing our duty,' one said to him.

'And I have done mine,' he replied, drawing himself to attention as they shot him twice, once in the head and the other through the heart. Some weeks later members of the British cabinet were told that Byrne had been 'the best Secret Service man we had'.

Fergus Bryan Molloy was gunned down in Dublin in late March by the Squad in broad daylight on South William Street. He had been offering to procure arms. He was a soldier working for Colonel Hill Dillon, the chief intelligence officer of the British army at Parkgate Street. The colonel's secretary, Lily Merlin, was supplying information to Collins, and she warned him of Molloy, who had already written to his sister in America that if anything happened to him, Liam Tobin would be responsible. On one occasion he asked Tobin in the Cairo Café to write down on Dáil Éireann notepaper the names and addresses of prominent members of Sinn Féin, like Count Plunkett and Countess Markievicz.

'We have to shoot that fellow,' Tobin warned Collins.

'Well shoot him so,' Collins replied.

On the day Byrne's body was returned to England, Alan Bell, the resident magistrate who had served on the secret committee which had called for 'the shooting of a few would-be assassins', opened a much publicised inquiry into Sinn Féin funds. He was empowered to examine bank accounts in order to locate money deposited in the names of a number of party sympathisers.

Bell stayed out in Monkstown and travelled into the city each day on a tram. A police guard escorted him to and from the tram each day, but he travelled into the city alone. He was coming into the city as usual on the morning of 26 March when four men approached him as the tram reached Ballsbridge. 'Come on, Mr Bell, your time has come,' one of the men said. Horrified passengers looked on as the Squad members dragged the elderly man into the street and shot him dead on the pavement. The killing of an old man like that provoked a storm of revulsion.

It was widely believed that he was killed because he was trying to find the National Loan money, though there were also published rumours that he had been investigating the attempt on the life of his friend, Lord French. One rather colourful story was published in the United States to the effect that Bell had arranged for a Scotland Yard detective to go to Mountjoy Jail, pose as a priest and 'hear' confessions of political prisoners there. The IRA supposedly learned of this and shot both Bell and the detective next day.

The fact that no detective was killed next day, or indeed in the whole month of March, did not prevent the publication of the story.

Despite his frail elderly appearance, Bell had posed an extremely dangerous threat to Collins. He had, in fact, directed Detective Inspector Redmond during hs brief stint in Dublin, and he was also one of the architects of the policy which led, as will be seen in the next chapter, to the killing of Tomás MacCurtain, the lord mayor of Cork. This was not brought out at the time, presumably because Collins was not in a position to release the information without endangering his source in Dublin Castle.

In any event, the bad publicity surrounding Bell's elimination had some advantages, as far as Collins was concerned, because it acted as a very public warning to various individuals not to go looking for the loan money. Despite early misgivings he achieved the goal of raising £250,000. In fact the loan was oversubscribed by some 40 per cent and more than £357,000 was collected. Of that the British captured only a mere £18,000. 'From any point of view the seizure was insignificant,' Collins wrote, 'but you may rely upon it we shall see to the return of this money just as someday Ireland will exact her full reparation for all the stealings and seizures by the British in the past.'

6

The Backlash

De Valera's overall approach to the controversy over the League of Nations led to difficulties with the leadership of the influential Irish-American organisation, the Friends of Irish Freedom. Its leaders, Judge Daniel Cohalan and John Devoy, resented his suggestion that the United States should renew efforts to make the world safe for democracy. That was sheer Wilsonian babble, as far as Cohalan was concerned.

Born in upstate New York of Irish parents, Cohalan was a controversial figure, detested in Democratic Party circles as a political turncoat. In the past he had been closely identified with the powerful Tammany boss, Charles F. Murphy, and had been a member of the New York delegations at the Democratic Party's national conventions of 1904 and 1908. In 1910 he was appointed to the New York Supreme Court and, together with Murphy, spearheaded an unsuccessful attempt to block Woodrow Wilson's quest for the Democratic nomination on his way to the presidency in 1912. Murphy soon made his peace with Wilson, but Cohalan did not. He bolted the party and supported Wilson's Republican opponent in 1916. Cohalan despised Wilson, and the feeling was quite mutual.

When the judge headed an Irish-American delegation which sought to make representations to Wilson before his departure for the Paris Peace Conference, the President insisted on Cohalan's exclusion. He gracefully withdrew and in the process greatly enhanced his own standing among Irish-American activists. He had not only stepped aside and borne Wilson's affront in the interest of the cause, but more importantly, he had been singled out as an opponent by the President himself, and this would become a valuable distinction in the coming months as Wilson's reputation plummeted in Irish-American circles.

Cohalan would undoubtedly have been delighted to use de Valera against Wilson, but the Irish leader was wisely unwilling to be used in such a way. He was anxious to be on friendly terms with both the Democrats and the Republicans, and he might have succeeded had he not tried to act as a power-broker, ready to deliver Irish-American support.

Cohalan and Devoy had already informed de Valera of their utter opposition to American membership of the League of Nations, even if Ireland were admitted to the organisation, so they therefore naturally resented his nationwide effort to depict 'men and women of Irish blood' as being prepared to support the Versailles Treaty in return for Wilson's recognition of the Irish Republic. De Valera had no mandate whatever to speak for Irish-Americans and his intervention was resented as outside interference in American politics. Cohalan tried to keep him out of Irish-American affairs, and when de Valera asked 'to be let into the political steps' the judge was planning, he was told not to 'go near the political end at all'.

'The trouble is purely one of personalities,' de Valera wrote to Griffith. 'I cannot feel confidence enough in a certain man [Cohalan] to let him have implicit control of tactics here without consultation and agreement with me.' In short, de Valera was insisting on having the final say on policy matters, though he was prepared to consult with Irish-American leaders. 'On the ways and means they have to be consulted,' he conceded, 'but I reserve the right to use my judgment as to whether any means suggested is or is not in conformity with our purpose.'

Whether the United States decided to join the League of Nations or not was basically none of his business. 'The fight for the League of Nations was purely an American affair attacked from a purely American angle,' de Valera admitted in a letter to the cabinet at home. He certainly had no right to say that people like Cohalan would support the Versailles Treaty under conditions that they had pronounced unacceptable. The two men developed a distinct personal dislike for each other. Cohalan felt that the Irish leader was interfering in American politics while de Valera felt that the judge was interfering in Irish affairs. A clash was therefore virtually inevitable.

In the summer of 1919 de Valera had refused to go along blindly with efforts to arrange for him to address the United States Congress. Cohalan had approached Senator William E. Borah of the Foreign Relations Committee with a view to making arrangements to secure an invitation for de Valera. But as Borah was an isolationist Republican and a strong critic of Wilson, de Valera believed the approach should be bipartisan, and he insisted that Senator James D. Phelan of California should be asked to co-sponsor the approach. De Valera subsequently met with Cohalan, Borah, and Phelan to discuss the matter but nothing ever came of it, much to the irritation of Cohalan, who believed they would have had a much better chance if the Irish leader had gone along with Borah.

De Valera's own reports to the cabinet in Dublin left no doubt that he had interfered in American affairs by presuming to speak for Irish-Americans during the controversy over the Versailles Treaty. On the other hand, the Cohalan faction interfered in Irish affairs when de Valera tried to reassure the public that Britain had nothing to fear from an independent Ireland. Many Americans had reservations about Irish independence because they felt an independent Ireland would pose security risks for Britain, their ally in the recent war. Congressman Tom Connolly of Texas contended, for instance, that the British could never permit Ireland to become independent because it would 'become the prey of every scheming nation in Europe'. De Valera tried to allay these fears by indicating that Ireland would guarantee Britain's legitimate security needs.

In the course of an exclusive interview with the *Westminster Gazette* on 5 February 1920, he explained there were four different ways of ensuring Britain's security. First, there could be an international guarantee of Ireland's neutrality as in the case of Belgium, or second, 'in a genuine League of Nations the contracting parties could easily by mutual compact bind themselves to respect and defend the integrity and national independence of each other, and guarantee it by the strength of the whole'.

The other two ways of guaranteeing that Irish independence would not endanger Britain's security had distinct American parallels. De Valera suggested that the London government could simply declare a doctrine for Britain and Ireland similar to the Monroe Doctrine used by the United States to insist against European encroachment on the independence of Latin American countries. The fourth idea was for Britain to agree to a treaty similar to the 1901 treaty between Cuba and the United States. The Americans had protected their interests then, according to de Valera, by demanding that the Cuban government promise it would 'never enter into any treaty or other compact with any foreign power or powers which shall impair or tend to impair Cuban independence, nor in any manner authorise or permit any foreign power or powers to obtain by colonisation or for military or naval purposes or otherwise, lodgment in or control over any portion of the said island'.

'Why doesn't Britain do with Ireland as the United States did with Cuba?' de Valera asked. 'Why doesn't Britain declare a Monroe Doctrine for her neighbouring island? The people of Ireland so far from objecting, would co-operate with their whole soul.'

In advocating the Cuban analogy de Valera had quoted from the first clause of what was known as the Platt Amendment, which had been incorporated into the 1901 treaty. He did not make any reference to other Platt clauses demanding that the United States should be granted naval and coaling stations in Cuba, as well as the right to intervene there for the preservation of the island's independence. De Valera did not intend the other clauses of the Platt Amendment to be part of his proposal. He actually intimated during the interview that he would not be in favour of allowing Britain to have Irish bases. In summarising his arguments, for instance, he said that 'it is not her national safety nor her legitimate security that

England wants to safeguard. By any of the four methods indicated she could have made provision for these. What she wants to make provision for, I repeat, is the perpetuation of her domination of the seas by her control of the great Irish harbours.'

Unknown to de Valera there was an arrangement between the *Westminster Gazette* and the *New York Globe* to share their material, so the interview appeared on the front page of the New York newspaper next day under the headline: 'Compromise Suggested by Irish'. The *Globe* mentioned that the salient features of the interview were de Valera's call not only for 'the opera- tion of a policy based on the American Monroe Doctrine' but also for 'the granting of complete independence to Ireland on the same basis as the independence granted to Cuba'. There was no suggestion in the report that the Irish leader was prepared to accept less than 'complete independence'.

He had achieved part of his objective. A *Globe* editorial in the same edition suggested that de Valera had offered 'a really convincing assurance' to 'the seemingly unanswerable argument' that Irish independence would be extremely damaging to Britain's security. The editorial concluded, how- ever, that the assurance in question actually introduced 'a new principle. It is a withdrawal by the official head of the Irish Republic of the demand that Ireland be set free to decide her own international relations.'

Although the Philadelphia *Irish Press* and the New York *Irish World* both welcomed de Valera's initiative, the *Gaelic American* condemned the proposals as an offer of surrender to Britain, and the *Globe* editorial was cited to support the charge. De Valera quickly clarified that he had only quoted the first clause of the Platt Amendment and was referring to it alone when he put forward the Cuban analogy. He had no hesitation in reaffirming that Ireland would give Britain that guarantee, because it would not be incom- patible with Irish independence, on which he said he had no intention of compromising. John Devoy, the editor of the *Gaelic American*, chose to dis- regard de Valera's clarification. 'When a part of a document is offered in evidence in court, or in negotiations,' Devoy declared in an editorial, 'the whole document becomes subject for consideration.' He basically wanted to put de Valera on trial in the columns of the *Gaelic American*.

Instead of replying to Devoy, de Valera took the extraordinary step of complaining to Cohalan. The judge had made no public comment on the controversy, yet de Valera essentially demanded that he dissociate himself from Devoy's views. De Valera wrote that he was planning to use 'the great lever of American opinion' as a wedge to achieve his aims in the United States. As the Irish-Americans were to be the thin edge of this wedge, he was anxious to satisfy himself that the metal at the point was of the right temper. 'The articles of the *Gaelic American* and certain incidents that have resulted from them, give me grounds for fear that, in a moment of stress the point of the lever would fail me,' he wrote. It was therefore vital he should know how the judge stood in the matter. 'I am led to understand that these articles in the *Gaelic American* have your consent and approval. Is this so?'

De Valera's letter was a naive piece of insensitive arrogance. He was in effect telling the judge that he intended to use him without so much as asking if he was willing to be used in such a manner. Understandably indignant, Cohalan replied he had no intention of being used as a lever for alien ends. And he warned that de Valera was making a serious mistake if he thought other Irish-Americans would allow themselves to be used in this way. The judge emphasised that he considered himself 'as an American, whose only allegiance is to America, and as one to whom the interest and security of my country are to be preferred to those of any and all other lands'.

'Do you really think for a moment that any self-respecting American citizen will permit any citizen of another country to interfere, as you suggest, in American affairs?' the judge asked. 'If so, I may assure you that you are woefully out of touch with the spirit of the country in which you are sojourning.'

The Irish leader was undoubtedly acting tactlessly by interfering in American politics, but then Cohalan was doing the same thing by injecting his views on what was essentially an Irish policy matter. 'A British Monroe Doctrine that would make Ireland an ally of England, and thus buttress the falling British Empire so as to further oppress India and Egypt and other subject lands would be so immoral and so utterly at variance with the ideals and traditions of the Irish people as to make it indefensible to them as it would be intolerable to the liberty-loving people of the world,' Cohalan wrote.

De Valera's critics were not confined to an Irish-American clique. Sinn Féin envoy Patrick McCartan was hostile to Devoy and Cohalan but he was decidedly uneasy about the *Westminster Gazette* interview. 'Apart from its malice there was little Devoy said with which we could in our hearts disagree,' McCartan wrote. 'Had he said in private what he spread over the pages of the *Gaelic American*, we might have tried to moderate his tone, but not to refute his argument.' De Valera had been needlessly antagonising people 'by betraying an unconscious contempt' for the views of others, according to McCartan. He noted that de Valera 'tends to force his own opinions without hearing the other fellow's and thus thinks he has co-operation when he only gets silent acquiescence'.

On the day that the United States Senate finally rejected the Versailles Treaty, Cohalan complained to a meeting of prominent Irish-Americans in New York that de Valera, who was present at the meeting, knew very little about American politics, yet consulted no one and by his arrogance alienated many people who had spent a lifetime helping the Irish cause. In the course of a thirty-minute tirade, the judge accused de Valera of interfering in American affairs and causing 'considerable friction' among Irish-Americans. He certainly had a valid point, but he continued in terms which showed that he himself was interfering in purely Irish affairs. He complained, for instance, that de Valera's controversial *Westminster Gazette* interview amounted to an offer of 'a compromise to England which would put Ireland in the position of accepting a protectorate from England, and consent to an alliance with that country which would align the race with England as against the United States in the case of war' between America and Britain.

When de Valera was invited to explain his own position to the meeting, he tactlessly blurted out that he was not in the United States a month when he realised the country was not big enough for himself and Cohalan, which prompted Archbishop William Turner of Buffalo to remark that the judge could hardly be expected 'to leave his native land just because the President had decided to come in'.

The meeting, which dragged on for ten hours, was acrimonious in the extreme. At one point Harry Boland went into hysterics and had to retire from the room to compose himself. 'De Valera's attitude was one of infallibility; he was right, everybody else was wrong, and he couldn't be wrong,' one witness recalled. 'I thought the man was crazy.' In the end the bishop persuaded the two factions to agree to a truce. The meeting broke up on the understanding that henceforth de Valera would not interfere in purely American matters, and Cohalan and Devoy would keep out of essentially Irish affairs.

But de Valera had no intention of upholding his side of the agreement. Within a week he was writing to Griffith asking the Dáil to secretly authorise him to spend between a quarter and a half a million dollars in connection with forthcoming elections in the United States. He wanted to keep the matter secret for the time being so as not to upset his fund-raising efforts. 'It is very important,' he wrote, 'that there should not be an open rupture until the Bond Drive were over at any rate.'

He was already being confronted with an internal problem. James O'Mara, the man that Collins sent out to help organise the bond-certificate drive, resigned over de Valera's arrogant behaviour. 'What on earth is wrong with Mr O'Mara?' Collins wrote to Boland. 'There always seems to be something depressing coming from the USA.' O'Mara agreed to withdraw his resignation following an appeal from Griffith, who noted that the resignation would be damaging to the movement.

There was also a degree of uneasiness at home over the *Westminster Gazette* interview. Father Michael O'Flanagan, a Sinn Féin vice-president, wrote to Collins complaining about the 'suspicion that we are prepared to desert our friends in a foolish attempt to placate our enemies. In the last resort we must rely not upon the people who wish to make the world safe for the British Empire, but upon those who don't.'

Despite his own reservations, McCartan backed de Valera over the Cuban controversy because he believed that repudiating him 'would irredemiably injure our cause in America' as well as hurt the cause at home by providing encouragement to the British. McCartan was therefore sent back to Dublin to explain to the cabinet what was happening in America. He found that Brugha, Plunkett, and Markievicz 'showed marked hostility' to the interview, but Griffith deftly limited discussion on the matter and secured cabinet acceptance of de Valera's explanation, with strong backing from Collins. The cabinet also authorised de Valera to spend the money he requested on the American elections.

In the following weeks de Valera concentrated on the recognition question as he toured the Deep South. He was trying to drum up public support to rescue a bill introduced in the House of Representatives some months earlier by Congressman William Mason, who had proposed that Congress allocate funds for a diplomatic mission to Ireland. Normally the President would first accord recognition and Congress would then authorise the funds for a diplomatic mission. In the case of the Mason bill the procedure was being reversed, but the novel approach ran into such determined opposition that it was necessary to abandon it.

The poet, W. B. Yeats, attended one of de Valera's rallies in New York in May 1920, but he was disappointed. He described de Valera as 'a living argument rather than a living man. All propaganda, no human life, but not bitter, hysterical or unjust. I judged him persistent, being both patient and energetic, but that he will fail through not having enough human life as to judge the human life in others. He will ask too much of everyone and will ask it without charm. He will be pushed aside by others.'

In some respects the assessment was prophetic, but de Valera was no pushover, as Cohalan and Devoy were to learn in the coming months. The campaign for recognition had suffered a serious setback with the failure of the Mason bill, but de Valera did not despair. It was an election year in the United States and he was already working on a scheme to enlist the support of a presidential candidate for Irish recognition in return for Irish-American votes. Although the Irish-Americans were a distinct minority in the United States, they possessed an inordinate political influence because they were concentrated in the large urban areas of the most populous states and tended to block vote as directed by their leaders.

In New York, the state with the largest number of electoral votes for the presidency, for example, the Irish-Americans were concentrated in New York city, where their support was crucial to any Democratic candidate, because upstate New York was heavily Republican. Thus, the Democratic candidate had to win well in New York city to carry the state, and this was highly improbable without the support of the Irish-American community. The 'Irish vote' tended to have the same kind of pivotal influence in other important states; hence the excessive influence exerted by the Irish-American political bosses within the Democratic Party. De Valera hoped to enlist that influence to further his aims. 'The Democrats will bid high for the Irish vote now,' he explained. 'Without it they have not the slightest chance of winning at the elections, unless something extraordinary turns up.'

While he thought the Democratic Party was Ireland's best hope, he did not write off the Republicans. 'Our policy here has always been to be as friendly with one of the political parties as with the other,' he wrote. If the Irish-American vote was important to the Democrats, it could be just as valuable to the Republicans, seeing that solid Irish-American backing could guarantee the Republicans victory in a number of very important states because it would deprive the Democrats of their traditional support; they would then need to pick up twice as many votes from elsewhere just to offset the loss of the Irish-Americans.

Consequently, de Valera was just as optimistic about the possibility of being able to bargain with a Republican candidate. In fact, he considered Senator Hiram Johnson, the California Republican, to be 'the best man available'. The only way 'to play the cards' for Ireland, de Valera believed, was to get a firm public commitment from a candidate to recognise the Irish Republic. He hoped to get such a commitment from Johnson in order that 'our people could start working for him', but the *Gaelic American* endorsed the California senator's candidacy without waiting for such a commitment.

De Valera resented Devoy's action; Johnson had been able to get what he was looking for without any commitment. 'It is disappointing to see a clear nap hand played poorly,' de Valera wrote. 'Sometimes when I see the strategic position which the Irish here occupy in American politics I feel like crying when I realise what could be made of it if there was real genuine teamwork for Ireland alone being done. As far as politics is concerned, the position is almost everything one could wish for.'

This amazing comment again betrayed his naive view of the political situation. The Irish-Americans considered themselves Americans first. Their 'Irish' prefix was indicative of their ancestry, not their allegiance. To have engaged in 'real genuine teamwork for Ireland alone' would have meant subordinating American interests to those of Ireland. De Valera was trying to set himself up as a power-broker in the selection of the US President by getting Americans to vote strictly on the grounds of what the man would do for Ireland.

All this was clearly a violation of his agreement to stay out of American affairs but, as previously stated, he never really intended to uphold his end of the agreement anyway. Under the circumstances another clash with the Cohalan–Devoy faction was virtually certain. The political truce collapsed in June 1920 when de Valera went to Chicago for the Republican Party's national convention, despite being asked to stay away. He was hoping to influence the Republicans to adopt a plank calling for recognition of the Irish Republic in the party's election platform.

His people opened offices across from the convention centre and published a daily newsletter. On the eve of the convention they organised a torchlight parade involving some five thousand marchers, who were afterwards addressed by de Valera. 'The Republicans must promise to recognise the Irish Republic,' he told them. 'All of Chicago wants this — I know the entire country wants this — I have been all over the country and I know.'

'There was no chance of offending America that we did not take,' McCartan later recalled. Their actions were so glaring that the *Chicago Daily Tribune* carried a cartoon of the Irish leader with the comment: 'De Valera is not really a candidate in this Convention.' When he tried to get a personal hearing before the party's subcommittee on resolutions, he was refused and his plank calling for official recognition was heavily defeated by a vote of twelve to one.

Cohalan managed to persuade the subcommittee to adopt a resolution by seven votes to six calling for 'recognition of the principle that the people of Ireland have the right to determine freely, without dictation from outside, their own governmental institutions and their international relations with other states and peoples'. But on learning of the acceptance of the Cohalan plank, de Valera objected and demanded it be withdrawn. The chairman of the subcommittee was so annoyed at this foreign interference that he reversed his own vote and killed the plank.

Afterwards de Valera explained that he had undermined the Cohalan resolution because it was too vague. 'It was positively harmful to our interests that a resolution misrepresenting Ireland's claim by understating it should have been presented,' he said. The plank was supposedly an understatement because it called, not for recognition of the Irish Republic, but merely for recognition of the Irish people's right to self-determination.

Before going to the United States, de Valera had stressed that Ireland was only seeking the right of self-determination. After his arrival in New York, he endorsed this policy, and he subsequently emphasised it by dwelling on the point in many of his American speeches. 'What I seek in America,' he said on more than one occasion, 'is that the United States recognise in Ireland's case, Ireland's right to national self-determination, that and nothing more.' Upon his return to Ireland at the end of 1920 he again emphasised the same theme in a series of interviews with foreign correspondents, as when he told a Swiss journalist that 'the principle for which we are fighting is the principle of Ireland's right to complete self-determination'. In addition he bitterly resented it the following April when Seán T. O'Kelly advised him to stop talking about self-determination and just call for recognition of the Irish Republic. The dispute in Chicago had nothing to do with principles: it was strictly a power struggle over who should speak for the Irish people and for the millions of Irish-Americans.

De Valera had already written home that he did not want anyone to think that he had 'become a puppet to be manipulated' by the judge. He did not want American politicians to get the idea Cohalan was 'the real power behind our movement — the man to whom they would have to go. Were I [to] allow myself to appear thus as a puppet, apart from any personal pride, the movement would suffer a severe blow. Those who hold aloof because of the plea that the Judge is running this movement would cry out that they were justified.' It is noteworthy that he mentioned his personal pride before the interests of the movement.

In view of the manner in which he was denied normal parental affection, de Valera grew up with a deep yearning for distinction and a nagging sense of inferiority which was perversely stirred by his sudden fame, a fame which owed so much to chance that it provided little sense of security. Had he been more secure in his own mind, he might not have looked on Cohalan's actions as menacing, but as things stood he felt his position threatened, and he had to show he was no longer insignificant. He may well have convinced himself that he was acting in Ireland's interest, but then, as he would show in the coming years, he had a facility for being able to convince himself that his own self-interest was in the national interest.

Following the Chicago debacle there were efforts to convene a conference to stop the feuding, but some of de Valera's own people wished to exclude him because he had been betraying 'an unconscious contempt' for the opinions of others by doing most of the talking and not allowing others to speak. De Valera also wanted a conference, but his aim was to reorganise Irish-Americans in order to inject the Irish question into the forthcoming national elections. In a letter to Bishop Michael J. Gallagher of Detroit, who was elected president of the Friends of Irish Freedom shortly after the Chicago debacle, de Valera suggested a convention of the Irish race should be held in some central point like Chicago in order to make arrangement for a fresh campaign.

Chicago was suggested as the site in an obvious attempt to break the stranglehold on the Friends of Irish Freedom that was enjoyed by Cohalan's supporters, most of whom were based in the New York area. But their resentment over Irish interference in American affairs was already very strong, and was further fuelled with the publication of some seized documents showing that the Dáil had authorised de Valera to spend a half a million dollars on the American elections. De Valera tried to take the mischief out of the report by issuing a statement emphasising that it was misleading to speak of the funds as intended for the American elections. 'In public and in private I have been scrupulously careful to avoid even appearing to take sides in the party politics of this country,' he declared. 'Apart from any possible illegality, it would obviously be bad taste on my part and most inexpedient.'

He seemed to be contending that he was staying above party politics by being prepared to back sympathetic candidates without regard to their party affiliation, but it was patently absurd for his authorised biographers to contend that he 'could never be accused of interference with American internal politics'. By his own admission he knew full well he was interfering in American politics in calling for the revision of the Versailles Treaty. Providing support for candidates in American elections would likewise have constituted an intervention in internal politics.

The Irish-American refusal to call a race convention before the November elections was understandable. Devoy considered the idea a blatant effort to remove himself and Cohalan so that de Valera could 'show that nobody in America amounts to anything and that he is the kingpin of the movement'. They did agree, however, to call a meeting of the national council of the Friends of Irish Freedom in New York on 17 September 1920. De Valera personally telegraphed each council member to attend, with the result that delegates from as far away as California came, but when he was unable to get his way, he walked out, trailed by supporters shouting 'follow the President'.

Outside, de Valera announced plans to found a new organisation, which, he said, should be under the democratic control of members throughout the country, instead of being run by a cabal in New York. 'We from Ireland simply ask this,' he said, 'that we should be accepted as the interpreters of what the Irish people want — we are responsible to them, they can repudiate us if we represent them incorrectly.'

Devoy sought to undermine de Valera by depicting Collins as the real Irish leader following the Big Fellow's interview with Carl W. Ackermann of the *Philadelphia Public Ledger* in August 1920. 'Michael Collins Speaks for Ireland', Devoy proclaimed boldly in a *Gaelic American* editorial. The weekly newspaper also carried a large front-page photograph of Collins in uniform (taken in 1916), with the caption, 'Ireland's Fighting Chief'. There was no doubt Devoy was hitting at de Valera, but Collins wanted nothing to do with it. 'Every member of the Irish cabinet is in full accord with President de Valera's policy,' Collins wrote to Devoy on 30 September. 'When he speaks to America, he speaks for all of us.'

These were not mere words. Collins actually went so far as to sever the IRB's connections with Clan na Gael a fortnight later. 'Let it be clearly understood,' he emphasised in a further letter to Devoy, 'that we all stand together, and that here at home every member of the cabinet has been an ardent supporter of the President against any and every group in America who have either not given him the co-operation which they should, or have set themselves definitely to thwart his actions.'

Collins could not have been more forthright in his support of de Valera's position. He obviously held the President in high esteem, and that affection was extended to de Valera's family. Although Collins was the most wanted man in the country, he regularly visited Sinéad de Valera and the children at their home in Greystones, County Wicklow. He brought her money and news from America, and he also played with the children. Sinéad de Valera sincerely appreciated his help. In later life she would go out of her way to tell members of the Collins family how much the visits had meant to her. She appreciated that he took the trouble to visit her personally, rather than sending messengers, as he could so easily have done.

He also arranged for her to visit the United States, but that may not have been one of his more helpful gestures, to judge, at least, from de Valera's reaction. He complained that his wife's place was at home with the children, and she promptly returned to Ireland. There were, however, some rather unseemly rumours about de Valera's relationship with his secretary, Kathleen O'Connell, whom he met in the United States. They had been travelling together, and it was rumoured they were having an affair.

On 16 November 1920 de Valera formally launched the new organisation in Washington, D.C. The American Association for Recognition of the Irish Republic prospered for some months and seemed to justify de Valera's belief that Cohalan's leadership was unacceptable to many Irish-Americans. In the following year the Friends of Irish Freedom suffered serious defections as its membership declined to about 20,000, while that of the new association soared to around half a million in the same period.

But any chance of securing official American recognition had already been dashed with the election of Senator Warren G. Harding as the next President of the United States in November 1920. There had been a noticeable shift among Irish-Americans to the Republican candidate even though he made no effort to woo votes on the Irish question. In fact, when asked during the campaign about his attitude towards the Irish issue, he came down clearly on the British side. 'I would not care to undertake to say to Great Britain what she must do any more than I would permit her to tell us what we must do with the Philippines,' Harding declared.

De Valera had failed dismally in his principal goal of securing official American recognition, as well as in his secondary aim of helping to end the developing split within Irish-American ranks. The split was wider than ever when he returned to Ireland in December 1920, but he did leave behind a viable organisation which was primarily dedicated towards serving the Irish cause, rather than using the Irish situation to serve American ends. His mission had certainly not been a total failure, because he collected over $5 million for the cause at home. Moreover, by his clever exploitation of the opportunities afforded for propaganda, he had secured invaluable publicity for the cause. As a result of this publicity the British government came under enormous pressure to negotiate an Irish settlement, if only to avoid Anglo-American difficulties.

Prior to 1920 the British cabinet was too preoccupied with other problems to devote much attention to Ireland, but the need to do something about the deteriorating situation gradually dawned on Lloyd George and his colleagues. During the early months of 1920 they set about changing their own policy and undertook a thorough spring-cleaning of the Dublin Castle administration. Sir Hamar Greenwood was appointed Chief Secretary, Sir John Anderson under-secretary, and Sir Alfred (Andy) Cope assistant under-secretary. General Sir Nevil Macready became commander-in-chief of British forces in Ireland, Major-General Henry Tudor took over at the head of the police, and General Sir Ormonde Winter became chief of combined intelligence services.

From the outset Greenwood was determined to follow a hard-line policy. Even before visiting Ireland he 'talked the most awful tosh about shooting Sinn Féiners at sight, and without evidence, and frightfulness generally', according to Sir Maurice Hankey, the cabinet secretary.

The British began to retaliate by using some of the IRA's tactics. In Cork during recent weeks, for instance, there had been the killings of Quinlisk and a number of constables, as well as the shooting of District Inspector MacDonagh. The police held Tomás MacCurtain responsible; he was both lord mayor of Cork and commander of the local IRA. On the night of 20 March, following the killing of another constable, a group of men with blackened faces forced their way into MacCurtain's home and shot him dead in front of his wife and daughter.

At the subsequent inquest there was evidence that the RIC had assisted the killers during the attack by cordoning off the area around the shop over which MacCurtain lived. The coroner's jury returned a verdict of murder against Lloyd George and various members of the British administration in Ireland, as well as District Inspector Swanzy of the RIC. He was one of a large number of Orangemen from Ulster stationed in Cork, and they were believed to have been implicated in the killing. Swanzy was transferred from Cork for his own protection.

Collins was deeply upset by the death of his friend, MacCurtain; they had been quite close ever since their internment together in Frongoch. 'I have not very much heart in what I am doing today, thinking of poor Tomás,'

Collins wrote to Terence MacSwiney. 'It is surely the most appalling thing that has been done yet.'

Two similar killings took place on following nights in the Thurles area, where the RIC also contained a strong contingent of Orangemen. Collins complained that the British and 'their agents here, whether military, police or civil, are doing all they can to goad the people into premature action'. It had been with difficulty that Mulcahy and Collins had persuaded MacCurtain not to go ahead with plans to stage a 1916-style rebellion in Cork to commemorate the fourth anniversary of the Easter Rebellion. Terence MacSwiney, who succeeded MacCurtain as lord mayor, would not be easily goaded. He was quite prepared to suffer. 'This contest is one of endurance,' he declared in his inaugural address. 'It is not they who can inflict most, but they who can suffer most who will conquer.'

The other side's capacity for suffering was already showing signs of stress. Members of the RIC were not prepared to put up with the social ostracisation and attacks to which they were being subjected. Resignations from the force were running at more than two hundred a month in early 1920. It was not long before the British found it necessary to bring in new recruits from outside. The first of these arrived in Ireland on 25 March 1920. They had been recruited so hastily that there was not time to get them proper uniforms.

All wore the dark green caps and belts of the RIC, but some had the dark green tunics with military khaki pants, while others had khaki tunics and dark green pants. Most were veterans of the Great War who had been unable either to find civilian employment or to adjust to civilian life. The ten shillings a day, all found, was a relatively good wage for the time, especially for men who were desperate for a job. In view of the colour of their uniforms and the ruthless reputation they quickly acquired, they were called Black and Tans after a pack of hounds. The more active undoubtedly welcomed the name, because they — like Dan Breen — tended to see their enemy in terms of hunting 'game'.

Faced with the choice of British or Irish terrorists, the Irish people preferred their own; they hid them and supported them. As a result the Black and Tans quickly began to look on all civilians as their enemy and acted accordingly, thereby further alienating the Irish people from the Crown government.

The week after the arrival of the first contingent of Black and Tans, the IRA intensified its campaign. At Collins's suggestion tax offices throughout the country were fire-bombed on the night of 3 April in an attempt to disrupt the British tax-collecting apparatus. Around the same time more than 350 unoccupied RIC barracks were burned to the ground.

When the British government discussed what to do about the Irish situation, General Macready advocated making the security forces mobile enough to surprise IRA bands, but Field Marshal Sir Henry Wilson, the chief of imperial general staff, dismissed this idea as useless. He wanted, instead, 'to collect the names of Sinn Féiners by districts; proclaim them on church doors all over the country; and whenever a policeman is murdered, pick five by lot and shoot them!' One could hardly imagine anything more likely to provoke the indignation of Irish people than to defile their churches in such a barbarous manner. The suggestion was a measure of the wooden stupidity of the Crown authorities when it came to dealing with Ireland.

'Somehow or other terror must be met by greater terror,' wrote Sir Maurice Hankey. And this is precisely what happened. When members of the new Dublin Castle administration met on 31 May to discuss the situation with Lloyd George and Minister for War Winston Churchill, the new Chief Secretary complained of 'thugs' going about shooting people in Dublin, Cork, and Limerick. 'We are certain that these are handsomely paid,' Greenwood said, 'the money comes from the USA.' According to him, Collins paid 'the murderers in public houses'.

'It is monstrous that we have 200 murders and no one hung,' Churchill cried. 'After a person is caught he should pay the penalty within a week. Look at the tribunals which the Russian Government have devised. You should get three or four judges whose scope should be universal and they should move quickly over the country and do summary justice.' It was ironic that he, of all people, should privately advocate imitating the Bolshevik system, against which he railed in his public speeches.

'You agreed six or seven months ago that there should be hanging,' he said to Lloyd George.

'I feel certain you must hang,' the Prime Minister replied, but he doubted that an Irish jury would convict any rebel of a capital offence. In the circumstances, he therefore advocated economic pressure.

'Increase their pecuniary burdens,' he said. 'There is nothing farmers so much dislike as the rates.'

'Why not make life intolerable in a particular area?' Churchill asked.

'We are at present in very much of a fog,' Macready explained. The old system of intelligence had broken down, as the DMP's 'morale had been destroyed by the murders'. There was no longer an effective detective division in Ireland, though he added that a new system was being built.

While the British were reorganising, Collins's network was able to settle an old score. On 15 June Joe Sweeney happened to be in the bar of the Wicklow Hotel when Collins stomped in.

'We got the bugger, Joe.'

'What are you talking about?' Sweeney asked.

'Do you remember that first night outside the Rotunda? Lee Wilson?'

'I'll never forget it.'

'Well,' said Collins, 'we got him today in Gorey.'

He had tracked Wilson to Gorey, County Wexford, where he was an RIC district inspector. He was shot dead that morning in revenge for his degrading treatment of Tom Clarke on the evening of the surrender in 1916.

'Sinn Féin has had all the sport up to the present, and we are going to have sport now,' Colonel Ferguson Smyth, the newly appointed RIC divisional commissioner for Munster, told the assembled police at the RIC station in Listowel on 19 June. A highly decorated veteran, he was scarred by the Great War in which he had been shot six times and had lost an arm as a result of his injuries. He seemed a rather embittered man as he advocated the RIC should shoot first and ask questions afterwards, but his remarks were obviously authorised because General Tudor was present.

'We must take the offensive and beat Sinn Féin at its own tactics,' Smyth said. 'If persons approaching carry their hands in their pockets or are suspicious looking, shoot them down. You may make mistakes occasionally, and innocent people may be shot, but that cannot be helped. No policeman will get into trouble for shooting any man.'

'By your accent I take it you are an Englishman, and in your ignorance you forget you are addressing Irishmen,' Constable Jeremiah Mee replied, appalled by the thought of such a policy. He took off his cap and belt and threw them on a table. 'These, too, are English,' he said. 'Take them.'

Smyth, a native of Banbridge, County Down, denied he was English. He ordered that Mee be arrested, but the constable's colleagues shared his indignation and ignored the order. Afterwards Mee drew up an account of what had happened and thirteen of those present testified to its accuracy by signing the statement.

Mee and a colleague met Collins and others in Dublin on 15 July. Those present included Countess Markievicz and Erskine Childers (who was editor of the republican news-sheet *The Bulletin*), together with the editor and managing director of the *Freeman's Journal*, which had recently published details of Smyth's speech and was being sued for libel as a result.

'I had always imagined that the IRA leaders who were "on the run" were in hiding in cellars or in some out of the way place far removed from the scene of hostilities,' Mee recalled. 'I was somewhat surprised then, as I sat with some of these same leaders, and calmly discussed the current situation, while military lorries were speeding through the street under the very windows of the room where our conference was taking place. As a matter of fact there seemed to be nothing to prevent anybody walking into that room and finding Michael Collins and Countess Markievicz.'

'For at least three hours we sat there under a cross-examination,' Mee wrote. The representatives of the *Freeman's Journal* were trying to build a defence against the libel action, and the republicans were seeking to exploit the Listowel incident for propaganda purposes. But Smyth never got the chance to press his libel suit. He was shot by the IRA on 18 July in the County Club in Cork city. He was hit five times and died at the scene. When the authorities sought to hold an inquest afterwards, they were unable to find enough people to serve on a jury.

In the coming months, Collins would milk the controversy surrounding Smyth's remarks in Listowel for all the affair was worth in the propaganda war by recruiting Mee and two of his colleagues for speaking tours of the United States. In a way it was ironic because the policy advocated by Smyth was not really much different from that being pursued by the IRA in general, and Collins in particular. 'We may make mistakes in the beginning and shoot the wrong people,' Pearse had written in the article in *An Claidheamh Soluis* which Collins had endorsed so enthusiastically.

Collins's intelligence network also traced District Inspector Swanzy to Lisburn, County Antrim, where he was shot dead on 22 August in revenge for the killing of MacCurtain. 'Inspector Swanzy and his associates put Lord Mayor MacCurtain away,' Collins later explained, 'so I got Swanzy and all his associates wiped out, one by one, in all parts of Ireland to which they had been secretly dispersed.'

The killing of Swanzy led to a massive outbreak of sectarian violence in Belfast and other towns in Antrim, as Roman Catholics were burned out of their homes in mixed areas, and some eight thousand Catholic workers were expelled from the shipyards and other industries. The Dáil retaliated by sanctioning a boycott of goods from Belfast.

IRA units in various parts of the country had begun attacking policemen, many on a random basis, as Breen and his colleagues had done at Soloheadbeg. One incident that caused particular revulsion was the killing of Constable Mulhern in Bandon, County Cork. He was shot in the local Catholic Church, where he had gone to attend Sunday mass on 25 July 1920. Others were shot, not because they had shown initiative against Sinn Féin or the IRA, but simply because they were policemen. When the Crown forces retaliated, it contributed to a vicious circle of violence.

Flying columns were established by the IRA in several areas to cope with the increasing mobility of Crown forces. Local leaders like Tom Barry and Liam Lynch in Cork, Tom Maguire in Mayo, and Seán MacEoin in the Longford area generally acted independently of IRA headquarters, but Collins was always quick to endorse their actions, and this created the impression that their efforts were being orchestrated centrally. As a result Collins was often credited with, or accused of, involvement in skirmishes that he only learned about later.

Dick Mulcahy looked on Breen and the Soloheadbeg gang as a kind of nuisance. Their wild, undisciplined approach to matters, especially their unauthorised killing of the two policemen on the day the Dáil was established, was resented. Even within the IRA, they were not generally welcome in Dublin. 'The only place in which they could find association and some kind of scope for their activities was on the fringe of Collins's Intelligence activity work,' according to Mulcahy. Collins adopted a warm and friendly attitude towards them. 'It would have been a comfort to them at all times compared with the natural attitude of Gearóid O'Sullivan and Diarmuid O'Hegarty,' Mulcahy wrote. Of course, Collins's 'rough breezy manner' afforded him 'greater flexibility in being able, while putting up with them when he liked, to get away with pushing them unceremoniously out of his way when he didn't want them'.

Lloyd George's initial hope of using economic pressure to turn the Irish people against the rebels by putting the cost of fighting on the local rates was undermined when Sinn Féin won control of all but five of the island's thirty-three county councils in June 1920. As a result the party controlled the striking of rates throughout all but the north-east corner of Ireland. Later that month Collins outmanoeuvred the British on the income tax front by getting the Dáil to establish a tax department. All Irish people were called upon to pay income tax to this new department rather than to the British government, and the Dáil promised to indemnify anyone against loss. The call was partly effective as people avoided Crown taxes by exploiting the chaos caused by the burning of tax offices in April. Some did pay the Sinn Féin regime, but most simply used the opportunity to evade income tax altogether.

With economic pressure holding little prospect for success, Lloyd George gave a virtual free rein to militants like Churchill and Greenwood. On 23 July 1920 Churchill told his cabinet colleagues it was necessary 'to raise the temperature of the conflict'. One of his pet schemes was to recruit 'a special force' of carefully selected men to act in Ireland. The cabinet authorised this during the summer, and advertisements were placed for a *corps d'élite* in which the recruits were supposed to be veteran officers from any of the services.

Known as Auxiliaries, they contained a mixture of fine men and scoundrels. On the whole they were more intelligent than the Black and Tans and received twice the pay. Like the Black and Tans they wore a blend of police and military uniforms, though with their own distinctive headgear, a glengarry cap. They were heavily armed; each man carried two revolvers, some on low-slung holsters, Wild West style, and they also had a rifle each, as well as a Sam Browne belt. They usually travelled in Crossley tenders, seated back to back in two rows, and they had at their disposal fast armoured cars with revolving turrets and Vickers machine guns. They were a formidable force as far as the IRA was concerned. Although sometimes accused of having started the counter-terror, the policy was already in operation for some time before the Auxiliaries took up duty in September 1920.

During August the Black and Tans revenged attacks on their forces by 'shooting up' towns and burning the business premises or homes of people known to be sympathetic to Sinn Féin. In towns like Bantry, Fermoy, Thurles, Limerick, Enniscorthy, Tuam, and other towns and villages, they rampaged about the streets, shooting indiscriminately into buildings, and generally terrorising the communities. In the process nine civilians were killed.

Although a hard-liner, Field Marshal Wilson was disgusted at the undisciplined conduct of the Black and Tans. 'I told Lloyd George that the authorities were gravely miscalculating the situation but he reverted to his amazing theory that someone was murdering two Sinn Féiners to every loyalist the Sinn Féiners were murdering,' Wilson wrote on 1 September. 'He seemed to be satisfied that a counter murder association was the best answer to Sinn Féin murders.'

Collins, for his part, saw the British terror as a kind of mixed blessing, in that it clearly drove any doubting nationalists into the arms of Sinn Féin. 'The enemy continues to be savage and ruthless, and innocent people are murdered and outraged daily,' he wrote on 13 August. 'Apart from the loss which these attacks entail, good is done as it makes clear and clearer to people what both sides stand for.'

Even the DMP betrayed signs of uneasiness with the British policy. Since it was implicit in Collins's attitude towards the force that policemen would not be attacked if they stayed out of political or military matters, representatives of the DMP approached Sinn Féin for a guarantee that they would not be shot at if they stopped carrying weapons. Collins was consulted and he agreed, provided they also ceased their supportive role of the military on raids. The DMP commissioner agreed and the force was effectively withdrawn from the ongoing struggle during October.

While the terror and counter-terror were spiralling, the British sent out peace feelers and quietly orchestrated press speculation about a possible settlement on the lines of Dominion Home Rule. Fearing that Lloyd George was merely exploiting the speculation in order to obscure the terrorist policies of British forces, Collins tried to scotch the unfounded rumours by giving his famous newspaper interview to the celebrated American journalist, Carl W. Ackermann, who had earlier interviewed Lenin during the Russian Revolution. Ackermann had sought a meeting with Collins because the British considered him 'the most important member of the Irish Republican cabinet'. (This was the interview that Devoy exploited in the *Gaelic American* to suggest that Collins was the real Irish leader.)

'There will be no compromise,' Collins told Ackermann, 'and we will have no negotiations with any British Government until Ireland is recognised as an independent republic.'

'But Mr Collins,' the reporter asked, 'would you not consider accepting Dominion Home Rule as an installment?'

'I see you think we have only to whittle our demand down to Dominion Home Rule and we shall get it. This talk about Dominion Home Rule is not promoted by England with a view to granting it to us, but merely with a view of getting rid of the Republican movement. England will give us neither as a gift. The same effort that would get us Dominion Home Rule will get us a Republic.'

Ackermann concluded his scoop with a prediction that 'there will be a real war in Ireland in the not-distant future'. A British officer told him 'the next few weeks will be decisive — one way or the other'.

The outrages continued. On the night of 20 September 1920, one of the Black and Tans was shot and killed in a pub in the village of Balbriggan, a short distance from Dublin. Afterwards his colleagues went on the rampage in the village, bayoneted to death two young men, viciously beat others with rifle butts, and burned down some twenty homes. When questions were asked in the House of Commons, Sir Hamar Greenwood, the Chief Secretary for Ireland, virtually condoned the police taking the law into their own hands.

'I found that from 100 to 150 men went to Balbriggan determined to avenge the death of a popular comrade shot at and murdered in cold blood,' Greenwood said. 'I find that it is impossible out of that 150 to find the men who did the deed, who did the burning. I have had the most searching inquiry made. But I cannot in my heart of hearts condemn in the same way those policemen who lost their heads as I condemn the assassins who provoked this outrage.'

The Sinn Féin regime was clearly getting the better of the propaganda struggle on the world stage, and the movement received enormous publicity when the new lord mayor of Cork, Terence MacSwiney, went on hunger strike to protest his imprisonment. He had been arrested in August after being found in possession of police codes personally given to him by Collins. Although there were eleven others on hunger strike in Cork around the same time, he got the most extensive publicity because he was an elected member of the British parliament. His seventy-four-day fast was given worldwide publicity, and Lloyd George came under pressure from all sides to do something about MacSwiney and the deteriorating situation in Ireland.

Collins took a keen interest in MacSwiney's condition and was in regular contact with Art O'Brien, the Sinn Féin representative in London, where Cork's lord mayor was imprisoned in Brixton Jail. 'As the days pass,' Collins wrote to O'Brien, 'we will marvel more and more at the fight being made by him and by our men in Cork.'

At one point, O'Brien reported that MacSwiney was deeply agitated by rumours that de Valera was going to announce that he would go on hunger strike himself, if the lord mayor died. MacSwiney believed the hunger strike would not prove effective again because the British realised that they had made a mistake in allowing things to go so far. In future they would force-feed hunger strikers, but those already on hunger strike were too far gone.

De Valera apparently never had any intention of making such a gesture. He felt very strongly that once anybody went on hunger strike, it was necessary to carry it through to its ultimate conclusion. A couple of years later when MacSwiney's sister Mary went on hunger strike, de Valera essentially insisted that she would hurt the cause if she did not persist, having started.

'When Terry was dying, knowing how conscientious he was and how good, I feared he might have some scruples about what he was doing, and intended giving him an official order to continue, as I might to a soldier running great risk on the battlefield,' de Valera wrote to her. 'For him to surrender having begun would have been not personal defeat, but defeat for the cause. Your cause is the same and may the God of Calvary give your spirit the necessary strength to endure to the last if need be and take you to Himself when your ordeal is ended.'

Collins, on the other hand, reportedly wrote to Terence MacSwiney suggesting that he had 'put up a glorious fight' and had done all that was humanly possible. 'The British Cabinet mean to finish this hunger strike weapon of ours, and do not intend to release you,' Collins reportedly wrote. 'I now order you to give up the strike as you will be ten times a greater asset to the movement alive than dead.' Seán Murphy, the republican diplomat, said that he saw the letter in the Big Fellow's own handwriting. He was visiting MacSwiney and the letter was passed around amongst his visitors. All of them thought Collins was right, with the exception of Terence's sister Mary, who would have 'no surrender'.

Although Dr Daniel Cohalan, the bishop of Cork, virtually sanctified the death of MacSwiney in 1920 by describing him as a martyr, he later rounded on Mary MacSwiney for having 'gambled on the life' of her brother in the apparent belief that the British would be compelled to relent and release him. 'She encouraged Terry to continue the strike,' Bishop Cohalan said. 'She never believed it would go to a fatal end. She thought he would be released, and that she would share in a sunburst of cheap glory.' Of course, there were republicans, like Ernie O'Malley, who thought that the lord mayor would be of more use to the movement if he were allowed to die rather than being freed in the final days. He hoped MacSwiney 'would not be released when his body was almost used up'.

Michael Fitzgerald was the first of the hunger strikers to die, and eight days later, on 25 October, Joseph Murphy, a seventeen-year-old, died the same day as MacSwiney. Though both Fitzgerald and Murphy were on the seventy-fifth day of their fast, their deaths received very little attention in comparison with the massive international coverage given to MacSwiney.

People around the world were greatly moved by his fortitude and determination. Among those who derived inspiration was Mahatma Gandhi in India, and another was Clement Attlee, the future British Prime Minister, who would be in power over a quarter of a century later when Gandhi used similar tactics in leading the Indian people to independence. Attlee was so moved by MacSwiney's gesture that he actually walked in the first part of his funeral in Britain.

While the MacSwiney drama was being played out, there was an intense debate raging in British government circles about the impact of their policy of counter-murder. In private Lloyd George 'strongly defended the murder reprisals', according to Sir Maurice Hankey, the cabinet secretary. 'The truth is that these reprisals are more or less winked at by the Government.' Sir Henry Wilson, the chief of imperial general staff, was blunt with Lloyd George and Andrew Bonar Law, the Conservative leader, when he had a ninety-minute meeting with them on 29 September 1920. 'I pointed out that these reprisals were carried out without anybody being responsible; men were murdered, houses burnt, villages wrecked,' Wilson noted in his diary. 'I said that this was due to want of discipline, and this *must* be stopped. It was the business of Government to govern. If these men ought to be murdered, then the Government ought to murder them. Lloyd George danced at all this, said no Government could possibly take this responsibility.'

Winston Churchill was concerned that the security forces were 'getting out of control, drinking, and thieving, and destroying indiscriminately'. He argued that the reprisal policy should be formally regularised. Instead of turning a blind eye while the Black and Tans burned or killed indiscriminately, he wanted it done officially and publicly acknowledged, with the full support of the British government. He wanted official hangings rather than shooting prisoners in cold blood and then contending they were killed while trying to escape.

After months of clamouring, he finally had his way with the hanging of Kevin Barry, who was executed on Monday, 1 November, All Saints Day. Barry, an eighteen-year-old university student, had been captured after a shoot-out in which a couple of British soldiers had been killed. It is hard to imagine how the British thought that making a martyr out of Barry would help their cause. In view of his age, there was strong public pressure for his sentence to be commuted. Collins tried to arrange for Barry's escape but all efforts failed, and the young man became, in the words of the popular ballad:

> Another martyr for old Ireland,
> Another murder for the Crown,
> Whose brutal laws may kill the Irish
> But can't keep their spirit down.

On the eve of Barry's hanging, Terence MacSwiney was buried in Cork. De Valera was speaking in the Polo Grounds baseball stadium in New York that day and he drew attention to the impending execution of Barry. MacSwiney and Michael Fitzgerald had sacrificed themselves for love of country, de Valera declared. 'The English have killed them,' he told the crowd. 'Tomorrow a boy, Kevin Barry, they will hang, and he alike, will only regret that he has but one life to give. Oh God!' De Valera then went on to quote W. B. Yeats:

> They shall be remembered forever,
> They shall be alive forever,
> They shall be speaking forever.
> The people shall hear them forever.

Tensions were running extremely high around the country that Sunday night. Collins was reportedly very upset about the situation, and the IRA were asked to make their presence felt. Maybe they could not save Barry, but they could make the British realise that the executions would not be taken lying down. There were over fifty attacks on police throughout the country that night, and seven policemen were killed in Kerry. Two Black and Tans, lured into a trap by local girls, were killed in Tralee and buried in the mud of the local canal at low tide.

The Tans retaliated by burning down the local County Hall the same night and enforcing a reign of terror in Tralee for the next nine days. On Monday they fired just over the heads of people coming from twelve o'clock mass at St John's Parish Church. John Conway, a fifty-seven-year-old painter and father of six, was killed by the Tans as he was returning from evening devotions. The authorities said that he died of heart failure but a bullet wound to his head was clearly visible, according to a journalist from *The Times* of London. He was one of a group of foreign journalists who stayed at the Grand Hotel in Tralee that Monday night. Others included representatives from Associated Press, *Le Journal* (Paris), the London *Daily News*, the *Manchester Guardian*, and the London *Evening News*. They had come from Cork following MacSwiney's funeral.

Hugh Martin of the *Daily News* ventured out into deserted streets, along with A. E. McGregor from the *Evening News*. 'Upon leaving the Grand Hotel we noticed a party of from twenty to twenty-five men standing on the opposite side of the road,' Martin reported. 'We greeted them and said we were journalists. They were Black and Tans.'

'What have you come for, to spy on us, I suppose!' one of the men remarked. McGregor explained that they had come to find out the facts about the burning of the County Hall. They were ordered to get indoors. During the night they could hear the noise of shop windows being broken as the Black and Tans attacked the business premises of people known to support Sinn Féin.

A French journalist with the group depicted a frightening situation. 'I do not remember, even during the war, having seen a people so profoundly terrified as those of this little town, Tralee,' M. de Marsillac, the London correspondent of *Le Journal* reported. 'The violence of the reprisals undertaken by representatives of authority, so to speak, everywhere, has made everybody beside himself, even before facts justified such a state of mind.'

Not knowing the fate of their two missing colleagues, the Tans were insisting that the two men should be released, and for the next eight days, people were ordered to stay indoors. Businesses were not allowed to open, the three local newspapers had to suspend publication, and all schools were shut. The security forces rampaged about the deserted streets firing shots in the air, or even firing blindly into windows as they drove up and down.

Tommy Wall, a twenty-four-year-old former soldier who had fought in France during the First World War, was standing at the corner of the main street around noon on Tuesday when some Tans told him to put up his hands. Being a former soldier who had fought for the Crown, he apparently thought he was safe, but one of the men hit him in the face with a rifle butt and told him to get out of the place. As he left they shot him fatally and declared that he was killed while trying to escape.

'All the afternoon, except for soldiers, the town was as deserted and doleful as if the Angel of Death had passed through it,' de Marsillac wrote. 'Not a living soul in the streets. All the shops shut and the bolts hastily fastened. All work suspended, even the local newspapers.'

'It is impossible for any person who has not been in the town to realise the terrible plight of the people,' the *Kerry People* reported when it returned to the streets afterwards. 'The privations, particularly in the case of the poorer classes, are appalling, and starvation has by now entered many a home.'

'The police in Ireland are themselves the victims of a condition of terrorism which is only equalled by the condition of terrorism that they themselves endeavour to impose,' Hugh Martin of the *Daily News* wrote. 'They are, for the most part, quite young men who have gone through the experience, at once toughening and demoralising, of fighting through a long and savage war. They are splendid soldiers and abominably bad policemen.'

'I do not blame the police or soldiers for the impasse,' Martin continued. 'But no honest man who has seen with his own eyes and heard with his own ears the fearful plight to which unhappy Ireland has been brought could fail to curse in his heart the political gamble that bred it or cease to use all the power of his pen to end it.'

On Friday, 5 November, Hamar Greenwood told the House of Commons that John Conway had died of natural causes, even though *The Times* had already reported that its correspondent had seen the obvious bullet wound in his temple.

'The vital fact in the tragedy is that while the Chief Secretary is repeating his stereotyped assurances that things are getting better, it is patent to the readers of newspapers the world over that they are getting daily worse,' the *Daily News* commented. 'At the moment the supreme need is to withdraw the troops. If the police cannot remain unprotected, let them go too. Ireland could not be worse off without them than with them. There is every reason to believe her state would be incomparably better.'

On the evening of 9 November the Black and Tans posted notices in Tralee that businesses would be allowed to open next morning. That night Lloyd George declared in his address at the Lord Mayor's Banquet at the Guildhall, London, that it was necessary to 'break the terror before you can get peace'. He left no doubt that he intended to persist with his policy of counter-terror, and he seemed confident he was getting the upper hand. 'We have murder by the throat,' Lloyd George declared. 'We had to re-organise the police and when the Government was ready we struck the terrorists and now the terrorists are complaining of terror.'

With events in Ireland under the international spotlight, speculation about a possible settlement commanded growing press attention. The British had been sending out peace feelers ever since July when a Conservative member of parliament made discreet approaches to Art O'Brien in London about the kind of terms that Sinn Féin would be looking for. Collins was rather dismissive of the approach. He predicted that nothing was likely to happen unless the United States was asked to intervene or 'offered her services as a mediator'.

Nevertheless Lloyd George continued to encourage peace feelers behind the scenes for the remainder of the year, through a number of people like John Steele of the *Chicago Daily Tribune*, a Mayo businessman named Patrick Moylett, and George Russell (Æ), the well-known writer. Peace speculation was boosted when former Prime Minister, H. H. Asquith, wrote to *The Times* in early October advocating that Britain offer Ireland 'the status of an autonomous dominion in the fullest and widest sense'.

Moylett came to Dublin for informal talks with Griffith in mid-October, and, upon his return to London, was invited by Lloyd George to sit in on a Foreign Office meeting at which it was suggested that the Dáil should select three or four people to visit London for preliminary discussions about a formal conference to resolve the Irish situation. Collins remained highly skeptical of the whole proceedings, and felt his suspicions were confirmed when Lloyd George started bragging about having 'murder by the throat'.

'I wonder what these people with their hypocritical good intentions and good wishes say to L. George's speech yesterday,' Collins wrote. 'So much for the peace feelers.'

Throughout most of 1920 Ireland was being infiltrated by British Secret Service agents intending to take on Collins and the IRA at their own game in line with the scenario outlined the previous December by the three-man committee on which Alan Bell had served. Most were recruited in London by Basil Thompson, the head of intelligence at Scotland Yard. They were known as the Cairo gang, because some of the more notorious among them hung out at the Cairo Café in Grafton Street.

Members of the gang lived in private houses and guest-houses scattered around the city, and they were given passes to allow them to move about after curfew. Jim McNamara from the DMP furnished the names of people with curfew passes and by a process of elimination Collins's network was able to narrow the list down to likely agents. Many of them stood out because of their English accents. They were mostly 'hoy hoy lah-di-dahs', according to Brigadier General Frank Crozier, the commander of the Auxiliaries. Collins, with the help of his own agents in the postal sorting office, had the mail of suspected members of the Secret Service intercepted and delivered to himself.

Amidst the intercepted correspondence was a letter from Captain F. Harper Shrove to Captain King on 2 March 1920. Even though the country was 'in a fearful mess', he wrote that they should be able to put up 'a good show' because they had 'been given a free hand'.

'Re our little stunt,' Shrove continued, 'there are possibilities.' In hindsight it became apparent that the killing of MacCurtain was part of their 'little stunt'. The Secret Service planned to exterminate prominent members of Sinn Féin and make it appear that they had been killed in an IRA feud. They had sent a threatening letter to MacCurtain on Dáil Éireann notepaper, seized the previous September in a raid on Sinn Féin headquarters. 'Thomas MacCurtain, prepare for death,' it read. 'You are doomed.'

In the following months most members of the Dáil received threatening letters. One was addressed to Collins at the Mansion House:

AN EYE FOR AN EYE.
A TOOTH FOR A TOOTH
THEREFORE A LIFE FOR A LIFE.

'I'm quite safe,' Collins joked. 'If they get me, I'll claim I haven't received my death notice yet.'

While Collins made light of the threat on his own life, he took the overall threat posed by the Secret Service very seriously. In fact, he infiltrated it with at least one agent of his own. Willie Beaumont, a former British army officer, joined the Secret Service to spy for Collins. The agents from Britain had to rely on touts for information, and Beaumont pretended that members of Collins's intelligence staff— Tom Cullen, Frank Thornton, and Frank Saurin — were his touts. He introduced them to, and they got to know, other Secret Service agents. On one occasion Cullen and Thornton were with Beaumont and David Neligan in a Grafton Street café when one of the Cairo gang joined them. 'Surely you fellows know these men — Liam Tobin, Tom Cullen and Frank Thornton,' he said. 'These are Collins's three officers, and if you can get them we could locate Collins himself.' Getting Collins had clearly become a prime goal of the Secret Service, and they were getting close. At least they now knew the names of his staff, though they were seriously handicapped in not knowing what any of them looked like.

One of the British Secret Service agents, going under the name of F. Digby Hardy, acted as an *agent provocateur*. He met Griffith and offered to set up his intelligence chief on Dun Laoghaire pier so that the IRA could kill him, but Collins was forewarned. Griffith invited reporters, including foreign correspondents, to a secret meeting on 16 September 1920. Before the meeting he briefed them about Hardy. 'This man admits he is in the English Secret Service, and offered to arrange for the presence of the Secret Service Chief at a lonely point on Dun Laoghaire pier,' Griffith told the reporters. 'He asked me to let him meet leaders of the movement, especially on the military side, and he is coming here this evening imagining that he is to meet some inner council of the Sinn Féin movement,' Griffith explained. 'I will let him tell you his own story, but I will ask the foreign gentlemen present not to speak much, lest the man's suspicion be aroused.'

Hardy duly arrived and told the gathering that he was a Secret Service agent and that upon his arrival in Ireland he had been met by Basil Thompson of Scotland Yard at Dun Laoghaire pier and given instructions to find Michael Collins. He offered to arrange another meeting with Thompson on the pier so the IRA could kill him. He also said that he could arrange to lead the Auxiliaries into an ambush and could locate arsenals of the Ulster Volunteer Force. If the IRA would give him information about Collins's whereabouts, he said he would withhold the information for a couple of days and could then impress his Secret Service superiors by giving them the information. 'And, of course,' he added familiarly, 'no harm would come to Mick.'

'Well, gentlemen, you have heard this man's proposal and can judge for yourselves,' Griffith intervened. He then proceeded to expose Hardy as a convicted criminal, with actual details of his criminal record. 'You are a scoundrel, Hardy,' he said, 'but the people who employ you are greater scoundrels. A boat will leave Dublin tonight at nine o'clock. My advice to you is — catch that boat and never return to Ireland.'

Griffith furnished the press with detailed inside information supplied by Collins about Hardy's criminal record. He had been freed from jail to work for the Secret Service, and it made for good propaganda to show that the British were using criminal elements to do their dirty work in Ireland.

Indeed, the Sinn Féin Propaganda Department would do such an effective job that many Irish people believed the British had opened their jails for any criminals prepared to serve the Crown in Ireland. This was absurd, but incidents like the Hardy affair certainly lent it credence.

The following week the Secret Service struck again. John Lynch, a Sinn Féin county councillor from Kilmallock, County Limerick, who had come to Dublin with National Loan money for Collins, was shot dead in his room at the Exchange Hotel on the night of 23 September. Secret Service agents claimed he had pulled a gun on them, but Collins dismissed this. 'There is not the slightest doubt that there was no intention whatever to arrest Mr Lynch,' he wrote. 'Neither is there the slightest doubt that he was not in possession of a revolver.' Neligan reported to Collins that Captain Bagally, a one-legged court-martial officer, had telephoned Dublin Castle about Lynch's presence in the hotel, and the men responsible for the actual shooting were two undercover officers using the names MacMahon and Peel, each a *nom de guerre*. There was some suggestion that John Lynch was mistaken for Liam Lynch, an IRA commandant, but that was hardly likely seeing that there was an extreme difference in their ages. John Lynch was simply a Sinn Féiner, and this had become a capital offence as far as the British Secret Service was concerned.

Griffith publicly charged the Secret Service with planning to kill moderates in Sinn Féin and give the impression that they were victims of an internal feud. In this way the movement's international support could be undermined. 'A certain number of Sinn Féin leaders have been marked down for assassination,' he said. 'I am first on the list. They intended to kill two birds with the one stone by getting me and circulating the story I have been assassinated by extremists because I am a man of moderate action.'

The British were particularly anxious to catch Collins, but he was proving extremely elusive. Bertie Smyllie, a journalist with *The Irish Times*, was sitting in a Dublin restaurant with a friend who seemed to know everybody. 'Suddenly I noticed that my companion had turned very pale,' Smyllie wrote later.

'Don't look round yet,' his friend whispered, 'Michael Collins has just come in.'

'I could not resist the temptation to have a look at the elusive "Mike". The man to whom my friend referred was small, thin, with mouse-coloured hair, and looked rather like a jockey. What he lacked in physique, however, he made up in facial ferocity, for a more villainous looking individual I never saw.'

'Are you sure that he is Collins?' Smyllie asked.

'Of course, don't I know him well!'

The same thing undoubtedly happened to many other people, and in time some of Collins's own people would deliberately sow the seeds of confusion. So many diverse descriptions of him added to his aura of elusiveness. Of course the Black and Tans were at a disadvantage in looking for him as they did not know him, but he was known to detectives of the DMP. Yet he had infiltrated them with his spy network, killed off their most efficient officers, and so terrorised the remainder that they were virtually impotent. They were afraid to arrest him for fear of the retaliation of the faceless people who were believed to be protecting him. For instance, Lady Gregory wrote that Collins was known to the police but whenever he felt threatened he would blow a whistle, whereupon hundreds of men would appear and he would vanish in the shuffle. Of course that was nonsense.

Brigadier Ormonde Winter, who took charge of intelligence at Dublin Castle, grudgingly admitted to holding 'a certain respect' for his enemies, among whom he singled out Collins as pre-eminent. 'Actuated by an intense patriotism,' Winter wrote, 'he combined the characteristics of a Robin Hood with those of an elusive Pimpernel. His many narrow escapes, when he managed to elude almost certain arrest, shrouded him in a cloak of historical romance.' As a result he was credited with exploits in which he had no involvement.

The ensuing notoriety was to cause problems for Collins, especially with Cathal Brugha. Although Brugha's reaction was widely attributed to jealousy, the charge was probably unfair because he was really a selfless character who never sought glory for himself. Brugha was 'as brave and as brainless as a bull', according to Richard Mulcahy, who as the IRA chief of staff acted as a kind of buffer between Brugha as Minister for Defence and Collins. As cabinet ministers, Collins and Brugha were equals in the Dáil. However, as director of intelligence of the IRA, Collins was answerable to Mulcahy, who in turn was answerable to Brugha. Mulcahy essentially allowed Collins to do his own thing, and Brugha resented the way Collins was operating. He was repulsed by the egotistical side of the Big Fellow's personality and the way he interfered in matters that were outside the scope of his official duties.

All British intelligence was being co-ordinated in Dublin Castle by Winter. With his monocle and greased black hair, plastered flat, he was like the prototype of a character in a spy thriller. 'A most amazing original' was how the assistant secretary at Dublin Castle, Mark Sturgis, described him. 'He looks like a wicked little white snake, and is clever as pain, [and] probably entirely non-moral.' In October Winter organised the Central Raid Bureau to co-ordinate the activities of his agents and the Auxiliaries. And they soon began to make their presence felt.

Major Gerald Smyth, a brother of the one-armed colonel shot in Cork in July, had returned from the Middle East to avenge the death of his brother. It was rumoured that he had been killed by Dan Breen. So when Winter's people learned that Breen and Seán Treacy were spending the night of

11 October at the Drumcondra home of Professor John Carolan, Smyth was selected to lead the raiding party. They burst into the house, but Smyth and a colleague were killed when Breen and Treacy shot blindly through their bedroom door before making a run for it. Although hit himself, Breen still managed to get away. He went up to a house at random and asked for help as he collapsed on the doorstep.

'I don't approve of gunmen,' he heard the man of the house reply. 'I shall call the military.'

'If you do I'll report you to Michael Collins,' came a woman's voice from inside the house. The threat obviously worked because word was passed to the IRA and Breen was collected and taken to the Mater Hospital, where doctors and nurses colluded to hide his identity and the nature of his wounds.

Another patient was Professor Carolan whom the raiding party had put up against a wall and shot in the head. He died of his wounds but not before making a full deathbed statement about what had happened. Treacy had escaped unscathed from Drumcondra only to be shot dead a few days later in a gunbattle in Talbot Street.

Despite his busy schedule and the risk involved, Collins took a keen interest in Breen's recovery. He visited him in hospital and arranged his transfer to the home of Dr Alice Barry in the south side of the city as soon as he was ready to be moved. Breen was there about a week when he heard a commotion outside the house and looked out to find the whole block cordoned off by the Auxiliaries. They were searching the houses as a crowd of spectators gathered.

'I concluded there was no chance for me,' Breen wrote. 'As I surveyed the mass of spectators, I recognised the figure of Mick Collins.' He had seen the troops moving in the direction of the house and had followed them in case Breen needed to be rescued. As it was, the Auxiliaries did not bother to search Dr Barry's home, and Breen was spared.

At one point the DMP thought they had found Breen's body, so Sergeant Roche of the RIC was brought up from Tipperary to identify him. David Neligan was given the gruesome task of accompanying Roche to the hospital morgue.

'That's not Dan Breen,' Roche said on being shown the body, 'I'd know his ugly mug anywhere.'

That evening Neligan mentioned the incident to Liam Tobin and added that he was due to meet Roche on Ormond Quay the following afternoon. To his horror next day, Neligan found four members of the Squad waiting for Roche.

'For Christ's sake, what has he done?' Neligan asked.

'I don't know,' one of the men replied. 'I've my orders to shoot him and that's what I'm going to do.'

Neligan pleaded with them, but it was no good. They shot and killed Roche in front of him. A witness reported that he had seen Neligan talking to one of the killers, and he had some difficulty extricating himself.

Neligan was rightly annoyed that the incident had jeopardised his cover as a spy. It demonstrated a dangerous blind spot in the Big Fellow's intelligence operations. As a man of action Collins was so anxious to get things done that he sometimes acted before the dust had settled to cover his agents' tracks.

In early October two American soldiers were shot and wounded by Crown forces in Queenstown (Cobh), and the Republican Publicity Bureau naturally exploited the incident in an effort to secure American publicity and hopefully provoke some Anglo-American difficulties. Collins furnished the Republican Publicity Bureau with a copy of a report from General Tudor to Dublin Castle suggesting that American sailors were engaged in smuggling arms. The report had been supplied by Jim McNamara, who was called to the commissioner's office and summarily dismissed from the police force. 'You are lucky,' Collins told him. There was obviously no hard evidence against McNamara, or he would not have been let go so easily. There was a danger, however, that he would be assassinated by the Secret Service. He therefore went 'on the run' to work with the Squad.

As of October 1920 the conflict had become extremely nasty. Collins was deeply upset when he learned that the Black and Tans had captured and tortured Tom Hales, a brother of Seán Hales, his closest friend in Frongoch. Another man tortured at the same time went mad and had to be committed to a mental asylum. Tom Hales managed to smuggle out an account of their ill-treatment, which included pulling out his nails with pincers.

'I was with Collins when he received the message,' Piaras Béaslaí recalled. 'He was beside himself with rage and pity, and, as he told me afterwards, could not sleep that night for thinking of it.' Collins himself wrote that the whole episode was something 'that no civilised nation can let pass unchallenged'. It was ironic that he should have been so upset because Tom Hales was the man who would organise the ambush to kill Collins at Béalnabláth less than two years later.

The torture of Hales was indicative of what Collins might expect if he fell into enemy hands. He was now the most wanted man in the country and the Cairo gang were getting close. 'We were being made to feel that they were very close on the heels of some of us,' Mulcahy explained.

In the first two weeks of November the Cairo gang detained some of Collins's closest associates. They had Frank Thornton for ten days, but he managed to convince them that he had nothing to do with the IRA. On the night of 10 November they just missed Mulcahy; he escaped out the skylight of Professor Michael Hayes's house in South Circular Road around five o'clock in the morning. Three days later they raided Vaughan's Hotel and questioned Liam Tobin and Tom Cullen, but they managed to bluff their way out of it. In a matter of days the IRA's chief of staff and the three top men of Collins's intelligence network had come close to being captured.

Collins prepared detailed files on suspected members of the Cairo gang. One of his sources, whom he merely referred to as 'Lt. G', helped identify the members of the gang. Collins planned on killing those he called 'the particular ones', and his spy suggested the morning of Sunday, 21 November, as the best time to strike. 'Arrangements should now be made about the matter,' Collins wrote to Dick McKee on 17 November. 'Lt. G is aware of things. He suggests the 21st. A most suitable date and day I think.'

Although Collins was not always as careful as he should have been about protecting the identity of his spies, he was religious about keeping their names to himself. In this case 'Lt. G' was apparently a woman typist at army headquarters. She always signed her notes to him with just the letter 'G', and he probably added the 'Lt.' to make it more difficult for anyone to guess her identity. People naturally assumed his agent was an army officer.

On Saturday night Collins met with Brugha, Mulcahy, McKee, and others to finalise arrangements in the headquarters of the printers' union at 35 Lower Gardiner Street, where the Dublin Brigade normally held meetings. Brugha felt there was insufficient evidence against some of those named by Collins. But there was no room for doubt in the cases of Peter Ames and George Bennett, the two men who had questioned Tobin and Cullen, nor with Captain Bagally and the two men who had shot John Lynch at the Exchange Hotel, MacMahon and Peel. Brugha authorised their killings along with eleven others.

'It's to be done exactly at nine,' Collins insisted. 'Neither before nor after. These whores, the British, have got to learn that Irishmen can turn up on time.' The killings were to be a joint operation of the Squad and the Dublin Brigade, under the command of Dick McKee.

After the meeting Collins, McKee, and some of the others went over to Vaughan's Hotel for a drink. There was a group of them in an upstairs room when Christy Harte, the porter, became suspicious of one of the hotel guests, a Mr Edwards, who had booked in three days earlier. He made a late-night telephone call and then left the hotel, a rather ominous sign as it was after curfew. Harte immediately went upstairs to where Collins and the others were gathered. 'I think, sirs, ye ought to be going.'

Collins had come to trust Harte's instincts and had no hesitation now. 'Come on boys, quick,' he said, and all promptly headed for the door.

Collins took refuge a few doors down in the top-floor flat of Dr Paddy Browne of Maynooth College at 39 Parnell Square. From there he watched the raid on Vaughan's Hotel a few minutes later. By then all the guests in the hotel were legitimately registered, with the exception of Conor Clune, a football supporter in Dublin for a game next day. He had come to the hotel with Peadar Clancy, and had apparently been forgotten. Clune was not registered. Although he was not a member of the IRA, he was obviously nervous when questioned because he made some rather inane comment about being prepared to die for Ireland, or something to that effect. He was therefore taken away for further questioning.

During the night McKee and Clancy were arrested where they were staying, but everything was already in train for the morning. Eleven different assassination teams took part. Some used church bells, and others waited for clocks to strike before they began the operations, exactly at nine o'clock. Each team contained a member of the Squad as well as an intelligence officer, assigned to search the bodies and rooms for documents.

Eleven of the Cairo gang were shot and killed at eight different locations, some in the presence of their families. Captain W. F. Newbury's pregnant wife was in the room with him at the time; the following week their child was stillborn. There was some confusion over whether or not Captain MacCormack of the Royal Army Veterinary Corps was on the list. He was shot dead in the Gresham Hotel, but Collins had no evidence against him. 'We have no evidence he was a Secret Service Agent,' he later wrote. 'Some of the names were put on by the Dublin Brigade.' This, of course, raised some questions about the clinical efficiency with which the attacks were supposedly carried out.

Also killed were two Auxiliaries who just happened to be passing the scene of one of the killings at 22 Lower Mount Street as the gunmen were trying to escape while a maid was screaming hysterically from an upstairs window. One of Lynch's killers had been shot there but his colleague managed to escape by barricading himself in his room while some twenty shots were fired into the door. Frank Teeling of the Dublin Brigade was captured by Auxiliaries.

Brigadier General Crozier, the commander of the Auxiliaries, was nearby and he visited the house on Mount Street. He then went to Dublin Castle to report what had happened. While there, word was received by telephone of the other killings.

'What!' the officer who answered the telephone exclaimed, turning deathly pale. He staggered as he turned around. 'About fifty officers are shot in all parts of the city,' he said. 'Collins has done in most of the Secret Service people.'

'In Dublin Castle panic reigned. For the next week the gates were choked with incoming traffic — all military, their wives and agents,' according to Neligan. One distraught agent, whose pals had been killed, shot and killed himself and was buried with the others in England, where they were given a state funeral, with services at Westminster Abbey.

Collins certainly had no regrets about what he had organised. 'My own intention was the destruction of the undesirables who continued to make miserable the lives of ordinary decent citizens,' he wrote. 'I have proof enough to assure myself of the atrocities which this gang of spies and informers have committed. Perjury and torture are words too easily known to them.' If he had another motive, he added, 'it was no more than a feeling such as I would have for a dangerous reptile. . . . That should be the future's judgment on this particular event,' he wrote. 'For myself my conscience is clear. There is no crime in detecting and destroying in war-time, the spy and the informer. They have destroyed without trial. I have paid them back in their own coin.'

'The attack was so well organised, so unexpected, and so ruthlessly executed that the effect was paralysing,' according to Neligan. 'It can be said that the enemy never recovered from the blow. While some of the worst killers escaped, they were thoroughly frightened.'

Two of those who escaped were Captain King and Lieutenant Hardy, who were particularly despised by the IRA because of their brutal treatment of prisoners; they were not in their residences when the hit teams called. Todd Andrews of the Dublin Brigade burst into King's room to find only his half-naked mistress. Shocked by the sudden intrusion, she sat bolt upright in bed and looked terror-stricken.

'I felt a sense of shame and embarrassment for the woman's sake,' Andrews noted, but the two Squad members with him were too frustrated at missing King to have any sympathy for the unfortunate woman.

'I was so angry I gave the poor girl a right scourging with the sword scabbard,' Joe Dolan recalled. 'Then I set the room on fire.'

Andrews was horrified at the conduct of Dolan and the other Squad member. They 'behaved like Black and Tans', he wrote. Hardy and King, on the other hand, gave vent to their rage by torturing and then killing McKee, Clancy, and Clune in Dublin Castle.

Elsewhere in the city the Auxiliaries went on a rampage at Croke Park, where they raided a football game and began firing indiscriminately into the crowd. Twelve innocent people, including one of the players on the field, were killed and dozens wounded. The Auxiliaries claimed that they were fired upon, as British soldiers would contend on another Bloody Sunday some fifty years later, but Crozier publicly refuted the claim afterwards. 'It was the most disgraceful show I have ever seen,' one of his officers told him. 'Black and Tans fired into the crowd without any provocation whatever.'

In London Lloyd George and members of the cabinet were very jittery, according to Sir Maurice Hankey. Greenwood provided weapons for all his domestic staff, though — unlike the Prime Minister — he was able to joke about his own predicament. 'All my household are armed,' the Chief Secretary told the cabinet, 'my valet, my butler, and my cook. So if you have any complaints about the soup you may know what to expect.'

There was good reason to be fearful. Brugha, it will be remembered, had raised a force to go into the House of Commons and kill as many members of the government as possible if conscription had been enforced in 1918, and he resurrected this plan as a possible response to the death of Terence MacSwiney; he still had not given up on the idea, and would raise it in the coming weeks.

In the interim, arrangements were made for a large-scale operation in Britain, where the IRA planned incendiary attacks on warehouses in the Liverpool and Manchester areas. On the day after Bloody Sunday Collins wanted to send an important message to the IRA in Britain and he arranged for Jeremiah Mee, who had been working for Countess Markievicz since his resignation from the RIC over the late Colonel Smyth's remarks in Listowel, to take the message personally. He was selected because he had a military look about him, but Mee had been trying to conceal this.

'What happened to your little moustache?' Collins asked.

Mee explained he shaved it off because the countess thought it looked too military.

'Be damn to her,' cried Collins. 'She should know by now that a military appearance is the best disguise for our men at the present time.'

He proceeded to outline the best way for Mee to behave in order to avoid detection. The advice provided a real insight into how Collins had been able to move about Dublin so freely in recent months. Dress up in spats with good creases on his pants and carry a walking stick and a supply of cigars, he told Mee. 'Get into friendly chat with some of the military officers,' he added. 'You can do this by passing round your cigars and even if they do not smoke cigars it will at least be an introduction and will save you being questioned or searched. That is how I get across myself and you should have no difficulty if you keep your head screwed on.'

Collins might well have gone himself except that he was anxious to pay his last respects to McKee and Clancy. Their deaths had been a terrible blow to him. They were 'two men who fully understood the inside of Collins's work and his mind, and who were ever ready and able to link up their resources of the Dublin Brigade to any work that Collins had in hand, and to do so promptly, effectively and sympathetically,' Mulcahy noted.

Collins was so upset by their deaths that he seemed to become quite reckless. He went to the Pro-Cathedral to dress the bodies in IRA uniforms and took a prominent part in the funeral. At one point he was actually filmed as he stepped out of the crowd to lay a wreath on the grave. Attached was a note signed by himself: 'In memory of two good friends — Dick and Peadar — and two of Ireland's best soldiers.' As he stepped forward, he overheard a woman. 'Look,' she said, 'there's Michael Collins.' He turned and glared at her. 'You bloody bitch,' he snarled.

Given his state of mind, it was a measure of his respect for Griffith that he was still ready to go along with Lloyd George's continuing peace feelers, even though he had no faith in them himself. Patrick Moylett had visited Dublin again in November and returned to London with a letter from Griffith, who was acting President during de Valera's absence, to the Prime Minister on the eve of Bloody Sunday. One might have thought the events of the next day would have killed the peace initiative at this point, but not at all. When Moylett met Lloyd George on the Monday, the Prime Minister did not seem unduly perturbed.

'They got what they deserved,' Lloyd George supposedly said. That, at any rate, was Moylett's story, but Art O'Brien, the Sinn Féin representative in London, warned Collins that the Mayoman was just a 'Big Blower' and a damn fool.

'Your view is shared by me,' Collins replied, 'but Mr Griffith thinks differently, therefore, I am keeping in touch with this man for the present.'

While Moylett was meeting with Lloyd George, the journalist John Steele was talking with Griffith about a possible cease-fire on both sides. 'I'll do all I can [to] stop murders but you must call off reprisals at the same time,' was Griffith's message for the Prime Minister. Lloyd George met George Russell on 26 November and told him that he would negotiate with anybody but Collins and somebody called 'Gallagher'. Presumably the Prime Minister was referring to Mulcahy, and either he or Russell got the name mixed up. Lloyd George's message to Russell was basically that he would call off military operations if there were three weeks of peace. Then negotiations could begin, though he indicated there were limits to what the British would consider. 'We will not tolerate a Republic,' he emphasised, 'but anything short of that.'

Whatever hope Lloyd George entertained for his proposals was seriously upset that day by the arrest of Griffith, who was picked up in a nationwide swoop of Sinn Féin supporters. A a result Collins took over as acting President.

7

Changing Places

Michael Collins was acting President for four hectic weeks, amid a welter of peace rumours, some of the bloodiest fighting in the conflict, the most widespread round-up of suspects since the Easter Rebellion, and the movement of the campaign to Britain for the first time. The strain was already tremendous. 'Those of us who were in constant touch with him always possessed the fear that he would collapse under it,' Seán Ó Muirthile wrote. Now those fears became all the more real when Collins — still deeply upset over the brutal killings of McKee and Clancy — assumed the extra strain of the presidency.

He was not in his new post two full days when the British-based IRA fire-bombed more than a dozen warehouses in the Liverpool docks area, causing millions of pounds worth of damage. That same day, 28 November, in Kilmichael, County Cork, Tom Barry led an IRA ambush on a convoy of Auxiliaries and killed seventeen of them. Collins was delighted with the Kilmichael attack. Lloyd George, who had proudly boasted of having 'murder by the throat', and clearly intimated that British forces were coming to grips with things in Ireland, was faced with irrefutable evidence that the rebels were far from finished. The last full week of November was, in fact, the bloodiest in Ireland since 1916.

On 1 December Lloyd George opened up a new peace channel, this time through the Irish-born Roman Catholic archbishop of Perth, Australia, Patrick J. Clune, a former chaplain-general to the Australian forces who also happened to be an uncle of Conor Clune, the young man who was arrested at Vaughan's Hotel on the eve of Bloody Sunday and killed the next day. The archbishop was asked to meet the Irish leaders in Dublin and sound them out about negotiations and a possible cease-fire.

Griffith, who met the archbishop in Mountjoy Jail, advised Collins against a meeting because of the danger that British agents might be watching Clune, but Collins met him without difficulty on 4 December at a school run by Louise Gavan Duffy on St Stephen's Green. Even if the Secret Service were keeping an eye on the archbishop, they would have considered his visit to her school quite natural as she was a daughter of Sir Charles Gavan Duffy, a former Young Ireland leader who had risen to the top in Australian politics after migrating there in the mid-nineteenth century.

'I wonder how it is that the archbishop sees Collins apparently without difficulty in Dublin and our intelligence fails to find him after weeks of search,' Mark Sturgis wrote in obvious exasperation.

Collins gave Clune a written outline of cease-fire terms agreeable to the Dáil cabinet. 'If it is understood that the acts of violence (attacks, counter attacks, reprisals, arrests, pursuits) are called off on both sides,' he wrote, 'we are agreeable to issue the necessary instructions on our side, it being understood that the entire Dáil shall be free to meet and that its peaceful activities be not interfered with.'

Before the archbishop could return to Britain, a figurative spanner was thrown in the works when six Sinn Féin members of Galway County Council called publicly for peace talks, and Father Michael O'Flanagan, a Sinn Féin vice-president, sent a telegram to Lloyd George essentially suing for peace. 'You state that you are willing to make peace at once without waiting for Christmas,' O'Flanagan wrote. 'Ireland is also waiting. What first step do you propose?'

Although both acts were unauthorised, Collins realised their significance immediately. He asked Pádraig O'Keeffe, the general secretary of the party, to inform the press 'that Father O'Flanagan acted without any authority from the Sinn Féin Standing Committee, and without consulting that body'.

'We must not allow ourselves to be rushed by these foolish productions, or foolish people, who are tumbling over themselves to talk about a "truce", when there is no truce,' Collins wrote.

The *Irish Independent* suggested a hitch had developed in secret talks because of the difficulty in organising a truce in which the safety of Collins could be assured. He forcefully denied the report and lashed out against the recent unauthorised overtures in a short letter to the newspaper's editor. 'My personal safety does not matter and does not count as a factor in the question of Ireland's right,' he explained. 'I thank no one for refraining from murdering me. At the moment there is a very grave danger that the country may be stampeded on false promises and foolish, ill-timed actions. We must stand up against that danger. My advice to the people is, "Hold fast."'

People in the movement were rushing 'to talk of truce' when there was no indication the British were ready to call off their aggression, he complained in another letter to the press. As far as he was concerned, the Irish side was merely acting in self-defence. 'If the aggression ceases there will be no longer any need for defence,' he argued. 'But is the aggression ceasing?'

'Everywhere the enemy has gone on with his attack,' Collins added, answering his own question. 'Let us drop talking and get on with our work.

. . . Everyone in Ireland has reason to be profoundly distrustful of British politicians of all schools, and we have learned to be more distrustful of their promises than of their threats,' he continued. 'Prepare to meet their threats, but let their promises be realised. Then, we can bestow thanks according to value.'

His scepticism was well-founded. When Archbishop Clune returned to London, he found Lloyd George's attitude had stiffened. Passions were so roused over the recent killings, the Prime Minister said, it was necessary to hold off on actual talks for a while longer. If the Irish would keep things quiet for about a month, he predicted, the atmosphere would be more conducive for negotiations. He also added it would help matters if Collins and Mulcahy left the country for a while. The archbishop concluded the British attitude had changed because they believed O'Flanagan's letter and the telegram from the six members of Galway County Council were indications Sinn Féin was 'showing the white feather'.

Clune heard the Prime Minister call a meeting with his hard-liners, and it was noteworthy that when Lloyd George spoke in the House of Commons on 10 December, he said that the 'extremists must first be broken up' before there could be a negotiated settlement, and he announced the introduction of martial law throughout the southern counties of Ireland. Next evening the Black and Tans and Auxiliaries ran amuck in Cork, burning much of the business centre of the city in a frightening rampage of arson and looting. The outcry was such that the government ordered a formal military inquiry.

When Clune returned to Mountjoy for further discussions with Griffith on 12 December, Collins was clearly disillusioned. 'It seems to me that no additional good result can come from further continuing these discussions,' he wrote to Griffith. 'We have clearly demonstrated our willingness to have peace on honourable terms. Lloyd George insists upon capitulation. Between these there is no mean, and it is only a waste of time continuing.'

Collins was afraid that their willingness to continue with such talks might be interpreted in Britain as an indication that the Irish side was desperate for peace because it was on the verge of collapse. 'Let Lloyd George make no mistake,' Collins continued, 'the IRA is not broken.'

Although Lloyd George's coalition government had been given a handsome majority in the last general election, his own political position was quite precarious because his Liberal Party had been decimated at the polls, and the Conservative Party, with which he was in coalition, had won an overwhelming majority within Westminster. Thus the Prime Minister was essentially a political prisoner of the Conservatives, who traditionally tended to take a hard line on Irish matters.

Clune was convinced Lloyd George was 'genuinely anxious' for a settlement and was being hampered by die-hards in his government, but their position had been weakened by the recent outrageous behaviour of Crown forces. 'The Cork burnings have strengthened his hands against the die-hards,' the archbishop argued. In addition, there was also the senseless killing of a Catholic priest, Canon Magner. He had been shot near Dunmanway, County Cork by the Black and Tans after he had stopped to help a local magistrate who was having car trouble. 'His sole offence was to have helped a Resident Magistrate to get his motor car going, and here comes a drunken beast of a soldier who makes him kneel down and shoots him,' Lloyd George told his cabinet.

Griffith tended to agree with Clune about the Prime Minister's desire for a settlement. 'Lloyd George apparently wants peace,' he wrote to Collins, 'but is afraid of his militarists.'

All this was 'being too credulous of Lloyd George's intentions', as far as Collins was concerned. 'My own feeling about Lloyd George is that we should not allow him to disassociate himself from his public actions, as Head of his Cabinet, and from the actions resulting from decisions of his Cabinet,' Collins wrote to Art O'Brien on 15 December 1920. 'Particularly on this side, there is far too great a tendency to believe that Lloyd George is wishful for peace, and that it is only his own wild men prevent him from accomplishing his desires.'

Nevertheless the archbishop now brought proposals from Dublin Castle that the British were willing to stop arrests, raids, and reprisals for a month in return for a cease-fire on the Irish side, but they were not prepared to agree formally that the Dáil should be allowed to meet. It was not that they wanted to prevent such meetings but rather they did not want to be seen to be formally approving of them.

'A truce on the terms specified cannot possibly do us any harm,' Collins wrote to Griffith. He had consulted Brugha and Stack and both were agreeable. Stack was ready to accept if Collins was, while Brugha merely insisted that 'it must be definitely understood that our peaceful activities are not to be interfered with'.

Just as everything seemed ready for a truce, the British again scuttled the process. On 13 December Father O'Flanagan sent another telegram to Lloyd George, this time asking for the opportunity to consult the two leading Irish spokesmen, de Valera and Griffith. Pointedly, he did not mention the acting President, Collins. It seemed like a snub to Collins and could only have encouraged the British to believe that there was opposition to the Big Fellow within Sinn Féin.

Collins was understandably annoyed and wrote to Griffith next day, complaining about people 'butting in'. He noted that O'Flanagan would look foolish if he went to the United States to see de Valera, seeing that de Valera had already made plans to return to Dublin as soon as possible. 'I suppose,' Collins wrote, 'Fr Michael feels that nobody is able to handle things quite like he is himself.'

Lloyd George responded that he would facilitate a meeting with Griffith at Mountjoy Jail, and the ordinary means of communication were open to de Valera. Clune returned to Griffith on 17 December with news that the British had appeared to harden their attitude again. Dublin Castle was now insisting that the IRA should first surrender its arms. This, of course, was tantamount to demanding capitulation, and Griffith told him without hesitation that it would not even be considered.

Next day Collins met Clune for a second time. 'Our interview was not a lengthy one,' Collins wrote. 'We had both practically speaking come to the conclusion that no talk was necessary, seeing that the new proposal from the British Government was a proposal that we should surrender.'

A number of factors contributed to Lloyd George's change of heart, but in the last analysis the main reason was unwillingness to confront his cabinet hard-liners, who were predicting that they were on the verge of victory. 'Stress was laid on the importance of doing nothing to check the surrender of arms at a time when the forces of the Crown had at last definitely established the upper hand,' Sir Maurice Hankey, the cabinet secretary, noted in his diary.

The talk about getting the upper hand was strengthened by the antics of Father O'Flanagan and the Sinn Féin members of Galway County Council clamouring for peace, followed by the bitter denunciation of ambushes by the Roman Catholic bishop of Cork, Daniel Cohalan, who announced the excommunication of anyone engaging in ambushes. 'Anyone who shall, within the Diocese of Cork, organise or take part in an ambush or in a kidnapping, or otherwise shall be guilty of murder or attempt at murder,' Bishop Cohalan said, 'shall incur by the very fact the censure of excommunication.'

'That is pretty serious,' Lloyd George noted. He saw the sermon as an indication that the hierarchy were turning away from Sinn Féin.

On top of all this the British had their own intelligence reports that de Valera was on his way back from the United States, and they believed that he would be easier to deal with than a militant like Collins. As things stood Clune told the British that Collins was 'the only one with whom business could be done', but they gave the archbishop the impression that they thought O'Flanagan and de Valera would be more ready to compromise.

The British cabinet was told on 20 December that de Valera would be landing at Liverpool that day and Lloyd George suggested that no effort should be made to arrest him.

'I cannot guarantee de Valera's safety now,' the Chief Secretary, Sir Hamar Greenwood declared.

'That is his look out,' the Prime Minister replied.

'How can you let de Valera loose when we have arrested Arthur Griffith?' Greenwood asked.

'That was a piece of impertinence on the part of the military and if it had not been for the fact that we want the support of the military we would have repudiated it,' Lloyd George explained.

Although there had been a number of British peace initiatives, the Clune talks had seemed to hold out the best prospect yet for negotiations, but O'Flanagan's interventions undoubtedly played into the hands of the British hard-liners. Archbishop Clune was eventually thanked for his help by Dublin Castle on 3 January 1921 and told that peace negotiations had been opened in another direction — through O'Flanagan, who went over to London and met Lloyd George four days later.

The Clune talks were only one of the things that Collins had to concern himself with during his month as acting President. He was still Minister for Finance, president of the IRB, and director of intelligence in the IRA. He was an administrative genius, able to compartmentalise all matters and keep them separate, while at the same time slicing through bureaucratic red tape. He believed in getting right to the heart of a matter and balked at the paper shuffling in which civil servants often spend so much of their time.

'Look here,' he wrote to the cabinet secretary, Diarmuid O'Hegarty, 'I am not going to have any more of the parcels of miscellanies dumped on me. If anything concerns this department, or the general aspect, it should be sent to me and no more about it — I have something else to do than to wade through a miscellaneous collection of cuttings, surmounted by a letter from the Propaganda Department to you, a letter from you to the Propaganda Department, and another letter to myself.'

'If a little common sense is applied, the situation will be very much simplified,' he declared. He had the neat, orderly mind of a trained civil servant. He liked his reports typed, or at least written in ink.

'For God's sake,' he wrote to one intelligence officer in the habit of sending pencilled reports, 'buy a pen and a bottle of ink.'

Collins returned an illegible report to another officer. 'What in Heaven's name is the use of mystifying me with a thing like this?' he asked. His own letters were a model of businesslike clarity — short and to the point, with numbered paragraphs for different items, and separate letters dealing with intelligence and financial matters.

His good friend Harry Boland used to irritate him by including Sinn Féin, IRB, and personal matters in the same letters, which caused problems if Collins wished to pass on the letters to someone else. But, try as he might, there was no way some people would adopt the kind of reporting habits Collins wanted. 'I undertook to fight for you, not to write for you,' Seán Mac Eoin snapped back in irritation one day.

'Got plenty of staff, Austin?' Collins asked one day on entering the office of Austin Stack, the Minister for Home Affairs.

'Yes,' replied the Kerryman.

De Valera under arrest at the end of the 1916 Easter Rebellion. His position as the senior surviving commandant of the rebellion was to give him a unique status in the coming years.

De Valera in Volunteer uniform.

WHO IS DE VALERA ?

CLARE - ABU,

AND

DE VALERA ABU.

Of American-Irish Spanish race
DE VALERA spat in England's face,
The gap of danger's still his place
To lead historic Clare's Dragoons.

Viva la for Ireland's wrong !
Viva la for Ireland's right !
Viva la in Sinn Fein throng,
For a Spanish steed and sabre bright !

DE VALERA is 34 years of age.   In Rockwell College distinguished as
an Athlete and Scholar.   Renowned as Professor in Blackrock College.
Prominent worker for Irish Language.   For further particulars apply to
the British Army, which made his acquaintance during Easter Week

UP IRELAND !

Published for the Candidate by his Authorised Election Agent, H. O'B. Moran, Solicitor
Limerick, and Printed and Published at the CHAMPION Works, Ennis.

Election poster for de Valera in Clare, 1917.

Three members of the Auxiliaries.

The house and shop of Tomás MacCurtain in Cork.

EAMON DeVALERA

PRESIDENT OF

THE IRISH REPUBLIC

Reserve, Wisconsin 18

➡

SATURDAY OCT.

PROGRAM

At High Noon. Memorial Mass for Indian Soldiers that are buried overseas. Sermon, Rev. P. J. O'Mahoney of Spooner.

At 2 p. m. President De Valera addresses the Indians after which he will be adopted into the Chippewa tribe.

At 3 p. m. Indian War and Tribal dances and games.

☞ Visitors are advised to bring lunches as there is no hotel or regular restaurant at the Indian village.

As this poster suggests, de Valera spoke in some unusual locations during his American tour of 1919–20.

De Valera speaking at Los Angeles, December 1919.

De Valera in Chicago, following the award of an honorary degree, 1919.

The Evening Herald of Monday, 22 November 1920, the day after Bloody Sunday.

Two images of Collins, taken only a few years apart, show the degree to which he aged under the strain of events. The first shows him in Volunteer uniform in 1916, aged twenty-six, the second just six years later, in August 1922, the last month of his life.

Michael Collins (left) and Harry Boland (right) in Croke Park in 1921.

Four of the five Treaty negotiators. (Left to right) George Gavan Duffy, Michael Collins, Arthur Griffith and Robert Barton.

As British troops march out, troops of the new Irish army march in to take possession of military installations in Dublin.

Collins sent an autographed copy of this photograph showing himself (left) and Harry Boland to Joe McGarrity, a crucial figure in the Irish-American Clan na Gael organisation. Collins has signed the print in Irish.

As Chairman of the Provisional Government, Collins speaks in front of O'Donovan's Hotel, Clonakilty, Co. Cork, 15 June 1922.

Collins and Richard Mulcahy walk in Arthur Griffith's funeral procession, August 1922. A week later, Collins himself was dead.

De Valera addressing a public meeting.

Following his ten years in the wilderness in the aftermath of the Civil War, de Valera returned to power in 1932. He is shown here in his office at Government Buildings.

By mid-century, de Valera was the dominant figure in Irish politics. Here he is shown address-ing an open-air meeting during the general election of 1948, in which he suffered his first defeat in sixteen years.

Grand old man and President of Ireland: Eamon de Valera in old age.

'Well I have just received the following,' Collins snarled, dumping a bundle of complaints on his desk. 'Your department, Austin, is nothing but a bloody joke.'

The rather sensitive Stack resented the remark. A few days later when someone referred to Collins as the Big Fellow, Stack betrayed a gnawing bitterness.

'Big Fella!' he said. 'He's no Big Fella to me.'

The nickname, born of derision, had become a term of affection, but there was no longer any affection between Collins and Stack. Their once warm friendship was developing into an extremely bitter rivalry in which Collins made no effort to spare the personal feelings of Stack, whom he would come to despise. Pádraig O'Keeffe noted it was easy to work with Stack. 'Of course,' O'Keeffe added pointedly, 'he did no work.'

Stack antagonised Collins by transmitting routine material through the IRA's express communications network. It was a kind of 'fast-track' service in which railwaymen carried sensitive IRA messages all over the country. Collins had set up the network and was very protective of it. He would not have minded it being used for something important, but resented Stack endangering the process just to transmit routine stuff.

Collins 'never crossed the bows of anybody who was doing work and particularly anybody in authority', wrote Mulcahy, who noted that Collins 'set himself out to serve unreservedly in every possible way'. He certainly had an excellent working relationship with Griffith while the latter was acting President, and with Mulcahy as chief of staff.

Collins was a demanding taskmaster, always pushing to get things done. He pushed everyone, especially himself. Throughout the movement people looked to him for action. 'There was no burden too big to put on Mick's shoulders,' Dan Breen wrote, 'and there was no job too small for him to do.'

'Whenever anybody wanted anything done they were told to see Mick,' Tom Barry noted. 'He was very good-hearted and generous, but he was also a man you could easily dislike. He was very domineering.'

'Get up and I'll wrestle you, you West Cork so and so,' Collins said to him one day. Barry was four stone lighter than him and had no intention of wrestling.

'Go and wrestle your own bloody weight,' he replied.

'Get up. Are you yellow?'

Barry got up and they wrestled before they both fell to the floor. 'The next thing was he caught me by the hair,' Barry explained. 'He had to be the top man.' Eventually the two of them were 'fighting in earnest on the bloody floor', before somebody separated them. 'But within a couple of minutes he was his laughing and affable self again.'

Witnesses were often embarrassed by the way Collins bullied his aide Joe O'Reilly. The latter was everything to him, confidant, messenger, nurse, sometime bodyguard, and the person who bore the brunt of the Big Fellow's rages when he left off steam as things went wrong, which was quite often for a perfectionist like Collins. They had been friends since their emigrant days in London, and O'Reilly was a perfect sidekick — totally devoted to Collins. At times, though, the bullying did get to him. O'Reilly would announce he was leaving, and Collins would act indifferently, making no effort to change his friend's mind.

——'Here!' Collins would say. 'Take this letter on your way.'

'Do you know what you're doing to that boy?' one woman asked Collins in disgust.

'I know his value better than you do,' he replied. 'He goes to Mass for me every morning. Jesus Christ, do you think I don't know what he's worth to me?'

O'Reilly always returned, of course, because in spite of everything he knew that Collins valued his services. Maybe the reason Collins would not ask him to stay was his recognition that nobody should be pressed to take the risks that O'Reilly took for him. Collins, in turn, trusted him with his life, because O'Reilly always knew where to find Collins; he was the only person who knew where Collins was sleeping on any given night.

Finding a bed for the night was usually a problem for someone like Collins. The Munster Hotel was the subject of regular raids, so it was too dangerous for him to stay there throughout 1920, and Vaughan's Hotel became much too dangerous after Bloody Sunday. Anyone putting him up for the night had to be particularly brave, because they were endangering their own lives and those of their families. He often stayed at the Rathgar home of Mrs O'Donovan, an aunt of Gearóid O'Sullivan, or on Richmond Avenue in Walter House, the home of a colleague's widowed mother. Collins had digs in Walter House for a time before moving to the Munster Hotel. He also stayed at 23 Brendan's Road with his secretary Susan Mason and her aunt, or with Patricia Hoey and her mother at 5 Mespil Road in the house where he had his intelligence office. Another of his safe houses was Furry Park, the home of Moya Llewelyn Davies. She was the daughter of James O'Connor, a Parnellite member of parliament, and her husband was a confidant of Lloyd George. With credentials like those, her home was one of the last places the security forces were likely to raid.

Nobody ever seemed to have suggested then that there was anything sexual between Collins and any of those women. At the time he did not show any interest in the opposite sex. Given his lifestyle and his precarious prospects, it was understandable he should have avoided entangling relationships. Later people would suggest there might have been something more to his relationship with some of those women, but nobody every produced a shred of evidence to substantiate their snide insinuations, or in some cases actual accusations. About all one can say at this juncture is that if Collins was sexually involved with any of them, he was certainly discreet.

De Valera, meanwhile, had planned to stay longer in the United States and had received cabinet approval for the idea, but he quickly changed his mind on hearing the news from Dublin that Griffith had been arrested and that Collins had been selected as acting President. De Valera arrived home just before Christmas and lost no time in complaining about the way the IRA campaign was being waged. 'Ye are going too fast,' he told Mulcahy. 'This odd shooting of a policeman here and there is having a very bad effect, from the propaganda point of view, on us in America. What we want is one good battle about once a month with about 500 men on each side.'

It was certainly insensitive of him to criticise the way the campaign had been run without, at least, waiting to consult a few people. Collins had his narrowest escape yet from arrest on Christmas Eve. The *Police Gazette: Hue and Cry* had come out that day with a good photograph of him taken the previous year on its front page. He had arranged a stag party with some friends at the Gresham Hotel, but the party was raided by the Auxiliaries, and all were questioned and searched.

'They were very suspicious of me,' Collins told friends next day. 'I was questioned over and over again. One officer actually drew an old photograph of me out of his pocket, and compared it with my face, drawing my hair down as it was in the picture. It was touch and go. They were not quite satisfied, and hesitated long before they left us.' Throughout it all Collins remained cheerful, and the raiding party eventually departed, leaving him to get very drunk indeed.

Relations between Collins and both Brugha and Stack were already seriously strained, and de Valera seemed to side with them in the coming days. He tried to send Collins to the United States and even got cabinet approval for the idea after Collins had refused to go. De Valera wrote a long letter to him on 18 January 1921 giving a plethora of reasons for the trip. In fact, he argued so strongly that Collins concluded the whole thing was a plot to get rid of him. 'That long whore won't get rid of me as easy as that,' Collins remarked.

In the following months a distinct strain developed in the relationship between de Valera and Collins. America had not been big enough for the Long Fellow and Daniel Cohalan, and it soon began to look like Ireland was too small for himself and the Big Fellow. While in the United States de Valera appeared to be particularly touchy about his role as the Irish leader. His dispute with Cohalan had centred on his own determination to show that he had to be consulted about anything to do with Ireland, because he was determined that all would realise that he was the real leader. Once he returned home, however, Collins appeared to pose a real threat to his leadership, because many people thought the Big Fellow was the real leader.

The year 1921 began badly for Collins when the home of Eileen McGrane at 21 Dawson Street was raided on New Year's Day. The British found a large cache of documents which she had been storing for him; among them were carbon copies of police reports typed by Ned Broy, who immediately came under suspicion. This undermined his value as a police source.

Although de Valera went into hiding following his return to Ireland, there was really no need as he was not wanted by the British. They could have arrested him virtually at will because they knew where he was living. But they could not find Collins despite frantic efforts. Auxiliaries frequently burst into bars and other public places shouting, 'Where's Michael Collins? We know he's here!'

John Foley — a former secretary to the lord mayor of Dublin and well known for his antipathy to Sinn Féin — was arrested while having lunch with a former high sheriff of Dublin, T. J. MacAvin, in Jammet's restaurant on 10 January 1921. 'Come on Michael Collins, you've dodged us long enough,' the arresting officer said.

Despite their protestations, Foley and MacAvin were taken to Dublin Castle, before they could convince the officer of his mistake. Ironically, Foley did not look anything like Collins.

The following week some Crown authorities again thought they had Collins when they arrested a barman in the Prince of Wales Hotel using the name of Corry. He turned out to be a Michael Collins all right. 'But,' *The Irish Times* noted, 'he is not the Michael Collins of IRA notoriety.'

The *Daily Sketch* reported that Collins had been shot off a white horse in trying to escape from Burgatia House on the outskirts of Rosscarbery, County Cork, on 2 February. The IRA had seized the house in order to attack a nearby police barracks, but the Black and Tans got wind of what was happening and surrounded the premises with some one hundred men. The IRA force nevertheless managed to break out without suffering any casualties. One Billy Sullivan escaped on a bay mare which stumbled and fell, but he was uninjured.

Collins, who was not within a hundred miles of the place, was particularly amused when his intelligence people intercepted a coded message asking for confirmation from Cork about the reported shooting.

'Is there any truth that Michael Collins was killed at Burgatia?' Dublin Castle asked.

'There is no information of the report re Michael Collins, but some believe he was wounded,' came the reply.

'We are hoping to hear further confirmation about poor Michael Collins,' the Big Fellow remarked facetiously in acknowledging receipt of the two telegrams.

There was a further news agency report on 8 February that Collins had been killed in an engagement in Drimoleague, County Cork. Such reports, which were obviously inspired by British sources, added considerably to his notoriety. Their frustrated forces were seeking to explain their failures by exaggerating the strength and the guile of their opponents. Following the Burgatia incident, for instance, the Black and Tans said the IRA had a force of some five hundred men in the house; *The Irish Times* credulously reported it, and Collins was credited with the most amazing feats. 'The English papers have been giving me plenty of notoriety,' Collins wrote to his sister Helena on 5 March 1921. 'The white horse story was an exaggeration.' It was not just an exaggeration, it was pure fiction.

The *Daily Sketch* described Collins as a 'super hater, dour, hard, [with] no ray of humour, [and] no trace of human feeling', according to himself. This probably reflected Dublin Castle's distorted perception of him and thus explained the British difficulty in finding him, because he was a very different type of person. He could be serious and intent, but generally he had a breezy, affable manner. He went out of his way to be friendly with British troops or police. If he saw an area condoned off he would go over and talk to the troops. 'There are several of these fellows I don't know yet,' he would say to colleagues.

When stopped or searched himself, he would be cordial with the troops or Auxiliaries, would smile at them and joke with them. He could do this with ease because he had spent most of his adult life in London. They naturally welcomed his friendliness in the hostile atmosphere permeating Ireland. 'You're a good sort anyway,' one of them said to him one day. He liked that; it appealed to his sense of humour. Such friendliness was the last thing the British expected of Michael Collins.

He liked to tell the story of talking to an Auxiliary in a Grafton Street pub one day. 'That man Collins, I wish I could nail him,' Collins said.

'Don't worry,' replied the Auxiliary. 'His days are numbered.' Collins related what happened with a roar of laughter and held up a calendar.

'See here,' he said to O'Reilly, 'how many days have I got to live?'

During early 1921 he had several narrow escapes of which the British were unaware, such as when the Auxiliaries raided 22 Mary Street, where he had his main finance office. They were primarily interested, however, in another office in the building. When he casually walked down the stairs, they merely searched him and then allowed him to leave the place.

One night he was staying at Susan Mason's house at 23 Brendan's Road when it was due to be raided, but the officer in charge of the raiding party mislaid his list in another house. In the course of a raid in Donnybrook, the officer had come across some love letters and was reading them when the woman to whom they had been sent entered the room and upbraided him for his ungentlemanly conduct. The embarrassed officer hurriedly stuffed the letters back into a drawer and inadvertently included his own list of houses to be raided that night. She found the list and passed it on to Batt O'Connor next day. It was then that Collins learned of his narrow escape.

He had another close call in Kirwin's bar one night when it was raided. He was with Sergeant Maurice McCarthy of the RIC who had just come down from Belfast with the latest police codes. Everyone in the bar was being searched but when McCarthy produced his RIC identification, the officer in charge invited him and Collins to have a drink. Had they searched Collins they would have found the codes.

It was widely believed there was a reward of £10,000 for the capture of Collins, which was as much as most Irish people could then expect to earn in a lifetime. The Black and Tans, for instance, were considered well paid, but the supposed reward amounted to more than they could earn in fifty years, working seven days a week and fifty-two weeks a year. As a result there was always the danger someone might betray Collins for the money. The British arrested Christy Harte and offered him his freedom and a size-able reward if he would telephone a certain number the next time Collins visited Vaughan's Hotel. Harte agreed, but promptly told Collins about the promise which he had no intention of keeping.

William Doran, the porter at the Wicklow Hotel, however, was apparently a different case. Collins learned that he had betrayed some people and had the Squad kill him. Doran had given some assistance to Collins in the past and his widow thought he had been killed by British agents. She therefore appealed to Sinn Féin for funds as she had three small children. For the children's sake, Collins ordered that she should not be told the true circum-stances of her husband's death and that she should be given the money. 'The poor little devils need the money,' he said. It was a humane response, but he did not have the authority for such a gesture. It was the kind of thing which raised questions about his handling of finances.

Brugha needled Collins relentlessly to provide the cabinet with a proper accounting of money allocated to purchase arms in Scotland. There was a discrepancy which Collins was unable to resolve. In the light of the pressure under which he was operating, together with the amount of money he had handled, the discrepancy was of little significance, other than as a weapon with which to attack his administrative credibility, if not his actual integrity.

Things got so bad that Mulcahy complained to de Valera about Brugha's attitude towards Collins.

'You know,' de Valera told him, 'I think Cathal is jealous of Mick. Isn't it a terrible thing to think that a man with the qualities that Cathal undoubtedly has would fall a victim to a dirty little vice like jealousy.'

A small, sincere, resolute man, Brugha was dedicated to the cause with the zeal of a fanatic. While he and others worked unselfishly, seeking no glory for themselves, he resented not only the press attention given to Collins, but also the way the Big Fellow had opinions on everything and delved in the affairs of colleagues. For instance, Collins was dismissive of a scheme that Brugha suggested to revive the Irish language.

'Perhaps you'd produce a scheme for Irish yourself, Mr Collins?'

'I will.'

'That's excellent.'

'And maybe it will surprise you,' said Collins.

Of course, the revival of the Irish language was not on the top of the Big Fellow's priorities. At the next meeting Brugha brought up the subject again. 'I believe Mr Collins's scheme for Irish will surprise us,' he said.

'Oh, shut up!' snapped Collins.

Yet with his well-organised intelligence network, he was particularly well placed to interfere in the legitimate ambit of others. He knew more about what was happening throughout the movement than anyone, and he was able to exert considerable influence through an IRB clique of fellow Corkmen in key administrative positions. For instance, he managed to have himself replaced as adjutant general of the IRA by Gearóid O'Sullivan, and as director of organisation by Diarmuid O'Hegarty, who also became secretary to the government, while Seán Ó Muirthile replaced Collins as secretary of the supreme council of the IRB. Collins's influence with them was based largely on their recognition of his enormous organisational talents.

'A vast amount of stuff could be assembled associating his smiling buoyancy, his capacity for bearing tension, clearness of mind, perfectly controlled calm, and a devil-may-carishness,' wrote Mulcahy. 'His clarity of mind and his whole manner and demeanour, together with his power of concentration on the immediate matter in hand, gave him a great power over men.'

Brugha so loathed Collins, however, that he was apparently unable to see, much less appreciate, those qualities which so many admired. He mistakenly believed Collins used his IRB position to acquire his influence, whereas, in fact, he acquired the position because he already had the influence as a result of his administrative ability. Much as Mulcahy disliked Brugha's attitude towards Collins, he never doubted Brugha's sincerity. 'He was naturally blunt and frank and was no more intending to intrigue than he was to diplomacy,' Mulcahy noted.

Maybe the way Collins interfered would have been more acceptable if he had not been so resentful of similar interference in his own areas. He seemed to think others should abide by certain rules, while he should be able to improvise as he went along.

'What the hell do you know about finance?' he snapped at Stack one day when the latter had the temerity to make some suggestion.

'I know more about finance, than you know about manner!' Stack snapped back.

Though Collins and Brugha both belonged to the militant wing of the movement, there was a difference in their militancy. Brugha was rather dull-witted, or as de Valera put it, 'a bit slow'. He basically reacted to events, whereas Collins provoked them. For instance, Brugha disapproved of the Soloheadbeg ambush which marked the beginning of the War of Independence, while Collins warmly approved of it and encouraged similar attacks throughout the country.

Collins had deliberately provoked the Black and Tan war in order to secure the support of the Irish people, but in the process he unleashed forces which he could not control and which would ultimately bring about his own death. Infuriated by the savagery of Crown forces, Brugha wanted to resurrect his old scheme to kill members of the British cabinet, but Collins realised that to react in that manner would be to make the same mistake that the British had made in Ireland; it would drive the British people into the arms of their militants. Hence Collins resolutely opposed Brugha's scheme.

'You'll get none of my men for that,' he declared.

'That's all right, Mr Collins, I want none of your men. I'll get my own.'

Brugha called Seán Mac Eoin, the leader of the IRA in Longford, to Dublin in March 1921 and outlined the scheme to him. Mac Eoin agreed somewhat reluctantly to lead the attack.

'This is madness,' Collins thundered when Mac Eoin told him about the plan. 'Do you think that England has the makings of only one cabinet?' He suggested Mac Eoin consult the chief of staff.

'I was appalled at the idea,' Mulcahy recalled. He told Mac Eoin to return to his command area and have nothing further to do with the pro- posed London project. On the train back, Mac Eoin was recognised and ran into a party of Auxiliaries at the railway station in Longford. He was shot and seriously wounded when he tried to make a break. His capture was a serious blow because he was probably the most effective IRA commander outside the Cork area.

'It is simply disastrous,' Collins wrote. 'Cork will be fighting alone now.'

Collins wrote that he 'would almost prefer that the worst would have happened' than that Mac Eoin should have fallen into the hands of the enemy. He immediately set about planning Mac Eoin's escape, as it was obvious the British intended to execute him as soon as he was fit enough to be tried and hanged.

While escape plans were being formulated, Collins suffered a devastating blow to his intelligence operations with the discovery of his office at 5 Mespil Road, where most of his documents were stored. He had just left for the evening on 1 April when the building was raided by the British. They were obviously acting on a tip. They found a considerable volume of material and staked out the office for his return next day. Patricia Hoey and her mother, who lived in the house, were held captive.

As they waited through the night Hoey's mother pretended to become seriously ill and the British summoned her doctor, Alice Barry, who managed to get word to Joe O'Reilly about the trap that had been set for

Collins and his staff. 'They waited for me all day Saturday,' Collins wrote to de Valera. 'The lady says they were so frightened they certainly would not have hit me in any case.' It was a touch of that raw vanity which some people found obnoxious.

The British had little to fear from Collins himself, as far as Brugha was concerned, because there was no evidence Collins ever fired a shot at any of them. In view of the regularity with which people were stopped and searched in the streets of Dublin during the War of Independence, Collins would rarely carry a weapon. This really required a considerable amount of courage, especially when one considers the fate of his friends Dick McKee and Peadar Clancy.

Men like Tom Barry and Liam Deasy, who visited Dublin during the early spring, marvelled at the fearless way in which Collins moved about the city. Although they had been in the thick of the fighting in west Cork, they found Dublin unnerving. Deasy and Gearóid O'Sullivan's brother, Tadhg, met Collins in Devlin's bar and soon found themselves at a race meeting in Phoenix Park, which was crawling with military and police. Yet Collins and his people showed no fear. 'Nothing would do him now but to bring us into the reserved stand where we stood shoulder to shoulder with the enemy,' Deasy noted.

'Good God!' Tadhg O'Sullivan exclaimed. 'These fellows are mad.'

That night they adjourned to Vaughan's Hotel. When someone warned Collins that it would be curfew time in twenty minutes, he was dismissive. 'To hell with curfew and them that enforce it,' he replied.

'They seemed to have no fear of arrest, or if they had, they did not show it,' Tom Barry wrote.

'Their lack of precautions was amazing and even made one angry,' Barry recalled. 'One night at about nine o'clock we ran into a hold-up by about fifty Auxiliaries.' They were each searched. 'I was next to Collins and he put up such a fine act, joking and blasting in turn, that he had the whole search party of terrorists in good humour in a short time.' Needless to say they were not detained, but Barry was critical that Collins had not taken the precaution of sending a scout ahead.

'Mick as usual guffawed and chaffed me about being a windy West Cork beggar,' Barry noted. 'Failing to see the joke, I told him crossly that it was quite true, I was a windy beggar, as I had a wholesome regard for my neck.'

As Príomh-Aire, de Valera's main function should have been to supervise the other ministers, but he had been out of the country for all but a couple of months since his election. Some of the departments proved to be little more than notional. Count Plunkett was Minister for Foreign Affairs, for instance, but he had never set up a department, so de Valera undertook the function himself. He essentially took over the duties and advised the secretary merely to consult Plunkett once in a while.

All representatives sent abroad by the Dáil were primarily engaged in propaganda, as their efforts to secure diplomatic recognition proved futile. The only country which had ever shown any inclination to recognise the Irish Republic was the Soviet Union, whose representatives in Washington had agreed to draft terms for a recognition treaty, but de Valera was afraid to proceed for fear the agreement with the Bolshevik government would damage the possibility of securing official American recognition. He therefore delayed, but tried to keep the Soviet representatives interested by secretly loaning their financially embarrassed mission some $20,000. In return, he received jewels as collateral, but the whole transaction remained a closely guarded secret for more than a quarter of a century.

De Valera looked on foreign affairs as primarily a matter of propaganda. On appointing Robert Brennan secretary of the department, for example, he instructed him 'to keep in touch with the Director of Propaganda'. It is as much his department as yours,' de Valera wrote. 'It is in fact what I have called the "Statistical" or permanent-value-department of propaganda.'

Even the Soviet Union had lost the interest it had shown the previous summer. Patrick McCartan was sent to Russia to negotiate a recognition treaty, but he found upon his arrival that the Bolshevik authorities were more interested in securing a trade agreement with Britain. When an Anglo-Soviet trade agreement was signed in March 1921 it effectively killed any chance of Soviet recognition of the Irish Republic, because the Russians had no intention of antagonising London by recognising the rebel regime in Dublin.

Other countries' desire to maintain friendly relations with Britain posed the most formidable barrier in the way of securing diplomatic recognition. In early 1921 there were rumours that the British had persuaded Pope Benedict XV to denounce the Irish republican regime. On 2 February 1921 de Valera wrote to Archbishop Patrick J. Hayes of New York to enlist his help in forestalling any such action by the Pope. 'I have what I must regard as sure information to the effect that the English have actually succeeded in impressing their views upon His Holiness and upon his advisers,' de Valera wrote. 'His Holiness is on the point of issuing what will be regarded as a condemnation of those who are nobly striving in the cause of their country's liberty and freely offering their lives as a sacrifice.'

Archbishop Hayes went to Rome and had talks with Monsignor Sebastiani of the Vatican secretariat. It seems the Irish fears had been well founded, but the intervention of Hayes, together with a personal appeal to the Pope himself by Archbishop Clune of Perth, was enough to persuade Benedict

XV to write to Michael Cardinal Logue in Armagh with an assurance that he would pursue neutrality on the Irish question.

As part of this propaganda de Valera deliberately portrayed himself as a moderate. In written statements and a number of interviews he gave to foreign correspondents, who were spirited to his hiding-place, he cultivated a moderate image. In his personal contacts with members of the IRA, however, he talked about engaging in major battles that could be best exploited for propaganda purposes in the United States. While it may have seemed strange to some that he should have been anxious to wage war in order to influence American opinion, his judgment was astutely based, because it was not the military actions of Collins or his men that worried the British government most, but American opinion, and this is where de Valera made his greatest contribution.

In January 1921 Lloyd George privately voiced disquiet over the effect his Irish policy was having on Anglo-American relations, especially after the British ambassador in Washington gave him 'a most gloomy account' of the American situation. 'In the interests of peace with America,' the Prime Minister said, 'I think we ought to see de Valera and try to get a settlement.'

Throughout the early months of 1921 the British were sending out peace feelers offering a settlement on the lines of Dominion Home Rule. Father Michael O'Flanagan met Lloyd George on 7 January, against the advice of de Valera, and had further meetings with the unionist leader Edward Carson at which the possibility of a settlement on the lines of Dominion Home Rule was suggested. De Valera showed a keen interest in the dominion concept and indicated that real dominion status would be acceptable to Ireland, seeing that Andrew Bonar Law, the Canadian-born leader of the Conservative Party, had said the dominions had 'the right to decide their own destinies'.

'Thus,' de Valera declared, 'the British Dominions have [had] conceded to them all the rights that Irish Republicans demand. It is obvious that if these rights were not being denied to us we would not be engaged in the present struggle.' He went on to stress that Sinn Féin was not an isolationist movement. The Dáil had already proved this by advocating the country's willingness to join the League of Nations. 'We are thoroughly sane and reasonable people, not a coterie of political doctrinaires, or even party politicians, Republican or other,' he emphasised.

Before going to America de Valera had taken a hard line on the Ulster question, as he spoke about kicking the unionists out or blasting them out of the way, but since the Government of Ireland Act, the 'Partition Act', had become law in December 1920, he modified his tone and talked about accepting a form of partition. 'There is,' he said, 'plenty of room in Ireland for partition, real partition, and plenty of it.' He suggested the island could be divided into administrative units and associated in a confederation like

Switzerland, where the cantons had much more local authority than was conferred by the Government of Ireland Act. 'It does not give Belfast and Ulster enough local liberty and power,' he said. 'In an Irish confederation they ought to get far more.'

On the issue of Britain's security, de Valera repeatedly emphasised a willingness to satisfy Britain's legitimate needs. 'Time after time,' he declared in March 1921, 'we have indicated that if England can show any right with which Ireland's right as a nation would clash, we are willing that these be adjusted by negotiations and by treaty.' After recognising Ireland's independence, he said, Britain could 'issue a warning such as the Monroe Doctrine, that she would regard any attempt by any foreign power to obtain a foothold in Ireland as an act of hostility against herself. In case of a common foe Ireland's manpower would then be available for the defence of the two islands.' He had, in fact, been saying that for more than a year, because the idea was at the heart of his famous *Westminster Gazette* interview.

He was following a carefully conceived policy. Privately he wrote that the 'best line to pursue' for propaganda purposes was to declare that Britain should 'propose a treaty with Ireland regarded as a separate state. Irish representatives would then be willing to consider making certain concessions to England's fear and England's interests.' By appearing moderate he was keeping pressure on the British to negotiate, with the result that he was definitely opposed to standing openly for a republic and nothing short of it.

'There is no use in saying that DÁIL ÉIREANN cannot negotiate on account of the mandate which is given to it,' de Valera wrote to Harry Boland. 'That simply means that Lloyd George will be put in a position of being able to force an Irish Party into existence to oppose us at the next elections on a platform of "freedom to negotiate".'

'In public statements,' he explained, 'our policy should not be to make it easy for Lloyd George by proclaiming that nothing but so and so will satisfy us. Our position should be simply that we are insisting on only one right and that is the right of the people of this country to determine for themselves how they should be governed. That sounds moderate, but includes everything and puts Lloyd George, the Labour Party and others on the defensive, and apologetic as far as the world is concerned.'

When Seán T. O'Kelly, the Irish representative in Paris, advised against the moderate approach, de Valera resented the advice. 'I wish,' the President wrote, 'he would confine himself to his own country, and I am sending him a message to that effect.' O'Kelly's wife, Cáit, was going to Paris, so de Valera asked her to explain the advantages of advocating a settlement on the lines of his *Westminster Gazette* interview, but her husband was still not persuaded.

'I have not the least wish or intention to make myself troublesome,' O'Kelly wrote to de Valera on 17 April 1921, 'but lest you should have to say later, why did not people protest in time, I hold seriously — and I shall be astonished if some others will not be found who think as I — I hold that the firm stand we take "on an Irish Republic or nothing" needs not change but development.'

The President was so impressed with his own ideas that he did not seem to understand how somebody like O'Kelly could disagree with him, except that his proposals had not been explained properly. He therefore sent an insolent letter to Cáit O'Kelly, rebuking her for apparently distorting what he had told her. If it were not for the possibility of such misrepresentation, he wrote, 'I would have regarded his letter as incomprehensible, and even worse. Considerable friction and very serious misunderstanding might have resulted. I can never allow such risks to be run again.' At the same time he sent a stern letter to O'Kelly himself telling him that all representatives abroad 'must carry out the instructions of the Department, whether they personally agree with the policy or not'. He added that 'it is only by resignation that the representatives can find a way out'.

Shortly afterwards de Valera did receive a resignation, and his handling of the whole affair was certainly of little credit to him. He had offered the post of ambassador to the United States to James O'Mara, but the latter declined because, as he explained privately, he could no longer 'hold any official position under the government of the Irish Republic whose President claims such arbitrary executive authority, and in whose judgment of American affairs I have no longer any confidence'. O'Mara not only refused the post of ambassador but also resigned as one of the three trustees of Dáil Éireann and announced he was standing down from the Dáil itself. Instead of just accepting the resignation, de Valera sent O'Mara a petulant telegram announcing he was being fired. It was a blatant example of de Valera's presumption of the arbitrary authority about which O'Mara had complained. Even if O'Mara had not already resigned, de Valera did not have the authority to remove him, seeing that he had been appointed by the Dáil.

A number of people within the movement were clearly worried by de Valera's conduct. Both Tom Barry and Ernie O'Malley, two of the IRA's more active field commanders, feared that he wished to call off the military campaign. They therefore deliberately exaggerated the strength of the IRA when they met him for the first time. He, on the other hand, surprised them by taking a different line from what he had been saying publicly. Privately he was still talking about taking on the British in major engagements. O'Malley remarked afterwards that the President was very poorly informed about the real military situation, which was hardly surprising, seeing that he had just been exaggerating the position himself.

Collins and Mulcahy later joked about some of de Valera's foolish questions. They were ridiculing the President behind his back, because they thought his plan of engaging the British in major battles was sheer lunacy. Collins had never had any intention of challenging the might of the British empire; he thought it made more sense to challenge its weakness. De Valera had already demonstrated in the United States not only a fanatical belief in everything he said or did himself, but also a prophet's indignation if anybody questioned him or his tactics. Just when he became aware that the Big Fellow was ridiculing him behind his back is not clear, but de Valera told his authorised biographers that from April 1921 onwards, 'Collins did not seem to accept my view of things as he had done before and was inclined to give public expression to his own opinions even when they differed from mine.'

On the other hand, of course, de Valera had begun questioning the Big Fellow's judgment on the very day of his return from the United States when he complained about the way the IRA campaign was being run. Collins might have expected better, because he had supported de Valera strongly in his troubles in the United States. He had accepted, without question, de Valera's assumption of the title of President of the Irish Republic, had sided with Griffith to stifle cabinet debate when Cathal Brugha and Constance Markievicz were critical of de Valera's *Westminster Gazette* interview, and had even severed the IRB's ties with Devoy and Clan na Gael because they had not backed the Long Fellow.

While de Valera was trying to sound moderate in public statements following his return to Dublin, Collins adopted a very different line. In another interview with the American journalist Carl W. Ackermann in early April 1921, he said the IRA was going to fight 'until we win'.

'What are your terms of settlement?' Ackermann asked.

'Lloyd George has a chance of showing himself to be a great statesman by recognising the Irish Republic.'

'Do you mean a Republic within the British Commonwealth of Nations or outside?' Ackermann asked.

'No, I mean an Irish Republic.'

'Why are you so hopeful?'

'Because I know the strength of our forces and I know our position is infinitely stronger throughout the world,' Collins explained. 'The terror the British wanted to instil in this country has completely broken down. It is only a question of time until we shall have them cleared out.'

'So you are still opposed to compromise?'

'When I saw you before I told you that the same effort which would get us Dominion Home Rule would get us a Republic. I am still of that opinion, and we have never had so many peace moves as we have had since last autumn.'

The British concluded there was a power struggle going on within Sinn Féin in which de Valera was little more than a figurehead, crying in the wilderness for a negotiated settlement, while Collins, the real leader, wanted to fight it out to the bitter end. 'De Valera and Michael Collins have quarrelled,' Lloyd George told his cabinet on 27 April. 'The latter will have a Republic and he carries a gun and he makes it impossible to negotiate. De Valera cannot come here and say he is willing to give up Irish Independence, for if he did, he might be shot.'

Lloyd George was actually in a precarious political position. Not only was he at the head of a coalition government in which his own party was in a distinct minority, but he was also under pressure from within his own wing of the Liberal Party to try to negotiate a settlement. He was able to mollify that pressure by stringing out his contacts with people like Father O'Flanagan and sending out his other peace feelers, and by having his people arrange secret meetings with de Valera for people like Lord Derby and Sir James Craig, who was shortly to become the first Prime Minister of Northern Ireland.

The secret meeting took place with Craig in Dublin on 5 May 1921, but nothing came of it. Each of them had been led to believe the other had asked for the meeting, so they waited for each other to begin.

'Well?' said de Valera.

'Well?' replied Craig.

A brief silence followed as they eyed each other across a table.

'I'm too old at this political business to have nonsense of this kind: each waiting for the other to begin,' de Valera said. 'And,' he later recalled, 'I started putting our case to him.'

Craig, who interjected to say that northern unionists considered the Union with Britain sacred, had difficulty getting a word in edgeways.

'Do you know how the Union was brought about?' de Valera asked, according to himself. 'And I started telling him about it.'

'After half an hour he had reached the era of Brian Boru,' according to Craig. 'After another half hour he had advanced to the period of some king a century or two later. By this time I was getting tired, for de Valera hadn't begun to reach the point at issue.' Craig therefore seized on an opportunity to suggest they draft a press release to the effect that they had met and exchanged views.

Dublin Castle had been predicting the IRA was on the verge of collapse since before Christmas, but by April this collapse seemed no nearer. 'The tenacity of the IRA is extraordinary,' Lloyd George's trusted aide Tom Jones wrote to Bonar Law. 'Where was Michael Collins during the Great War? He would have been worth a dozen brass hats.'

While the Big Fellow's bold statements undoubtedly contributed to the impression that the IRA was full of fight, and in turn undermined the credibility of Dublin Castle, they also undermined de Valera's efforts to get the British to the conference table. De Valera therefore moved to whittle away at Collins's power base, with the help of Brugha. The Squad was amalgamated with the Dublin Brigade, and Collins was replaced by Stack as the designated substitute in the event of anything happening to the President.

Lloyd George had emphasised that he wanted to negotiate but he felt it would be pointless talking with de Valera, because Collins was the real leader, and he was afraid of the political repercussions among Conservatives if he talked with Collins. 'The question is whether I can see Michael Collins,' he told the newspaper magnate Lord Riddell. 'No doubt he is the head and front of the movement. If I could see him, a settlement might be possible. The question is whether the British people would be willing for us to negotiate with the head of a band of murderers.'

When the British cabinet discussed the possibility of a truce on 12 May 1921, the Prime Minister remarked that 'de Valera does not agree with the gun business' but he was being spied upon by Collins, who was depicted as being 'against compromise'. Churchill, who had been one of the most vocal proponents of the British terror, was now showing distinct signs of wavering. 'We are getting an odious reputation,' he declared, adding that it was 'poisoning' Britain's relations with the United States. He was therefore in favour of a truce. But there was no point in having a truce without trying to negotiate a settlement, and Austen Chamberlain, the newly elected leader of the Conservative Party, saw no point in this 'as long as de Valera is at the mercy of Michael Collins'.

'You can't make a truce without meeting with Michael Collins,' declared Lord Fitz Alan, who had recently taken over as Lord-Lieutenant from Lord French. 'We can't have that.'

The cabinet divided, with Churchill and four other Liberal Party ministers in favour of a truce, while Lloyd George sided with the Conservative majority. But a fortnight later the British had to reconsider the Irish situation in the light of further developments.

On 24 May Brigadier General Frank Crozier, who had recently resigned as head of the Auxiliaries, went public with a blistering attack on the conduct of some of his own men and the Black and Tans. He admitted they had fired into the crowd in Croke Park on Bloody Sunday without provocation. Maybe the pressure on the British government would not have been as great if the Crown forces were being seen to make progress, but the reverse was evident. Next day the IRA attacked the Custom House in Dublin in what was the Irish side's largest single operation since the Easter Rebellion. As a result the casualty figures of the Crown forces soared. The seventy-two police and soldiers killed that month made a mockery of Greenwood's repeated predictions that the IRA was on the verge of collapse.

The IRA in Dublin was virtually decimated with the killing of five members and the capture of some eighty more during the attack on the Custom House. Next day, Thursday, 26 May, Crown forces raided Collins's office at 22 Mary Street just after lunch and narrowly missed him. He had transferred his intelligence office there following the raid on Mespil Road and would normally have been there at the time, but had a foreboding during lunch with Gearóid O'Sullivan and decided not to return to the office that afternoon. 'I ought to have been there at that precise moment,' Collins wrote a few days later. 'They depended too much on my punctuality.' But Bob Conlon, his messenger boy was arrested and taken to Dublin Castle.

'They did not ill-treat him,' Collins explained with characteristic vanity, because they 'thought if they did that M. C. would murder them all.' In fact, however, they did mistreat the boy, by using thumbscrews on him. And Collins found himself just one step ahead of the Crown forces in the following days. 'I may tell you the escape of Thursday was nothing to four or five escapes I have had since,' he wrote to de Valera on 1 June. 'They ran me very close for quite a good while on Sunday evening.'

By this stage another shadowy figure had come into the picture. Andy Cope had been appointed assistant under-secretary at Dublin Castle some time earlier with the aim of making contact with the republicans. He was in written contact with both de Valera and Collins. Indeed, it has been suggested that he was actually meeting Collins at this stage. William Darling, who later became chancellor of Edinburgh University, was serving with the military in Dublin Castle at the time. He recalled a strange incident one night when he was sent out to an accident in Newry as 'a high official' was involved. A police car was in collision with a larger vehicle containing the official. When Darling arrived he found a group of men standing around with the official. They had been going from Belfast to Dublin and Darling invited them to join the official for the journey back.

There were three of them cramped into the front seat and the man beside him could feel the gun that Darling was carrying.

'Are you carrying a gun?' the man asked.

'I am.'

The man then guessed at Darling's name but was wrong, so he said he was one of two other people. This time he was right.

'Do you know me?'

'No,' Darling replied. 'I think I know your friends, but I don't know you.'

'I am Michael Collins.'

Darling was astounded. 'Are you the Michael Collins whom the British police have made famous?'

'What do you mean by that?'

'A police force has a duty to apprehend criminals,' Darling explained. 'If they fail to apprehend criminals one defence is to say that the criminal whom they cannot apprehend is the most astute, remarkable, astonishing criminal in history, and so I say: "Are you the Michael Collins whom the British police force have made famous?"'

Collins laughed at that. They talked on the way to Dublin and Darling drove them to 'an hotel in one of Dublin's squares'. The high official, presumably Cope, went into the hotel with the other two, while Collins and

Darling went into the hotel bar and had a couple of bottles of stout and chatted together until the official was ready to leave.

'That was an astonishing thing meeting Michael Collins,' Darling remarked in the car.

'What do you mean?' the official asked.

'You knew that was Michael Collins with whom I sat in the car.'

'Collins!' the official exclaimed. He knew he was in contact with people on the fringe but never suspected that Collins was with them. They went back into the hotel, but the Big Fellow was gone. Later, when Collins came out publicly after the truce, Darling realised that the man that night was indeed Collins.

Although the IRA had suffered devastating losses in Dublin as a result of the attack on the Custom House, it was a calculated military risk, deliberately taken for its political effect. The venture seemed to justify de Valera's long-held conviction that major confrontations would be more effective on the propaganda front, because it made a mockery of repeated British assertions that the IRA was on the brink of collapse. In the face of all the publicity the British government was forced to change its policy.

The initial British reaction was to decide to declare martial law throughout the twenty-six counties and intensify their campaign. Collins learned through his cousin in Dublin Castle that the British were going to triple the strength of their forces in Ireland and intensify their operations, especially their searches and internment. 'All means of transport, from push bicycles up, will be commandeered, and allowed only on permit,' he warned de Valera.

Before implementing such a policy, however, Lloyd George was advised to make a genuine effort to negotiate a settlement. Otherwise, Jan Christiaan Smuts, the South African Premier, predicted, irreparable damage would be done to relations within the British Commonwealth. Smuts played a large role in persuading the British to offer peace talks. It was decided to use the occasion of the opening of the new Northern Ireland parliament by King George V on 22 June to foreshadow the more conciliatory approach.

This process was nearly upscuttled the same day when de Valera was arrested by British soldiers. As was mentioned, he had left instructions that Austin Stack should take over as acting President in the event of his arrest, which was a clear de-motion for Collins, who had taken over the previous December. To make matters worse, Collins despised Stack, who had a reputation for being a bit of a bungler, but Stack never got the chance to take over because de Valera was released within a matter of hours and was asked to await a communication from the British government. This was an invitation from Lloyd George for himself and anyone he wished to accompany him to come to London for talks with himself and Craig 'to explore to the utmost the possibility of a settlement'.

De Valera saw the simultaneous invitations to himself and Craig as a trap. Meeting with Craig on an equal basis would, for one thing, afford tacit recognition to partition. Moreover, he was afraid Lloyd George would use the inevitable differences between Belfast and Dublin to blame the Irish for the failure of the talks. Before responding to the invitation, therefore, de Valera said he would have to consult with the Irish minority, and he invited Craig and four unionists, elected to parliament for Trinity College, to meet him.

Smuts came to Dublin for secret talks on 5 July 1921 with the aim of getting an idea of the kind of peace settlement that the Dáil wanted, so that he could pass on the information to Lloyd George. De Valera explained to him that before there could be any talks, there would have to be a truce, and he also insisted that he would not take part in three-way talks that included Craig.

'What do you propose as a solution of the Irish question?' Smuts asked.

'A republic,' de Valera replied.

'Do you really think that the British people are ever likely to agree to such a republic?'

Such a status was so desirable, de Valera explained, the Irish side would agree to be bound by treaty limitations guaranteeing Britain's legitimate security needs, but he emphasised they would not be prepared to accept any limitations on dominion status. In short, he insisted the Irish people should have the choice between a 'republic plus treaty limitations and dominion status without limitations'.

'We want a free choice,' de Valera emphasised. 'Not a choice where the alternative is force. We must not be bullied into a decision.'

'The British people will never give you this choice,' Smuts replied. 'You are next door to them.' He then talked about the difficulties in South Africa following the Boer War and noted that when the people were subsequently asked if they wanted a republic, 'a very large majority' preferred free partnership with the British empire. 'As a friend,' Smuts added, 'I cannot advise you too strongly against a republic. Ask what you want but not a republic.'

'If the status of dominion rule is offered,' de Valera replied, 'I will use all our machinery to get the Irish people to accept it.'

Smuts reported on his Irish visit to a cabinet-level meeting in London next day. It was decided to accede to de Valera's demands for both a truce and the exclusion of Craig from the conference, but it was left to de Valera to take the initiative for Craig's exclusion. He did this by agreeing to meet the Prime Minister to discuss 'on what basis such a conference as that proposed can reasonably hope to achieve peace'.

The truce came into effect at noon on 11 July 1921. De Valera selected a delegation consisting of four cabinet colleagues, Griffith, Stack, Plunkett, and Robert Barton, as well as Erskine Childers, the acting Minister for Propaganda, to accompany him along with a number of others. On the evening of the truce, Collins tried to insist on his own inclusion in the negotiating team, but the President flatly refused to have him. This led to some bitter words between them.

De Valera's authorised biographers later contended that he feared the negotiations 'might end in a stalemate and that war might be resumed, so he saw no reason why photographers should, at this stage, be given too many opportunities of taking pictures of Collins'. The latter never accepted this explanation because, for one thing, it could not be squared with de Valera's attempt to send him to the United States earlier in the year.

Having been demoted in favour of Stack, of all people, Collins was now being ignored for people like Laurence O'Neill, the lord mayor of Dublin, and the Dáil deputy, Robert Farnan, who had been invited along with his wife. In addition, there were two secretaries, one of whom was Kathleen O'Connell. The delegation set up headquarters at the Grosvenor Hotel, but de Valera and Kathleen stayed with the Farnans in a private house acquired for them.

'At this moment,' Collins wrote in despondence, 'there is more ill-will within a victorious assembly than ever could be anywhere else except in the devil's assembly. It cannot be fought against. The issues and persons are mixed to such an extent as to make discernibility an utter impossibility except for a few.'

8

Preparing for
Peace Talks

As arrangements were being finalised for his meeting with the British, de Valera intimated privately that he would prefer to meet Lloyd George 'alone'. The Prime Minister jumped at the opportunity, and they had four private meetings during the next seven days.

The first of the four private meetings took place at 10 Downing Street on the afternoon of 14 July 1921. Immediately afterwards the Prime Minister dictated a note to his private secretary, Edward Grigg, indicating that de Valera had been more inclined to listen than he had expected and had 'listened well'. The same evening, however, he gave a very different account to another secretary, Geoffrey Shakespeare, as the latter drove him to an official dinner.

'I listened to a long lecture on the wrongs done to Ireland starting with Cromwell, and when I tried to bring him to the present day back he went to Cromwell again,' the Prime Minister said. 'It reminded me of a circus roundabout when I was a boy. I used to sit on a rocking horse that raced round and round after the horse in front, and when the roundabout came to rest I was still the same distance from the horse in front as when I started. That's how I ended with de Valera.'

Lloyd George, of course, was never renowned for his honesty. The account dictated to Grigg was probably the more accurate, because on this occasion de Valera had come to listen, but it was the fanciful version given to Shakespeare which found credence. Indeed it would come back to haunt de Valera in later years.

From the outset of the talks the Irish leader's aim was to show as little as possible of his own hand while trying to get the British to make some definite proposals. 'You will be glad to know that I am not dissatisfied with the general situation,' he wrote to Collins after a second meeting next day. Lloyd George had indicated he would be making a definite offer. 'The proposal will be theirs,' de Valera explained. 'We will be free to consider it without prejudice.'

'You confirm exactly what I was thinking about,' Collins replied in a letter exuding his own personality next day. 'Apart from the little unpleasant things on Monday evening,' he wrote, referring to their disagreement before de Valera left for London, 'have you got some little value from the talk?' He did not record his advice to de Valera, so there is no way of knowing whether that advice was heeded, but there can be little doubt that the Big Fellow did not take the President's advice about keeping a low profile himself.

'Their civilian and military heads have said that it would not be wise for Michael Collins to appear too publicly,' Collins wrote. He was therefore determined to go right into the Lion's den by requesting permission to visit his brother in the internment camp on Spike Island in Cork harbour. 'They said they could not be responsible for my safety in the Martial Law area, which means that they could not and would not be responsible for my non-safety,' he continued. 'The whole thing is an effort on their part to make us believe that they have irresponsible forces. My effort, of course, is the very contrary, and it will be seen later how I mean to make them responsible.'

Although Collins realised that the British were unlikely to make an acceptable offer at this early stage, he warned de Valera not to reject the proposals without allowing the Dáil to consider them. This would afford the Irish side the opportunity of demanding the release of all imprisoned members of the Dáil so that they — the democratically elected representatives of the people — could consider the offer. Several deputies had already been released since the truce, but Collins was particularly anxious to secure the release of Seán Mac Eoin, who was under sentence of death. 'No matter how bad the terms are,' Collins wrote, 'they would be submitted to a full meeting' of the Dáil.

De Valera had a third meeting with Lloyd George on 18 July. The Prime Minister began by observing that the notepaper on which de Valera had written to him was headed 'Saorstát Éireann'. What did Saorstát mean? he asked.

'Free state,' replied de Valera.

'Yes,' remarked the Prime Minister, 'but what is the Irish word for republic?'

De Valera was taken aback. Although his own command of the Gaelic language was not nearly as complete as he liked to pretend to non-speakers, he must have known that the leaders of the Easter Rebellion had used the term Poblacht na hÉireann (Republic of Ireland); but he now played dumb, possibly because he had no convincing explanation as to why the original term had been dropped and Saorstát adopted instead in 1919.

'Must we not admit that the Celts never were Republicans and have no native word for such an idea!' Lloyd George exclaimed triumphantly. He was content that Saorstát Éireann could be used in any agreement, provided the literal translation — Irish Free State — was used. He promised to send formal settlement proposals to de Valera before their next meeting.

There was widespread press speculation at this stage about de Valera's willingness to compromise, which was hardly surprising after he had spent six months making conciliatory gestures. *Le Matin*, the Paris newspaper, now quoted him as having supposedly said he would drop the word republic provided Ireland was given 'the substantial equivalent' to it. This was no doubt a leak inspired by somebody close to the talks, but de Valera denied making the statement or anything like it. 'The press give the impression that I have been making compromise demands,' he said. 'I have made no demands but one — the only one I am entitled to make — that the self-determination of the Irish nation be recognised.'

The formal British proposals, which were delivered to the Irish delegation on the night of 20 July, offered the twenty-six counties a form of dominion status, limited by defence restrictions curtailing the size of the Irish army, prohibiting a navy, and according Britain the right to obtain whatever facilities it might desire in time of war or international crisis. The proposals also included an insistence on free trade between Britain and Ireland, as well as a stipulation that the new Irish state should 'allow for full recognition of the existing powers and privileges of the parliament of Northern Ireland, which cannot be abrogated except by their own consent'.

On discussing the British terms with Lloyd George next day, de Valera indicated a willingness to accept unfettered dominion status as he had in his discussion with Smuts a fortnight before in Dublin and with various journalists earlier in the year, but he complained that the latest proposals did not even amount to an offer of dominion status, because the restrictive conditions meant that Ireland would have an inferior status to existing dominions like Canada and South Africa.

The Irish leader explained that he would agree to 'the status of a dominion *sans phrase*, on condition that Northern Ireland would agree to be represented within the all-Ireland parliament', according to Lloyd George. 'Otherwise, de Valera insisted that the only alternative was for the twenty-six counties to be a republic.'

'This means war,' the Prime Minister warned.

Refusing to be intimidated, de Valera became quite dismissive of the British offer. At one point he actually said he would not 'be seen taking these things home'. That stunned the Prime Minister, who had been threatening to publish proposals despite an agreement that neither side would do so without the prior approval of the other. 'Aren't you going to give me a considered reply?' Lloyd George asked.

'I'll give you a considered reply if you keep your part of the bargain.' If the British desired counter-proposals in the form of a considered reply, they would have to wait for it and keep their own offer secret in the meantime. With that de Valera departed, leaving the British document behind him. He later sent word to Downing Street to forward the proposals to him in

Dublin. In effect, he not only called Lloyd George's bluff but also made good his own threat not to be seen carrying the proposals home with him.

Of course, Lloyd George was more concerned with international opinion than with what the Irish people thought. He was not optimistic about de Valera coming up with an acceptable alternative. 'There is, I fear, little chance of his counter-proposals being satisfactory,' the Prime Minister wrote to King George V that day, 'but I am absolutely confident that we shall have public opinion overwhelmingly upon our side throughout the Empire and even in the United States when our proposals are published.'

The British proposals were a significant advance on anything previously offered to Ireland, so de Valera had to be careful. He knew the Irish side could not win an actual war with Britain and unless the Irish people were given some alternative other than 'continuing the war for maintenance of the Republic', he later admitted, 'I felt certain that the majority of the people would be weaned from us'. Hence he had to come up with an alternative for which the Irish people would be prepared to fight.

He hoped to persuade all concerned to agree to a settlement in which Britain would acknowledge Ireland's freedom and the Irish people would then freely accept the same *de facto* status as the dominions, without formally being a member of the British Commonwealth. He had not yet worked this out fully in his own mind when he presented his idea to the cabinet on 25 July. In fact, he had not even thought of a name for the plan.

It was a particularly thorny meeting, and things were not helped by his poor chairmanship. His cabinet meetings lacked discipline. Instead of considering one thing at a time, he tended to deal with everything together in the hope of reaching a general consensus. This would have been extremely difficult at the best of times, but it was almost impossible in a cabinet of eleven headstrong ministers, who were often joined by obstinate understudies. The discussions tended to ramble and they were often quite inconclusive. Ministers frequently came away with conflicting opinions about the outcome of discussions.

At the meeting on 25 July, Arthur Griffith and W. T. Cosgrave said the British offer was better than they had expected and Eoin MacNeill welcomed it, while Collins described it as 'a step forward', but Austin Stack was very critical, and Erskine Childers was also hostile. J. J. O'Kelly suggested that relevant documents should be circulated so that everyone could give the issues more consideration. Constance Markievicz agreed with him.

Cathal Brugha sat silently until de Valera asked him for his views after everyone else had spoken. Normally a quiet, reserved man, he nevertheless had definite views and did not believe in mincing words. Resolute and utterly fearless, he was prone to obstinacy. When he spoke everybody knew exactly where he stood. 'I haven't much to add,' Brugha said, looking straight at de Valera, 'except to say how glad I am that it has been suggested that we circulate these documents and consider them fully before we meet again, if for no other reason than to give you and the great masters of English you keep at your elbow an opportunity of extricating us from the morass in which ye have landed us.'

'We have done our best,' de Valera replied, 'and I have never undertaken to do more than my best.'

'We have proclaimed a Republic in arms,' Brugha reminded him. 'It has been ratified by the votes of the people, and we have sworn to defend it with our lives.'

'The oath never conveyed any more to me than to do my best in whatever circumstances might arise.'

'You have accepted a position of authority and responsibility in the Government of the Republic,' Brugha said striking the table with his fist. 'You will discharge the duties of that office as they have been defined. I do not want ever again to hear anything else from you.'

The meeting adjourned shortly afterwards and did not resume until two days later. By this time de Valera had decided to call his plan, External Association. He presented his colleagues with a memorandum arguing that 'the Irish people would be ready to attach themselves as an external associate to that partial league known as the British Commonwealth of Nations'. With this he overcame Brugha's objections, and the members of the government unanimously agreed that External Association would be acceptable.

Although Collins had been showing moderation within the government, he remained uncompromising in public. Indeed, he made another of his unauthorised pronouncements on 6 August, when the British announced the release of all members of the Dáil with the exception of Mac Eoin. Without as much as consulting anyone, Collins issued a statement warning 'there can and will be, no meeting of Dáil Éireann' without Mac Eoin's release.

De Valera had hoped to work quietly behind the scenes, believing it would be easier to secure the prisoner's release if the British were not forced to back down publicly, but the intervention by Collins destroyed any chance of this. De Valera therefore declared publicly that he could 'not accept responsibility for proceeding further in the negotiations' unless Mac Eoin was freed. The British cabinet promptly backed down and freed Mac Eoin.

In view of the fuss kicked up over the Mac Eoin affair, it was ironic that de Valera did not bother to consult the Dáil before formally rejecting the British offer in a letter to Lloyd George on 10 August 1921. 'On the occasion of our last interview,' he wrote, 'I gave it as my judgment that Dáil Éireann could not and the Irish people would not accept the proposals of your Government. I now confirm that judgment.' But the Dáil had not even met, and did not convene until the following week when it was presented with a *fait accompli* and was asked simply to endorse the reply.

At the time the Dáil was composed largely of people selected by the leadership of Sinn Féin to represent the party. Since independent thinkers could be difficult to handle, the individuals selected were those who would give unquestioning support to party leaders. As a result all initiative was invariably left in the hands of the few recognised leaders. The general body of the Dáil approved decisions rather blindly and took much for granted. As one member observed, 'nothing could well be less democratic in practice than the government which we recognised as the government of the Irish Republic'.

In his letter to the Prime Minister, de Valera stated that the restrictive conditions, which were unheard of in the case of the dominions, would be an interference in Irish affairs. 'A certain treaty of free association with the British Commonwealth group, as with a partial league of nations, we would be ready to recommend,' he wrote, 'had we an assurance that the entry of the nation as a whole in such an association would secure it the allegiance of the present dissenting minority, to meet whose sentiments alone this step could be contemplated.' The Irish factions would settle partition among themselves without resorting to force, if the British would just stand aside. 'We agree with you,' he added, 'that no common action can be secured by force.'

Back in 1918 de Valera had concluded that the British undermined the Irish Convention by assuring Ulster unionists that they would not be coerced. Bolstered by the assurance, unionists insisted on having their own way and, when the nationalists balked, the Convention inevitably ended in failure. 'It was evident to us,' de Valera wrote shortly after the Convention, that 'with the "coercion-of-Ulster is unthinkable" guarantee, the Unionists would solidly maintain their original position.' Thus when he gave Lloyd George a similar assurance on 10 August 1921, he was obviously accepting that some form of partition would be a part of any settlement.

The general election of May 1921 had resulted in Sinn Féin candidates being returned unopposed in all constituencies except Trinity College Dublin. Sinn Féin boycotted the opening of the Southern parliament in late June, and instead convened the second Dáil in public session in the Round Room of the Mansion House on the morning of 16 August. The hall was crammed and the atmosphere stifling when de Valera entered ceremoniously, followed by the rest of his ministry in Indian file. The gathering rose to give them a rapturous welcome. The President sat facing the general body as the Speaker read out the oath to the Republic in Gaelic, allowing the deputies to repeat it after him. For some, including de Valera, it was the first time they took the oath, obliging them to 'support and defend the Irish Republic . . . against all enemies, foreign and domestic'.

For many of the press this would be their first glimpse of Collins. Bertie Smyllie of *The Irish Times* remembered the previous October in the Dublin restaurant when a friend pointed to a small man with a fierce look and the build of a jockey and told him it was Collins. 'For nearly a year,' Smyllie wrote, 'I guarded the guilty secret of having been within touching distance of the most badly "wanted" man in Ireland.' Now he was about to learn the truth.

> I scanned the assembly in vain for the gentleman of the restaurant. None of the members resembled him in the very least, and I was just beginning to be afraid that Mr Collins was a myth after all, when the Clerk of the House began to call the roll. 'Mícheál Ó Coileáin' was the first name on the list.
>
> Here was no emaciated little jockey-man, furtive of eye, and hang-dog of look. A big, burly, broad-shouldered individual, with a shock of pitch black hair and a broad smile, walked across the floor and signed the register. All my preconceived ideas were shattered. I could not have been more completely taken aback if the Moderator of the General Assembly had answered to that name.

'At first sight Mr Collins is decidedly disappointing,' one reporter noted. 'He does not look a bit like a mystery man. And the stories we used to hear about him! One, I remember was that he had slipped up a chimney to escape arrest. I should like to see that chimney, for Mr Collins does not weight an ounce under fourteen stone. He is of more than average height, although you would not describe him as tall. His face is round and somewhat O'Connellesque, with a sharpish nose and a largely mobile mouth. A phrenologist would give him good marks for his head, and he has a fine pair of eyes, which are set off by arching brows. One misses that aggressive firmness that hits you when you look at Mr Arthur Griffith. Mr Collins can be firm enough when he pleases, but it is impulse rather than resolution that makes him dig his heels into the ground.'

De Valera delivered a short presidential address in which he spoke 'with great emphasis and obvious sincerity', according to one experienced reporter. Speaking off the cuff he caused a bit of a stir when he talked about the unmistakable answer given by the people in the recent general election. 'I do not say that the answer was for a form of government so much, because we are not Republican doctrinaires,' he said, 'but it was for Irish freedom and Irish independence, and it was obvious to everyone who considered the question that Irish independence could not be realised in any other way so suitably as through a Republic.'

In a further speech next day he elaborated by emphasising his personal readiness to compromise on partition and defence, as well as on the issue of association with the British Commonwealth. 'I would be willing to suggest to the Irish people to give up a good deal in order to have an Ireland that could look to the future without anticipating distracting internal problems,' he said. The unionists in the six counties were 'Irishmen living in Ireland', so he would be prepared to give up a lot to win them over. 'We are ready,' he emphasised, 'to make sacrifices we could never think of making for Britain.'

Having publicly indicated his willingness to compromise, he went even further in the following days when the Dáil met in private session. In the course of a rather rambling discussion on 22 August, he told deputies to realise that if they were determined to make peace only on the basis of recognition of the Republic, then they were going to be faced with war, except that this time it would be a real war of British reconquest, not just a continuation of limited military coercive measures 'in support of the civil police' to force some people to obey the law. In short, he was saying the War of Independence had not been a real war at all.

Although de Valera's remarks were couched in terms of outlining stark realities so the Dáil could decide the best course for itself, there was absolutely no room for doubt about his readiness to compromise, even on important issues like the partition question. He then gave the private session an idea of what he had meant when he talked publicly about making sacrifices for a secure settlement.

'The minority in Ulster had a right to have their sentiments considered to the utmost limit,' he explained, according to the official record. 'If the Republic were recognised he would be in favour of giving each county power to vote itself out of the Republic if it so wished.' The only other choice would be to coerce Northern Ireland, and he was opposed to such coercion because, for one thing, it would not be successful and, anyway, he warned, attempting to coerce the majority in Northern Ireland would be to make the same mistake the British had made with the Irish people as a whole.

On the issue of Commonwealth membership, he told deputies 'they could not turn down what appeared to be, on the face of it, an invitation to join a group of free nations provided it was based on the principles enunciated by President Wilson'. And he also indicated they would have to make concessions to satisfy Britain's security requirements.

'It was ridiculous of course to say that because Ireland was near Britain she should give Britain safeguards,' de Valera admitted. 'But,' he continued, 'America demanded such strategic safeguards from the small island of Cuba.' If security concessions were refused, Britain would depict the Irish as unreasonable, America would agree, as would the international community generally, and then 'England would be given a free hand to deal with Ireland'. The Irish people's natural moral right to their own island would be eradicated, just as the rights of the American Indians had been trampled on in North America. 'Look at America,' he said ominously, 'where are the natives? Wiped off the face of the earth.' The same thing could happen in Ireland. 'Unfortunately,' he added, 'they were very far away from living in a world where moral forces counted.' It was 'brute force' which mattered.

If the deputies insisted on securing recognition of the Republic as a totally independent country, they would be acting like prisoners in jail going on hunger strike to secure their freedom. If they won, they would have their freedom, but if they lost, they would be dead and have nothing. His choice of imagery was particularly significant because he personally had always been opposed to going on hunger strike.

De Valera gave only a vague outline of the kind of compromise alternative he had in mind. He demanded what amounted to a blank cheque to negotiate whatever agreement he thought fit, subject only to its subsequent approval by a majority of the Dáil. With the Dáil due to go back into public session for the formal election of the President, he told the secret session he wanted his own position clearly understood before allowing his name to be put forward.

'I have one allegiance only to the people of Ireland and that is to do the best we can for the people of Ireland as we conceive it,' he declared. 'If you propose me I want you all to understand that you propose me understanding that that will be my attitude.' All questions would be discussed, he said, 'from the point of view absolutely of what I consider the people of Ireland want and what I consider is best from their point of view'.

One deputy interjected to object to the President's stated willingness to allow each of the six counties to vote itself out of the Irish Republic, but de Valera reaffirmed his position. He would be ready to consider allowing counties or provinces to vote themselves out. 'I do not feel myself bound to consider anything,' he emphasised next day. 'I will not accept this office if you fetter me in any way whatever.'

'I cannot accept office except on the understanding that no road is barred, that we shall be free to consider every method,' he stressed again at another point. 'For example, the question of voting out of counties or provinces. That would be a way, if that came up, a way in which a certain result could be obtained. I would be ready to consider that.'

'We must be free to consider and above suspicion to deal with every situation that arises,' he emphasised. 'The policy of the Ministry will be that which they consider would be best for the country. The Ministry itself may not be able to agree and in such a case the majority would rule. Those who would disagree with me would resign.'

Although de Valera maintained throughout his life that he got into politics with the aim of avoiding partition, and he maintained for decades that ending partition was his main goal, he was obviously quite prepared to use the issue as a bargaining chip to secure more freedom for the South in 1921.

Brugha had said at the cabinet meeting of 25 July that the President had no right to consider anything which was not in line with allegiance to the Irish Republic: de Valera's latest remarks were a patent effort to ensure such an argument would have no validity in future. He concluded by proposing the Dáil adjourn for the day. No time was allowed for any debate on what he had said; there was no room for discussion, as far as he was concerned. If the deputies wanted him as President they had to accept his terms; otherwise, they should elect somebody else.

Before the election for President, however, there was a discrepancy to be cleared up about his actual title because, as de Valera himself admitted, 'no such officer had been created'. Back in 1919 he had simply assumed the title of President without the authority of the Dáil, which had elected him Príomh-Aire (Prime Minister). Now the discrepancy was somewhat obliquely tackled by slipping the term 'President' into a constitutional amendment limiting the size of the cabinet to seven specified officers — 'the President who shall also be Prime Minister' and the Ministers for Foreign Affairs, Home Affairs, Defence, Finance, Local Government, and Economic Affairs. De Valera was then duly elected President and he nominated Griffith, Stack, Brugha, Collins, Cosgrave, and Barton to the respective cabinet posts.

Following the appointment of his government de Valera released the text of a letter he had sent to Lloyd George the previous day confirming 'the anticipatory judgment' of the Dáil's rejection of the British offer. Exploiting the occasion with some theatrics to bolster his own carefully cultivated image of passionate sincerity, he explained it had been agreed with the British to publish the communication at noon and, as it was two minutes short of the appointed time, he waited in silence for the two minutes.

He then read the letter which concluded by intimating that the British should convene a conference to negotiate a democratic peace settlement. 'To negotiate such a peace, Dáil Éireann is ready to appoint its representatives, and, if your Government accepts the principle proposed, to invest them with plenary powers to meet and arrange with you for its application in detail.'

The conference was initially due to meet in Inverness, Scotland, on 20 September, but a wrangle developed over the Irish letter of acceptance. Lloyd George cancelled the conference and there followed a protracted exchange of letters and telegrams as he and de Valera sought to find an agreeable basis for the conference. There were essentially two points at issue in their correspondence. Initially de Valera stated that the conference should consider Ireland's right to self-determination, while Lloyd George insisted that it could only consider the detailed application of his July offer. De Valera promptly modified his demand to a request that the scope of the discussions be unconditional, but Lloyd George held his ground. In six of his seven communications he stressed that only the July proposals could be considered, but in his final telegram he backed down and agreed the conference could 'explore every possibility' of settlement 'with a view to ascertaining how the association of Ireland with the community of nations known as the British Empire may best be reconciled with Irish national aspirations'. This formula was essentially a compromise on their original positions, but de Valera seemed to get the better of the dispute because he had taken the more flexible stand.

The second point at issue involved recognition of Irish sovereignty. 'Our nation has formally declared its independence and recognises itself as a sovereign state,' de Valera wrote, in accepting the initial invitation to the Inverness conference. 'It is only as the representatives of that State and as its chosen guardians that we have any authority or powers to act on behalf of our people.' It was the publication of this letter which prompted Lloyd George to cancel the conference.

Although de Valera explained he was only stating that the Irish representatives recognised their own government, Lloyd George wanted no confusion on the point. There would be no question of his government affording recognition to the Dáil regime or even acknowledging that the Irish recognised their own regime as sovereign. He stressed this point in his telegram on 29 September when he extended another invitation for the Irish side to send representatives to a conference, this time in London.

De Valera's acceptance of this invitation involved dropping the self-recognition stand, though he did try to confuse the issue by stating that 'our respective positions have been stated and are understood'. This was an attempt to give the impression he was still holding to his earlier position, but his remarks were not a condition. They were a statement of fact, which could only be logically interpreted as an admission that he understood and accepted Britain's insistence that there could be no conference if he formally persisted with his claim of self-recognition.

'The communication of September 29th from Lloyd George made it clear that they were going into a conference not on the recognition of the Irish Republic, and I say if we all stood on the recognition of the Irish Republic as a prelude to any conference we could very easily have said so, and there would be no conference,' Collins later contended. 'What I want to make clear is that it was the acceptance of the invitation that formed the compromise. I was sent there to form that adaptation, to bear the brunt of it.'

During the protracted correspondence between de Valera and Lloyd George, the question of who would represent the Irish side was debated at length in cabinet. It was generally felt that de Valera should lead the delegation, but he declined for several reasons.

For one thing, if Lloyd George tried to use the kind of strong-arm tactics he used in July, de Valera contended the delegation could always use the necessity of consulting him as an excuse to prevent it being rushed into any hasty decisions. There were, however, much broader considerations.

'There seemed, in fact, at the time to be no good reason why I should be on the delegation,' he wrote. 'There was, on the other hand, a host of good reasons why I should remain at home. One had, above all, to look ahead and provide for the outcome of the negotiations. They would end either in a "make" or "break" — in a settlement based on the accepted cabinet policy of External Association, or in a failure of the negotiations with a probable renewal of war. In either case I could best serve the national interest by remaining at home.'

'If the outcome were to be the settlement we had envisaged, that based on External Association,' he continued, 'it was almost certain that it would be no easy task to get that settlement accepted wholeheartedly by the Dáil and by the Army.' He had already got a taste of the kind of bitterness such a proposal could generate, not only from Brugha's vitriolic outburst at the cabinet meeting on 25 July, but also during the controversy following his *Westminster Gazette* interview in the United States. External Association was essentially a more developed version of the idea first propounded in that controversial interview.

By not taking part in the negotiations, de Valera believed he would be in a better position to influence radical republicans to accept a compromise agreement. 'My influence,' he argued, 'would be vastly more effective if I myself were not a member of the negotiating team, and so completely free of any suggestion that I had been affected by the "London atmosphere".' In emphasising this point an allusion was made to Woodrow Wilson's failure to get the United States Senate to ratify the Versailles Treaty following his involvement in the Paris peace talks.

Those negotiating would inevitably have to compromise, but even this might not be good enough in the last analysis. Consequently, by staying at home, he would be in a position to rally both moderates and radicals to fight for an absolute claim, instead of a less appealing compromise. 'Were there to be a "break" with any substantial section of our people discontented and restless, the national position would be dangerously weakened when the war resumed. I was providing for this contingency much better by remaining at home than by leading the delegation.'

Throughout the struggle his primary role within the movement at home had been as a unifying figure. He had tried to be all things — a moderate among moderates and a radical among militants. And, as he wished to maintain that role, it made good sense not to get too involved in the nitty-gritty of the negotiations. In the last analysis his decision to stay in Dublin was based on sound, and selfish, political grounds. He knew that those who went were likely to become scapegoats — with the radicals if they compromised, and with the moderates if they did not. 'We must have scapegoats,' de Valera told his government.

Later in trying to justify his decision, he sought to rationalise his selfish considerations by cloaking them in the national interest, but in the process he seemed to argue a little too much. He contended, for instance, that by staying at home he could play his part 'in keeping public opinion firm' and also 'in doing everything possible to have the Army well organised and strong'. Such reasons sounded rather hollow coming from someone who had spent most of the Black and Tan period in the United States.

Griffith, Collins, and Cosgrave rejected the President's arguments. They insisted he should head the delegation. A vote was therefore taken. When Stack, Brugha, and Barton supported de Valera, the vote was a tie and he was therefore able to use his own vote to exclude himself. He then proposed that Griffith and Collins should lead the delegation, even though he knew that they were more amenable to the British terms than any other members of the cabinet.

'That Griffith would accept the Crown under pressure I had no doubt,' de Valera admitted to a friend a few months later. 'From the preliminary work which M. C. [Collins] was doing with the IRB, of which I had heard something, and from my own weighing up of him I felt certain that he too was contemplating accepting the Crown.'

Stack made 'a weak kind of objection', according to himself. He complained that 'both gentlemen had been in favour of the July proposals'. They objected. They had not advocated accepting the British terms. Well, Stack explained, he got the impression that Griffith only wanted some modifications. 'Yes,' said Griffith, 'some modifications.'

Griffith agreed to act as chairman of the delegation, but the President had trouble persuading Collins. 'I was somewhat surprised at his reluctance for he had been rather annoyed with me for not bringing him on the team when I went to meet Lloyd George earlier on in July,' de Valera recalled. 'I now considered it essential that he should be on the team with Griffith.'

'They by themselves alone, it seemed, would form a well balanced team,' the President continued. 'Griffith would, I thought, have the confidence of the "moderates" and Collins that of the IRB and the Army.' He added that 'with these two as the leaders no one could suggest that the delegation was not a strong and representative one'. Collins had a number of reasons for not wishing to be a part of the delegation. Like de Valera, some were selfish, but he did not mention those to the cabinet.

'Of course,' he later wrote, 'we all knew that whatever the outcome of the negotiations, we could never hope to bring back all that Ireland wanted and deserved to have, and we therefore knew that more or less opprobrium would be the best we could hope to win.' Nobody could be expected willingly to court such infamy, and Collins was no exception. 'I had got a certain name, whether I deserved it or not,' he later told the Dáil, 'and I knew when I was going over there that I was being placed in a position that I could not reconcile, and that could not in the public mind be reconciled with what they thought I stood for, no matter what we brought back.'

'For my own part,' Collins explained on another occasion, 'I anticipated the loss of the position I held in the hearts of the Irish people as a result of my share in what was bound to be an unsatisfactory bargain. And to have and to hold the regard of one's fellow countrymen is surely a boon not to be lost, while there is a way to avoid it.'

Instead of arguing on those lines, however, Collins actually made many of the same points in favour of his own exclusion that de Valera had already made for not going himself. He could be of use to the delegation if he were 'kept in the background (against all eventualities) to be offered in a crisis as a final sacrifice with which to win our way to freedom'.

'For three hours one night, after the decision had been made to send a delegation to London, I pleaded with de Valera to leave me at home and let some other man take my place as a negotiator,' Collins recalled. 'The point I tried to impress on de Valera was that for several years (rightly or wrongly makes no difference) the English had held me to be the one man most necessary to capture because they held me to be the one man responsible for the smashing of their Secret Service organisation, and for their failure to terrorise the Irish people with their Black-and-Tans.' It really did not matter whether the legend was true, or was simply the product of press sensationalism. 'The important fact,' he emphasised, 'was that in England, as in Ireland, the Michael Collins legend existed. It pictured me as the mysterious active menace, elusive, unknown, unaccountable, and in this respect I was the only living Irishman of whom it could be said.' In effect, Collins was arguing that he was seen as the real leader; so he would be in a better position to influence republicans to accept a compromise if he was not involved in the negotiations. Since the British considered him a treacherous gunman, the delegation could always delay in order to consult him or demand further concessions to placate him. The Irish delegation would thereby be able to get the best possible terms from the British.

De Valera was not impressed. 'His argument,' according to Collins, 'was that aside from whatever truth might be in my view the menace I constituted was of advantage to us.' That was how de Valera explained the situation, but his insistence on the inclusion of Collins was motivated not so much by the belief that he would be an asset to the delegation as the realisation that it would be too risky not to include the real architect of the Black and Tan war. Collins, after all, had been questioning the President's judgment on military and political matters in the lead-up to the truce and had bitterly resented his exclusion from the delegation that went to London in July. Moreover, he had deliberately stampeded the President in the matter of demanding Mac Eoin's release, and de Valera, with his acute sensitivity to criticism, was no doubt suspicious of the implied criticism in the Big Fellow's lavish praise of James O'Mara in the Dáil on 26 August.

De Valera made little more than passing reference to O'Mara's contribution in his report on American fund-raising, but Collins, who was responsible for sending O'Mara, pointedly singled him out in his report as Minister for Finance. 'But for the pioneering work done by Mr James O'Mara, they would not have been nearly so successful in raising the money abroad,' Collins told the Dáil. Probably very few people in the Dáil would have understood the significance of what Collins said about O'Mara, but it certainly would not have gone over the head of somebody as touchy as de Valera. The best way of committing Collins to any settlement terms, therefore, was to have him as part of the negotiating team.

Collins suggested that Stack should go, but the latter refused. So did Brugha, which was just as well as far as de Valera was concerned.

'Cathal is the honestest and finest soul in the world, but he is a bit slow at seeing fine differences and rather stubborn, and the others would not seek to convince him, but would rather try to outmanoeuvre him, and there would be trouble,' de Valera explained afterwards.

'If I were going myself,' he added, 'I would certainly have taken him with me.'

'It is not a question of individuals now,' the President told Collins at the time. 'It is a question of the nation and you and I and the cabinet know that the British will not make their best offer in your absence.'

Despite his reservations, Collins relented. 'It was a job that had to be done by somebody,' he said. In the past he had never shirked responsibility and now was no different, even though he was warned by several people not to trust de Valera. On the other hand, however, the President had courageously confronted the Dáil hard-liners by emphasising his unwillingness to exclude the possibility of any kind of settlement, and he had sent Harry Boland to the United States to prepare opinion there for a compromise settlement.

'I had no choice,' Collins explained afterwards. 'I had to go.' But he made it clear to everyone that he was going against his better judgment.

After Collins accepted, the cabinet next sought three men 'to work in well' with Griffith and himself. Barton, the only other member of the cabinet to be included, felt he was chosen for propaganda purposes because he was a wealthy Protestant landowner. Two lawyers, George Gavan Duffy and Éamonn Duggan, were included as 'mere legal padding', according to de Valera.

Throughout the remainder of his life, de Valera went to great pains trying to justify his actions in relation to the selection of the delegation.

While the reasons he gave to the cabinet were undoubtedly factors, there were other reasons that he was only prepared to elaborate on privately. In December 1921 he explained these in some detail in a letter to Joe McGarrity, and again to Lord Longford more than forty years later.

He admitted to McGarrity that he knew that Griffith and Collins were more amenable to the British proposals, but he selected them because he thought they would be 'better bait for Lloyd George — leading him on and on, further in our direction. I felt convinced on the other hand that as matters came to a close we would be able to hold them from this side from crossing the line.'

De Valera had it all worked out in his own mind. He had Erskine Childers appointed chief secretary to the delegation. He believed that Childers would have a strong influence over Barton, who was like a younger brother. The two of them were double first cousins. Childers's father and Barton's mother had been brother and sister, as had Barton's father and Childers's mother, but Childers's parents had died when he was quite young and he had been reared by Barton's parents, with the result that Barton and he were as close to brothers as any two cousins could be.

The President, who believed that Childers would hold sway over his younger cousin, wrote that the two of them 'would be strong and stubborn enough as a retarding force to any precipitate giving away by the delegation'. If de Valera really suspected that Griffith and Collins would be weak, however, why did he not include Childers in the delegation proper? It was idiotic to think that a secretary would be able to control the delegation through his influence with Barton, especially when de Valera had questions about Barton's ability to cope with pressure. Shortly before the truce, for instance, he actually wrote to Collins that he thought that Barton was on the verge of a breakdown. Yet a few months later he supposedly relied on him to restrain Griffith and Collins.

Childers was really included not so much to hold Griffith and Collins as to keep an eye on them. De Valera made the mistake of assuming he could control them himself, even though he had saddled them with the full responsibility of negotiating a settlement by insisting that the cabinet give them full plenipotentiary powers.

When the Dáil was asked to ratify the selection of the representatives, Cosgrave moved that the President should head the delegation himself. But the proposal was promptly undermined by his own assistant minister, Kevin O'Higgins, who endorsed de Valera's decision. Griffith was then ratified as chairman, but when the name of Collins was submitted for formal ratification, he explained that he 'would very much prefer not to be chosen'. He said that he believed de Valera should head the delegation.

'To me the task is a loathsome one,' Collins said. 'If I go, I go in the spirit of a soldier who acts against his judgment at the orders of a superior officer.'

If he was not President and as such a symbol of the Republic, de Valera said, he would go himself. But as this was now out of the question, it was 'absolutely necessary that the Minister for Finance should be a member' because he 'was absolutely vital to the delegation', de Valera emphasised. That settled the matter. The nomination of Collins was put to the Dáil and promptly approved. The other names were then approved without any discussion.

Following his selection, however, Gavan Duffy objected to the plenipotentiary powers being given to the delegation. He thought they were too broad and he moved that they should be curtailed, but de Valera — who had twice previously threatened to resign if full and unfettered plenipotentiary powers were denied to the delegation — was insistent. He said the Dáil would be able to reject the treaty after it was signed, if it proved unsatisfactory. 'Remember what you are asking them to do,' the President said. 'You are asking them to secure by negotiations what we are totally unable to secure by force of arms.' With that Gavan Duffy withdrew his motion.

Members of the delegation were furnished with credentials signed by de Valera authorising them 'to negotiate and conclude on behalf of Ireland, with the representatives of His Britannic Majesty, George V, a Treaty or Treaties of Settlement, Association and Accommodation between Ireland and the community of nations known as the British Commonwealth'.

The President thought he could prevent the delegation signing anything that he did not want by having the cabinet issue them with the following secret instructions:

(1) The Plenipotentiaries have full powers as defined in their credentials.

(2) It is understood however that before decisions are finally reached on the main questions that a despatch notifying the intention of making these decisions will be sent to the Members of the Cabinet in Dublin and that a reply will be awaited by the Plenipotentiaries before the final decision is made.

(3) It is also understood that the complete text of the draft treaty about to be signed will be similarly submitted to Dublin and reply awaited.

(4) In case of break the text of final proposals from our side will be similarly submitted.

(5) It is understood that the Cabinet in Dublin will be kept regularly informed of the progress of the negotiations.

Since the Dáil had already conferred full plenipotentiary powers, the instructions from the cabinet, an inferior body, were not legally binding in any instance in which they limited the powers of the delegation. Indeed, from the instructions themselves, it would seem that they were not intended to limit those powers, because the first of the instructions basically re-affirmed that the delegation had the full authority 'to negotiate and conclude' a treaty. There was, of course, a moral obligation to try to comply with the instructions, which had been accepted as a kind of informal under-standing. In fact, the word 'understood' was used in each of the three clauses that might be seen as limiting the delegation's authority.

The instructions were obviously issued to ensure that de Valera would ultimately have a kind of control over the delegation. 'I expected to be in the closest touch with it,' he wrote. 'In fact, it was my intention to be as close almost as if I were in London.'

In short, de Valera wanted his bread buttered on both sides. He wanted the real power, or ultimate control over the delegation, while he was putting all of the responsibility for whatever happened on the members of the delegation. He provided them with an incomplete document known as Draft Treaty A, in which External Association was outlined in treaty form.

It envisaged Britain not only recognising Ireland as 'a sovereign independ-ent state' but also renouncing 'all claims to govern or to legislate' for the island. In return, Ireland would become externally associated with the British Commonwealth, enjoying equal status with the dominions and being separately represented at imperial conferences. Instead of the common citizenship of the dominions, External Association would substitute reciprocal citizenship — the subtle difference being that Irish people would be Irish citizens rather than British subjects, but they would enjoy the same rights and privileges as British subjects while residing within the British Commonwealth, and British subjects would enjoy reciprocal rights with Irish citizens while resident in Ireland.

The President had thought it necessary to seek reciprocal rights because he was afraid of losing the sympathy of Irish people throughout the British empire, if the Dáil looked for a settlement that would make Irish immi-grants aliens within the Commonwealth. In many respects the distinction between reciprocal and common citizenship represented on a personal level the distinction between External Association and dominion status at the national level. External Association was designed to ensure that Ireland would legally have 'a guarantee of the same constitutional rights that Canada and Australia claimed', according to de Valera.

His controversial *Westminster Gazette* interview was the inspiration for another aspect of Draft Treaty A, which called for the British Common-wealth to guarantee 'the perpetual neutrality of Ireland and the integrity and inviolability of Irish territory'. In return Ireland would commit 'itself to enter into no compact, and take no action, nor permit any action to be taken, inconsistent with the obligation of preserving its own neutrality and inviolability and to repel with force any attempt to violate its territory or to use its territorial waters for warlike purposes'. Once ratified by the respective parliaments the treaty would be registered with the League of Nations at Geneva and the dominions would try to get 'the formal recognition of Ireland's neutrality, integrity and inviolability by the League of Nations in conformity with the similar guarantee in favour of Switzerland'.

In spite of its title, Draft Treaty A was not really a serious effort to draw up a draft treaty, as has often been suggested. It was strictly a negotiating document which the Irish delegation would present in response to the British proposals of 20 July. De Valera proposed a series of contingency documents be drafted. Draft Treaty B would be the document the delegation would publish as the Irish alternative in the event the negotiations collapsed, while Draft Treaty S would be the document the plenipotentiaries would use for internal purposes as their prospective treaty.

De Valera gave Gavan Duffy and Childers partially completed copies of Draft Treaties A and B, but he did not attempt to advise them on Draft Treaty S. 'We must depend on your side for the initiative after this,' he wrote to Griffith. The choice of the term 'your side' was possibly an unconscious reflection of the division within the cabinet even at that early stage.

As far as negotiating tactics went, de Valera's advice was that the most difficult issue, the question of the Crown, should be left until last.

'Supposing they refuse to do this?' Griffith asked.

'Well, you can put it to them that we ought first of all discuss the things there will be no great dispute about.'

'But supposing they insist on considering the question of the Crown first?'

'You can only use your powers of persuasion. After all, they cannot want to have a break on the first day.'

Griffith pressed for further advice. 'Well,' said de Valera, 'there you have the situation. You'll have to make the best of it.'

'Oh, wait now,' cried Griffith. 'That won't do!'

'Why?'

'It's not enough to say "make the best of it".'

'I'm not talking about a settlement,' de Valera explained. 'I'm talking about the method of handling the negotiations. You see, if we get them to concede this and this and this and this, and then come to a stumbling-block, like the question of the Crown, which they say is a formula, then we can put the question before the world and point out that they want to renew the war on us for a formula.'

In the days following the selection of the delegation there were some ominous developments as far as Collins was concerned. He was the one who had reorganised what became known as the IRA in the aftermath of the Easter Rebellion, but now de Valera announced that he was reorganising it again in view of the influx of tens of thousands of volunteers following the truce. One of his first acts was to have Stack take over as assistant chief of staff of the IRA, as part of a restructuring of the general headquarters staff. Stack had actually been appointed to the post in November 1919 when he was getting on with Collins, but he never functioned in the position. Brugha not only was determined that Stack should now function as deputy chief of staff, but seemed even more determined to ensure that Mulcahy or Collins did not get their way.

'Before you are very much older, my friend,' Brugha wrote to Mulcahy on 6 September, 'I shall show you that I have as little intention of taking dictation from you as to how I should reprove inefficiency or negligence on the part of yourself or the D/I, [director of intelligence, Collins] as I have of allowing you to appoint a deputy chief of staff of your own choosing.' His real grievance against Mulcahy was that the latter had not been 'controlling' Collins for a considerable time. Stack was therefore being inserted to control the Big Fellow.

When Mulcahy insisted on appointing Eoin O'Duffy instead, Brugha warned that 'the whole General Staff will be appointed by the Cabinet on the recommendations of the Minister for Defence'. The headquarters staff, which was intensely loyal to Collins, resolutely resisted the efforts to impose Stack. People like Liam Lynch and Seán Russell, who would later break with Collins and Mulcahy, strongly supported them in this controversy which dragged on for the next three months.

In the midst of what was going on many people urged Collins to stay in Dublin. 'I had warned Collins not to go unless de Valera also went,' Tim Healy wrote, 'but he was too unselfish and unsuspecting to refuse.' Whatever about being unselfish, he was far from unsuspecting, though he did try to give a contrary impression afterwards. 'Before the negotiations began,' he later contended, 'no doubt of de Valera's sincerity had place in my mind.'

There were mixed feelings within the supreme council of the IRB. Harry Boland was strongly in favour of Collins going. 'From what I have learned since I came back from America,' Boland wrote to an IRB colleague, 'you will not succeed in overthrowing the British militarily. If it is a question between peace and war, I'm for peace. If there are negotiations, I think "Mick" should go, and I'll tell you why — in my opinion a "gun man" will screw better terms out of them than an ordinary politician.'

Other IRB people were decidedly uneasy about de Valera staying at home while insisting that Collins should go. 'There were certain members of the Supreme Council who thought there was something sinister behind the suggestion,' Seán Ó Muirthile, the secretary of the supreme council, wrote. They therefore warned Collins.

'We had the temerity to tell him that he was likely to be made a scapegoat in the matter,' Ó Muirthile recalled.

'Let them make a scapegoat or anything they wish of me,' Collins replied. 'We have accepted the situation as it is, and someone must go.' He went with his eyes open.

'You know the way it is,' Collins wrote to his trusted aide, Joe O'Reilly, on the day the conference began in London. 'Either way it will be wrong. Wrong because of what has come to pass. You might say the trap is sprung.'

9

The Treaty Negotiations

The Irish delegation was housed in two separate buildings at 22 Han's Place and at nearby 15 Cadogan Gardens, where the delegation had its offices. Collins and the younger men stayed at Cadogan Gardens, while the women and older men resided at Han's Place.

Lloyd George met the Irish delegation at 10 Downing Street on 11 October 1921 and shook hands warmly with each of the plenipotentiaries and then led them to the cabinet room, where members of the British delegation were already seated. This procedure had been followed to avoid a possible scene, as the Prime Minister was afraid the Irish might balk at shaking hands with Sir Hamar Greenwood, the Chief Secretary for Ireland, and some of the British were obviously not enamoured with the possibility of shaking hands with Collins, the man they considered the head of the murder gang.

Greenwood was seated at the end of the British side of the table with Sir Laming Worthington-Evans, the Secretary of State for War, next to him. At the other end of the same side sat Sir Gordon Hewart, the Attorney General, with Churchill, then Colonial Secretary, next to him, followed by Lord Birkenhead, the Lord Chancellor. Lloyd George took up his place in the centre on Birkenhead's right, and two secretaries, Tom Jones and Lionel Curtis, sat on either side of the Prime Minister in chairs that were slightly withdrawn from the table. Sir Austen Chamberlain, the Conservative leader, would normally sit on his right, but he was absent from the opening conference due to a back ache.

In all there were seven plenary sessions during the next two weeks of the conference. Collins said very little at any of the four sessions during the first week, which was taken up with general discussions on the July proposals.

From the outset the British took the offensive by insisting that their July proposals would have to form the basis of any agreement. The Irish representatives, on the other hand, were trying to get External Association, even though they only had 'a hazy conception of what it would be in its final form', according to Barton. 'What was clear was that it meant that no vestige of British authority would remain in Ireland. The compromise would be as regards our foreign relations.' Initially therefore the Irish followed de Valera's line in trying to hold back on the question of the Crown, until they knew what they were 'going to get in exchange for some accommodation regarding it.'

Collins was clearly ill-suited to this type of negotiating. He had little time for the endless beating around the bush. 'I've come to call a spade a spade,' he wrote on the opening day. 'It's the only name I know it by.' But, of course, he soon found it impolitic to be as candid as he would have liked. As a result he found the first day with its two plenary sessions particularly trying. 'I never felt so relieved at the end of any day, and I need hardly say I am not looking forward with any pleasure to resumption,' he wrote to de Valera. 'Such a crowd I never met.'

He was obviously deeply troubled. He had a reputation for being anti-clerical ever since his emigrant days in London when he called for the extermination of the Roman Catholic clergy, or in the GPO when he mocked Volunteers who sought a priest to make what they feared might be their last confession during the Easter Rebellion. It may well have been indicative of the weight upon his mind that he went to early-morning mass and communion at a nearby church each day of the negotiations.

The task confronting the relatively inexperienced Irish negotiators was a formidable one, especially for Collins. At thirty-one he was easily the youngest of the delegates on either side of the conference table. All the others were in their forties or fifties. Nevertheless he was soon to find himself in the un-enviable position of sharing much of the leadership responsibility over a divided delegation that obviously lacked the full confidence of the cabinet at home. Yet he had to face a determined British delegation consisting of an experienced and seasoned team of negotiators, headed by Lloyd George, backed up by the most powerful men in the Conservative Party as well as his own wing of the Liberal Party.

Collins quickly found that he formed a rapport with Birkenhead, but he disliked others with a varying intensity. Of course all of them were pro-fessional politicians and most were lawyers — two types of people for whom Collins had a distinct aversion. He was convinced the genial Lloyd George — whom he found 'particularly obnoxious' — and Winston Churchill, the Prime Minister's Liberal colleague, were both unprincipled individuals who would do anything for political gain.

'Churchill was as rude as could be', according to Barton, who noted that the future British leader 'sat through the conference making paper boats and looking quite hostile. He always looked at us as if he would be glad to cut our throats, a very different attitude from Lloyd George, who was so affable.'

Chamberlain was more formal and reserved, but Collins disliked him because he was very cold and seemed like a snob who looked down on the Irish representatives. Collins had contempt for Greenwood, the Chief

Secretary for Ireland and the most vocal defender of the Black and Tans. He also disliked Hewart, but apparently left no account of his attitude towards the only other member of the British delegation, Worthington-Evans.

Initially the conference concentrated on issues like defence, finance and partition, with the Irish delegation contending that the restrictive conditions in the British proposals really amounted to a denial of the dominion status supposedly being conferred. Ireland could not enjoy that status if it were compelled to make unprecedented concessions because, for one thing, the dominions were supposedly completely free, with the right to leave the British Commonwealth, if they wished.

'Bonar Law said that the dominions could vote themselves out of the British Empire,' Collins noted.

'All that means is that we might not undertake military operations against the dominions which did so,' replied Lloyd George.

'What would happen in that case probably is civil war in the dominion, which was in South Africa's case,' Churchill interjected.

'You are asking more from us than from them in this naval business,' Collins contended.

'No,' the Prime Minister insisted. After some further discussion, he proposed setting up 'a sub-committee to go into the naval and air defence'.

'We would like that very much,' Collins replied.

Three different sub-committees were established to consider defence, finance, and questions relating to violations of the truce. Collins was the only Irish plenipotentiary on the three sub-committees. As the finance sub-committee only met once and its deliberations were inconclusive, the other two were more important. On those Collins was helped by some of his own men like Emmet Dalton, J. J. O'Connell, Eoin O'Duffy, and Diarmuid O'Hegarty, together with Erskine Childers, who soon proved to be a particularly unhappy choice, because he was 'altogether too radical and impractical' in the estimation of Collins.

Childers was not in any way shy about pushing his own strong views. On the third day of the conference, he was with Collins when they met Churchill and the First Sea Lord, Admiral David Beatty, who was about to leave for the United States, where he was to represent Britain at the Washington Naval Conference.

'Now, gentlemen,' Childers began, 'I mean to demonstrate that Ireland is not only no source of danger to England, but from the military standpoint, is virtually useless.'

'This announcement staggered me probably more than it did the other two,' Collins recalled. 'It was ridiculous balderdash. I felt like wanting to get out of the room, but I naturally realised that I must make the pretence of standing by my colleague. Churchill and Beatty exchanged glances, and then gave Childers their attention again.'

'Take the matter of Irish bases for English submarine chasers,' Childers continued. 'From the viewpoint of naval expediency Plymouth is a far better base than any port on the Irish coast.'

'You really think so?' Beatty asked.

Childers insisted such was the case. 'For instance,' he said, 'supposing Ireland were not there at all?'

'Ah,' replied the admiral with a smile, 'but Ireland is there.'

'And how many times have we wished she were not!' interjected Churchill.

While the hypothetical approach adopted by Childers would have been appreciated by the more theoretical mind of a mathematician like de Valera, it had no appeal for the practically minded Collins, who did not even bother to relate the details of the hypothetical argument. He felt the British destroyed it. Using a map marking the locations of ships sunk by U-boats during the Great War, Beatty demonstrated that in some situations certain Irish ports would obviously be more strategic than Plymouth for anti-submarine warfare. Childers had no real answer.

'I had an idea,' Collins continued. Pointing to the French coast, he suggested that Le Havre would make 'an excellent base for British forces engaged in hunting submarines'.

'Quite so,' replied the admiral with another smile, 'but we can't take the French port!'

'If that constitutes duress,' Collins later explained, 'I admit we were under duress. But to my way of thinking it is plain talk, right talk, and the kind of talk I prefer my opponents to use.'

Shortly after the meeting Collins wrote to Kitty Kiernan, who had by then become his fiancée, that he preferred people to be open. 'I would like people to say what they themselves think and mean,' he wrote. Yet even at that early stage of the conference he had found himself having to support arguments in which he did not really believe.

This happened again on 18 October when Childers insisted that Ireland should have the right to defend herself. He was claiming, in essence, that the denial of this right was a denial of Ireland's 'existence as a nation'. But in a memorandum submitted to the British before the meeting, he conceded that 'Ireland would be very unlikely to plan the building of submarines which are eminently an offensive weapon out of harmony with her purely defensive policy.'

As far as Collins was concerned, however, this concession made a non-sense of the Irish arguments. He felt the right to have a navy to defend the island was useless if Ireland was not allowed to have submarines, seeing that the Irish people simply could not afford to build and sustain a regular navy. Believing that attack was the best method of defence, Collins thought that submarines, which were comparatively inexpensive to build and cheap to run, were the country's only hope of defending itself properly.

Some might have thought that Ireland was too poor to have a navy, but Collins had declared in a speech as early as 17 February 1918 in Ballinamuck, County Longford, that within three years of independence the country would be able to have ten submarines and 'they would make England keep her Dreadnoughts and Super-Dreadnoughts in their own ports'.

By renouncing the right to have submarines, however, Childers effectively undermined the Irish case by conceding 'a point that really mattered. This cannot be stated too emphatically,' Collins later contended.

He realised, of course, that concessions would have to be made on defence, or he would not have allowed Childers to present the memorandum to the British in the first place. The difference between himself and Childers was that once Collins recognised the necessity to concede a point, he was prepared to carry the concession to its logical or practical conclusion. Yet, like one of those politicians he so despised, he now went through the motions of arguing the case for the country's right to defend itself. 'As a practical man,' he asked Churchill, 'do you think that we are going to build a big navy?'

'Honestly, I do not,' replied Churchill, 'and why then should we get into these depths? Why should these questions be raised?'

'It is we really who are dealing with this in a practical manner,' Collins continued. But he did not believe in what he was arguing. He was therefore deeply uneasy within himself.

'Trouble everywhere,' he wrote to Kitty Kiernan next day. 'Last night I escaped all my own people and went for a drive alone.' He admitted to feeling quite lonely and made arrangements for her to spend some time in London with him.

Collins was finding the negotiations especially trying in that he obviously felt he had to act as a politician himself. 'To be a politician,' he wrote to a friend, 'one needs to have the ability to say one thing and mean another; one needs to be abnormally successful at the "art" of twisting the truth. Can you wonder that I think and think yet never manage to achieve peace of mind?' He was afraid that anything he might say would likely be twisted and used against him. 'I do not in the least care for the false atmosphere of these discussions,' he wrote.

In this frame of mind he tended to become undiplomatically irritable. During one sub-committee meeting, Emmet Dalton recalled that Churchill was making a forceful case about Irish violations of the truce.

'Have we any answer to these?' Collins scribbled a note to Dalton.

'No,' Dalton replied.

Collins then listened for a while longer before suddenly becoming exasperated and slamming his fist on the table. 'For Christ sake,' he said to Churchill, 'come to the point.'

His loquacious counterpart was momentarily speechless. He sat there with a stunned expression on his face. At that point Collins erupted with an infectious laugh. Even Churchill soon joined in the laughter, thereby dissipating much of the force from his carefully prepared case.

Yet this was only a moment of light relief for Collins who was otherwise deeply agitated. He was finding it necessary to hide his true feelings not only from the British but from some of his own colleagues, especially Childers, who was keeping in touch with the members of the cabinet in Dublin. It would not be long before Collins would come to the conclusion that those in Dublin were the 'real problem' in the search for a settlement.

There was no Ulster clause in Draft Treaty A, for example, and the delegation had to deal with the question at the fourth plenary session of the conference before the clause had arrived. Griffith did most of the talking for the Irish side, with Collins and the others merely interjecting, while Lloyd George did most of the talking for the British.

The Ulster question had undermined Gladstone and it would have defeated his own government if he had not introduced partition, the Prime Minister contended. 'Ulster was arming and would fight,' he said. 'We were powerless. It is no use ignoring facts however unpleasant they may be. The politician who thinks he can deal out abstract justice without reference to forces around him cannot govern.' He added that he tried to persuade Craig and Carson to accept a united Ireland but they refused.

'They said their followers would desert them if they did,' Lloyd George explained. 'It is a mistake to assume that the population of Ulster for the time being is opposed to partition. It is not. I am glad that de Valera has come to the conclusion which we favoured that force is not a weapon you can use. It would break in your hands. We should have a terrible civil war and you would draw men from all parts into the vortex of the whirlpool. Mr Collins shakes his head. He knows Ireland. I know Great Britain and the Empire. It would resolve itself into a religious war. You do not want to begin your new life with a civil war which would leave you with despoliation in its train. Therefore I am glad that we are agreed that force is impossible.'

From early on it became apparent that the Irish negotiating position had been weakened by de Valera's assurance ruling out the use of force. Lloyd George was content to allow Dublin induce Belfast to agree to unity by any peaceful means. 'We promise to stand aside and you will have not only our neutrality but our benevolent neutrality,' he emphasised.

'It is not intended to use force, not because Ulster would not be defeated in a fight,' Collins said, 'but because defeat would not settle the matter.' He made it clear, however, that some provisions would have to be made for many of the nationalists who had been included in Northern Ireland against their will. 'If we are not going to coerce the North East corner, the North East corner must not be allowed to coerce,' he emphasised. 'There might,' he added, 'be a plan for a boundary commission or for a local option, or whatever you may call it.'

A few days later Collins went on to predict that there would be civil war if Northern Ireland retained the whole of the six counties. Nationalist representatives were prepared to meet with the unionists and be reasonable with them, he maintained, 'but if they refused our proposal and declared they were going to hold our people under their control, then freedom of choice must be secured in order to enable the people to say whether they would come with us or remain under the Northern Parliament'.

The Prime Minister asked what would be done about isolated nationalist areas within unionist strongholds, such as west Belfast. 'It would be necessary to make a deal,' Griffith explained. Very well, Lloyd George replied, the Irish could deal among themselves. But Griffith insisted that the British would have to arrange the deal, because they had created the problem in the first place.

The financial issue — Britain's demand that Ireland should contribute to its war debt — never really posed a serious problem during the London conference. It was eventually entrusted to separate negotiations, but the manner in which Collins dealt with the issue when the sub-committee on finance met for the first and only time on 19 October provides a typical example of his unsuitability for such negotiations.

Instead of countering the British demand by building a case to lead the British to the point where they might, of their own accord, suggest an acceptable compromise, Collins began by suggesting a compromise himself. He contended that, as Ireland had been grossly overtaxed during the nineteenth century, the new state should now start out with a clean slate. 'If we go into all past details,' he said, 'you will find that you owe us money. I say let us get rid of all these details, and let us treat the past as the past.'

The British did not buy his suggestion. But Collins persisted. 'I will put some arguments that may surprise you,' he said.

'Mr Collins will never surprise me again,' replied Worthington-Evans.

'According to my figures, our counter-claim works out at £3,940,000,000,' Collins declared.

The British were staggered. 'I suppose that dates from the time of Brian Boru,' the Chancellor of the Exchequer exclaimed. 'How much did we owe you then?'

'Oh no,' replied Collins, 'it is the capital sum since the Act of Union. Of course I have included in my calculations your restrictions on our capital development.'

Finding himself poorly prepared and his advisers out of their depth, Collins secretly enlisted the services of Joseph Brennan, who had been serving with the British administration in Ireland. Even though Brennan was technically on the Crown side, Collins was always prepared to enlist the help of such Irishmen, regardless of their past political affiliation. Indeed, such people had formed the backbone of his intelligence system. 'Never mind what the record of these people was in the past,' Collins told Childers, 'let us assume now that they are in the Irish cause up to their necks.'

His choice of advisers, however, caused him some problems with those remaining in Dublin. De Valera wrote that Brugha felt he was in charge of defence and that consequently the advisers on defence 'should have been summoned through him' so he 'would like to know why that course was not followed'. Likewise, the President added, the constitutional advisers should have been summoned through Stack. Griffith responded accepting the principle. By then nearly all of the advisers had already been chosen, so it did not matter. Yet it was another instance in which the delegation did not challenge an apparent infringement of its powers. The plenipotentiaries were only answerable to the Dáil, which appointed them, and certainly not to the individual members of the cabinet.

If Collins saw ominous implications in the President's letter, these were only minor to the sense of foreboding he must have felt next day when the delegation learned from the morning press that de Valera had sent an open telegram to Pope Benedict XV in response to an exchange of messages between the Pope and King George V. In responding to a message from the Pope, the British King had expressed the hope that the negotiations would 'achieve a permanent settlement of the trouble in Ireland and may initiate a new era of peace and happiness for my people'. De Valera complained that this implied the Irish strife was an internal British problem and the Irish people owed allegiance to the King, whereas Ireland had already declared her independence.

Although de Valera's inference was not unreasonable, the King's message was really vague enough to be interpreted differently. The whole matter was ambiguous, as the President himself admitted in his own telegram to the Vatican. He had actually used the King's message as an excuse to reproach the Pope, whose telegram was the really irritating one from the Irish standpoint. 'By this message,' de Valera explained to Griffith, 'the Vatican recognised the struggle between Ireland and England as a purely domestic one, for King George, and by implication pronounced judgment against us.'

Under the circumstances, it was understandable that Griffith and Collins should be annoyed that while they were involved in tense and delicate negotiations, the President had — without even warning them — revived the self-recognition issue by insulting the British King in an attempt to chide the Pope. But the affair also had a deeper significance in that it fuelled Collins's uneasiness by confirming his suspicions that de Valera was preparing the ground to lay all the blame for any compromises on the delegation by covering up the fact that he had already compromised on the self-recognition issue by agreeing to the conference. Moreover, the publication of the telegram brought the allegiance question to the fore in the negotiations, much to the chagrin of Griffith and Collins.

They only managed to stall the British a little longer by agreeing to present the Irish delegation's first formal proposals the following week. Before tackling the issue, they sought counsel from the cabinet. Childers was instructed to write to Dublin for advice on the best way of approaching the allegiance problem. He explained to the President that the delegation felt it could respond with an outright refusal to consider allegiance, or they could 'obtain a field of manoeuvre and delay the crucial question' by saying that 'they would be prepared to consider the question of the Crown', if agreement were reached on all other issues. But the cabinet never responded.

That weekend Collins returned to Dublin and pleaded with de Valera to go back to London with him, but the President refused on the grounds that there was no necessity at the time. He added, however, that he would go later if it could be shown that his presence was really required. In an undated letter written to a friend during the negotiations, Collins alluded to his growing distrust of de Valera. 'I was warned more times than I can recall about the ONE,' he wrote. 'And when I was caught for this delegation my immediate thought was of how easily I walked into the preparations. But having walked in I had to stay.'

The uneasiness that Collins felt about his cabinet colleagues at home was compounded by Childers sending reports to Dublin. These included his own observations even when those conflicted with the views of the leaders of the delegation. Collins described the reports as 'masterpieces of half-statement, painting a picture far from the true state of things'. He also surmised — correctly as it turned out — that Childers was also sending secret messages to de Valera.

This was an intolerable situation. Griffith had personally detested Childers for years, and now Collins came to look on him as a kind of spy within the delegation. They therefore decided to eliminate him from the actual discussions by secretly suggesting to Andy Cope that Lloyd George should invite them to a private discussion after one of the plenary sessions of the conference. Lloyd George jumped at the opportunity of cutting out Childers, whom he considered a retarding force. The seventh plenary session of the conference was pretty much like the others. It discussed the Irish counter-proposals in a general way, with no significant progress, except in the area of defence.

Birkenhead contended that if Dublin afforded Britain the defence facilities which the Royal Navy considered necessary, no enemy of Britain would recognise Irish neutrality, with the result that the right to remain neutral that the Irish were claiming would be 'reduced to a shadow — a meaningless trophy which would give you nothing'.

'We accept the principle that your security should be looked after, though the working out of the details might be very difficult,' Griffith replied.

'Britain had won on defence,' Frank Pakenham (later Lord Longford) declared in *Peace by Ordeal*. If this was so, then they had really won before

the negotiations had ever begun, because de Valera had long ago acknowledged that Ireland would accommodate Britain's legitimate security needs.
That had been at the very heart of his controversial *Westminster Gazette*
interview as well as many of his subsequent statements. Griffith's acceptance
of the principle was merely an affirmation of the line already taken.

———————————

The first informal meeting between the leaders of the two delegations took
place after the seventh plenary session of the conference on 24 October. The
other members of the Irish delegation did not know that it was actually
Collins who had asked for the meeting, so they were unaware that it was
their colleagues — not the British — who had inspired the rationalisation
of the conference, which never again met in plenary session. Instead there
were twenty-four informal sub-conference meetings, at which no
secretaries were present. Childers was thereby totally excluded from the
sub-conference meetings, while Barton was invited to only three of them
— all of which were in the final thirty-six hours of the conference.

In his account of the day's discussions Griffith merely reported that
Collins and himself 'were asked to see Lloyd George and Chamberlain this
evening'. He did not bother to mention that they themselves had asked that
they should be asked. Instead he let people believe that the British had asked
for smaller meetings because Lloyd George supposedly thought that the
Irish hostility towards Greenwood — whom Collins described as 'a man
who earns my personal detestation' — was having an unhelpful effect on
the discussions.

At the first sub-conference meeting Griffith said that the Irish delegation
could not accept the Crown. But, he added, if everything else was satisfactory, he would 'undertake to recommend it'.

'What does it involve?' Collins asked.

'The oath of allegiance,' replied Lloyd George.

'That's a pretty big pill,' said Collins, 'Cannot we have an oath to the
constitution?'

Afterwards Lloyd George confidently predicted that the Irish would
accept the Crown. 'If we came to an agreement on all other points,'
Griffith explained in his report to Dublin, 'I could recommend some form
of association with the Crown.'

Even though the form that this connection would take was not
mentioned, de Valera assumed Griffith was thinking of allegiance. So when
the Dublin-based members of the cabinet met to consider the report on
25 October, the President asked whether anyone present would be willing

to give allegiance to the British Crown. All answered in the negative, including Kevin O'Higgins.

De Valera therefore warned the delegation that agreeing to allegiance was out of the question. 'If war is the alternative we can only face it,' he wrote, 'and I think that the sooner the other side is made to recognise it, the better.'

Griffith and Collins were furious. They considered the warning an unjustifiable interference with their powers. When they had Childers ask for advice on the question some days earlier, none had been forthcoming, yet when they took one of the courses outlined by Childers, they were, in effect, admonished. Griffith therefore drafted a strong letter of protest and insisted that the whole delegation sign it. 'We strongly resent, in the position in which we are placed, the interference with our power,' he wrote. 'Obviously, any form of association necessitates discussion of recognition in some form or another of the head of the association.'

De Valera was stunned by the tone of the protest. 'There is obviously a misunderstanding,' he replied. 'There can be no question of tying the hands of the plenipotentiaries beyond the extent to which they are tied by their original instructions. These memos of mine, except I explicitly state otherwise, are nothing more than an attempt to keep you in touch with the views of the cabinet here on the various points as they arise. I think it most important that you should be kept aware of these views.'

The President soon came to appreciate the delegation's approach. He realised that a form of recognition would indeed be compatible with External Association, and he enthusiastically endorsed the idea, eventually persuading Brugha and Stack to agree to recognise the King as head of an association to which Ireland would be externally linked.

The Irish side, especially those in Dublin, tended to underestimate the weakness of Lloyd George's political position at the head of a coalition in which his own party was in a distinct minority, while the Conservatives enjoyed an overwhelming majority within parliament. In the coming days there would be two separate challenges to the government — one, a back-bench revolt in the House of Commons, and the other at the Conservative Party conference in Liverpool.

Many Conservatives, or Unionists as they were more commonly called at the time, were anxious to withdraw their support from the coalition and set up a government of their own. Unionist die-hards, led by people like Colonel John Gretton and Captain C. C. Craig, a brother of the Prime Minister of Northern Ireland, tabled a motion of censure against the government over its Irish policy. The challenges were not something that could be dismissed lightly, especially as there was an obvious leader waiting in the wings. Earlier in the year Bonar Law had stepped down as leader of the Conservative Party and resigned from the cabinet for health reasons, but his health had since improved dramatically. Now he was ready to take up where he had left off. He had always been a particularly strong supporter of the Irish unionists, with the result that the Conservative dissidents had an obvious candidate in him, seeing that he had the experience and the political stature to form a government.

With the censure vote due to be taken on 31 October 1921, Lloyd George was anxious to get a distinct indication from the Irish delegation that a settlement was possible in order that he might keep a majority of the Conservatives in line. He therefore had a private meeting with Griffith at Churchill's home on the eve of the censure motion.

Lloyd George had long preferred social settings for negotiations. 'If you meet for social purposes,' he explained during the Versailles Treaty negotiations, 'you can raise a point. If you find you are progressing satisfactorily, you can proceed, otherwise you can drop it. Much business can be done in that manner.' He would make considerable progress while closeted alone with Griffith during the next couple of weeks.

The influence of Churchill's role in the negotiations was later exaggerated by many people. He did not play that big a part in the talks. He attended only four of the sub-conference meetings — the one at his home and three others were in the last thirty-six hours before the Treaty was signed. None of his own team really trusted him. Even his Liberal colleague, Lloyd George, only included him in the delegation because he was too dangerous to leave out. Had Churchill really got on very well with Collins, he would undoubtedly have played a much greater role in the negotiations.

Much has been made of this meeting in Churchill's home. 'Griffith went upstairs to parley with Mr Lloyd George alone,' Churchill recalled. 'Lord Birkenhead and I were left with Michael Collins meanwhile. He was in his most difficult mood, full of reproach and defiance, and it was very easy for everyone to lose his temper.'

Collins looked on Churchill as a political animal who would 'sacrifice all for political gain'. Churchill was 'inclined to be bombastic' and 'full of ex-officer jingo', according to Collins, who wrote that he did not 'actually trust him'.

'You hunted me night and day,' Collins exclaimed. 'You put a price on my head.'

'Wait a minute, you are not the only one,' said Churchill, who took down a framed copy of a reward notice for his own recapture after he had escaped from the Boers some twenty years earlier. 'At any rate it was a good price — £5,000. Look at me — £25 dead or alive. How would you like that?'

'He read the paper, and as he took it in he broke into a hearty laugh,' Churchill continued. 'All his irritation vanished. We had a really serviceable conversation, and thereafter — though I must admit that deep in my heart there was a certain gulf between us — we never to the best of my belief lost the basis of a common understanding.'

Birkenhead was the member of the delegation with whom Collins got on best. He had the reputation of being the staunchest unionist on the British side, while Collins was supposedly the staunchest republican on the Irish side. They were the people whose followers were the most extreme and if there was to be a settlement, they would be seen as the people who compromised most. Hence they understood each other.

'I prefer Birkenhead to anyone else,' Collins wrote on 15 November. 'He understands and has real insight into our problems — the Dublin one as much as another.'

It was a strange relationship because Collins generally disliked lawyers. He felt that people like Gavan Duffy were so enamoured with the sound of their own voices that they talked too much and overelaborated just to hear themselves talk. Collins did not have the patience to listen to that kind of thing, with the result that he was pleasantly surprised to find that Birkenhead — reputed to have one of the most brilliant legal minds of his day — was a very different type of person. 'If all the British delegation had his capacity for clear thinking, capacity for work and getting ahead, things would be much easier,' Collins wrote. Describing the Lord Chancellor as 'a good man', he summed him up as a 'Lawyer, but with a great difference. Concise.'

Birkenhead had been one of Sir Edward Carson's staunchest backers in the fight against Home Rule and had led the prosecution team at the trial of Sir Roger Casement in 1916. The Casement case came up in conversation, and Birkenhead arranged for Collins and Duggan to see the notorious 'black diaries' in which Casement recorded details of some of his homosexual activities. When a public clamour was raised to save him from the gallows following his trial, the British leaked extracts of the diaries to the press in order to discredit Casement and stop the humanitarian campaign on his behalf. This was followed by a campaign in Irish nationalist circles charging the British with having forged the diaries, but Collins had no doubts about their authenticity after he saw them.

While Collins was closeted with Birkenhead and Churchill downstairs, Griffith was upstairs holding out the possibility of accommodating the British on association, the Crown, and defence, if the British could assure 'the essential unity' of Ireland. This was the kind of talk Lloyd George had wanted to hear. 'If I would give him personal assurances on these matters,' Griffith reported, 'he would go down and smite the die-hards and fight on the Ulster matter to secure essential unity.'

Lloyd George was 'in an expansive and optimistic mood' that night as Geoffrey Shakespeare drove him back to Downing Street. 'We have really made progress tonight for the first time,' the Prime Minister said. 'I really feel there is a chance of pulling something off.'

Griffith had agreed to provide the Prime Minister with a personal letter of assurance, which could be used to bolster wavering Conservative support. 'Provided I was satisfied on every point,' Griffith wrote, 'I was prepared to recommend recognition of the Crown, the formula in which this recognition was to be couched to be arrived at at a later stage.' He also agreed to recommend free partnership with the British Commonwealth, the formula defining the partnership to be arrived at later.

When Barton, Gavan Duffy, and Childers saw the proposed letter, they objected strongly. They felt that such a letter, even if signed only by Griffith, would commit the whole delegation, and they argued that it conceded too much to the British. Collins and Duggan took little part in the argument, which became quite heated. Next morning Gavan Duffy put his objections in writing.

Having already agreed to write a personal letter to Lloyd George, Griffith refused to back down on that point, but he did agree to redraft the letter to secure the approval of the whole delegation. This was accomplished by stating that in return for Irish unity he was 'prepared to recommend that Ireland should consent to a recognition of the Crown as head of the proposed Association of free states'.

Griffith and Collins discussed this letter with Lloyd George, Birkenhead, and Chamberlain on 2 November. The British tried to get them to drop the indefinite article — 'a' — from the phrase 'a recognition of the Crown', but Griffith refused. He also rejected an amendment stipulating that he would recommend that Ireland agree to be associated within the British Commonwealth, but he assented when the British suggested 'free partnership with the other States associated within the British Commonwealth'.

'I was prepared,' the final version of Griffith's letter to Lloyd George read, 'to recommend a free partnership with the other States associated within the British Commonwealth, the formula defining the partnership to be arrive at in later discussion. I was, on the same condition, prepared to recommend that Ireland should assent to a recognition of the Crown as head of the proposed Association of free States.' All this, of course, 'was conditional on the recognition of the essential unity of Ireland'.

'The tactical course I have followed,' Griffith explained to de Valera, 'has been to throw the question of Ulster against the question of association and the Crown. This is now the position: the British Government is up against Ulster and we, for the moment, are standing aside. If they secure Ulster's consent we shall have gained "essential unity" and the difficulty we shall be up against will be the formula of association and recognition. You will observe my words, which they accept, is consistent with External Association and external recognition.'

Despite strong representations from Gavan Duffy on 4 November, de Valera refused to demand that the conference go back into plenary session.

As far as he was concerned, everything was going beautifully according to plan. Griffith and Collins were acting as bait for Lloyd George, and Childers and Barton were preventing them from going too far. In fact, the President warmly endorsed the way the delegation had been handling things.

'I have been of the opinion from the very beginning of the negotiations that if the conference has to break the best issue to break on would be "Ulster", provided we could so manage it that "Ulster" could not go out with the cry "attachment to the Empire and loyalty to the Throne",' de Valera wrote to Griffith on 9 November. 'There can be no doubt whatever that the Delegation has managed to do this admirably. The danger now is that we shall be tempted, in order to put them more hopelessly in the wrong, to make further advances on our side. I think, as far as the Crown–Empire connection is concerned, we should not budge a single inch from the point to which the negotiations have now led us.'

Lloyd George was initially confident that he could persuade Craig to accept the principle of Irish unity. On Saturday, 5 November, Craig 'discussed conditions under which an all-Ireland parliament would function', according to Lloyd George. 'But when he came again on Monday afternoon he had changed: Under no circumstances could Ulster look at an all-Ireland parliament.' Craig, who had just come from a meeting with Field Marshal Wilson and Worthington-Evans, was utterly intransigent.

Lloyd George was despondent and talked seriously about resigning. 'I had about half an hour with him alone during which he paced up and down the cabinet room, more depressed than I had seen him at all since the negotiations began,' Tom Jones noted in his diary.

'Craig will not budge one inch,' the Prime Minister said. 'He is sending for his cabinet as he will not be responsible alone for turning our offer down. This means, therefore, a break on Thursday. I would like you to see Griffith and Collins and prepare them for it. I shall go out. I will not be a party to coercing the South.'

'What about Bonar?' Jones asked. 'Isn't he helping you?'

'No, he is not. He's had six months' rest and has come back and is busy.'

'I always knew he was fanatical on Ulster but,' Jones said, 'I thought with peace in sight he would take a statesman's view on the situation.'

When Lloyd George talked about resigning, he was not thinking in terms of retiring but of stepping down as a tactic to provoke a political crisis. He thought that Birkenhead and Chamberlain would continue to support him and that the Conservatives might not then be able to form a government without the support of their leader in either of the houses of parliament, but Churchill warned him that Bonar Law would take up the challenge. 'Why should he not do so?' Churchill asked. 'The delusion that an alternative Government cannot be formed is perennial.'

This advice merely emphasised the weakness of the Prime Minister's position. He felt that he could not even rely on Churchill, who was from his wing of the Liberal Party. 'I cannot rely on Winston in a crisis,' Lloyd George told Jones. 'I never could.' Jones was convinced that the Prime Minister was serious about resigning. He therefore urged him to stall.

'There is just one other possible way out,' Lloyd George said. 'I want to find out from Griffith and Collins if they will support me on it; namely that the 26 Counties should take their own dominion parliament and have a Boundary Commission.' He asked Jones to sound them out on this.

Next day Jones talked with Griffith and Collins for about an hour and a half at the Grosvenor Hotel. 'Collins was obviously very much upset at the news but it is much harder to tell what Griffith feels about anything as he keeps himself well in hand,' wrote Jones, who now tried to enlist the two Irishmen in a bid to save the British government as there was a danger that Bonar Law might be able to take over as Prime Minister without a general election.

'I then threw out the suggestion of the southern parliament plus Boundary Commission as my own and asked them what did they think of it,' Jones continued. 'Griffith said that they preferred a plebiscite. Collins did not like the suggestion at all because it sacrificed unity entirely. I agreed, but what was the alternative? Chaos, Crown Colony Government, Civil War. We were bound to try every device to avert that. Griffith was not alarmed at the proposal and I left promising to sound the P. M. upon it.'

Jones told Griffith and Duggan next day that Lloyd George 'was prepared to play the Boundary Commission as an absolutely last card if he felt sure that Sinn Féin would take it, if Ulster accepted'.

'It is not our proposal,' Griffith replied, 'but if the P. M. cares to make it we would not make his position impossible. We cannot give him a pledge, but we will not turn him down on it. We are not going to queer his pitch. We would prefer a plebiscite, but in essentials a Boundary Commission is very much the same.'

On 12 November Lloyd George met privately with Griffith and explained that he wished to put the Boundary Commission idea to Craig. If the latter rejected a Boundary Commission, it would make it more difficult for the British Conservatives to support him because Belfast would then be in the position of demanding self-determination for the six counties yet denying the same right to the nationalist population of the area, even though the nationalists formed a greater proportion of the population of Northern Ireland than the unionists did in the island as a whole. The Prime Minister said his position would be undermined, however, if the Irish delegation publicly repudiated the proposal after he made it.

Griffith assured him, as he had already assured Jones, that he would not publicly repudiate the proposal. To make sure there was no confusion on the point, the Prime Minister had Jones outline the Boundary Commission idea in a memorandum. When this was shown to Griffith next day, 13 November, he assented to its contents.

Griffith had already reported fully on his private meeting with Lloyd George the previous day. In fact, it was his longest report of the whole conference, but he did not subsequently mention that he nonchalantly approved the memorandum shown to him by Tom Jones. It only confirmed what he had already reported, so he possibly attached no significance to the document. He did not even mention it to Collins. The latter had returned to Dublin that weekend, along with Barton, Duggan, and Childers. While there, Childers made another futile attempt to get de Valera to intervene to stop the sub-conference set-up.

Again the President refused to interfere. Not only that, but the cabinet basically endorsed the way things were being handled in London. 'Whilst the utmost co-operation should exist between Dublin and London,' the cabinet concluded on 13 November, 'the plenipotentiaries should have a perfectly free hand but should follow original instruction re important decisions.' Collins and Barton were present at that meeting, as were Duggan and Childers, who had been invited to sit in as observers.

In the following days Griffith, who was unfortunately ailing and would be dead within a year, actually asked Collins to take over the effective leadership of the Irish team, but they both felt that the move would have to be kept secret. 'He and I recognise,' Collins wrote, 'that if such a thing were official it would provide bullets for the unmentionables.'

The two of them frequently discussed their apprehensions about those in Dublin. 'You realise what we have on our hands?' Griffith asked.

'I realised it long ago,' replied Collins.

'We stand or fall in this together,' said Griffith.

Collins agreed. As a youngster he had admired Griffith greatly. Now he was proud to be working with him, notwithstanding the obstacles facing them. It was the one redeeming feature in the whole situation as far as he was concerned. The longer the negotiations continued, the more critical Collins became of the cabinet at home.

'From Dublin,' he wrote, 'I don't know whether we're being instructed or confused. The latter I would say.' But this was not totally fair. When de Valera had expressed the views of the cabinet on 25 October, his letter had been bitterly resented. Hence his reluctance to give further advice was understandable.

———

During the talks Birkenhead told Sir Archibald Salvidge, an influential Conservative, that Collins and Churchill were 'bosom friends', but this should be viewed within the context in which the conversation took place. At the time Birkenhead was terrified that the Conservative Party conference was going to call on the party to withdraw from government. Salvidge was known to be leaning in that direction and, as he was an extremely influential political boss in the Liverpool area, his support was considered crucial at the party conference in Liverpool. Birkenhead therefore went to plead in person with him not to pull the plug on the government because, he contended, there was a real chance of a settlement.

In explaining the situation he exaggerated the role being played by Churchill, by saying that Collins was being won over by Churchill, who was seen as a political adventurer by Conservatives. The son of a former leader of the Conservative Party, Churchill had abandoned the Tories to join the Liberals. That he would get on with Collins would hardly have been surprising to a Conservative, but it would have been something altogether different if Birkenhead had admitted that he himself was getting on well with Collins. This might have alarmed Salvidge to the possibility that it was Collins who was winning over Birkenhead and not the other way round. The Conservatives were already deeply suspicious of people like Lloyd George and Churchill, and the news that Birkenhead might be going soft on the Irish nationalists would undoubtedly have fuelled their uneasiness. Indeed, if one examines the starting positions of both sides, it is possible to make the case that Collins actually influenced Birkenhead more than the other way round.

Since Collins used a forthright negotiating approach in which he tended to press for an acceptable compromise almost from the outset of any discussion, it is possible to determine the extent to which his willingness to compromise was influenced during the protracted negotiations. There was, in fact, as will be seen later, no really significant shift in his views on the major issues — partition, association, the Crown, and defence.

He undoubtedly gave different impressions to different people. When a nationalist deputation from Northern Ireland called on him during the negotiations, for instance, he indicated that partition would not be acceptable in any form. There was 'no principle whatever to justify' the cutting off of the six counties, he explained. 'In operation it would be a manifestation of the tribalistic interpretation of the principle of self-determination reducing it to an absurdity unless as originally enunciated the nation was understood as the unit — no other unit is possible in practice.' Yet he had already indicated a readiness to the British to recognise the separation of the area in the north-east in which the unionists had a majority.

He was obviously misleading somebody. But whom? Was he fooling the British by feigning a readiness to accept repartition, or the nationalist deputation by pretending to be unwilling to accept any form of partition? In the light of subsequent events, it is not possible to answer these questions with any degree of assurance. Indeed, it is not beyond the bounds of possibility that he was deceiving both, and himself into the bargain.

Collins was playing a complicated and dangerous game in deliberately giving different impressions to different people. On the allegiance question, for example, he obviously tried to convey the idea that he was prepared to take a firmer stand against the British than was apparently the case.

'They'll give us *anything practically* but say they must preserve the link of the Crown,' he explained in a letter home at the beginning of the third week of the conference. 'A very nominal thing is all they want.'

'Go to the devil says I in effect,' he wrote. Yet he was not the kind of man to be bothered about nominal things, and it was intrinsically unlikely that he would have felt differently at this stage.

There can be no doubt from his private correspondence that he had firmly come to the conclusion that dominion status was the most they could expect to get for the time being. He wanted to accept it, but dared not admit this openly, because neither he nor Griffith really knew how far they could go with those in Dublin.

'What do we accept?' Griffith asked him.

'Indeed what do we accept?' Collins wondered. If they accepted any British terms, he was afraid it would be considered 'a gross betrayal or a similar act of treachery'. He was already in favour of a settlement on dominion lines. 'Dominion status will be to a large extent beneficial to us,' he wrote to a friend on 2 November 1921. 'I do not look on the above as being anywhere near a finalised solution. It is the first step. More than this could not be expected.'

Collins was so intent on concealing his views from those in Dublin that there was very little mention of his contributions in any of the Irish reports of the negotiations. This allowed for speculation about the role which Lady Hazel Lavery played in the negotiations.

Hazel Lavery was a society flirt. She was an American who married the Irish painter Sir John Lavery, who was much older than her. She was actually ten years older than Collins, but was a strikingly good-looking woman who claimed to be in her mid-thirties. She had become enchanted with the Irish cause some years earlier and sought a meeting with Collins by persuading her husband to ask the Big Fellow to sit for a portrait.

Hazel Lavery passed on the invitation through Collins's sister Hannie, but it was quite late in the negotiations — 18 November, in fact — before he went to Lavery's studio at Cromwell Place. 'One morning he walked into my studio, a tall young Hercules with a pasty face, sparkling eyes and a fascinating smile,' Sir John Lavery wrote. 'I helped him off with a heavy coat to which he clung.'

'There is a gun in the pocket,' Collins said excusing himself casually.

Lavery noted that Collins sat uneasily, always facing the door. That night Collins described the sitting in a letter to Kitty Kiernan. It was 'absolute torture', he wrote, 'as I was expected to sit still, and this, as you know, is a thing I cannot do'.

Hazel Lavery took a fancy to Collins and figuratively threw herself at him. It is not unreasonable to assume that, notwithstanding his denials, the virile thirty-one-year-old may have availed of her sexual favours, but this does not mean she influenced his views on the negotiations.

History is replete with peripheral figures who believed that they had a vital input in critical events in which their involvement was actually little more than token. Hazel Lavery's biographer Sinéad McCoole wrote that 'the Laverys' friends believed Hazel played a central diplomatic role during the Treaty negotiations, particularly as an influence on Collins', but Collins had already indicated the kind of settlement he was seeking and the most her influence could have done was merely to reinforce his convictions.

In the video, *The Shadow of Béal na Bláth*, Colm Connolly contended that Hazel Lavery played a vital role in getting Churchill and Collins together, but this is absurd because Collins and Churchill attended only three sub-conference meetings together. The first of those at Churchill's home was almost three weeks before Collins even met Hazel Lavery, and the others were on the final day of the negotiations.

Sinéad McCoole contended that 'Collins was a welcome guest at the Laverys' and would often stay late into the night reading books from their shelves.' But there were in fact only eighteen nights between the time he first went to Cromwell Place and the signing of the Treaty, and Collins spent at least six of those in Dublin or travelling to and from Dublin. It seems much more likely therefore that while this friendship began towards the end of the negotiations, it grew as a result of meeting after mass at Brompton Oratory, where Collins went every morning. The relationship would have blossomed afterwards, and those Cromwell Place dinner parties that Collins attended, according to McCoole, were probably during the visits that Collins made to London after the signing of the Treaty.

Collins was extremely busy at the time. He returned to Dublin most weekends. During November the dispute over the appointment of a deputy chief of staff of the IRA came to a head. Mulcahy had continued to insist on the appointment of Eoin O'Duffy instead of Stack, while Brugha continued to demand that the whole general staff be appointed by the cabinet on the recommendation of himself as Minister for Defence. Mulcahy stated that his acceptance of the post of chief of staff had been contingent on the cabinet's acceptance of all of his recommendations. 'If the Ministry decide to make an appointment to such an important Staff position against my judgment,' he warned, 'I cannot accept the responsibility attaching to any position on the Staff.'

The whole thing reached a proverbial boiling-point at a meeting on 25 November 1921. De Valera suggested a compromise in which O'Duffy would be deputy chief of staff, acting on Mulcahy's behalf, while Stack would be 'Cathal's ghost on the Staff'. During the ensuing discussion O'Duffy, who was prone to hysterics, indignantly took the objection to his appointment as an affront to himself. 'After a very short time,' Mulcahy continued, 'Dev rose excitedly in his chair, pushed the small table in front of him and declared in a half-scream, half-shout: "Ye may mutiny if ye like, but Ireland will give me another Army", and he dismissed the whole lot of us from his sight.'

It was against the backdrop of this kind of turmoil behind the scenes at home that Collins was so uneasy in London. To make things worse, he was really arguing on points on which he had no real conviction himself. Even though he was already inclined towards full dominion status, for instance, he still argued for External Association, which he depicted as simply a means of ensuring that Ireland would have the same *de facto* status as Canada. To back up his argument he outlined the situation, as he saw it, in a personal memorandum.

'The only association which it will be satisfactory to Ireland, to Great Britain and the dominions for Ireland to enter will be one based, not on the present technical legal status of the Dominions, but on the real position which they claim, and have in fact secured,' Collins argued. 'In the interest of all the associated states, in the interest above all of England herself, it is essential that the present *de facto* position should be recognised *de jure*, and that all its implications as regards sovereignty, allegiance, [and] constitutional independence of the governments, should be acknowledged.'

Collins went on to argue that External Association 'might form the nucleus of a real league of nations of the world'. Even though there had been a clear swing towards isolationism in the United States, he suggested that the Americans might even be willing to enter such a league if it were 'more fully recognised how far the claim of the Dominions to independent statehood had matured, and the progress which had been made in finding ways in which independent nations may act in concert'. Under the circumstances it was hardly surprising that Chamberlain described the memorandum as 'extraordinarily interesting though sometimes perverse and sometimes Utopian'.

When the British came back on 29 November with an offer to include in the proposed treaty any phrase desired by the Irish to ensure that Ireland would have the same *de facto* status as Canada and the other dominions, they essentially offered the assurance that Collins was seeking. 'With this offer,' Griffith wrote, 'they knocked out my argument.' He might just as well have written that they demolished de Valera's argument, which Collins and himself had been dutifully pressing.

At this point the negotiations were coming to a conclusion. Lloyd George informed Griffith and Collins that he would present the Irish delegation with the final terms in the form of a draft treaty on Tuesday, 6 December.

'They proposed to send their final proposals to Craig and ourselves on Tuesday,' Griffith reported. 'We objected. We should see them beforehand. They agreed to send us them on Thursday evening [1 December], but formally to hand them to us Tuesday.'

Craig told Stormont that he had been authorised by the Prime Minister to issue a statement. 'By Tuesday next,' Craig explained, 'either the negotiations will have broken down or the Prime Minister will send me new proposals for consideration by the Cabinet.'

The British draft treaty, delivered to the Irish delegation on the night of 30 November, offered the Irish Free State, as Ireland would be known, the same status as the dominions in 'law and practice'. The exceptions, which really limited Irish freedom in relation to that of existing dominions, were in matters of trade and defence. The British insisted on free trade and also stipulated that the coastal defence of Britain and Ireland would 'be undertaken exclusively' by the British, who would retain control of four specified ports and such other facilities as might be desired 'in times of war or of strained relations with a foreign Power'. The British and Irish armies were to be the same size in relation to each other as each was to its country's population. Another specific difference was the form of the oath to be taken by all members of the Free State parliament, who would swear 'allegiance to the Constitution of the Irish Free State; the Community of Nations known as the British Empire; and to the King as head of the State and of the Empire'.

On the Ulster question the draft treaty gave a fleeting recognition to Irish unity in that it applied to the whole island even though the representatives of Northern Ireland were not even consulted, but the proposals protected their interests by stipulating that the area could opt out of the Irish Free State and retain its existing status. In that event, however, a Boundary Commission would be established to adjust the boundary of Northern Ireland 'in accordance with the wishes of the inhabitants, so far as may be compatible with economic and geographic conditions'.

Keeping true to de Valera's assessment of him as 'an intellectual Republican', Childers argued forcefully against the British terms, which he contended were too like the July proposals. He presented the delegation with an elaborate memorandum arguing that the legal and constitutional positions of the dominions were 'two wholly different things'.

Using Canada as a model, Childers pointed out that its legal status was that of 'a subordinate dependent of Britain holding her self-governing rights under a British Act of Parliament, which can legally be repealed or amended without Canada's consent'. But, he added, Canada's constitutional position under Britain's unwritten constitution was something quite different: it was an independent country in total control of its own affairs. Although Canadians swore allegiance directly to the British Crown and were subject to the royal veto, Childers argued that 'in fact the Crown has no authority in Canada. It signifies sentiment only,' because 'the Canadian owes obedience to his own constitution only.' In short, he wrote, 'Canada is by the full admission of British statesmen equal in status to Great Britain and as free as Great Britain.'

Childers contended that the British had no intention of offering Ireland the same status as Canada, seeing that they were demanding certain trade and defence concessions from Ireland that were unheard of in the case of Canada. But even if those demands were dropped, Ireland could not enjoy the same status as the Canadians because the essence of freedom in the case of Canada was guaranteed by their distance from Britain. The British were simply too far away to enforce their legal edicts. Ireland, on the other hand, was close enough that the law, which distance rendered unenforceable in Canada's case, 'could be enforced against Ireland so as to override the fullest constitutional freedom nominally conferred'.

The Childers memorandum, which was basically a detailed argument of de Valera's reasons for proposing External Association in the first place, was essentially the same as that put forward by Collins a week earlier and by Griffith that Monday, except that Childers spelled out the actual freedom enjoyed by Canada in much greater detail. In fact, he did such a good job of outlining the Canadian position that much of what he wrote was later used to support acceptance of the British offer guaranteeing Ireland the same *de facto* status as Canada.

Griffith and Collins discussed the draft treaty with the British on 1 December, and they got the guarantee of *de facto* dominion status strengthened to read that the Irish Free State would have the same status as Canada in 'law, practice and constitutional usage'. The addition of the term, 'constitutional usage', was specifically to exploit the real position enjoyed by Canada. Collins also objected to the latest oath and proposed the following one instead:

> I . . . do solemnly swear to bear true faith and allegiance to the Constitution of the Irish Free State as by law established and that I will be faithful to His Majesty King George in acknowledgment of the Association of Ireland in a common citizenship with Great Britain and the group of nations known as the British Commonwealth.

Such an oath would be explicitly in line with Childers's assessment of the *de facto* situation in Canada, where he contended that each 'Canadian owes obedience to his own constitution only'. The word 'faithful' was specifically included in order to denote equality between the monarch and those taking the oath, as opposed to allegiance normally owed to one's sovereign. Although the oath involved common citizenship, which was tantamount to acceptance of indirect allegiance and also membership of the British Commonwealth, the British rejected the proposal. It was accepted later with some minor alterations, but this is getting ahead of the story.

Before accepting the British terms, the Irish representatives were obliged to consult the cabinet in Dublin in line with the third paragraph of their instructions. Barton and Gavan Duffy, who were opposed to the British terms, did not want the bother of returning to Dublin. But the others insisted that the whole delegation should return for a meeting with the cabinet in line with their instructions. The negotiations had reached a critical stage and everyone knew that the conference was supposed to be concluded by the following Tuesday.

Arrangements were made for a cabinet meeting at the Mansion House on Saturday morning, 3 December 1921. Griffith returned to meet de Valera on Friday night, while Collins stayed on with Childers for some talks with the British on financial matters.

De Valera had been touring the country, inspecting IRA units. This was essentially ceremonial but with a purpose. He was subtly getting the men to recognise that the army was under political control as they paraded by and gave him the salute as President. He cut off his tour to return to Dublin on Friday night. He insisted on driving all the way himself and was very tried when he reached Dublin at 10.30 p.m. Griffith arrived about thirty minutes later and their meeting lasted for two hours.

'First of all I got a document from Mr Griffith which I said I will never sign,' de Valera recalled later. 'I will not sign it.' It was a strange thing for him to say, unless he was expecting to take over the leadership of the delegation at the last moment.

Griffith again emphasised that he was not going to break over the Crown, but de Valera later told his authorised biographers that he was too tired at the time to argue the matter. He therefore postponed further discussion until the cabinet meeting next morning.

Meanwhile Collins was doing such an effective job of hiding his own attitude that Childers could not determine where the Corkman stood on the proposals. This was hardly surprising seeing that Collins had become thoroughly distrustful of Childers, whose 'advice and inspiration' he described as 'like farmland under water — dead'.

He and Childers set out for Dublin that evening and crossed from Holyhead on the mail-boat, but it was delayed *en route* by an accident and had to return to port, with the result that it did not eventually dock in Dublin until shortly before the cabinet was due to convene. A sleepless night was certainly not the best preparation for the arduous meetings that were to follow.

Collins had asked to see the available members of the supreme council of the IRB but, because of the delay, he was unable to meet them as planned. Instead, he telephoned Seán Ó Muirthile from the Mansion House to pick up a copy of the draft treaty while the cabinet was meeting.

In addition to the cabinet members, Gavan Duffy and Duggan were invited to sit in on the meeting, as were Kevin O'Higgins and Childers, while Colm Ó Murchadha attended as acting secretary to the cabinet in the absence of Diarmuid O'Hegarty in London.

At the outset each member of the delegation gave his views on the draft terms. Griffith explained he was in favour of accepting them, and he emphasised that he would not break on the question of the Crown. Barton, on the other hand, argued against acceptance on the grounds that the proposals were not Britain's last word, that they did not really give full dominion status, and that there was no guarantee of unity. Gavan Duffy agreed with him, but Duggan concurred with Griffith.

There was some confusion about the attitude of Collins, who was obviously still trying to keep his views to himself, especially in the presence of Brugha and Stack. Childers noted in his diary that 'Collins was difficult to understand — repeatedly pressed by Dev but I really don't know what his answer amounted to.' Stack later recalled that 'Collins did not speak strongly in favour of the document at all.' But Ó Murchadha described him as being 'in substantial agreement' with Griffith and Duggan in arguing that rejecting the 'Treaty would be a gamble as England could arrange a war in Ireland within a week'. Collins did say, however, that further concessions could be won on trade and defence, and he suggested the oath should be rejected.

At the President's invitation, Childers criticised the proposals. Confining himself to the defence clauses, he denounced them saying that they meant the Free State's status would be less than that of a dominion. Barton asked him if the dominions would support the Free State in any question involving status, seeing that any British infringement in Irish affairs might be seen as setting a precedent affording Britain the right to interfere in the domestic affairs of the other dominions.

No,' replied Childers. So long as those defence clauses remained, he felt the Free State would not really be a dominion at all. 'I said,' he recalled, 'we must make it clear that we had a right to defend ourselves.'

Griffith suggested consulting a constitutional lawyer to interpret the significance of the stipulation that the defence of Irish coastal waters would be undertaken 'exclusively' by the British. At this point Childers adopted a distinctly censorial tone.

'I said,' he wrote in his diary, 'two such lawyers had been brought by him to London and had been there for some time and could have been consulted.'

De Valera contended that 'exclusively' clearly meant 'a prohibition on us which could not be admitted', Childers continued. 'He said he differed from me in that he thought it natural for them to demand facilities on our coast as being necessary. I said I didn't disagree in this but we had to keep up our principles.'

Brugha then created 'an unpleasant scene', according to Childers. Observing that Griffith and Collins had been doing most of the negotiating, Brugha asked who was responsible for the sub-conference set-up in which some of the delegation were not in complete touch with what was happening. Someone replied that the British had invited Griffith and Collins, and Brugha remarked that the British had selected 'their men'. Griffith was furious. He stood up and went to where Brugha was sitting and demanded that the outrageous remark be withdrawn, but Brugha refused at first.

Collins, too, was angry, but he contained himself. 'If you are not satisfied with us,' he said to Brugha, 'get another five to go over.'

Barton then came to the defence of his colleagues. Not withstanding his own dislike of the sub-conference set-up, he said that Griffith and Collins had been negotiating with the 'knowledge and consent' of the full delegation. Brugha then withdrew his remark, but Griffith insisted it be entered in the record. The damage had been done and an air of tension prevailed throughout the rest of the day's discussions.

De Valera avoided personalities in criticising the draft treaty, which he rejected mainly on the grounds that the oath was unacceptable. 'The oath,' he later wrote, 'crystallised in itself the main things we objected to — inclusion in the Empire, the British King as King of Ireland, Chief Executive of the Irish State, and the source from which all authority in Ireland was to be derived.' He also criticised the fact that Northern Ireland would be allowed to vote itself out of the Irish state. While he could have understood accepting dominion status in return for an end to partition, he complained that the proposals afforded neither one nor the other. He therefore suggested the delegation should return to London, try to have the draft treaty amended and, if necessary, face the consequences of war.

At 1.30 the cabinet broke for lunch. During the recess Collins had a hurried meeting with Ó Muirthile, who explained that their IRB colleagues had reservations about the oath, together with the defence and partition provisions of the British terms. He gave Collins an alternative oath suggested by his IRB colleagues. As it was comparatively similar to the one already suggested by Collins to the British, it was likely that the wording was actually suggested by somebody who was aware of the lines on which Collins was thinking.

The cabinet reconvened at three o'clock and Barton appealed to de Valera to join the delegation on the grounds that it was unfair to ask Griffith to break on the Crown when he was unwilling to fight on the issue. The President later said that he was seriously considering the suggestion but was reluctant to go because 'my going over would be interpreted as anxiety on our part and likely to give in. I did not want this interpretation to be placed on my action, and that extra little bit I wanted to pull them and hoped they could be pulled could not be done if I went and therefore I was balancing these.'

Griffith — who never lost an opportunity of declaring that he would not break on the issue of the Crown — emphasised his own attitude. When as many concessions as possible had been gained, he said that he would sign the agreement and go before the Dáil, which was the body to decide whether it should be war or not.

'Don't you realise that, if you sign this thing, you will split Ireland from top to bottom?' Brugha interjected.

'I suppose that's so,' replied Griffith. He was obviously struck by the implication of Brugha's words. 'I'll tell you what I'll do. I'll go back to London. I'll not sign the document, but I'll bring it back and submit it to the Dáil and, if necessary, to the public.'

De Valera was satisfied with this. He later said that he would 'probably' have gone to London but for Griffith's undertaking not to sign the draft treaty. It never seemed to have occurred to him that he did not have the authority to join the delegation, seeing that he had not been selected as a plenipotentiary by the Dáil, as had the members of the delegation.

Although various defects were pointed out in the draft treaty during the seven hours of discussion, the oath was the single item that evoked most criticism. In fact, with the exception of Griffith, every member of the cabinet voted for its rejection.

Unfortunately, Ó Murchadha's brief notes did not reflect much of the criticism. For example, he never mentioned any of Cosgrave's contributions. But about thirty minutes before the meeting broke up, Cosgrave declared that he would not 'take that oath'. There followed a discussion in which the cabinet was asked to suggest an alternative.

Brugha objected to any oath unless the British were, in turn, willing to swear to uphold the agreement. De Valera also questioned whether an oath was necessary but, on being told that the British were insisting on one, he sought an acceptable formula to replace the oath in the draft treaty. 'It is obvious that you cannot have that or any like "and the King as head of the State and the Empire",' he said. 'You could take an oath of true faith and allegiance to the Constitution of Ireland.'

'I started trying to get some sort of oath,' de Valera explained afterwards. 'Here is the oath I refer to, "I, so and so, swear to obey the Constitution of Ireland and to keep faith with His Britannic Majesty, so and so, in respect of the Treaty associating Ireland with the states of the British Commonwealth."'

'Nothing doing,' Brugha snapped, 'there is going to be no unanimity on such an oath as that.'

'Surely Cathal, you can't object to taking an oath if you agree to association,' de Valera said.

Stack agreed with the President, so he, too, tried to persuade Brugha that such an oath would be acceptable.

'Well,' Brugha sighed in resignation, 'you may as well swear.'

'At the end of the discussion on the oath,' Childers recalled, 'I expressly raised the point myself as to whether scrapping the oath in the draft meant scrapping the first four clauses of the British draft, that is to say the clauses setting out Dominion Status.'

'Yes,' replied the President, so Childers was satisfied. But Collins never heard the exchange.

Before the meeting concluded some decisions were taken hurriedly. It was decided that the delegation should return to London with the same powers and instructions. If the oath was not amended, the draft treaty would be rejected regardless of the consequences. If this led to the collapse of the conference, Griffith was advised to say that the matter should be referred to the Dáil, and he was to try to blame the Northern unionists for the impasse, if possible.

It was also decided that the trade and defence clauses should be amended, according to Childers, who noted that no specific suggestion was made about how to change the trade provisions. But de Valera did advocate that the British should be given 'two ports only' instead of the four they were demanding.

'All this amendment business was too hurried,' Childers noted in his diary, 'but it was understood by Barton, Duffy, and me that amendments were not mandatory.' They were 'only suggestions'.

De Valera later emphasised this point himself in the Dáil. 'I did not give, nor did the cabinet give, any instructions to the delegation as to any final document which they were to put in,' he said.

The division within the delegation seemed even deeper following the cabinet meeting. The two elements did not even return to London together that night. Barton, Gavan Duffy, and Childers took a boat from the North Wall, while Griffith, Collins, and Duggan went on the mail-boat from Dún Laoghaire.

In his biography of Collins, Rex Taylor quoted from the record of undated exchanges between Griffith and Collins during the latter stages of the negotiations.

'I will not agree,' Collins declared, 'to anything which threatens to plunge the people of Ireland into a war — not without their authority.'

'Still less do I agree to being dictated to by those not embroiled in these negotiations.' It was significant that he placed more emphasis on his objection to being 'dictated to' than on his objection to plunging the country into war. After all he, more than anybody else, was responsible for provoking the Black and Tan war. Now his ego had become involved.

'If they are not in agreement with the step which we are taking, and hope to take, why then did they themselves not consider their own presence here in London?' asked Griffith. 'Brugha refused to be a member of this delegation.'

'Supposing,' Collins continued, 'we were to go back to Dublin tomorrow with a document which gave us a Republic. Would such a document find favour with everyone? I doubt it.'

'So do I,' remarked Griffith. 'But sooner or later a decision will have to be made and we shall have to make it.'

'There's a job to be done and for the moment here's the place,' Collins wrote to Kitty Kiernan upon his return to London. 'That's that.'

Early next morning, Sunday, 4 December, Childers, with help from Barton and later Gavan Duffy, drew up alternative proposals. On seeing that these included External Association, Collins immediately objected. He thought the British guarantee about according the *de facto* status of Canada had been acceptable to the cabinet. He noted that nobody had talked about pressing again for External Association. He was right. There had been no such discussion, but the President had responded affirmatively when Childers asked if the suggested alterations to the oath also applied to the first three clauses of the British proposals. When Childers mentioned this exchange, Collins could not remember it, but Griffith confirmed that it had taken place. Collins was understandably furious. Such an important issue — indeed, what ultimately became the vital issue — should not have been determined by a simple answer to an almost throw-away question from a secretary.

Part of Collins's confusion was undoubtedly contributed to by his re-collection that de Valera had proposed an oath that was consistent with dominion status. Together with Griffith and Duggan, he recalled that the President had suggested that they could 'recognise the King of Great Britain as Head of the Associated States'. This could be interpreted to mean that the King was head of each state individually as well as the head of the combined association of states.

Barton and Childers contended, however, that de Valera had proposed recognising the King only as 'Head of the Association'. Barton produced his notes, but these proved inconclusive because he had simply written 'Head of the Assoc.' Childers, on the other hand, actually recorded in his diary that the President had suggested 'King of the Associated States'. Moreover, Ó Murchadha's notes were identical with the version remembered by Griffith, Collins, and Duggan.

When de Valera later contended that he had said 'Association' and not 'Associated States', he found himself in the embarrassing position of con-fronting formidable evidence. He actually damaged his own case during a secret session of the Dáil by recalling what he had said a fortnight earlier. 'I do swear to recognise the King of Great Britain as Head of the Associated States,' he said. 'That is the way I expressed it verbally, meaning the association of states.'

As this form of the oath was rejected by the British anyway, it is not really of much importance, except that the whole controversy does help to illustrate why Collins could have wondered whether Dublin was trying to advise or confuse the delegation. He was so annoyed over the confusion about re-proposing External Association that he became quite obstreperous.

Childers essentially accused him of 'deliberately' trying to make the new document 'unreasonable' by insisting that 'Dev had said that only two ports [and] nothing else' could be conceded to the British. Notwithstanding his position as a secretary, Childers took issue with Collins. 'I protested against making Dev's words ridiculous,' he noted.

Griffith, Collins, and Duggan initially refused to present the counter proposals to the British. They said it would be a waste of time, seeing that the British had already rejected External Association on numerous occasions. Barton and Gavan Duffy were determined to press ahead, and Griffith eventually agreed to go with them to Downing Street that Sunday afternoon, but Collins and Duggan refused.

'I did not attend this conference,' Collins wrote next day, 'for the reason that I had, in my own estimation, argued fully all points.' In addition, he had already shown his hand to the British by suggesting an oath that was consistent with Irish membership of the British Commonwealth.

The British again flatly rejected External Association, as Collins predicted. Then Gavan Duffy blurted out that the Irish 'difficulty is coming into the Empire'. At that point the conference broke down. The two sides announced that they would submit their final proposals the following day, and they would formally announce that the conference had collapsed.

Tom Jones tried desperately to salvage the situation during the night. He had a private meeting with Griffith, whom he found 'labouring under a deep sense of the crisis'. The Irish chairman 'spoke throughout with the greatest earnestness and unusual emotion'. Collins and himself were in favour of the British terms, but needed something further to offer the Dáil. Their position would be simplified, Griffith said, if the British could get Craig to give 'a conditional recognition, however shadowy, of Irish national unity in return for the acceptance of the Empire by Sinn Féin'. If the British delegation could obtain an assurance that Northern Ireland would agree to unity, he said that Dublin would give all the safeguards the Northern majority needed and the Boundary Commission could be scrapped. With a Northern acceptance of unity, he was confident he could get the Dáil to accept a treaty with an oath that would be acceptable to the British. He added that Barton and the doctrinaire republicans could then be ignored, because 90 per cent of the gunmen would follow Collins.

Without the support of Collins, however, Griffith did not have a chance of getting the Dáil to accept the British terms. He therefore asked Jones to arrange a meeting so that Lloyd George could have a 'heart to heart' talk with Collins. Jones then left and arranged a meeting with the Prime Minister for the following morning, Monday, 5 December, but Griffith had great difficulty persuading Collins to attend. Collins was so annoyed over the confusion in Dublin that he was refusing to have anything further to do with the negotiations. It was not until just before the meeting with Lloyd George was due to begin that he finally relented and agreed to go to Downing Street. In fact, he had been so determined not to attend that he was some fifteen minutes late for the meeting, which was most uncharacteristic as he had a virtual obsession about punctuality.

During the meeting Collins emphasised he was 'perfectly dissatisfied' with the British terms regarding Northern Ireland. He said the British government should get the position clarified by pressing Craig for a letter specifying the conditions under which unity would be acceptable, or else rejecting it outright. At that point, according to Collins, Lloyd George said that Collins himself pointed out on a previous occasion that the North would be forced economically to come in. Collins continued:

> I assented but I said the position was so serious owing to certain recent actions that for my part I was anxious to secure a definite reply from Craig and his colleagues, and that I was as agreeable to a reply rejecting as accepting. In view of the former we would save Tyrone and Fermanagh, parts of Derry, Armagh and Down by the Boundary Commission, and thus avoid such things as the raid on the Tyrone County Council and the ejection of the staff. Another such incident would, in my view, inevitably lead to a conflict, and this conflict, in the nature of things (assuming for instance that some of the Anglo-Northern police were killed or wounded) would inevitably spread throughout Ireland. Mr Lloyd George expressed a view that this might be put to Craig, and if so the safeguards would be a matter for working out between ourselves and Craig afterwards.

The Prime Minister was willing to consider objections to the financial, trade, and defence clauses of the British draft treaty. He also offered to consider a new oath, if the Irish delegation accepted the clauses concerning dominion status.

'Finally,' Collins concluded his report, 'the conversation developed into a statement by Mr Lloyd George to the effect that were Clauses 1 and 2 accepted he would be in a position to hold up any action until we had, if we desired to do so, submitted the matter to DÁIL ÉIREANN and the country. I left it at that saying that unless I sent word to the contrary some members of the delegation would meet him at 2 o'clock.' Arrangements were then made for members of the two delegations to meet that afternoon.

This time Barton accompanied Griffith and Collins, and they met with the Prime Minister, Chamberlain, Birkenhead, and Churchill. From the outset Griffith tried to concentrate on the Ulster question by demanding that the Irish delegation should know whether Craig would accept or reject Irish unity. The British replied that Griffith was going back on his previous promise not to let them down on the Boundary Commission proposal.

'Collins said,' according to Barton, 'that for us to agree to any conditions defining the future relations of Great Britain and Ireland prior to Craig's giving his assent to the unity of Ireland was impossible, that to do so would surrender our whole fighting position. That every document we ever sent them had stated that any proposals for the association of Ireland with the British Commonwealth of Nations was conditional upon the unity of Ireland. That, unless Craig accepted inclusion under the all-Ireland Parliament, the unity of Ireland was not assured and that if he refused inclusion we should be left in the position of having surrendered our position without having even secured the essential unity of Ireland.'

Lloyd George became excited and accused the Irish side of trying to use the Ulster question to break off the talks when the real difficulty was the opposition in Dublin to membership of the British Commonwealth. He accused Griffith of going back on the promise of not repudiating the Boundary Commission proposal, and he produced the explanatory memorandum that Griffith had approved in November.

'What is this letter?' Barton whispered to Collins.

'I don't know what the hell it is.'

'Do you mean to tell me, Mr Collins, that you never learnt of this document from Mr Griffith?' Lloyd George asked.

The memorandum outlining the Boundary Commission proposal was then passed across the table to Collins and Barton, both of whom were seeing it for the first time. Collins said nothing.

'I have fulfilled my part of the bargain,' the Prime Minister declared. 'I took the risk of breaking my party. You in Ireland often bring against us in England the charge of breach of faith. Now it is for you to show that Irishmen know how to keep faith.'

'I said I would not let you down on that, and I won't,' Griffith replied. He no longer felt able to hold out on the Ulster question, but he argued that it was unfair to hold the rest of the Irish delegation to his private promise.

The discussion changed to other subjects, and the British agreed to accept the proposed oath that Collins had handed to Lloyd George that morning with only some minor changes; it was effectively the same as the one the British had rejected on 1 December. They also agreed to other concessions such as dropping the stipulation that the British would 'exclusively' have the right to defend the seas around Ireland. They agreed that the Irish could have vessels for fishery protection and to combat smuggling. They also agreed that this aspect of the agreement would be reviewed in five years 'with a view to the undertaking by Ireland of a share in her own coastal defence'. Lloyd George also offered to drop the British demand for free trade between the two countries, if the Irish delegation would agree to the rest of the proposals.

Griffith said he would sign the agreement, but he contended that it was unfair to ask his colleagues to sign before they knew where Craig stood.

'Do I understand, Mr Griffith, that though everyone else refuses, you will nevertheless agree to sign?' Lloyd George asked.

'Yes, that is so, Mr Prime Minister.'

'That is not enough,' Lloyd George said, sensing that he had the Irish delegation at his mercy. 'If we sign, we shall sign as a delegation and stake the life of the Government on our signature. Is the Irish delegation prepared to do the same?'

At this point Lloyd George knew that Barton was the one he had to convince. He therefore turned to Barton.

'He particularly addressed himself to me,' Barton reported, 'and said very solemnly that those who were not for peace must take the full responsibility for the war that would immediately follow refusal by any delegate to sign the Articles of Agreement.'

'I have to communicate with Sir James Craig tonight,' Lloyd George said dramatically as he raised two envelopes. 'Here are the alternative letters which I have prepared, one enclosing the Articles of Agreement reached by His Majesty's Government and yourselves, and the other saying that the Sinn Féin representatives refused the oath of allegiance and refused to come within the Empire. If I send this letter, it is war — and war within three days! Which letter am I to send? Whichever letter you choose travels by special train to Holyhead, and by destroyer to Belfast.

'The train is waiting with steam up at Euston. Mr Shakespeare is ready. If he is to reach Sir James Craig in time we must have your answer by 10 p.m. tonight. You can have until then, but no longer to decide whether you will give peace or war to your country.'

The Irish delegation withdrew to consider its next move. 'Michael Collins rose looking as though he was going to shoot someone,' Churchill recalled. 'I have never seen so much pain and suffering in restraint.'

As Collins left he was accosted by newsmen, who were aware that the deadline to inform Craig was approaching. They asked if the Irish delegation would be returning later that evening.

'I don't know,' Collins replied.

'Has the conference finished?'

'I don't know that either.'

On their way back to the headquarters Collins told Barton of his intention to sign. The surprise with which the latter greeted the decision was a measure of the extent to which Collins had hidden his real views in recent weeks. Although Duggan, too, was in favour of signing, Barton and Gavan Duffy held out for a time.

Geoffrey Shakespeare, who was waiting to take the letter to Craig, later wrote that he 'never understood why the Irish accepted the ultimatum at its face value. Why did they not call the bluff?'

Lloyd George was undoubtedly bluffing when he insisted that all the members of the Irish delegation had to sign the agreement. Collins must have known this. First of all the Prime Minister had told him and Griffith the previous week that he planned to present Britain's final terms to Craig at the same time as they would be given to the Irish delegation. The British were apparently going to follow the same procedure that was used with the Versailles Treaty in 1919. It had been given to the German delegation and published some weeks before it was actually signed. It was only to facilitate Griffith and Collins that the British handed over the draft treaty the previous Wednesday. Consequently Griffith and Collins must have known that Lloyd George's schedule simply called for the British to send Craig a copy of their final terms by the next day — not necessarily a signed agreement. Moreover, Lloyd George had told Collins that morning that he would allow the draft treaty to be referred to the Dáil before signing, if the Irish delegation was prepared to recommend dominion status.

In Griffith's case the ultimatum was insignificant because he had agreed to sign before it was issued. And it would have been out of character for Collins to desert him at that point. He had already agreed that the two of them were in the negotiations together to the bitter end. But he did not explain to Barton that he thought the threat of immediate and terrible war was probably bluff. Instead, he went along with the bluff in order to ensure that all of the delegation signed, as this would make it easier to get the agreement accepted in Dublin.

Without Barton's vote, for instance, Collins realised there would be little chance the cabinet would accept the Treaty, because de Valera, Brugha, and Stack would likely oppose the agreement. If Barton joined them, then the majority of the cabinet would be opposed to the British terms and the Dáil would probably not be given any more say than it had with the July proposals, which were formally rejected in the name of Dáil Éireann before the Dáil had even convened to discuss them.

Having been entrusted by the Dáil with the responsibility of negotiating an acceptable settlement, Griffith and Collins saw it as their duty to sign when they were convinced the terms would be acceptable not only to a majority of the Dáil but also to a majority of the Irish people. Moreover, they thought an unwinnable war would inevitably follow the collapse of the conference.

'Unquestionably, the alternative to the Treaty, sooner or later, was war,' Collins later wrote. 'To me it would have been a criminal act to refuse to allow the Irish nation to give its opinion as to whether it would accept this settlement or resume hostilities.'

Some notes drawn up by Collins during the latter stages of the London conference give a clear insight into his thinking. He was convinced Ireland would benefit from dominion status, which he did not consider 'as being anywhere near a finalised solution. It is the first step,' he wrote. 'More than this could not be expected.'

'I am never of the opinion that the majority of the Irish people will be against such a treaty as we have in mind,' he observed. 'It is a question of greater influence — de Valera will command, I think, a large part of what was formerly the Volunteer Organisation.' Believing that there would be opposition in Dublin from 'those who have in mind personal ambitions under pretence of patriotism', Collins still thought that 55 to 60 per cent 'of all concerned' would support the Treaty.

Collins had told the Dáil cabinet on Saturday that he was in favour of accepting the British draft, with the exception of the oath. Back in London the British accepted the oath that he proposed with the approval of the IRB. Thus the only remaining stumbling block was removed.

Shakespeare realised that the demand for the Irish delegates to sign that night was part of a bluff, but this did not mean that he thought they could have won further concessions, as has been inferred. 'Lloyd George was not bluffing in refusing further concessions,' Shakespeare wrote. 'He had gone to the limit, and there was nothing more to offer.' The Prime Minister was afraid, however, that if the 'Irish delegates went back without signing or expressing an opinion, the atmosphere in Dublin would have influenced them and the Treaty would have been lost'. Hence the ultimatum.

That evening Shakespeare dined with Lloyd George alone. 'Either they sign now or negotiations are off,' the Prime Minister told him. 'If there is a break we will put into Ireland a large force and restore order. I told them as much and it is now up to them to choose between peace and war.'

Referring the final terms back to the cabinet in Dublin before signing was not at issue. Nobody even thought of telephoning Dublin, according to Barton. All were satisfied they had fulfilled their instructions in referring the draft treaty to the cabinet that weekend. Consequently none of them thought they had any further obligation to consult the cabinet in Dublin. They had been given full plenipotentiary powers 'to negotiate and sign' an agreement, so the moment of truth had come. They had to make up their own minds.

The delegation convened in the upstairs living-room at Han's Place at around nine o'clock that Monday evening. It has been suggested that it was Lady Lavery who persuaded Collins to sign, but that is absurd. If he did meet her that evening, it was sometime after 7.30 when they left Downing Street and before nine o'clock when the delegation gathered to discuss the Treaty at Han's Place. She certainly did not drive him back to Downing Street later that night, as her husband wrote in his memoirs. Collins returned to Downing Street with Griffith and Barton.

In these memoirs Sir John Lavery wrote: 'Michael Collins stood firm to the last minute. He seemed to have lost his temper. Even I, whose head was never really out of the paint-pot, could see that he who loses his temper in argument is lost, and told him so, but I failed to convince him. Eventually, after hours of persuasion, Hazel prevailed. She took him to Downing Street in her car that last evening, and he gave in.'

Possibly the meeting between the Laverys and Collins that Lavery was talking about took place on the Sunday afternoon while Griffith, Barton, and Gavan Duffy were at Downing Street. Hazel Lavery met Collins after mass a number of mornings and she might actually have driven him to the private meeting with Lloyd George the following morning. In that event she may well have played a significant role in persuading Collins to stand by his own beliefs.

'Would we, or would we not, come within the Community of Nations known as the British Empire?' that was the question the members of the Irish delegation had to answer, according to Griffith.

Griffith 'spoke almost passionately for signing', according to Childers, who noted that Collins said virtually nothing during the argument, which was 'long and hot'. On three occasions Griffith, Collins, and Duggan were 'on the point of proceeding to sign' without the others but Barton stalled them. The argument went on for so long that the delegation was still at Han's Place more than an hour after the time-limit set by Lloyd George had expired.

When eleven o'clock passed without any sign of the Irish representatives returning, the British became uneasy. 'We had doubts as to whether we would see them again,' the Prime Minister recalled afterwards. He realised that much depended on Collins. 'If only Michael Collins has as much moral courage as he has physical courage,' Lloyd George said to his colleagues, 'we shall get a settlement. But moral courage is a much higher quality than physical courage, and it is a quality that brave men often lack.'

Collins had already made it clear to his colleagues that he took a bleak view of the IRA's prospects of success if the cease-fire collapsed. He was convinced it would not be possible to attain further success by physical force and his own effectiveness as intelligence chief was ended, seeing that his main agents within Dublin Castle had all been uncovered. In addition, he would not be able to move about Dublin with the same ease as he had before the truce because he was now well known to the British, who would have little difficulty recognising him.

'He knew that physical resistance, if resumed, would collapse and he was not going to be the leader of a forlorn hope,' Barton explained years later. 'He intended to live to fight again.' At one point during the discussion at Han's Place, Collins pointed out that there had only been about two thousand active volunteers, and he asked if Barton wished to send them out to be slaughtered.

'Barton,' said Duggan, 'you will be hanged from a lamp post in the streets of Dublin if your refusal to sign causes a new war in Ireland.'

Barton was shaken. He did not place much store in Duggan's opinion, but he did feel that 'Collins was in a better position to appraise our military position than anyone else.' He therefore asked to be allowed to consult privately with Childers.

As they left the room, Collins apparently was tired of all the arguing. He had made up his own mind and he went downstairs to wait for the others, while Childers and Barton talked together on the landing.

It seemed de Valera's assessment of Childers's influence over Barton was proving accurate. When the two of them were alone, Barton asked for the advice of his cousin, who promptly urged him to hold out as it was a matter of principle. Childers added that his own wife would agree with them.

'Molly will be with us,' he said.

This suddenly brought home to Barton that the women of Ireland, who had already suffered so much, were being given no say. He decided to sign in order that the Dáil would have a chance to consider the agreement.

'Well,' he said, 'I suppose I must sign.'

Although Barton admitted some hours later that the 'allusion to Molly's support for refusal to sign' had been the 'deciding element' in his decision, Childers still believed the main factor had been Barton's 'belief that war was really imminent and inevitable — real war'. In other words, the remark about Molly Childers was little more than the last straw!

Kathleen McKenna, one of the secretaries with the delegation, later wrote that Collins actually fell asleep while he waited downstairs for the others. Griffith and Barton eventually came down and the three of them returned to Downing Street. If it had been so important that all of them sign that night, then surely Duggan and Gavan Duffy would also have been there. In fact, Gavan Duffy did not sign until many hours later and Duggan never actually signed the British copy of the Treaty. He had returned to Dublin with the Treaty and it was necessary to cut his signature from a dinner menu he had autographed and attach that to the document. So having everybody sign the agreement was clearly not that important.

When Collins signed around 2.20 in the morning of 6 December, he was aware of the likely consequences for himself.

Immediately after signing, Birkenhead turned to Collins. 'I may have signed my political death-warrant tonight,' he said.

'I may have signed my actual death-warrant,' Collins replied.

Within minutes the Irish delegates emerged from No. 10 Downing Street looking very tired and grave.

'Have you anything to say?' a reporter asked Collins.

'Not a word,' he replied sharply.

He was obviously deeply troubled. Some hours later he wrote a truly prophetic letter to a friend:

> Think — what have I got for Ireland? Something which she has wanted these past seven hundred years. Will anyone be satisfied at the bargain? Will anyone? I tell you this — early this morning I signed my death warrant. I thought at the time how odd, how ridiculous — a bullet may just as well have done the job five years ago.
>
> I believe Birkenhead may have said an end to his political life. With him it has been my honour to work. Those signatures are the first real step for Ireland. If people will only remember that — the first real step.

10

The Dáil Debate

'In the creation of the Irish Free State we have laid a foundation on which may be built a new world order,' Collins told an Associated Press correspondent on the day the Treaty was signed. This, of course, was pure hyperbole. Just because Ireland was supposedly being accorded the *de facto* status of the dominions was hardly grounds for thinking that the British Commonwealth would become a league of free nations in which even the United States would participate. Yet Collins now declared that 'Ireland would be a link to join America and Britain. And with America in this League of Free Nations, what country would wish to stay outside?'

Harry Boland issued a particularly positive statement in the United States. 'After centuries of conflict the Irish nation and the British have compromised their difference,' he announced. 'A treaty of peace has been signed and an agreement reached between the representatives of the Irish nation and the representatives of the British Empire, an agreement which restores Ireland to the comity of nations.'

Boland later claimed that the actual terms of the Treaty had not been published when he issued that statement, but they had been published on 8 December when he issued a further statement blasting Judge Daniel Cohalan and Diarmuid Lynch of the Friends of Irish Freedom for criticising the Treaty. Of course, de Valera's views were not yet known. When he spoke out, they all switched sides.

De Valera was in Limerick when he first heard that the Treaty had been signed. His initial reaction was one of delight, according to himself. Because of Griffith's promise not to sign the draft treaty the previous Saturday, the President assumed the British must have capitulated. 'I never thought that they would give in so soon,' he remarked to those with him.

It was only that evening as he was about to attend a cultural gathering in Dublin that Éamonn Duggan and Desmond FitzGerald arrived from London with a copy of the Treaty, which Duggan handed to the President. When de Valera showed no interest in the document, Duggan asked him to read it.

'What should I read it for?' de Valera asked.

'It is arranged that the thing be published in London and Dublin simultaneously at eight o'clock and it is near that hour now,' replied Duggan.

'What,' said the President, 'to be published whether I have seen it or not?'

'Oh well, that's the arrangement.'

After reading the terms of the Treaty de Valera summoned a meeting of the available members of the cabinet. 'I am going to pronounce against the Treaty,' he declared. He added that he intended to demand the resignations of Griffith, Collins, and Barton from his government upon their return. Stack and Brugha agreed with him, but Cosgrave objected.

'I don't agree with that,' declared Cosgrave, insisting that the plenipotentiaries should be allowed to explain what had happened before any pronouncement was made. Cosgrave actually felt that the President welcomed his intervention because he readily agreed to hold his hand until the whole cabinet could meet.

A full meeting was called for 8 December 1921, and a press release was prepared. 'In view of the nature of the proposed treaty with Great Britain,' it read, 'President de Valera has sent an urgent summons to members of the cabinet in London to report at once so that a full cabinet decision may be taken.'

Desmond FitzGerald, the Minister for Publicity, was surprised at the tone of the release. 'This might be altered Mr President,' he said, entering the cabinet room. 'It reads as if you were opposed to the settlement.'

'And that is the way I intended it to read,' replied de Valera. 'Publish it as it is.'

FitzGerald was amazed. 'I did not think he was against this kind of settlement before we went over to London,' he whispered to Stack.

'He is dead against it *now* anyway,' replied Stack. 'That's enough.'

It was like a cry of triumph. FitzGerald thought Stack was gloating that he and Brugha had persuaded the President to abandon his more moderate views while the delegation was in London.

Many people thought de Valera would be in favour of the terms of the Treaty, in view of his moderate pronouncements during the summer when he made it clear that he was no doctrinaire republican. He had sent the delegation to London to secure 'the status of a dominion', and they had returned with essentially 'dominion status'. Thus they had a right to expect the President's support, but Collins knew it would not be forthcoming.

Any doubts that FitzGerald had that de Valera would have been in favour of such terms would have been dispelled the following week when the President indicated that he would have rejected the Treaty if he had been consulted in advance. 'I would have said, "No",' he explained, 'though I might not have said "No" before. I would have said "No" in the circumstances because I felt I could have said "No" with advantage to the nation.'

The first thing Collins did upon arriving in Dublin was to ask Tom Cullen how his own men viewed the Treaty.

'Tom, what are our fellows saying?' he asked.

'What is good enough for you is good enough for them,' Cullen replied.

Although this represented the attitude of many people, there were already ominous signs. The previous evening in London the delegation had been given a tumultuous send-off by Irish exiles. Childers recorded that he was 'nearly rushed to death' by the enthusiastic crowd. So Collins found it 'in a sense prophetic' that there was no welcoming crowd and 'no signs of jubilation' on reaching Dublin next morning. Instead, the few people about 'seemed strangely apathetic'.

'This lack of jubilation among the people was dispiriting enough,' Collins continued, 'but it was nothing compared with the open hostility we faced in the cabinet drawing-room of the Mansion House.' De Valera was waiting there, looking gaunt and depressed, while Stack was in a blazing mood and Brugha was 'the personification of venom'.

The ensuing cabinet meeting, which recessed three times, lasted through the afternoon and into the late evening. Frank Gallagher was in the next room with the press, and he said he frequently talked loudly in an effort to cover 'the raised voices' in the cabinet room.

The merits and drawbacks of the Treaty were examined, but not in any great detail, according to Stack, who noted that the main topic of discussion was the circumstances under which the plenipotentiaries had signed the agreement.

Griffith refused to 'admit duress by the British', which was accurate in his case, seeing that he had agreed to sign before Lloyd George issued his infamous ultimatum. Collins, on the other hand, said that if there had been duress it was only 'the duress of the facts'.

'I did not sign the Treaty under duress,' he later wrote, 'except in the sense that the position as between Ireland and England, historically, and because of superior forces on the part of England, has always been one of duress.' He added that 'there was not, and could not have been, any personal duress.'

But both Barton and Gavan Duffy said they had been intimidated into signing. They admitted that Lloyd George had not attempted coercion in the sense of physically threatening them. 'The form of duress he made use of,' according to Barton, 'was more insidious and in my opinion, a more compelling duress, for Mr Lloyd George, knowing already from Mr Griffith himself that he was prepared to sign, demanded that every other delegate should sign or war would follow immediately, and insisted that those who refused to sign must accept the responsibility.' As far as Barton was concerned, his refusal to sign would have meant going against the wishes of the majority of the delegation, and accepting 'personal responsibility for the slaughter to ensue' without having a chance 'to consult the President, the cabinet in Dublin, the Dáil, or the people'. Barton actually blamed de Valera for what had happened. The President, he said, had vacillated from the beginning and had even refused to go to London when he asked him to do so on Saturday. The problem was, Barton declared, *'we were not a fighting delegation'*.

Had it not been for Griffith's undertaking not to sign the draft treaty on Saturday, the President said that he would have gone to London himself and rejected the British terms. 'I *would* have gone and said "Go to the devil. I will not sign."'

He later told Lord Longford that he might have understood the delegation giving up independence for an end to partition, but 'you have neither this nor that'.

At one point someone said: 'Supposing Ulster came in on the Treaty basis, would you agree to it?'

'That was the one consideration that might affect his judgment,' according to Childers, who noted, 'This surprised me.'

The cabinet voted to endorse the Treaty by the narrowest margin possible. Griffith, Collins, and Cosgrave lined up in favour, while the President, Brugha, and Stack were in opposition. It was therefore Barton's vote which made the difference. Even though he was personally opposed to the agreement, he explained that he felt bound to vote for it, seeing that he had agreed to recommend it to the Dáil by signing it in London.

Kevin O'Higgins, who did not have a vote in cabinet, said that while the Treaty should never have been signed, it should be supported because it was important to preserve a united front. Diarmuid O'Hegarty, the cabinet secretary, even interrupted to make a strong appeal to the President not to oppose the Treaty, but Childers called for a protest in the Dáil against 'the irrevocable step of signing away independence'.

Although repeatedly pressed, de Valera rejected the suggestion that he not speak out publicly. Speaking 'at great length', he explained that he had been working for unity by seeking a form of association which people like Brugha and Stack could accept, but that had been thrown away without the permission of the cabinet. Still 'he did not despair of winning better terms yet', according to Childers.

Stack appealed to the delegation 'not to press the document on the Dáil'. At one point he turned to Collins. 'You have signed and undertaken to recommend the document to the Dáil,' he said. 'Well, recommend it. Your duty stops there. You are not supposed to throw all your influence into the scale.' If the agreement was rejected, Stack argued, they would be in an even stronger position than before. 'Will you do it?' he asked.

'Where would I be then?' Collins snapped.

The cabinet was irrevocably split. De Valera announced he would resign if the Dáil accepted the Treaty, while both Griffith and Collins said they would do the same if it was rejected. Back in August de Valera had told the

Dáil that the policy of his cabinet would be to do 'that which they consider would be best for the country. The Ministry itself may not be able to agree and in such case the majority would rule.' But now he was insisting that it should be submitted to the Dáil and that they should all carry on in cabinet until the Dáil could vote on the agreement.

Following the meeting de Valera issued a 'Proclamation to the Irish People'. 'The terms of the agreement are in violent conflict with the wishes of the majority of the nation as expressed freely in successive elections during the past three years,' he declared. 'I feel it is my duty to inform you immediately that I cannot recommend the acceptance of this Treaty either to Dáil Éireann or to the country. In this attitude I am supported by the Ministers for Home Affairs and Defence.'

'The greatest test of our people has come,' he concluded. 'Let us face it worthily, without bitterness and above all without recriminations. There is a definite constitutional way of resolving our political differences — let us not depart from it, and let the conduct of the Cabinet in this matter be an example to the whole nation.'

Though the first hurdle in the ratification process had been cleared, Collins was obviously troubled after the cabinet meeting. He called at Batt O'Connor's home, where he had been a frequent visitor during the terror, but now he was unsure of his welcome. When O'Connor opened the door, Collins did not walk in as usual but stood on the doorstep 'with a strange expression' as he waited to be invited in.

'Come in,' said O'Connor somewhat puzzled. 'What are you waiting for?'

'I thought you would have no welcome for me, Batt,' replied Collins. Of course, he was welcome, but he was so upset that he was unable to relax. Too agitated to sit down, he strode around the room, gesturing animatedly with his hands flaying the air. Should the Treaty be defeated, he said that he would move back down the country.

'I will leave Dublin at once,' he said bitterly. 'I will go down to Cork. If the fighting is going to be resumed, I will fight in the open, beside my own people down there. I am not going to be chivvied and hunted through Dublin as I have been for the last two years.'

'You have brought back this Treaty,' O'Connor argued. 'It is a wonderful achievement. The people want it. They must at least be given the chance to say what they think of it. Then if they reject it (only they will not reject it) you will have done your part, and will have no responsibility for the consequences.'

'I will accept their verdict,' Collins declared.

Next day de Valera met Childers, Barton, and Gavan Duffy and explained that he planned to draw up an alternative to the Treaty. It was a 'revelation' to Childers to find that the President was thinking of a document that had more appeal to the extremists than to the moderates. 'His nerve and confidence are amazing,' Childers noted. 'Seems certain of winning.'

When the supreme council of the IRB met to consider the Treaty on 10 December, Collins chaired the meeting at which Liam Lynch was the only dissenting voice. Lynch was sorry that he felt conscientiously compelled to differ with Collins, but he nevertheless felt that his opposition would not strain their friendship.

'I admire Mick as a soldier and a man,' Lynch wrote. 'Thank God all parties can agree to differ.'

Although the supreme council endorsed the Treaty, it decided that all members who were Dáil deputies would be free to vote as they saw fit. The IRB was not going to try to compel its members to vote for ratification.

Griffith and Collins were undoubtedly helped by the negative reaction to the Treaty in Belfast. Sir James Craig expressed 'grave dissatisfaction and alarm' to the Stormont parliament. Its members were irate that the Treaty had been signed with representatives of Sinn Féin representing the whole island. Northern Ireland was included without even consulting its representatives.

'We protest against the declared intention of your Government to place Northern Ireland automatically in the Irish Free State,' Craig wrote to Lloyd George. 'It is true that Ulster is given the right to contract out, but she can only do so after automatic inclusion in the Irish Free State.'

Among the defence provisions, Belfast Lough was mention as one of the four Treaty ports to be retained by the British. 'What right has Sinn Féin to be recognised as parties to an agreement concerning the defences of Belfast Lough, which touches only the loyal counties of Antrim and Down?' Craig asked indignantly.

He could hardly have been reassured when Andrew Bonar Law expressed the belief that the Boundary Commission clauses would lead to the transfer of Fermanagh and Tyrone to the Irish Free State. And Lloyd George seemed to confirm the assessment himself in the House of Commons.

'There is no doubt,' the Prime Minister said, 'certainly since the Act of 1920, that the majority of the people of the two counties prefer being with their Southern neighbours to being in the Northern Parliament. Take it either by constituency or by Poor Law Union, or, if you like, by counting heads, and you will find that the majority in these two counties prefer to be with their Southern neighbours — What does that mean? If Ulster is to remain a separate community, you can only by means of coercion keep them there, and although I am against the coercion of Ulster, I do not believe in Ulster coercing other units.'

'Our Northern areas will be so cut up and mutilated that we shall no longer be masters in our own house,' Captain C. C. Craig, the Northern Prime Minister's brother complained. He was positively vitriolic about the Treaty, as was Sir Edward Carson.

When one remembers that de Valera had merely asked for the British to stand aside and let the Irish settle the issue between themselves, the indignation of the unionists complaining about the way the agreement had been signed with Sinn Féin representatives on behalf of the whole island without even consulting Belfast probably helps explain why the Treaty's Southern critics had so little to say about the partition clauses.

———————————

There was a great air of anticipation on 14 December 1921 when the Dáil convened in the main hall of University College at Earlsfort Terrace, Dublin. The division within the cabinet immediately manifested itself in the seating arrangements which saw de Valera, Brugha, and Stack positioned to the left of the Speaker, while Griffith, Collins, and the other members of the delegation took up their seats across the floor. Most members of the general body sat facing the Speaker, with the public gallery behind them, while some 110 journalists from around the world were crammed together at the other end of the hall behind the Speaker's chair.

Following the roll-call there was supposed to be a motion to go into private session, but de Valera rose to say a few words first. It was but a fore-taste of what was to come during the following days. Whenever he wanted to say something he just interrupted as if he had a right to determine procedure himself. During the thirteen days of public and private debate, he interrupted the proceedings more than 250 times. It was, no doubt, a measure of his standing that he was allowed to interrupt so often. Many of those interruptions were admittedly very brief interjections, but some were quite lengthy.

His opening remarks were patently dishonest. Speaking the few perfunctory words in Irish, he said that his command of the language was not as good as he would like and he would therefore speak in English, because he would be better able to arrange his thoughts. Then he proceeded to tell the Dáil in English that he was not going to continue in Gaelic because some of those present could not understand the language.

He quoted the instructions to the plenipotentiaries and noted that they had not fulfilled the provision stipulating that the 'complete text of the draft treaty about to be signed' would be submitted to the cabinet in Dublin and a 'reply awaited'.

Collins, who had shaved off his moustache within the previous twenty-four hours, looked younger than ever as he rose to refute the suggestion that the members of the delegation had exceeded their authority, or violated their instructions. They 'did not sign as a treaty', he argued but merely signed a document 'on the understanding that each signatory would recommend it to the Dáil for acceptance'. The document, which was officially headed 'Articles of Agreement for a Treaty between Great Britain and Ireland,' would not effectively become a treaty until it had been ratified.

A vital consideration in signing, as far as Collins was concerned, was the fact that there was so little difference between what the rest of the cabinet wanted and what the British were offering. In order that the circumstances would be better understood he wanted the fullest possible disclosure of all documents relating to the negotiations. He was therefore annoyed when the President acted selectively in reading the secret instructions given to the delegation without even mentioning the credentials conferred at the same time.

Standing with his hands in his pockets, Collins began speaking slowly but firmly. While sitting his eyes had glimmered softly, but one reporter noted that as he became more intense they narrowed.

'If one document had to be read,' Collins said with his jaw set determinedly and his voice vibrant with the intensity of his feelings, 'the original document, which was a prior document, should have been read first. I must ask the liberty of reading the original document which was served on each member of the delegation.'

'Is that the one with the original credentials?' de Valera asked.

'Yes,' replied Collins.

'Was that ever presented?' the President asked. 'It was given in order to get the British Government to recognise the Irish Republic. Was that document giving the credentials of the accredited representatives from the Irish Government presented to, or accepted by, the British delegates? Was that seen by the British delegates or accepted by them?'

It was a dramatic moment as de Valera stood there facing Collins across the floor. The credentials had not been given to the British, but the important point, as far as Collins was concerned, was that they were given to the delegates by de Valera himself. Collins was not therefore about to get sidetracked on the issue.

'May I ask,' he said almost jocularly to the Speaker, 'that I be allowed to speak without interruption?'

'I must protest,' the President insisted. But the Speaker called for order and de Valera sat down.

Continuing with dramatic effect Collins read the credentials signed by the President himself. Those specifically stated that the delegates had been conferred with plenipotentiary powers 'to negotiate and conclude' a treaty with Britain. Collins did not stress the word 'conclude', but the reading of the terms of reference seemed to create a profound impression on all those present in the hall.

From his slow, measured tones, Collins gradually built himself into a crescendo of anger and indignation as he repeated that the credentials should have been read along with the instructions so that members of the Dáil would be in a position to judge the issue on its merits. He said that he had refrained from trying to influence members of the Dáil before it met to consider the agreement, even though he knew that he was being vilified by opponents of the agreement.

'I have not said a hard word about anyone,' he emphasised as he rapped the table in front of him. 'I have been called a traitor.'

'By whom?' de Valera asked.

The atmosphere was electric as Collins ignored the question. 'If there are men who act towards me as a traitor I am prepared to meet them anywhere, any time, now as in the past,' he declared.

People were heard to murmur throughout the room. De Valera sat staring at Collins while ministers and deputies became restless. But then the tension dissipated as Collins changed the subject and continued in a more ordinary tone. Even though he was opposed to a private session, he said he would accept one.

'If there is anything, any matter of detail, if, for instance, the differences as they arose from time to time, should be discussed first in private, I am of the opinion that having discussed it in private I think we ought then to be able to make it public,' he said. In short they could discuss these matters privately to clear up any misunderstandings, but then they should be free to explain their own points of view. 'I am willing to go as far as that, that is only detail. But on the essentials I am for publicity now and all along.'

The debate drifted as various members argued whether or not to go into private session. Although de Valera wanted one, Brugha — demonstrating that sincerity and independence which even Collins admired — objected. Then suddenly the President revived the controversy over the credentials by charging that Collins had earlier wished 'to lay stress on the word "conclude"'. In effect, he was contending that Collins had implied that the Dáil had no right to reject the Treaty.

'No, sir,' Collins said emphatically. He had already made it clear that the Dáil was free to reject the agreement. Yet de Valera persisted.

'What is the point then of raising the original credentials, if the word "conclude" did not mean that when you had signed it was ended?' the President asked. But nobody asked why de Valera had included the word in the first place. If he had agreed with the Treaty, would he have contended that the Dáil had no right to reject it?

Griffith settled the issue by pointing out that while the delegates had been given the authority to commit the Dáil to a treaty, they had not done so. Neither they nor the British signatories had bound their nations by the signatures. 'They had to go to their parliament,' he said, 'and we to ours.'

After the Dáil went into private session, the President again referred to the powers of the delegation. Although some people were confused about those powers, he left no doubt that the delegation had the right to sign the agreement. 'Now I would like everybody clearly to understand that the plenipotentiaries went over to negotiate a Treaty, that they could differ from the cabinet if they wanted to, and that in anything of consequence they could take their decision against the decision of the cabinet.' He actually stressed the same point in the Dáil four different times during the debate.

In short, de Valera's position was that the delegation had a right to sign but should not have done so in view of the undertaking given by Griffith at the cabinet meeting not to sign the draft treaty. Collins admitted that Griffith had said he would not sign 'that document', but claimed he had fulfilled that commitment because the document eventually signed had been altered significantly, with the result that 'a different document was signed'. If this was the case, however, the new document should have been submitted to the cabinet in accordance with the instructions. There could be no doubt that Griffith had broken the undertaking involved in either his acceptance of the instructions or his declaration at the cabinet meeting on 3 December that he would not sign the draft terms being discussed.

De Valera felt let down on this matter. He was annoyed that they had not only signed without consulting him again but also published the text of the agreement. 'They not merely signed the document but, in order to make the *fait accompli* doubly secure,' de Valera wrote, 'they published it hours before the President or their colleagues saw it, and were already giving interviews in London and proclaiming its merits and prejudicing the issue at the time it was being read in Dublin.'

The President was obviously annoyed that the plenipotentiaries had not taken their lead from him. 'I was captaining a team,' he told the private session of the Dáil on the first afternoon of the debates, 'and I felt that the team should have played with me to the last and I should have got the chance which I felt would put us over and we might have crossed the bar in my opinion at high tide. They rushed before the tide got to the top and almost foundered the ship.'

'A captain who sent out his crew to sea, and tried to direct operations from dry land!' Collins remarked to those about him.

'I am excusing myself to the Dáil as the captain of the ship and I can only say it is not my fault,' de Valera continued. 'Had the Chairman of the delegation said he did not stand for the things they had said they stood for, he would not have been elected.' Here the President's argument was patently disingenuous. He knew well where Griffith stood when he proposed him for the delegation, and he also knew where Collins stood. That was why he sent Childers to keep an eye on them.

They could hardly be blamed for concluding that de Valera had been acting like a cautious schemer who preferred to stay on the sidelines, at least until the crucial moment. It was as if he was waiting to see how the negotiations would develop before committing himself. In the event of failure he could always blame them. As long as the plenipotentiaries had to refer to him before signing, he could always include some extra demand and get the credit by appearing to rescue the talks at the last moment.

During the afternoon session Collins called several times for the release of various documents relating to the latter stages of the negotiations so deputies could determine for themselves the difference between the signed terms and what the others wanted. In particular, he argued that the counter-proposals which were presented to the British on 4 December should be 'put side by side' with the Articles of Agreement. Otherwise people were likely to think that de Valera, Stack, and Brugha had been standing for an isolated republic, whereas Collins himself believed the difference was not worth fighting over.

De Valera had come prepared to explain exactly what he wanted. He produced his own alternative, which Collins dubbed Document No. 2, and the name stuck. The President made the startling admission that it was 'right to say that there will be very little difference in practice between what I may call the proposals received and what you will have under what I propose. There is very little in practice but there is that big thing that you are consistent and that you recognise yourself as a separate independent State and you associate in an honourable manner with another group.' He contended that if the Dáil stood by his counter-proposals, the British would 'not go to war for the difference'. In other words, both Collins and de Valera were saying that the difference was not worth fighting over.

'I felt the distance between the two was so small that the British would not wage war on account of it,' de Valera explained. 'You may say if it is so small why not take it. But I say, that small difference makes all the difference. This fight has lasted through the centuries and I would be willing to win that little sentimental thing that would satisfy the aspirations of the country.'

Document No. 2 included External Association on the lines of the proposals put forward by the delegation during the final weeks of the London conference. There was no oath in the new document, but there was a stipulation that 'for the purposes of the Association, Ireland shall recognise His Britannic Majesty as head of the Association'. Britain would be afforded the same defence concessions, except that instead of stipulating that the two countries would reconsider the defence clauses in five years, the alternative stated that coastal defence would be handed over 'to the Irish Government, unless some other arrangement for naval defence was agreed upon by both Governments'. The partition clauses were also included practically verbatim in the alternative document, except that there was a declaration to the effect that 'the right of any part of Ireland to be excluded from the supreme authority of the National Parliament and Government' was not being recognised.

In other words, de Valera explained, the alternative would not 'recognise the right of any part of Ireland to secede', but for the sake of internal peace and in order to divorce the Ulster question from the overall Anglo-Irish dispute, he was ready to accept the partition clauses of the Treaty, even though he found them objectionable from the standpoint that they provided 'an explicit recognition of the right on the part of Irishmen to secede from Ireland'.

'We will take the same things as agreed on there,' the President told the Dáil. 'Let us not start to fight with Ulster.'

Collins welcomed Document No. 2 because it confirmed his contention that the delegation had practically achieved its aim. 'The issue has been cleared considerably by the document the President has put in,' he explained. The alternative was basically in line with the proposals put forward by the delegation during the latter stages of the conference.

'We put this before the other side with all the energy we could,' Collins said. 'That is the reason that I wanted certain vital documents and these will show that the same proposals that the President has now drafted have been put already.' Consequently he thought it would be pointless trying to get the British to accept Document No. 2. They would not even listen to any delegation that went back and tried to substitute the alternative for the Treaty. He predicted the British would say, 'You can go to the devil; you can't speak for anyone: you can't deliver the goods.' But he did not elaborate with details right then because he intended to do so when the public session reconvened.

De Valera appeared to confirm this assessment of his own proposals. 'No politician in England would stand by them,' he admitted. 'Because they would have the same difficulty in legally ratifying this proposed Treaty that I hold our delegates have in ratifying it here constitutionally. It would not be a politician's peace but a people's peace.' He subsequently made the same statement in public.

In some respects Collins believed the Treaty was actually better than Document No. 2. Describing the External Association clauses of the alternative as a dangerously loose paraphrase of the Treaty, he later complained that Ireland would be committed to an association so vague that Britain might be able to press for control of Irish affairs as a matter of common concern amongst the countries of the British Commonwealth. Ireland would not have the same status as the dominions, so the latter would not have a vested interest in ensuring that the Dublin government would not be forced to make special concessions to Britain. Such concessions would not establish a precedent for relations between Britain and the dominions as would be the case under the terms of the Treaty. Thus Collins believed that Document No. 2 'had neither the honesty of complete isolation' nor the advantages of 'free partnership'. He admitted there were restrictions in both the Treaty and the President's alternative. '*But,*' he added, '*the Treaty will be operative, and the restrictions must gradually tend to disappear as we go on, more and more strongly solidifying and establishing ourselves as a free nation.*'

De Valera quickly realised that he had made a tactical error in introducing Document No. 2. He therefore withdrew the document at the end of the private session.

When Collins entered the Dáil for the resumption of the public session the following Monday, 19 December 1921, something was obviously wrong. He was not smiling as usual. Instead he looked sour and he slammed his attaché case down on the table in front of him before taking his seat.

On opening the session the Speaker announced that the President wished to inform the Dáil that Document No. 2 was 'withdrawn and must be regarded as confidential until he brings his own proposal forward formally'. Griffith and Collins objected vociferously before the Speaker made it clear that he was not ruling on the issue. Each individual deputy would be free to decide whether or not to comply with de Valera's request.

Griffith formally proposed the motion 'That Dáil Éireann approves the Treaty between Great Britain and Ireland, signed in London on 6 December 1921.' In the course of his speech he complained about not being able to refer to Document No. 2 and also the fact that some people were representing themselves as having 'stood uncompromisingly on the rock of the Republic — the Republic, and nothing but the Republic'.

'It has been stated also here,' he continued, 'that the man who won the war — Michael Collins — compromised Ireland's rights. In the letters that preceded the negotiations not once was a demand made for recognition of the Irish Republic. If it had been made we knew it would have been refused. We went there to see how to reconcile the two positions and I hold we have done it.'

The motion to approve the Treaty was seconded by Seán Mac Eoin. Then de Valera spoke.

'I am against this Treaty because it does not reconcile Irish national aspirations with association with the British Government,' he declared. 'I am against this Treaty, not because I am a man of war, but a man of peace. I am against this Treaty because it will not end the centuries of conflict between the two nations of Great Britain and Ireland.'

The President, who never even alluded to the partition question, kept his remarks very general as he contended that the Treaty was 'absolutely inconsistent with our position; it gives away Irish independence; it brings us into the British Empire; it acknowledges the head of the British Empire, not merely as the head of an association but as the direct monarch of Ireland, as the source of executive authority in Ireland'. The oath was the only aspect of the Treaty to which he took specific exception during his speech.

De Valera's opposition to the oath was by no means straightforward. He had already told the private session that he had suggested that the Irish people could swear 'to keep faith with His Britannic Majesty'. Moreover during the Dáil debate he told an American correspondent, Hayden Talbot of the Hearst newspaper chain, that his problem was not with swearing to be 'faithful to the King'. He did not find the word 'faithful' objectionable at all because he said it could be taken in the context of 'the faithfulness of two equals' to uphold a bargain. His real problem with the oath was in swearing 'allegiance to the constitution of the Irish Free State as by law established'. This, he argued, would be tantamount to swearing direct allegiance to the Crown, seeing that the law which would establish the Free State constitution would be enacted by the British parliament in the name of the Crown. The Provisional Government, which would take over the administration of Ireland from the British, would not be set up by the Dáil, but by the Southern Irish parliament established under the Partition Act passed at Westminster. Thus the Provisional Government would derive its authority from the British King in whose name parliament had passed the Partition Act in the first place. In addition the Free State constitution, which would be drafted by the Provisional Government, would be enacted at Westminster, with the result that if the British had the acknowledged right to enact the Irish constitution in the name of their King, then it would automatically follow that they could amend the constitution if they wished. They would, in effect, be legally able to act in the King's name to interfere in Irish affairs at will.

Collins did not speak until immediately after a lunch-time break. As the Dáil reassembled there was a great buzz of excitement and expectation. 'At the back of the hall visitors, clergymen and telegraph messengers crushed forward to hear,' according to the *Freeman's Journal*. 'A Japanese journalist was wedged in the crowd, and three coloured gentlemen from Trinidad — medical students — leant forward to view the scene' when Collins rose to continue the debate. He was the focus of everyone's attention. 'His flashing eyes, firm jaw, and thick black hair, through which he ran his fingers from time to time, were all revealed under the dazzling light of the electroliers.'

'Mr Collins was passionate, forcible, and at times almost theatrical,' according to *The Irish Times*. Although he had a prepared speech before him, he rarely consulted it. Now and again he would rummage among his papers, feel his smooth chin, or toss his hair with one of his hands. At times he stood erect and at other times he leaned forward. He spoke slowly until aroused by the intensity of his conviction, and then, vibrating with emotion, the words would come in a torrent.

Early in the address he complained that a deputy had suggested the delegation had broken down before the first bit of British bluff. 'I would remind the deputy who used that expression,' Collins said indignantly, 'that England put up a good bluff for the last five years here and I did not break down before that bluff.'

'That's the stuff,' someone shouted while the gathering applauded.

Collins said that he was recommending the Treaty as one of the signatories. 'I do not recommend it for more than it is,' he emphasised. 'Equally I do not recommend it for less than it is. In my opinion it gives us freedom, not the ultimate freedom that all nations desire and develop to, but the freedom to achieve it.'

As a result of the guarantee of the 'constitutional status' of dominions like Canada and South Africa, he contended that those countries would be 'guarantors of our freedom, which makes us stronger than if we stood alone'. He admitted that allowing Britain to retain four ports was a 'departure from the Canadian status', but he felt the Free State's association with the dominions on an equal footing would ensure that Britain would not use the ports 'as a jumping off ground against us'. He also admitted the partition clauses were 'not an ideal arrangement, but if our policy is, as has been stated, a policy of non-coercion, then let somebody else get a better way out of it'. He had planned to compare the Treaty with Document No. 2 but explained that in deference to the President's request, he would not make use of his prepared arguments.

'Rejection of the Treaty means that your national policy is war,' Collins continued. 'I, as an individual, do not now, now more than ever, shrink from war. The Treaty was signed by me, not because they held up the alternative of immediate war. I signed it because I would not be one of those to commit the Irish people to war without the Irish people committing themselves.' This was a rather ironic statement coming from him in the light of his own role in deliberately trying to precipitate a state of general disorder back in 1919.

According to one seasoned parliamentarian, Collins's speech was worthy of a lawyer as well as a politician. 'It was big enough for a trained statesman. I was surprised by its precision and detail, and rhetoric,' Tim Healy wrote. Interspersing the speech with some wry humour, Collins observed that one deputy had complained the Free State could not enjoy the same freedom as Canada because that freedom was largely dependent on that country's distance from Britain. 'It seems to me,' Collins continued, alluding to the same deputy, 'that he did not regard the delegation as being wholly without responsibility for the geographical propinquity of Great Britain to Ireland.'

The speech also contained what may well have been a subtle effort to depict some of his leading opponents as something less than fully Irish. 'I am a representative of Irish stock,' Collins said. 'I am the representative equally with any other member of the same stock of people who have suffered through the terror in the past. Our grandfathers have suffered from war, and our fathers or some of our ancestors have died of famine. I don't want a lecture from anybody as to what my principles are to be now. I am just a representative of plain Irish stock whose principles have been burned into them, and we don't want any assurance to the people of this country that we are not going to betray them. We are one of themselves.'

Few people would have failed to notice that some of the leaders on the other side of the floor, like the American-born de Valera with his Spanish father, or Childers and Brugha with their English backgrounds, were not able to boast of such strong Irish ancestry.

It was a trying day for Collins, who afterwards explained to his fiancée that it was 'the worst day I ever spent in my life'. He wrote that 'the Treaty will almost certainly be beaten and no one knows what will happen. The country is certainly quite clearly for it but that seems to be little good, as their voices are not heard.'

According to Desmond Ryan, who witnessed the proceedings as a journalist, the debate developed into 'one long wrestle between ghosts and realities with all the stored up personal spleen of five years flaming through the rhetoric'. Numerous speakers argued that the various dead heroes would never have accepted the Treaty, but Collins decried the practice. 'Out of the greatest respect for the dead,' he complained, 'we have refrained from reading letters from relatives of the dead. We have too much respect for the dead.' He thought that deputies should not presume to speak for those deceased, though he was understanding when Kathleen Clarke, the widow of one of the 1916 leaders, personally told him that evening that she was going to vote against the Treaty because she believed her late husband would have wished to do so. 'I wouldn't want you to vote for it,' Collins told her. 'All I ask is that if it is passed, you give us the chance to work it.'

With Christmas approaching and no likely end to the debate in sight, the Dáil decided to recess on 23 December until 3 January 1922. During that time the press, which was solidly behind the Treaty, encouraged local bodies to endorse the agreement, and more than twenty county councils responded in a unanimous show of support. But the struggle for ratification was to become a long-drawn-out affair.

During the Christmas recess Labour Party leaders took the initiative to try to avoid a division in the Dáil on the question of the Treaty. They suggested the Dáil should allow the Treaty to become operative by passing legislation to establish the Southern parliament as a committee of the Dáil so that the Provisional Government would also derive its authority from the Dáil. De Valera's strongest objections could be surmounted in this way and the Irish people would be given an opportunity of evaluating the Treaty in practice.

From a practical standpoint Collins really did not care whether Irish freedom was legally derived from the British or anyone else, so long as that freedom was real. He therefore welcomed the Labour Party initiative. 'I think they are the basis of something that can be hammered into an agreement,' he told the Labour representatives on 23 December. Griffith, too, was hopeful on Christmas Day, but de Valera rejected the plan two days later.

Nevertheless Collins was not prepared to forget about the initiative so easily. When the Dáil reconvened on 3 January he suggested the Treaty be accepted without a division and the Dáil then authorise the establishment of the Provisional Government so that it could demonstrate the extent of the country's freedom. 'If necessary,' he said to those across the floor, 'you can fight the Provisional Government on the Republican question afterwards.'

'We will do that if you carry ratification, perhaps,' the President replied, spurning the suggestion.

Interviewed that evening, Collins explained that he was not asking his opponents to do anything dishonourable:

> They are not asked to abandon any principle; they may, if need be, act as guardians of the interests of the nation — act as guarantors of Irish requirements, and act as censors of the Government of the Irish Free State. The Government of the Irish Free State may have difficulties in carrying on and in fulfilling promises contained in the Treaty. If these promises are less in their working out than we who are standing for the Treaty declare, then there is a glorious opportunity for the present opponents of the Treaty to show their ability to guard the Irish nation and to act on its behalf. At the present moment we ask not to be hampered, and if we do not achieve what we desire and intend, we shall willingly make room for the others, and they will have no more loyal supporters than ourselves. This is the one way of restoring unity in the Dáil and to preserve [it] as a body truly representative of the Irish people.

However, de Valera had plans of his own. Next day he released a revised version of Document No. 2 and gave notice of his intention to move it as an amendment to the resolution calling for the approval of the Treaty, even though it had already been agreed that there could be no amendments until the Treaty had been voted on first. This raised the spectre of extending the already drawn-out debate further by allowing each of the more than one hundred deputies to speak again — this time on the amendment. 'If that takes place,' one Cork deputy complained, 'we will go on for ever, or at least till the people come in and pull us out.'

Collins argued that the vote should be taken on the Treaty first, and he was supported by Kevin O'Higgins, but the President was determined to get his own way.

'I am responsible for the proposals and the House will have to decide on them,' he declared. 'I am going to choose my own procedure.'

The Dáil was staggered. Griffith rose and responded in a cold, intent manner. 'I submit it is not in the competence of the President to choose his own procedure,' he declared. 'This is either a constitutional body or it is not. If it is an autocracy let you say so and we will leave it.'

'In answer to that I am going to propose an amendment in my own terms,' the President maintained. 'It is for the House to decide whether they will take it or not.' He seemed to want to 'hurl another few words across the floor, but the soothing hand of a supporter from the bench behind tapping him gently on the shoulder had a calming effect', a reporter wrote. The undignified spectacle was thus mercifully ended and the Dáil recessed for the evening.

Immediately afterwards nine backbenchers representing various shades of opinion — among them Seán T. O'Kelly, Liam Mellows, Paddy Ruttledge, Eoin O'Duffy, and Michael Hayes — met at O'Kelly's home in an effort to find a formula that would prevent a complete split within Sinn Féin. With only Mellows dissenting, they came up with a proposal in line with the idea that opponents should abstain from voting against the Treaty and allow the Provisional Government to function, drawing its powers from the Dáil, while de Valera would remain as President in order 'that every ounce can be got out of the Treaty'.

Griffith and Collins accepted the plan that night, but O'Kelly was unable to contact de Valera. Unfortunately the atmosphere next morning was poisoned by a savage attack on de Valera in the *Freeman's Journal*, whose political correspondent accused him of 'arrogating to himself the rights of an autocrat'.

'It seems as though he wanted to wreck the Dáil before a vote could be taken, and then carry the devastating split as far as his influence could reach, throughout the length and breadth of the land,' the correspondent continued. 'The worst disaster which has befallen Ireland since the Union is imminent, and can only be averted by the deputies who love their country more than they love Mr de Valera, refusing to share his terrible responsibility.'

In the same issue there was also a vitriolic editorial denouncing him for his 'criminal attempt to divide the nation' by pressing 'an alleged alternative' that contained 'all the articles for which the Treaty had been assailed by the "ideal orators of Dáil Éireann"'. Erskine Childers was accused of being the architect of the President's proposals. 'It is the curse of Ireland at this moment that its unity should be broken by such a man acting under the advice of an Englishman who has achieved fame in the British Intelligence Service.' The editorial continued:

> These are the men for whom the nation is to put aside Arthur Griffith, Michael Collins, and Richard Mulcahy.

When the fight was on Mr de Valera and Mr Erskine Childers fell accidentally into the hands of the military.

They were immediately released.

That was the time there was £10,000 for the corpse of Michael Collins.

The Irish people must stand up, and begin their freedom by giving their fate into the hands of their own countrymen.

Whether or not Collins had wished to draw attention to the President's foreign background in his own Dáil speech a fortnight earlier, he quickly dissociated himself from the *Freeman's Journal's* attack. He not only denounced it in the Dáil but also complained to the editor that he did not want his 'name associated with any personal attack on those who are opposed to me politically in the present crisis'.

De Valera remained deeply irritated by the attack. Flatly rejecting the backbench initiative, he insisted that Document No. 2 be accepted instead.

Next morning, 6 January, the Dáil went back into private session in order to consider the initiative, but the President was adamantly opposed. 'I am going to settle all this thing by resigning publicly at the public session,' he stated banging the table in front of him. 'I am not going to connive at setting up in Ireland another government for England.'

When the public session reconvened in an air of expectation on the afternoon of 6 January, the President began by announcing his resignation in the course of a truly extraordinary speech. 'Even in his happiest moments Mr de Valera has scarcely surpassed himself in declaratory power,' one reporter noted. The remarkable address claimed the full attention of the whole Dáil.

De Valera began slowly and deliberately, but his voice became charged with emotion as he defended his alternative. 'Now, I have definitely a policy,' he explained, 'not some pet scheme of my own, but something that I know from four years' experience in my position — and I have been brought up among the Irish people. I was reared in a labourer's cottage here in Ireland.'

The Dáil applauded. This was obviously the President's answer to the snide questioning of his credentials as an Irishman by the *Freeman's Journal*. 'I have not lived solely amongst the intellectuals,' he continued. 'The first fifteen years of my life that formed my character were lived among the Irish people down in Limerick; therefore, I know what I am talking about; and whenever I wanted to know what the Irish people wanted I had only to examine my own heart and it told me straight off what the Irish people wanted.'

This was not some morbid state of megalomania. No doubt there was a strong element of ambition and personal vanity in his argument, but also there was his conviction that he knew better than anybody else what was best for the Irish people. He knew the Irish people did not want the Treaty, and he was determined to wreck it. Hence he announced his resignation as President and said the Dáil would have 'to decide before it does further work, who is to be the Chief Executive in this Nation'. And he was going to stand for re-election.

'If you elect me and do it by a majority,' he said, 'I will throw out that Treaty.' This was a naked attempt to turn the whole Treaty issue into a personal vote of confidence. His manoeuvre evoked so much criticism that he felt compelled to withdraw his resignation, but not before making some self-righteous remarks. It was then proposed and seconded that the standing orders should be suspended in order to discuss the crisis caused by the President's resignation. Collins was enraged.

'The other side may say what they like, and they may put in any motion they like, and they may take any action they like, but we must not criticise them. That is the position that we have been put into,' he declared. 'We will have no Tammany Hall methods here. Whether you are for the Treaty or whether you are against it, fight without Tammany Hall methods. We will not have them.' He went on to complain that the backbench initiative to avoid a division had been frustrated by 'three or four bullies'.

De Valera objected to the use of the term bullies and the Speaker asked Collins to withdraw the remark. There followed an uneasy silence. Collins seemed to seek inspiration from the papers in front of him. Almost a minute passed before he responded.

'I can withdraw the term,' he said slowly and deliberately, 'but the spoken word cannot be recalled. Is that right, sir?'

A showdown with the Speaker had been averted. Deputies laughed and the gathering applauded. But Brugha, who felt that he was one of those alluded to as a bully, was unhappy with the way the remark was withdrawn.

'I don't know to whom he referred when he mentioned this word "bullies",' Brugha said. 'Possibly he may have referred to me as being one of them. In the ordinary way I would take exception and take offence at such a term being applied to me, but the amount of offence that I would take at it would be measured by the respect or esteem that I had for the character of the person who made the charge. In this particular instance I take no offence whatever.'

If the standing orders were suspended, however, Brugha said that Collins and the others should be free to discuss Document No. 2.

'In that case I am satisfied,' Collins replied.

But Griffith was not. He accused the President of violating the agreed procedure. 'He agreed that I should wind up the discussion,' Griffith explained. 'I have listened here for days — during all that time — to arguments and attacks on my honour and the honour of my fellow delegates and I have said nothing. I have waited to wind up this discussion.'

'Why we should be stopped in the middle of this discussion and a vote taken on the personality of President de Valera I don't understand,' Griffith continued. 'And I don't think my countrymen will understand it.'

'I am sick and tired of politics,' de Valera responded, 'so sick that no matter what happens I would go back to private life. I have only seen politics within the last three weeks or a month. It is the first time I have seen them and I am sick to the heart of them.' Depicting himself as straight and honest in the face of the twisted dishonesty of his opponents, he continued, 'it is because I am straight that I meet crookedness with straight dealing always. Truth will always stand no matter from what direction it is attacked.'

Of course, it was disingenuous of de Valera to feign innocence about the seedier side of politics. He had been up to his neck in such politics while in the United States and, arguably, he had more political experience than anyone else in the Dáil. In fact, he refuted his assertion of innocence in the same speech by referring to his American experiences. 'I detest trickery,' de Valera said. 'What has sickened me most is that I got in this House the same sort of dealing that I was accustomed to over in America from other people of a similar kind.' It was particularly significant he should compare his critics in the Dáil with his opponents in the United States, because there was a remarkable similarity between his attitude towards the Treaty and his actions during the Republican Party's national convention at Chicago in June 1920.

'It was a case of Cohalan and his machine over again,' he wrote to McGarrity.

'Insinuations about me have hurt me,' de Valera told the Dáil. 'I am straight with everybody and I am not a person for political trickery; and I don't want to pull a red herring across. If there is a straight vote in this House I will be quite satisfied if it is within forty-eight hours.'

'One of the most irritating features of Mr de Valera's behaviour at this time,' Piaras Béaslaí wrote, 'was that, having used every device of a practical politician to gain his point, having shown himself relentless and unscrupulous in taking every advantage of generous opponents, he would adopt a tone of injured innocence when his shots failed, and assume the pose of a simple sensitive man, too guileless and gentle for this rough world of politics.'

Maybe Collins would have been willing to allow the debate to be diverted, but Griffith was not ready to allow it. It was a political ploy to defeat the Treaty by turning it into a personal vote of confidence in de Valera.

Just as he knew there was no realistic chance of securing diplomatic recognition in the United States in 1920, de Valera knew no British politician would now be prepared to accept his alternative proposals in

Document No. 2. 'No politician in England would stand by them,' he admitted, repeating publicly what he had told the private session before Christmas. 'It would be a document that would give real peace to the people of Great Britain and Ireland and not the officials. I know it would not be a politicians' peace. I know the politician in England who would take it would risk his political future, but it would be a peace between peoples.'

For the Dáil to have accepted the President's suggestion that the Treaty be rejected and Document No. 2 presented to the British instead would have been as foolhardy as he was naive if he really believed that the propaganda campaign advocated by him had any more chance of success than the pathetic failure of his comparatively similar effort to win over the American electorate in 1920 after the Chicago debacle. A successful campaign in 1922 would have needed the sympathetic understanding of at least some sections of the press, and there was little chance of securing this, seeing that the only organs which opposed the Treaty had done so on the grounds that the agreement was too generous towards Sinn Féin. Not one Irish daily newspaper supported de Valera's position, and there was little prospect of getting international support because even American opinion was strongly in favour of the settlement.

Next day the *New York Times* carried an editorial that was bitterly critical of de Valera:

> Apparently he essayed a Napoleonic or Cromwellian stroke in resigning, at the same time that he demanded re-election with all power placed in his hands; but when this failed, he talked and acted like a hysterical schoolgirl. Whatever happens in Ireland, de Valera seems to have hopelessly discredited himself as a leader. Narrow, obstinate, visionary and obviously vain, he has now, in his representative capacity, wrought immense harm to the Ireland of his professed entire devotion.

Harry Boland, who had just returned from the United States to vote against the Treaty, admitted that 'the great public opinion of America is on the side of this Treaty'. Indeed, he added, the American press had adopted 'a unanimous attitude in favour' of it. There was even strong support among some of de Valera's supporters in the United States. The president and vice-president of the American Association for Recognition of the Irish Republic had, for instance, come out in favour of the agreement. So initially had Boland, but he told the Dáil on 7 January that he had issued his statement before the Treaty was published in the United States. He said that he had made the mistake of assuming the Treaty would be favourable because de Valera had assured him nothing less than External Association would be acceptable. But this did not explain why, after the terms were published, he actually denounced Daniel Cohalan and Diarmuid Lynch of the Friends of

Irish Freedom for criticising the agreement. Cohalan and Lynch had, ironically, been among the first to denounce the Treaty, but they subsequently
supported it after they learned de Valera was opposed to it. Such vicissitudes
certainly lent credence to the idea that personalities figured largely in the
controversy.

At one point during his address Boland turned to Collins. 'Is this, in your
opinion, a final settlement of the question between England and Ireland?'

'It is not,' Collins replied.

After Boland finished, Joe McGrath spoke and told how Boland had told
him back in August that he was going to America on de Valera's behalf 'to
prepare the American people for something short of a Republic'.

De Valera objected that what he meant was that, instead of 'an isolated
Republic', External Association would have to be accepted. 'It was because
I was honest and wanted to be honest with the American people that I said
that an isolated Republic would have to be changed into some sort of association,' he added.

Stripped of its polemical distortions and insinuations, the debate centred
on bizarre irrelevancies. Despite the national significance and momentous
implications of the Treaty, it was painfully obvious that personalities were
playing an inordinate role in determining how people were lining up on the
issue. On the one side people were backing de Valera, while on the other
side they were gathering behind Collins.

It was the personality of the Big Fellow which loomed largest during the
closing speeches. Winding up the debate on the anti-Treaty side, Cathal
Brugha delivered a speech that quickly turned into a tirade against Collins,
whom he described as 'merely a subordinate in the Department of Defence'.

Amid cries of 'Shame' and 'Get on with the Treaty', Brugha complained that Collins had originated the stories that there was a price on his
head, and the press had built him into 'a romantic figure' and 'a mysterious
character' which he was not. But it was Griffith's reference to Collins
as 'the man who won the war' that was most irritating to Brugha, who
actually questioned whether Collins 'had ever fired a shot at any enemy
of Ireland'.

For his part, Griffith made no apology for his earlier reference to Collins
when he wound up the debate moments later:

> I said it and I say it again; he was the man that made the situation;
> he was the man, and nobody knows better than I do, how, during
> a year and a half, he worked from six in the morning until two
> next morning. He was the man whose matchless energy, whose
> indomitable will, carried Ireland through the terrible crisis; and
> although I have not now, and never had, an ambition about either
> political affairs or history, if my name is to go down in history I

want it associated with the name of Michael Collins. Michael Collins was the man who fought the Black and Tan terror for twelve months until England was forced to offer terms.

The Dáil erupted with a roar of approval and thunderous applause. It was without doubt the most emotional response of the whole debate. Deputies who had listen to Brugha's invective in embarrassed silence obviously jumped at the opportunity of disassociating themselves from those bitter remarks.

Griffith's speech was described by one journalist as 'by far the most statesmanlike utterance that has been made in the Dáil'. He made some telling points in favour of the Treaty.

'The principle I have stood for all my life is the principle of Ireland for the Irish people. If I can get that with a Republic, I will have a Republic; if I can get that with a monarchy, I will have a monarchy. I will not sacrifice my country for a form of government,' he concluded. 'I say now to the people of Ireland that it is their right to see that this Treaty is carried into operation, when they get for the first time in seven centuries, a chance to live their lives in their own country and take their place among the nations of Europe.'

As the proposer of the resolution calling for the Dáil's approval of the Treaty, Griffith was supposed to have the last word before the vote was taken, but de Valera again violated the procedure.

'Before you take a vote,' he said, 'I want to enter my last protest — that document will rise in judgment against the men who say there is only a shadow of difference.' He was obviously calling on deputies to reject the Treaty in favour of his own Document No. 2.

'Let the Irish nation judge us now and for future years,' cried Collins.

The clerk of the Dáil began calling the roll in the order of constituencies. Armagh came first, so it fell to Collins to cast the first vote. With a faint smile he rose, paused momentarily, and answered slowly 'Is toil'. The clerk continued through the other names, with deputies voting either 'Is toil' or 'Ní toil'.

When the names of the deputies from Cork were reached, Collins was again called upon to vote, but he declined to do so on the grounds that he had voted already. Likewise, when de Valera was called upon to vote for his second constituency, he declined, by shaking his head slowly and smiling across at Collins. But Griffith protested against the disenfranchisement of his second constituency.

It took about ten minutes to complete the voting and another couple of minutes before the announcement was made that the Treaty had been approved by sixty-four votes to fifty-seven. There was no real demonstration within the hall, but when news filtered outside there was a wave of enthusiastic cheering in the street, where a crowd of some hundreds had gathered. The cheering continued for some minutes and seemed to stir those inside the chamber.

'It will, of course, be my duty to resign my office as Chief Executive,' de Valera said. 'I do not know that I should do it just now.'

'No,' cried Collins.

'There is one thing I want to say,' the President continued. 'I want it to go to the country and to the world, and it is this: the Irish people established a Republic. This is simply approval of a certain resolution. The Republic can only be disestablished by the Irish people. Therefore, until such time as the Irish people in regular manner disestablish it, this Republic goes on.'

Collins called for a committee of public safety to be set up by both sides of the Dáil to preserve order. Some people thought de Valera was going to respond favourably until Mary MacSwiney intervened to denounce the vote just taken 'as the grossest act of betrayal that Ireland ever endured'. 'There can be no union between representatives of the Irish Republic and the so-called Free State,' she declared.

De Valera announced he would like to meet 'all those who voted on the side of the established Republic' the following afternoon, and Collins repeated his appeal for 'some kind of understanding' between the two factions 'to preserve the present order in the country'.

'I would like my last word here to be this,' de Valera responded. 'We have had a glorious record for four years, it has been four years of magnificent discipline in our nation. The world is looking at us now —'

At this point he broke down, buried his head in his hands, and collapsed sobbing into his chair. It was a very emotional scene. Women were weeping openly, and Harry Boland was seen with tears running down his cheeks, while other men were visibly trying to restrain their tears.

'So far as I am concerned,' Brugha declared, 'I will see at any rate that discipline is kept in the Army.'

'Do you know, in spite of all,' Collins said afterwards, 'I can't help feeling a regard for Cathal.'

11

Towards the Civil War

Following the Dáil's acceptance of the Treaty, Collins sought to implement it as quickly as possible as a means of enlisting popular support. Convinced of the Treaty's enormous possibilities, he believed he could win over sceptics by demonstrating that the agreement could be used as a stepping-stone to complete independence.

At every step, however, he was confronted by the determination of his opponents. De Valera had first stated that the Treaty was a matter for the cabinet, but when the cabinet approved, he said it was a matter for the Dáil, and now that the Dáil had approved it, he contended that it could only be ratified by the Irish people.

'The resolution recommending the ratification of a certain treaty is not a legal action,' he told the meeting of anti-Treaty deputies at the Mansion House on 8 January 1922. 'That will not be completed until the Irish people have disestablished the Republic which they set up of their own free will.'

He had already indicated his intention of resigning as President, but he told the Mansion House gathering that he intended to run again on a platform of 'no co-operation with pro-treaty leaders' on matters relating to the implementation of the Treaty. At this meeting it was decided to set up Cumann na Poblachta (Republican Association), which amounted to a new party within Sinn Féin, but other than deciding on its name and defining its general aim as 'defending the Republic', little was done to organise it.

While some journalists may have taken de Valera's threat to retire from politics seriously, J. L. Garvin of *The Observer* refused to believe it. In a widely circulated article, republished in the *New York Times*, he described the President as 'a Robespierre who would send the dearest of his former friends to the guillotine for a formula and eat his dinner afterwards with self-righteousness'.

Collins responded to de Valera's resignation next day by proposing that the President be replaced by a committee of public safety consisting of representatives from both sides until a general election could be held. But de Valera rejected this as unconstitutional. 'This assembly must choose its executive according to its constitution,' he insisted.

Kathleen Clarke surprised many at this point by proposing de Valera for re-election as 'President of the Irish Republic'. But Collins was ready for the move.

'We expected something like this,' he said. 'We would have been fools if we had not anticipated it.' If de Valera was re-elected, he warned, 'everybody will regard us a laughing stock'.

De Valera explained that he would 'carry on as before and forget this Treaty', if he was re-elected. 'I do not believe that the Irish people, if they thoroughly understood it, would stand for it,' he added.

It was not just his arrogance that critics found offensive, but also the smug, self-righteous way in which he sought re-election. It was as if he was saying that he wished to go back to private life but, because he was more intelligent than most Irish people and could see things that they could not understand, he would condescend to serve them. 'Remember,' he said, 'I am only putting myself at your disposal and at the disposal of the nation. I do not want office at all.'

'I do not ask you to elect me,' he said, re-emphasising the point moments later. 'I am not seeking to get any power whatever in this nation. I am quite glad and anxious to get back to private life.'

If de Valera won, Collins said that he would quit. 'I will go down to the people of South Cork and tell them that I did my best, that I could bring the thing no further, "and now you can elect a representative who will carry the Irish nation further".'

'There is only one man who can lead us properly and keep us all together,' Brugha interjected. 'If Eamon de Valera did not happen to be President who would have kept Arthur Griffith, Michael Collins and myself together?'

'That is true,' replied Collins. 'It is not today or yesterday it started.'

'I only wish to God we could be brought together again under his leadership,' Brugha continued. 'I only wish it was possible.'

'It is not, though,' said Collins.

In a cold, reasoned response, Griffith depicted de Valera's tactics as a 'political manoeuvre to get round the Treaty'. It was an attempt to exploit the emotions of deputies. 'There is no necessity for him to resign today,' Griffith added. 'His resignation and going up again for re-election is simply an attempt to wreck this Treaty.'

In accordance with the Treaty, a Provisional Government was to be set up in Dublin Castle to take over the administration of the country from the British regime, and de Valera was now suggesting that the pro-Treaty people form a Provisional Government while he would remain on as President of Dáil Éireann as a kind of reserve. 'If the Provisional Government goes to

Dublin Castle and takes on the functioning we will not interfere with them,' he said. 'Let them deal with their government as they please.'

As nobody else had been nominated for President, Stack argued that de Valera 'has been re-elected unanimously'.

'Well, I am voting against anyway,' Collins declared.

Another deputy supported Stack's argument, but de Valera objected. 'I cannot, naturally, stand for that,' he said.

Collins tried to nominate Griffith, but the Speaker ruled the Dáil would have to vote on de Valera's nomination first. As the roll was called, de Valera refused to vote in an apparent effort to dramatise his contention that he did not want the office. This might easily have been a very costly gesture, because the vote was extremely close. He was only defeated by sixty votes to fifty-eight. If just one more deputy had voted in favour instead of against de Valera, his own vote would have given him victory by sixty votes to fifty-nine. His abstention, however, would have led to a tie and the Speaker, Eoin MacNeill, who was pro-Treaty, would probably have voted against the nomination.

The problems of implementing the Treaty in the face of obstructionist opposition became apparent when Collins proposed Griffith as 'President of the Provisional Executive', rather than as President of the Dáil or of the Irish Republic. Article 17 of the Treaty stipulated that 'a meeting of members of Parliament elected for constituencies in Southern Ireland' should meet to select a Provisional Government — all the members of which had to signify in writing their acceptance of the Treaty.

Collins wished the Dáil to authorise the establishment of the Provisional Government so that it would have continuity from the Irish people. He did not care if the British contended its authority was derived from Westminster. That made no practical difference. But de Valera was adamant that the Dáil could not transfer any of its authority, or do anything to implement the Treaty, without the prior approval of the Irish people. He was contending, in effect, that until the Treaty was ratified there would have to be two Irish governments — the Dáil executive, which would be recognised under Irish law, and the Provisional Government, which would take over the adminis-tration at Dublin Castle and would thus only be recognised under British law.

This whole argument now centred around the actual title of the chief executive and it was ironic that de Valera, of all people, should be so obstinate over the title, seeing that he had changed the title of his own office from Príomh-Aire to President back in 1919 without even consulting his colleagues. Indeed he waited for more than two years before requesting the Dáil to regu-larise the constitutional position with an oblique amendment in August 1921.

The wrangle over the title was unresolved until next day when de Valera was given his own way. 'If I am elected,' Griffith told the Dáil, 'I will occupy whatever position President de Valera occupied.'

'Hear, hear,' exclaimed de Valera. He had won his point. 'I feel that I can sit down in this assembly while such an election is going on.'

Minutes later, however, he changed his mind and announced that he was walking out of the Dáil 'as a protest against the election as President of the Irish Republic of the Chairman of the Delegation who is bound by the Treaty'. Accompanied by his supporters, he then walked out of the chamber in what could only be described as a contemptuous insult towards what he insisted was the sovereign assembly of the nation. It was all the worse in the face of a most conciliatory attitude adopted by his opponents.

Collins was indignant. 'Deserters all!' he shouted at those leaving. 'We will now call on the Irish people to rally to us. Deserters all!'

Countess Markievicz turned and shouted towards Collins and Griffith: 'Oath breakers and cowards.'

'Foreigners — Americans — English,' snapped Collins.

'Lloyd Georgeites,' cried Markievicz. Mary MacSwiney also shouted something but her words were drowned out amid cries of 'Up the Republic' and the counter-taunts of those remaining in the chamber. The sorry spectacle was mercifully ended as the last of the protesters left the chamber.

Griffith was then elected without any further opposition. He proceeded to call a meeting of the Southern parliament, but in obvious deference to the de Valera group, he did not do so as President of the Dáil, but as chairman of the delegation which had negotiated the Treaty. In theory the Southern parliament was a much smaller body than the Dáil, seeing that everyone elected to Stormont was entitled to sit in the Dáil, but in practice this made little difference because, with just one exception, all the deputies who took their Dáil seats had been elected in the twenty-six counties. The one exception was Seán Milroy, a pro-Treaty deputy from County Fermanagh.

Members of the second Dáil had been elected under the machinery to set up the Southern parliament, which was supposed to set up the Provisional Government. It was therefore summoned but only pro-Treaty deputies and the unionists elected for Trinity College turned up at the Mansion House on Saturday, 14 January. A Speaker was elected and a motion to approve the Treaty was proposed by Piaras Béaslaí and promptly agreed without a division. A further motion was then approved ratifying the appointment of an eight-man Provisional Government under the chairmanship of Collins.

All of this had been agreed in advance by the Dáil cabinet. They were just going through the motions of duplicating everything to satisfy both de Valera and the British. It was really only a cosmetic exercise. Others might have highlighted the significance of the occasion with some kind of ceremonial address, but not Collins. 'We did not come here to speak, but to work,' he said.

Griffith said a few words about the difficulties on the road ahead and the assembly then adjourned, never to meet again. The whole thing was over in three-quarters of an hour.

Ever since the establishment of the Dáil there had been two administrations in Ireland — the Dáil and the Crown regime at Dublin Castle. In theory this arrangement was continuing, with Collins and the Provisional Government taking over at Dublin Castle. But, with the exception of Griffith and Mulcahy, members of the Dáil cabinet were appointed to the same portfolios in the Provisional Government with the result that the two administrations were effectively being combined under the dual leadership of Griffith and Collins. They had worked well together both while de Valera was in the United States and again during the Treaty negotiations. Hence the dual set-up, insisted on by de Valera, was never likely to be much more than a minor inconvenience.

De Valera declared next day that he would never take the Treaty oath. 'We will continue every resistance against outside authority that has been imposed on the Irish people,' he said. 'We have a perfect right to resist by every means in our power.'

'Even by war?' a reporter asked.

'By every means in our power,' de Valera insisted.

In the coming weeks while de Valera railed against the Treaty — 'It is not a stepping-stone, but a barrier in the way of complete independence,' he argued in an interview with the International News Service on 15 January 1922 — Collins would try to implement it in order to convince the people of the benefits.

Collins sought to do this by taking over from the British in order to facilitate their earliest possible withdrawal. He met with Sir John Anderson, one of the under-secretaries of state, to make preliminary arrangements for the hand-over of power. It was not a particularly memorable meeting, except for one brief exchange. While Anderson and Collins were closeted together, Judge John Wylie, the man who had prosecuted the 1916 leaders, entered the room.

'You met the Judge before, of course?' Anderson asked.

'That's the damn silliest question I ever heard,' the Big Fellow replied. 'Would I be here if I'd met the Judge before?'

As part of the transitional process Collins and his team of ministers went to Dublin Castle on 16 January. Officially, they were there to receive their commissions from the Lord-Lieutenant, but this aspect was deliberately obscured. Inside the Castle they were met by the other under-secretary of state, Sir James MacMahon.

'We're glad to see you, Mr Collins,' MacMahon said.

'Like hell you are,' the Big Fellow growled.

The heads of the various departments met their new bosses in the under-secretary's room. The two groups sat across from each other, eyeing one another suspiciously. The civil servants were struck by the youth of the members of their new government. One of the civil servants noted that

Collins was 'cordiality itself, and there was none of the "top dog" attitude about him'. This, of course, was typical of him. The Big Fellow would show off by reserving his insolence for their bosses, people like MacMahon, or the army commander, General Sir Nevil Macready.

The resolution approving the Treaty was formally handed by Collins to the Lord-Lieutenant, who delivered a short address. Afterwards Collins bounded from the Castle into his taxi and returned to the Mansion House, where he issued a statement. He had just received his commission from the representative of the British King. In effect, he had at least temporarily abandoned the republican stance taken in 1919, but he made no mention of this. Instead he had the exquisite audacity to put his own particular spin on the proceedings: 'Members of Rialtas Sealadach na hÉireann [Provisional Government of Ireland] received the surrender of Dublin Castle at 1.45 p.m. today,' he announced. 'It is now in the hands of the Irish nation.' Thereafter, even historians would refer to what happened that day as 'the surrender of Dublin Castle'.

The task confronting Collins and his colleagues was a formidable one. There they were, 'eight young men in the City Hall standing amidst the ruins of one administration, with the foundations of another not yet laid, and with wild men screaming through the keyhole', according to Kevin O'Higgins. 'No police force was functioning through the country, no system of justice was operating, the wheels of administration hung idle, battered out of recognition by the clash of rival jurisdictions.'

Collins was personally taking on mammoth responsibilities. As well as being Minister for Finance in the Dáil, he assumed the duties of Finance Minister in the Provisional Government, which meant that he was in charge of fourteen different offices or departments, such as the treasury, internal revenue, board of works, and customs and excise. These would normally be taxing enough for any politician, but Collins also assumed the chairmanship of a committee to draw up the new constitution, and as Chairman of the Provisional Government, he had to oversee the transition of the overall structures of government, which necessitated frequent visits to London. In addition, he was still director of intelligence in the army, as well as president of the supreme council of the IRB. On top of all these he was required to play an arduous political role in defending his new regime against the constant sniping of his political opponents.

On 11 January several prominent officers had served notice on the Minister for Defence, Richard Mulcahy, demanding that he call an army convention, or they would do so themselves. The signatories included four members of the headquarters staff — Rory O'Connor, Liam Mellows, Seán Russell, and Jim O'Donovan.

Many of the ordinary Volunteers felt that they should have a much greater say about future events. Anti-Treaty elements controlled most of the

IRA units outside Dublin and they were anxious that the army should break away from the Dáil and revert to its previous independent status. In response to their demands, Mulcahy summoned a meeting of the headquarters staff and divisional commandants to discuss the situation on 18 January.

The anti-Treaty officers demanded that a full convention be convened on 5 February to select an executive that would take over supreme control of the army from the Minister for Defence. Ernie O'Malley explained that he would not recognise the authority of either the Minister for Defence or the new chief of staff, Eoin O'Duffy, who replaced Mulcahy after the latter became Minister for Defence. O'Malley's remarks were a blatant repudiation of de Valera's statement a few weeks earlier that the army owed full allegiance to the Dáil through the Minister for Defence.

De Valera personally protested against holding the convention, but O'Connor was not prepared to heed him. 'It doesn't matter to me what he said,' O'Connor commented. 'Some of us are no more prepared to stand for de Valera than for the Treaty.'

At the meeting on 18 January Collins appealed to the anti-Treaty officers to hold the line, for the time being, because the British could not be expected to hand over facilities to the IRA if the latter withdrew its allegiance to the Dáil. For the next six months Collins would play a double game. Publicly he would stand for the Treaty, while privately he tried to convince the anti-Treaty militants that he was as determined as ever to rid the country of the British, only now he was attempting to do so by peaceful means. 'My idea is that if we can get our own army we can tell the British to go to hell,' he told anti-Treaty officers.

In reality he was acting in much the same way he had conducted himself throughout the Black and Tan period. When in a tight situation he would go up to the enemy and talk with them as if he were a sympathiser. Playing this double game came quite naturally to him, but now he seemed to be playing it with everyone — at times possibly even with himself.

He wanted the anti-Treaty officers to trust him, but some of them no longer had any time for him. Jim O'Donovan, the director of chemicals, actually sparked an unseemly row. 'You are a traitor,' he snapped at Collins, 'and you should have been court-martialled long since for treason.'

Collins jumped to his feet in indignation. Even many of the anti-Treaty people present were incensed. There were shouts of 'Apologise' and 'Withdraw'.

'I will not withdraw the word,' O'Donovan insisted. 'It is true.'

Although most of the anti-Treaty people present wished to set up their own independent headquarters, Liam Lynch would not hear of this, and he was supported by Frank Aiken. Eventually it was decided that a full convention of the IRA would be held in two months' time. The meeting agreed that in the meantime the IRA headquarters would be run by a four-man committee with two members from each side of the Treaty divide. Mulcahy, who was to preside over the committee, did not like the arrangement, but he agreed to it in order to buy time. It never really amounted to much anyway, because Ernie O'Malley, one of the anti-Treaty duo, was so determined to break away from the Dáil that he never even attended a meeting.

Afterwards Collins was obviously troubled by the growing rift between himself and his former colleagues. 'I am more sorry than you are that the President and Harry are on the other side from myself,' he wrote to a friend of Boland. 'I believe they have missed the tide, for, were it not for taking the bold course I am certain this country would have been split by contending factions, whether we liked it or not. If there be but good will on all sides I am convinced we may still bring the whole thing to final success. In any case, we are going forward, the English are evacuating this country, and surely no one will claim that we can possibly be worse off when that evacuation is complete.'

He was in fact playing the same double game on both the political and military fronts. On 30 January he established a committee under his own chairmanship to draw up a constitution. Although he presided over the committee for the first meeting in the Shelbourne Hotel, he handed over the actual drafting to a panel of experts under Darrell Figgis, who was appointed vice-chairman. Other members included James Douglas, Hugh Kennedy, James Murnahan, James MacNeill, Professor Alfred O'Rahilly, Kevin O'Shiel, and John O'Byrne.

'You are not to be bound by legal formalities but to put up a constitution of a Free State and then bring it to the Provisional Government who will fight for the carrying of it through,' Collins told them. 'It is a question of status and we want definitely to define and produce a true democratic constitution. You are to bear in mind not the legalities of the past but the practicalities of the future.'

Collins maintained contact with members the committee, but essentially left the detailed drafting to them. He attended only one other meeting. In notes to Douglas, he indicated that he wanted a constitution that would be short, simple, and easy to alter as the final stages of complete freedom were achieved. He desired that it should contain only what was necessary to establish constitutional machinery to govern Ireland and suggested the committee omit everything already covered in the Treaty, such as the oath and the clauses dealing with the Governor-General. He also said that the authority of the constitution should rest solely upon authority derived from the Irish people, and that no phrase was to appear which vested executive powers in the King. In short, he was asking the committee to draw up a republican document that would be acceptable to the British.

Collins must have known that this was essentially an impossible task. Although he did not intend that the actual constitution should be ready before June, he asked them to have a rough draft prepared by the end of February. He apparently intended to use this draft constitution to placate the opponents of the Treaty and, then, once the people ratified the Treaty at the polls in April, the constitution would be completed. If he did not use this kind of deception, he warned the British, the Irish people would reject the Treaty.

'If they did not have an election till after the Constitution was drafted,' Collins told the British on 5 February, 'the Treaty would be beaten in Ireland.'

That same evening he met General Sir Nevil Macready to discuss the withdrawal of British forces. He was trying to get the British to believe that he was only stringing along the more militant anti-Treaty elements until he could get the people to ratify the Treaty. At the same time he was giving the anti-Treaty people the impression that he was only stringing along the British until he could get them to withdraw their forces. Once the British had withdrawn, he indicated to his militant friends, it would be a lot easier to change the obnoxious aspects of the Treaty unilaterally. Of course, he could not announce this publicly, because it would scupper the withdrawal.

———————

One of the areas of enormous potential in the Treaty concerned the partition question. Collins was convinced it contained the means of ending partition, because the Boundary Commission could, if implemented properly, render Northern Ireland an unviable entity; hence, he thought that this could be used as a lever to persuade the unionists to agree to a form of unity with safeguards for their own interests.

While he was in London to discuss the transfer of power to the Provisional Government, Collins met Craig on 21 January 1922. They talked about the possibility of closer relations between their respective governments.

'Can we come to some agreement — some agreement which will allay the horror of the past, calm down the people, try to encourage the best elements throughout the whole of Ireland, and then leave the road open in some future time for the Ulster people whether they will come into your Free State or whether they will not?' Craig began. 'It is for you to decide your future policy.'

For three hours they discussed various issues affecting the future of the island. 'We were able to put our joint names to a document,' Craig explained. By so doing, he contended, the Free State effectively recognised Northern Ireland and established a precedent for talks between 'Irishmen who wished well to their common country'.

They decided to try to settle the boundary issue by mutual agreement, instead of relying on the Boundary Commission, and Collins agreed to have the Belfast boycott 'discontinued immediately'. In return, Craig promised 'to facilitate in every possible way the return of Catholic workmen — without tests — to the shipyards as and when trade enables the firms concerned to absorb the present unemployed'.

They also discussed the Council of Ireland, which was supposed to be set up under the Government of Ireland Act to co-ordinate matters of common concern between the Dublin and Belfast governments. Craig suggested that it should be scrapped and replaced by joint meetings of the two cabinets, but Collins rejected this because he did not want to recognise the Northern government formally as there would be nothing to bargain with later. Collins proposed instead joint meetings of the two parliaments, but Craig argued that the time was not ripe for this. In the end they merely agreed to try 'to devise a more suitable system than the Council of Ireland for dealing with problems affecting all Ireland'. They also agreed to meet again in Ireland to discuss the thorny question of prisoners.

On just about every issue Collins appeared to concede, but he was happy enough, as was Craig. Believing that it was necessary to either fight the North or make peace with it, Collins had decided to try the peaceful road first. It seemed as if the Big Fellow was making monumental concessions, but in reality his magnanimous gesture on the boycott was of little practical significance. As far as he was concerned the boycott had been 'comparatively ineffective', and he had concluded that it would be better to replace it with tariffs, if necessary. Hence he was careful to include a stipulation in their agreement that the whole thing was without prejudice to future consideration of tariffs by the Dublin government.

Yet it soon became apparent that one or both of them had been engaging in some wishful thinking about the other's position.

'With regard to the Boundary Commission I think I have satisfied him, and he has satisfied me, that it is far better that the two controlling interests should meet together and work out a boundary which will be agreeable to those who are living on that boundary rather than have an artificial line, which may leave behind it constant irritation and a great deal of trouble with which we have been afflicted in the past,' Craig told a unionist gathering at the Ulster Hall on 27 January.

'I can promise you here today that there will be agreement on the matter,' the Northern Prime Minister added. 'He and I will be faithful to the bargain we have entered into, and there will be no disturbance of those people who would desire to go from under our flag to the Free State.'

Craig's use of terms like 'our land' and 'common country' certainly looked hopeful, as did his acceptance that there would be no hindrance of those wishing to give allegiance to the Free State. When Craig said that to him, Collins thought he was talking about people in the border areas staying put and simply transferring their allegiance to Dublin, but Craig actually envisioned those people transferring themselves physically to the twenty-six counties.

'I will never give in to any rearrangement of the boundary that leaves our Ulster area less than it is under the Government of Ireland Act,' Craig told the cheering unionist throng at the Ulster Hall.

Collins was giving up the right to arbitration in relation to the boundary dispute and agreeing to suspend the boycott, in return for Craig's promise that the Roman Catholics dismissed from the Belfast shipyards would eventually be rehired. Because of an economic slowdown at the time, they could not be re-employed for some time. Thus, Collins really got nothing but platitudes. It looked like a poor bargain, and the confusion led to suspicion of bad faith on both sides.

The confusion was understandable enough. Craig had been led by the British to believe that the Boundary Commission was designed merely to redraw the border so that pockets of Protestants in Counties Monaghan and Donegal could be included in the North, in return for similar-size pockets of Roman Catholics so that the overall area of Northern Ireland would remain the same. Collins, on the other hand, was convinced that all the nationalist areas adjacent to the border would be transferred.

When Collins met Craig for a second time on 2 February, their talks broke down over the extent of territorial revision that might be expected from the Boundary Commission. Collins contended that 'large territories' would be involved 'and not merely a boundary line', as Craig was given to understand privately by several British ministers.

Most people in the Dáil accepted Collins's interpretation, which explains why there had been so little opposition to the partition clauses of the Treaty. Why did people so readily accept this interpretation?

For one thing, Lloyd George had indicated during the Treaty debate in the House of Commons that counties like Fermanagh and Tyrone could only remain within Northern Ireland by force, and he made it clear that he was opposed to such force. And Collins indicated privately that he had received some kind of informal assurance from the British during the negotiations.

During the Treaty debate in the Dáil, for instance, Collins used to meet regularly with IRB colleagues like Seán Ó Muirthile, Joe McGrath, and P. S. O'Hegarty. One evening O'Hegarty mentioned he was surprised at how the anti-Treaty people were essentially ignoring the partition issue.

'It's an astonishing thing to me,' he said, 'that in the attack on the Treaty practically nothing is said about partition, which is the one real blot on it.'

'Oh, but that is provided for,' Ó Muirthile replied. 'Didn't you know?'

'How is it provided for?' O'Hegarty asked. 'Ulster will opt out.'

'Before they signed,' Ó Muirthile explained, 'Griffith and Collins got a personal undertaking from Smith [Birkenhead] and Churchill that if Ulster opted out they would get only four counties and that they would make a four-county government impossible.'

O'Hegarty looked over at Collins, who grinned. 'That's right,' he said.

Tim Healy told a relatively similar story. In the final week of the Treaty negotiations he informed William O'Brien that he dined with Lloyd George and Churchill. Healy told them that Northern Ireland's right to secede was 'likely to be intolerable to Irish national sentiment'. But, according to Healy, Churchill remarked that there was no need to worry on that point, because the government was ready to appoint a Boundary Commission that would 'ensure the transfer to the Free State of the counties of Tyrone and Fermanagh, South Armagh, and (if I remember rightly) South Down, together with the towns of Londonderry, Enniskillen and Newry, and the inevitable result being that Sir James Craig, with the three counties left to him, would be compelled ("compelled" or "forced" was quite certainly the word used) to follow the example'.

'That,' said Healy, 'is a statement of supreme importance. Do you mind repeating it, so as to enable me to transmit it to those men. I cannot imagine anything better calculated to silence their objections.'

Healy took down Churchill's words in shorthand. 'Am I to understand,' he asked, 'that that assurance is endorsed by the Prime Minister?'

'It certainly is,' Lloyd George replied.

Healy read his shorthand notes to O'Brien, who later said that this was the crucial point in the negotiations. But the records of the actual discussions do not back that up. The sticking points in the negotiations concerned the Crown and the association questions. O'Brien's story of Healy's impact on Griffith and Collins was only third hand.

As a Northern Protestant and a member of both Griffith's cabinet and the Provisional Government, Ernest Blythe had a deep personal interest in the Ulster situation, but he dismissed the suggestion that any such assurance had ever been given, because he believed that Griffith and Collins would undoubtedly have mentioned it in cabinet.

'I was present at a good many cabinet meetings with both in the early months of 1922, and I never heard either of them say anything of the kind,' Blythe explained. 'Of course both believed in making our maximum claim and both hoped for the best, and people may have confused what they said we should claim with what they believed we might get.'

Blythe was present when Kevin O'Higgins actually asked Lloyd George what the twenty-six counties was likely to get from the Boundary Commission.

'Who am I to say what a judicial commission will decide?' the Prime Minister replied.

In his own account of his private meeting with Lloyd George hours before the Treaty was signed, Collins indicated that the Prime Minister had referred to predictions made by Collins himself. 'He remarked that I myself pointed out on a previous occasion that the North would be forced economically to come in,' Collins reported.

Lloyd George had not disagreed with the assessment, but that is something vastly different from guaranteeing that the territory would actually be transferred. If the British were prepared to give such an assurance, Collins should have secured documentary evidence of the promise.

Seán Mac Eoin later stated that Collins actually got a commitment from Birkenhead in writing 'that if the Six Counties opted out of the all-Ireland parliament, the British Government agreed that instead of one representative on the Boundary Commission they would accept Collins's nomination of their man and this gave the Free State two members instead of one. This would rectify the situation in Ireland's favour.'

'Collins gave me that letter to read,' Mac Eoin continued. But he added that this letter vanished after Collins was killed. It seems strange that nobody else ever mentioned seeing that document.

Blythe dismissed the story. 'If you knew Seán Mac Eoin even fairly well,' Blythe wrote, 'you would know that he inclines to give play to his imagination and his sense of the dramatic when he is talking about other people and wants to make his story sound a little sensational. I venture to say that no one knowing him even fairly well would attach any importance to testimony from him which, on a matter not directly concerning himself, was intrinsically unlikely. Birkenhead may, like all men, have been foolish in some respects, but he certainly was not enough of a blithering idiot to write a letter of the kind suggested. Whatever he may have done during negotiations by way of innuendo or private hint to suggest vaguely the possibility of substantial transfers to the Free State we can be sure that he did not speak as suggested by Mac Eoin.'

Birkenhead was actually one of the ministers who was privately assuring the unionists that large areas would not be involved in the Boundary Commission transfer. 'The real truth is,' he wrote to Arthur J. Balfour, 'that Collins, very likely pressed by his own people and anxious to appraise at their highest value the benefits which he had brought to them in a moment of excitement, committed himself unguardedly to this doctrine, and that it had no foundation whatever except in his overheated imagination.'

'At no time was there any question of being misled by Mr Lloyd George,' Collins declared on 3 February 1922. 'I never went on any opinion of his on the subject. It was a matter for the inhabitants of the areas involved and for them only.'

The stories about a secret assurance were therefore probably fanciful, but they were the kind of stories that people wished to believe. There can be no doubt that Lloyd George deliberately allowed Collins to expect the transfer of large areas, and he even encouraged this with his remarks during the Treaty debate in the House of Commons.

By mid-February Griffith feared that London 'were backing off' on the Ulster question. 'If the British Government stands firmly on this situation,' he wrote to Collins, 'we'll [be] saved. Otherwise disaster.'

Collins complained to Churchill of provocation in Northern Ireland, after five members of the IRA were charged with possession of arms in early January 1922. They had fired shots at a funeral over the grave of a comrade. At the time they were supposed to have until 28 February to surrender their arms. Collins was particularly annoyed that special police constables had been drafted into nationalist areas like Newry, where they were 'hunting down and tracking every person suspected of having nationalist sympathies and in general doing their best to make trouble'. He argued that the provocation was 'apparently part of a determined plan to exasperate nationalist feeling beyond endurance, and thereby stir up strife and chaos between neighbours'. But then, as we will see later, Collins himself was already stirring up things in the North behind the scenes.

On the domestic front de Valera increased the political temperature on 12 February with the first of a series of political rallies around the country. He was introduced to the crowd from a platform under the Parnell monument in O'Connell Street by Count Plunkett as 'President de Valera — head of the Irish Republic'. He was welcomed by the huge crowd, but it was made up of 'what railway people call "novelty traffic"', according to Tim Healy. 'There was a great curiosity and no enthusiasm.'

De Valera told the crowd that the Irish people would not accept the Treaty because it was signed under duress. 'We, Irish Republicans, feel no more bound by that agreement signed in that fashion than the nationalists of the generations that have passed felt themselves bound by the equally infamous Act of Union,' he said. 'The independence and unity of Ireland have been hopelessly compromised unless you prevent it.'

Gradually de Valera would begin to harp on the drawbacks of the partition issue, which he had showed a willingness to accept during a private session of the Dáil before the Treaty negotiations. 'As far as I was concerned,' he said, 'I would rather have taken the old Council of Ireland Bill for the whole of Ireland than the fullest measure of Home Rule for twenty-six counties. I have made my position as regards partition clear in the Ard Fheis speech of 26 October. It was clear to the Chairman of the Delegation when he went to London, because in the draft Treaty there was a proposal with regard to the six counties.'

In fact there was no clause in Draft Treaty A when the delegation went to London, and his public stance on the issue was merely a negotiating posture. The following Sunday, 19 February, de Valera held a similar rally in Cork at which he raised the political temperature further.

'If the Treaty was signed under duress the men who went to London broke faith with the Irish people,' he declared. 'If it was signed without duress they were traitors to the cause.'

It was particularly volatile stuff. He said the country was 'in greater danger' than at any time in the last seven hundred and fifty years, because 'for the first time in that period a suggestion was being made to give Britain democratic title in Ireland'. He therefore challenged the Provisional Government to fulfil its promise to provide a constitution that would give the Irish people complete freedom.

'Let them make the boast good,' de Valera said, 'frame it, and then come before the people and they would know what they were voting on.'

Over three thousand delegates gathered at the Mansion House a couple of days later for the Sinn Féin Ard Fheis, which was dominated by the personalities of de Valera and Collins. 'As long as I have been working in the Sinn Féin movement,' de Valera said in his opening presidential address, 'I have never had a partisan idea in my mind and I hope I will die without being a partisan in that sense.'

During the Treaty negotiations he had been insisting on the unqualified allegiance of the IRA to the government, but now that he was in opposition, he called for two separate armies. 'I have sufficient faith in the Irish people to believe that they can divide without turning on one another,' he said.

Most of the anti-Treaty animosity at the Ard Fheis was directed at Collins. At one point de Valera looked straight at him. 'There are people who talk of Ireland being a mother country but who are content to make here the illegitimate daughter of Britain.'

The main issue before the conference was a resolution proposed by de Valera stipulating that 'the Organisation shall put forward and shall support at the coming Parliamentary elections only such candidates as publicly sub-scribe to it, and pledge themselves not to take an oath of fidelity to, or owe allegiance to, the British King'.

Collins argued repeatedly for the chance to demonstrate the benefits of the Treaty. 'If there is any false dealings with us by England,' he declared, 'they will find I am not a Redmond or a Dillon to deal with.' His supporters relished this kind of bravado.

'Some people say that England cannot now make war on this country,' he added. 'I know that England can go to war, and will go to war, and is at this moment watching for an opportunity to go to war with us.'

'It is for the Irish people to say whether they will have the Treaty or not,' Brugha interjected. 'Put it to the Irish electors and let them decide, whether Mr Collins decided to resign or not. Let the British put someone else in Mr Collins's place.'

There were loud shouts of 'Withdraw!'

'The people of South Cork put me there, not the British,' Collins replied amid the uproar.

Confusion reigned for some moments before de Valera announced that Brugha would withdraw his statement in substance. 'I had no intention and

I have no intention of offending Mr Collins,' Brugha said. 'Mr Collins has been put in that position as a result of the Treaty in London.'

'By whom?' some people shouted.

'By the majority of Dáil Éireann,' Brugha conceded, and the gathering applauded. 'Is that sufficient now?'

There were cries of 'Yes' from around the hall.

The day's proceedings dragged on for some nine hours. Although Michael Hopkinson has argued that there was very probably a pro-Treaty majority at the Ard Fheis, because of the make-up of the standing committee elected in January, the organisation outside Dublin was largely in the hands of militants. Collins actually admitted that the anti-Treaty faction probably had a majority, and he was therefore facing defeat. Towards the end of the day's deliberations, he suggested that they should adjourn for three months to allow passions to cool and give people a chance to see how things were developing in Northern Ireland. Afterwards he and Griffith got together with de Valera and Stack and hammered out a formal agreement.

It stipulated that the elections would be postponed for three months 'in order to avoid a division of the Sinn Féin Organisation'. Several other reasons were also given, such as allowing the Treaty signatories to draft a constitution that would be published before the election, so that the people would be better able to decide between the Republic and the Free State before voting. During the three-month delay all departments were to be allowed to function as before the signing of the Treaty.

'These articles,' de Valera told the Ard Fheis next day, 'have been signed by President Griffith and myself, Michael Collins and Austin Stack. Four of us have signed these articles of agreement, and we have agreed that we present them to you without speeches.' Naturally, they received the over-whelming approval of the convention.

The first weekend following the árd fheis de Valera was again campaigning against the Treaty, this time in Limerick and Ennis. In the circumstances, the pro-Treaty side could not afford to allow him to do all the running. They felt compelled to respond on behalf of the Treaty.

Collins and Griffith therefore addressed a massive rally near Trinity College Dublin the following Sunday, 5 March. Although it was a blustery day with showers, a huge crowd gathered between the college and the old parliament building, now housing the Bank of Ireland. Students gathered on the roof of the college and there was hardly room for people to move by 3 p.m. when the proceedings were to begin.

There were several minutes of cheering when Collins mounted the platform under the portico of the bank opposite Thomas Moore's statue. He took off his hat and coat and walked to the front of the platform and stood there with his hands on the wooden rail until the cheering died down. He then began in a deep, clear voice, and his words were broken only by applause, except for a group of women hecklers.

The speech was a fine blend of emotional appeal and logical argument. He had hoped to have the new constitution ready so that the real benefits of the Free State would be apparent for all to see, before taking the case for the Treaty to the public, but because of de Valera's regular rallies against the Treaty throughout the country, it had become necessary to speak out now.

After meeting with Lloyd George the previous July, de Valera recognised that 'the Republican ideal' was 'physically impossible' for the time being and therefore surrendered that ideal, according to Collins. 'We were sent to make a Treaty with England,' he said. 'Everyone knew then, and it is idle and dishonest to deny now, that in the event of a settlement some postponement of the realisation of our full national sentiment would have to be agreed to.' But now de Valera and his supporters were saying that they were again standing for the Republic.

'What has happened since to account for the burial of the Republican ideal and its subsequent resurrection?' Collins asked.

'Jealousy,' someone shouted from the crowd.

'I will tell you what has happened since. The Treaty has been brought back,' he continued. 'We could not beat the British out by force, so the Republican ideal was surrendered. But when we have beaten them out by the Treaty, the Republican ideal, which was surrendered in July, is restored.'

He accused de Valera and other critics of exploiting the situation. 'They are stealing our clothes,' Collins said. 'We have beaten out the British by means of the Treaty. While damning the Treaty, and us with it, they are taking advantage of the evacuation.'

Figurative speech was often used by de Valera as an effective oratorical device. In Limerick the previous week, for instance, he had said that the Irish people were like a party that had set out to cross a desert, but on coming to an oasis, some of them argued that they should lie down and stay there, and be satisfied and not go on. 'Yes,' Collins now countered, 'we have come by means of the Treaty to a green oasis, the last in the long weary desert over which the Irish nation has been travelling. Oases are the resting place of the desert, and unless the traveller finds them and replenishes himself he never reaches his destination. Ireland has been brought to the last one, beyond which there is but a little and easy stretch to go. The nation has earned the right to rest for a little, while we renew our strength, and restore somewhat our earlier vigour. But there are some amongst us who, while they take full advantage of the oasis — only a fool or a madman would fail to do that — complain of those who have led them to it. They find fault with it. They do nothing to help. They are poisoning the wells, wanting now to hurry on, seeing the road ahead short and straight, wanting the glory for themselves of leading the Irish nation over it, while unwilling to fill and shoulder the pack.'

'We are getting the British armed forces out of Ireland,' he added. 'Because of that evacuation our opponents are strong enough and brave enough now to say: "They are traitors who got you this. We are men of principle. We stand for the Republic" — that Republic which was physically impossible until the traitors had betrayed you.'

'Have we betrayed you?'

'No,' the crowd roared.

Collins justified his support of the Treaty with detailed arguments on the freedom to achieve freedom, but this time he went further than ever before in relation to the Northern aspect of the agreement. 'We must remember,' he said, 'that there is a strong minority in our country up in the North-East that does not yet share our national views, but has to be reckoned with. In view of these things I claim that we brought back the fullest measure of freedom obtainable — the solid substance of independence.'

'The arrangement in regard to North-East Ulster is not ideal,' he said. 'But then the position in North-East Ulster is not ideal. If the Free State is established, however, union is certain.' Rejecting the Treaty, on the other hand, would 'perpetuate partition'.

'Destroy the Free State now and you destroy more even than the hope, the certainty of union,' he continued. 'You destroy our hope of national freedom, all realisation in our generation of the democratic right of the people of Ireland to rule themselves without interference from any outside power.' Britain believed that it could not concede the Republic at that time without breaking up the Commonwealth. 'But she will acquiesce in the ultimate separation of the units, we amongst them, by evolution, which will not expose her and not endanger her. We must have a little patience. Have we not gained great things for our country?'

'We claim that the solid substance of freedom has been won, and the full power of the nation to mould its own life, quite as full for that purpose as if we had already our freedom in the Republican form,' Collins declared.

'The solid substance of freedom' about which Collins was speaking was Britain's formal agreement according the Irish Free State the same *de facto* status as the dominions. 'Our position cannot be challenged by England,' he argued, because it would be challenging the status of Canada, South Africa, and the other dominions, and 'such a challenge would disrupt her Empire at once'.

'War, though necessary and noble, for necessary and noble ends, has terrible effects incidental to it, not only material ruin, but moral effects when prolonged unrighteously; a tendency to lose balance and judgment, to forget or misinterpret the real objective of the national struggle, to grow to believe that strife, even fratricidal strife, is noble in itself. Such things must cease as soon as our freedom is secured, or the nation will perish.'

On the next seven weekends Collins travelled from Dublin to political rallies in Cork, Skibbereen, Waterford, Castlebar, Wexford, Naas, and Tralee. The first of his rallies outside Dublin was fittingly in Cork city, the following weekend.

Accompanied by Fionán Lynch, Seán Mac Eoin, Seán Milroy and J. J. Walsh, he was greeted on Saturday afternoon by a large crowd at Glanmire Station and was taken through the city in triumph, behind a number of bands, much to the annoyance of some armed anti-Treaty men. They tried to disrupt the proceedings by firing shots in the air as he was being driven through Patrick's Street.

'The people came out of their own free will to express their feelings, and they came without canvassing and without organisation,' Collins said afterwards. 'I knew that I was as good an interpreter of the desires of the people of Cork as anyone, and I am glad my interpretation was confirmed.'

Afterwards armed men attacked one of the bands and threw some instruments into the River Lee off North Gate Bridge. One enraged band member jumped into the cold water to recover the drum as it floated downriver.

During the night anti-Treaty militants dismantled the two platforms and threw the wooden planks into the river. Next morning the place around Turner's Hotel, where Collins was staying, was littered with slogans in red paint calling on people to stand by the Republic. There were also a number of white flags strategically placed in prominent positions, and some of the planks from the platforms could still be seen floating in the Lee. After Sunday mass Collins and his colleagues tried to visit the graves of Tomás MacCurtain and Terence MacSwiney, but their way was barred by some twenty armed men who threatened to shoot any of them who entered the Republican Plot.

Elsewhere, special excursion trains from Fermoy, Newmarket, and Youghal were held up by armed anti-Treaty militants, who kidnapped the drivers and firemen, leaving the passengers stranded. Had those trains made it to Cork, however, there would hardly have been room for the extra people because, as it was, a crowd of about fifty thousand people turned up that afternoon for the rally on Grand Parade.

Every vantage point was taken. As the crowd waited for the rally to begin, one young man began climbing the fountain to take down a white flag from its pinnacle. As he was about to remove the flag a shot rang out and, to the horror of spectators, the young man fell into the empty basin, but he was not injured. Shortly afterwards another young man shinned up a tram pole, topped by another flag. As he neared the top another shot was fired but, much to the amusement of the crowd, he ignored the flag and continued to the top and sat on the crossbar. The laughter of the crowd promptly turned to cheering as Collins and his colleagues made their way to the main platform. It was a most impressive sight.

'Old people who have seen Parnell, O'Brien and Redmond meetings all say that they never see anything like yesterday's display,' Collins gloated next day. He delivered a rousing speech that was typical of the Big Fellow, sprinkled with bravado, and indignant swipes at de Valera, who had had the effrontery to suggest in Cork, three weeks earlier, that Collins was, in effect, either a coward or a traitor. That was some charge from the man who had not only spent most of the terror in the United States but had also refused to go to London.

The anti-Treaty organ, *Poblacht na hÉireann,* concluded that there was a deliberate insinuation of cowardice against de Valera when Collins referred back to some of de Valera's remarks during the Treaty debate in the Dáil. 'While the captain was away from the ship — that time in America — there was a hurricane blowing,' Collins said. 'The helm had been left by the captain in the hands of those very same incompetent amateurs who afterwards, in the calm water, had the ship on the rocks, and while he was away, somehow or other, we steered safely through those troubled waters, the roughest through which the ship of the Irish nation had to be navigated in all her troubled history.'

The IRA had worn down the British, but it did not defeat them militarily. Hence in negotiating the Treaty, the Irish side was not able to dictate terms. He left no doubt that they would have stood out for better terms, if they had been strong enough to secure them. What they got was the freedom to develop. Prior to the truce, for instance, it was not safe for any man to walk the streets with his hands in his pockets. 'I put up my hand,' he said raising his hands with a laugh, 'as often as anybody, but not if I had anything in my pocket.' While the crowd loved this kind of bravado, it was not his rhetoric that was best remembered but the irresponsibility of about a dozen anti-Treaty agitators who skirted around the periphery of the gathering, firing shots into the air and shouting, 'Up the Republic'.

Collins remarked on the wonderful composure of the crowd. 'If there had been a stampede,' he said, 'women and little children would have been trampled under.'

That evening when he went over to the home of his sister, Mary Collins Powell, he was accosted by a gunman.

'I have you now,' the gunman said, but Mac Eoin disarmed him.

'Will I shoot him?' Mac Eoin asked.

'No,' replied Collins. 'Let the bastard go.'

Although de Valera was initially happy with the Ard Fheis agreement postponing the election until after the publication of the constitution, he soon changed his mind and began adopting delaying tactics. He demanded that the electoral register be updated, which would necessitate an even longer delay than the three months agreed at the Ard Fheis. He contended that the existing register 'contains tens of thousands of names that should not be on it, and omits several tens of thousands that should be on it — the latter mainly those of young men who have just attained their majority, who were the nation's most active defenders in the recent fight, and whose voice should certainly not be silenced in an election like the pending one, in which the fate of their country and the ideals for which they fought are to be determined'.

Griffith, showing signs of exasperation, refused a further delay. He was convinced the request had nothing to do with the democratic rights of the unfranchised, but was merely a ploy to stall the elections in order to avoid certain defeat. Griffith pointed out that while President as recently as the previous November de Valera had been instrumental in having the register updated. 'In face of this fact you now come forward to assert that the register is invalid,' Griffith wrote in an open letter. 'The public can draw its own conclusion.' If a new register were 'begun now an election would be impossible for the next six months', Griffith argued. 'This would suit the game of those who desire to muzzle the Irish electorate, but I cannot be a party to any muzzling order.'

'You propose muzzling them,' de Valera replied. 'I simply demand a proper register on the existing franchise, so that all who are entitled to vote may be permitted to vote. You would deprive the young men of their right because you believe that their votes would be cast against the London Agreement.'

De Valera's own conduct in recent months and especially in the following days and weeks certainly raised serious doubts about his commitment to democracy. On 15 March, for instance, he issued a manifesto announcing the formation of a new organisation, Cumann na Poblachta, which he said should be translated as 'the Republican Party Organisation'. Composed of anti-Treaty deputies, it was not supposed to supersede Sinn Féin, but there was no doubt that this party within the party added to the growing split within the movement as he set out on what would be the most controversial tour of his whole career.

'They tell you, you will be prosperous,' he warned a gathering in Dungarvan next day. 'Wait till you see the burden they will try to place upon you. You will want to fight for your rights whether you like it or not; if you don't fight to-day you will have to fight to-morrow, and I say when you are in a good fighting position, then fight on.'

While de Valera was calling on people to fight on, Collins was in his native west Cork proclaiming that 'Dublin Castle has been surrendered into my hands for the Irish nation.' He told the cheering crowd in Skibbereen that 'the British game is up. Dublin Castle has fallen, and with it will have gone all bureaucratic regulations and tyrannies that the people of Ireland suffered from.' With the British departing, who was de Valera proposing to fight against?

De Valera answered that question himself in both Carrick-on-Suir and Thurles next day, St Patrick's Day. Speaking in Thurles he told a crowd which included a contingent of armed IRA that if the Treaty was ratified, they would have 'to wade through Irish blood, through the blood of the soldiers of the Irish government, and through, perhaps, the blood of some members of the government in order to get Irish freedom'.

Next day in Killarney he suggested that he was not just talking about the current generation of Volunteers but also future generations. 'These men, in order to achieve freedom, would have to, as I said yesterday, march over the dead bodies of their own brothers. They will have to wade through Irish blood.'

'It is not peculiar in our time to have Volunteers and men who are willing to give up their lives for the freedom of their country,' he explained. 'Their aspirations will continue, and the next generation will strive to do it, and the road will be barred by their own fellow-countrymen and feeling that they have a right to complete freedom, they will not allow that to stand in the way. Therefore, they will oppose even the troops of an Irish Government set up in accordance with that, because it will be felt that, even if the Treaty were ratified, it would not be ratified with your free will, but under the threat of war.'

By this time his remarks had set off a fire-storm of criticism in both the Irish and international press. His speech was widely interpreted as threatening civil war, or even attempting to incite one. 'Mr de Valera has shocked the whole country,' The Times of London declared.

De Valera indignantly refuted that he was trying to incite civil war. He contended that he was merely assessing the situation realistically and refuting the argument that the Treaty contained the freedom to achieve freedom. He accused his critics of using his words to do the very thing of which they were accusing him.

'You cannot be unaware,' he wrote to the editor of the Irish Independent, 'that your representing me as inciting the civil war has on your readers precisely the same effects as if the inciting words were really mine.'

There were around seven thousand people in Tralee on Sunday, 19 March, when de Valera took a swipe at the press, by complaining that newspaper owners had 'an influence altogether disproportionate to their personal worth'. When making up their minds, he said, people should not allow themselves to be hypnotised by newspapers, but should conclude that something was more likely to be false if they read it in the newspaper.

Although de Valera was widely blamed for inciting the IRA, he was, in fact, rapidly losing his sway over the organisation. Under the influence of Collins and the IRB, most of the headquarters staff were pro-Treaty, while divisional commanders and the rank and file of the Volunteers were strongly anti-Treaty, especially in those areas that had been most active in the struggle against the British. The more militant, like Rory O'Connor, the director of engineering, had little time for de Valera any more. He had already declared that he was no more prepared to stand for de Valera than for the Treaty. He wanted an IRA convention called to elect a new leadership, but the headquarters staff — realising their own position was tenuous at best — procrastinated. De Valera tried to make the best of his own weak position by siding with those asking for a convention. He again suggested that the IRA should split on Treaty lines.

Many people mistakenly thought de Valera was the actual instigator when O'Connor — claiming to represent 80 per cent of the IRA — announced at a press conference on 22 March 1922 that an army convention would be held in four days' time, in defiance of the Dáil cabinet and headquarters staff. He added that the IRA, which had freely submitted to the authority of the Dáil, would be withdrawing its allegiance, because the Dáil had exceeded its authority by approving the Treaty.

'There are times when revolution is justified,' O'Connor said. 'The armies in many countries have overturned governments from time to time. There is no government in Ireland now to give the IRA a lead, hence we want to straighten out the impossible position which exists.'

The convention was being called to set up a new executive to issue orders to the IRA throughout the country. 'In effect,' he said, 'the holding of the convention means that we repudiate the Dáil.'

'Do we take it that we are going to have a military dictatorship then?' a reporter asked.

'You can take it that way, if you like,' O'Connor replied.

As the convention was being held, Collins went to Waterford for a political rally. Trenched roads, cut wires, a burned platform, and the stealing of band instruments were features surrounding his visit. Supporters of Collins felt that the aggressive and obstructionist tactics of their opponents were in fact indicative of the Treaty's inherent popularity.

The first sign of trouble was when the train carrying Collins, Ernest Blythe, Joe McGrath, and Seán Milroy was delayed for over an hour at Ballyhain Station, because the communication wires with Mullinavat had been cut. This necessitated a porter walking eight miles. When the party finally got to Waterford, the band to welcome them was unable to play because their instruments had been commandeered by armed men earlier in the day. Several tar barrels that were burning as a welcome were thrown in the river, and the platform that had been erected for them was sprinkled with petrol and set on fire.

Collins spoke, instead, from an upstairs window of the Town Hall. There were frequent interruptions from hecklers, but he parried those effectively, much to the delight of the crowd. 'I have had occasion to give plain talk to some of those slackers during the past few years; to those who were civilians in war, and who are warriors in peace and I perceive that some of you know nothing about freedom,' he said.

From a house on the other side of the mall, a banner with 'Long Live the Republic' was unfurled.

'I am not ashamed to see that flag flying,' Collins said. 'I can afford to look at it, and that is more than some of you can do.'

The crowd loved it. He was responding to good effect, but the interruptions continued.

'If you with the black hat down there were as brave this time twelve months as you are now, perhaps we need not be here today.'

In his address Collins was particularly critical of de Valera's recent speeches. 'While it was perfectly justifiable for any body of Irishmen, no matter how small, to rise up and make a stand against their country's enemy,' he argued, 'it is not justifiable for a minority to oppose the wishes of the majority of their own countrymen, except by constitutional means.'

'He states it was to future generations he was referring when he spoke of "civil war" and "wading through Irish blood" in order to get Irish freedom,' Collins continued. 'No one can speak for the next generation and no one can tie the hands of the next generation.' The Treaty was merely the freedom to achieve the desired freedom and any talk of future generations having to wage civil war to undo the Treaty was not just nonsense, but dangerous nonsense.

'Whatever Mr de Valera's meaning, the effect of his language is mischievous and, while I do not want needlessly to labour the point, I do want to make it clear to him that a leader must not be unmindful of the implications of his words,' Collins said. 'This is more than usually emphatic at this moment, when we are speaking to people just emerging from a great national struggle with their outlook and their emotions not in a normal state.'

'If Mr de Valera really wishes to convince the public that he did not mean to indulge in violent threats and in the language of incitement, and wants to wipe out the impression caused by his speeches, he must take instant action,' Collins continued. 'His explanation, as published, will not do. He must press home the foregoing truths to all his supporters, and he must publicly disassociate himself from the utterances of the former Ministers of Defence and Home Affairs, and from such mutinous views as those expressed by Commandant Roderick O'Connor.'

'Freedom under the Free State is definite and practical,' he added. 'It is there waiting for you to grasp it, if you will. If you prefer Mr de Valera's policy, which he tells you is now a Republic, can he give it to you? That is the question which the Irish people must put to themselves and answer.'

They were now being intimidated and threatened with civil war, if they decided to accept the Free State. 'Nobody knows better than Mr de Valera that the Treaty gives freedom to achieve freedom,' Collins insisted. 'The whole of his present position is founded upon that fact. He is already using the freedom won to shout for a Republic.'

It was indeed a measure of the new freedom that over two hundred delegates were free that day to attend the convention called by Rory O'Connor. They met throughout the day and into the night in the Oak Room of the Mansion House. The small gathering outside was indicative of their meagre popular support, but they went ahead anyway and formed a new executive with Liam Lynch as chief of staff. Henceforth there were two armies, both claiming to be the IRA, at least for the time being.

The pro-Treaty elements retained their headquarters at Beggar's Bush Barracks, while the others — branded as Irregulars by their opponents and the press — set up their headquarters in a building that they seized from the Orange Order in Parnell Square. Each claimed to be the regular or official IRA, but for the sake of convenience, and in order to avoid confusion, the pro-Treaty element will be referred to as the Free State army or Free Staters, and the anti-Treaty faction, the IRA or Republicans.

On 30 March Rory O'Connor and his men raided the offices of the *Freeman's Journal* and wrecked the equipment, and then boldly issued a statement justifying their actions. 'I was, with my associates, responsible for the suppression of the *Freeman*,' O'Connor announced. 'A free press is admirable, but "freedom of the press", according to the view of the *Freeman*, is the right to refuse publication of articles with which its proprietors do not agree, and the right to undermine the army and seduce it from its allegiance to the Republic.'

Although de Valera later said that he 'heartily disagreed' with O'Connor's repudiation of the Dáil, he nevertheless publicly defended O'Connor's patently undemocratic behaviour in a series of press interviews in the coming weeks.

The British were naturally alarmed about the IRA split and the way things were developing. As Colonial Secretary Churchill was now charged with dealing with Irish relations. He concluded that the Provisional Government 'were obviously afraid of a break with their extremists and have not shown themselves on any single important occasion capable of standing up to them'.

'The Irish have a genius for conspiracy rather than government,' Churchill wrote. 'The government is feeble, apologetic, expostulatory; the conspirators active, audacious and utterly shameless.'

Collins had a very difficult meeting in Castlebar that weekend. He would have needed all the experience of the previous public meetings to prepare him for what happened in Mayo. Motor cars and trains were held up to prevent Treaty supporters from getting to the meeting.

A train from Ballina had to be cancelled, but its prospective passengers were luckier than the three hundred people who set out from Sligo at about 11.30 that morning. At Swinford they were informed that the rails had been lifted down the line, about two miles from Kiltimagh. It was three o'clock before they were able to continue their journey. Then they were held up by fourteen armed Republicans, who forced the gangers to lift the rails again at the spot where they had just been replaced. The passengers therefore held a rally of their own on the spot. Ben Ryan, one of the speakers, told them that the tracks had been lifted by men who were lifting the 'rails of their beds' while Michael Collins was fighting the Black and Tans. The train had to reverse to Swinford before returning to Sligo, which it reached about nine o'clock.

Meanwhile the Castlebar meeting was a particularly stormy affair with persistent interruptions, some quite dramatic. As Collins was speaking from a makeshift platform on the back of a lorry, a motor car drew up beside him and a solicitor named Campbell from Swinford produced a list of type-written questions to which he demanded answers. Collins invited him to hand over the questions and there was a brief private exchange between the two of them.

'He won't give them to me,' Collins shouted to the crowd and then tried to take up his address where he had been interrupted. But Campbell shouted him down, demanding that he answer the questions. When a local priest called for order, Campbell suggested the priest should not interfere and proceeded to declare that Collins was a faithful subject of King George.

'Your conduct is worthy of your record,' Collins responded angrily. 'You took good care to be in jail when there was danger.'

Suddenly there was further commotion as some men tried to drive the lorry away with the platform. Alex McCabe, one of the pro-Treaty deputies on the platform, drew his revolver and threatened the would-be hijackers, and there were some moments of electrifying tension. Numerous revolvers were produced. Portions of the crowd took flight, and an anti-Treaty officer in uniform announced they were going to arrest McCabe. An angry scene ensued, as another priest pleaded with the uniformed officer and his men.

Charles Byrne, a tall, young Dubliner, dashed through the highly strung crowd, pursued by officers in uniform. He raced down a side street, and several shots were fired. Many women screamed, and some even fainted. One woman was wounded by a bullet, but the crowd around the lorry held their ground. In the brief lull that followed Collins proceeded with his address, only to be interrupted again.

'Aren't you ashamed of the man who shot the woman?' a uniformed officer shouted.

'Everyone here knows I am not responsible for that,' the Big Fellow replied, and the crowd cheered.

Another anti-Treaty officer then announced that the meeting was being 'proclaimed in the interests of peace'. Somebody started up the lorry, and Collins promptly jumped off as the vehicle was driven away, much to the consternation of the platform guests, who included a number of women and priests. Thus the meeting ended in disarray.

Collins went to a hotel with some colleagues. The officer who had proclaimed the meeting came by to explain that he had done so strictly in the interests of peace. He added that none of the Collins party would be allowed to leave the hotel until they had surrendered their guns, but this order was rescinded by Michael Kilroy, the divisional commandant.

Although de Valera was widely blamed for the disruptive tactics of the anti-Treaty people, because he had initially stoked the radical Republican passions, he was no longer able to control them, if, indeed, those people would ever have obeyed him. He was pretending to lead while he was, in fact, being dragged along by his supposed followers. He made approving statements to conceal his differences with them and he soon found himself compelled to serve his own initial folly. He was like a man floundering in quicksand, sinking deeper every time he tried to move. He was trying to assume a position of real leadership with his statements approving of the actions of the anti-Treaty militants, but each time he found himself outmanoeuvred as his erstwhile supporters moved on inexorably towards civil war.

'If Dáil Éireann attempted to set up a Provisional Government as the Government of this country, then, I tell you that that Government will not be obeyed, and further that that Government will not function,' de Valera declared in Dún Laoghaire on 6 April 1922. 'If the Irish people were allowed a free choice,' he told another gathering the following weekend, 'they would choose by an overwhelming majority exactly what these armed forces desire.' As far as he was concerned, it was wrong to talk about free elections with the British threat of war hanging over the electorate.

'The threat of war from this government is intimidation operating on the side of Mr Griffith and Mr Collins as sure and as definite as if these gentlemen were using it themselves, and far more effective, because indirect and well kept in the background,' he declared. 'Is our army to be blamed if it strives to save the people from being influenced by, and from the consequences of, giving way to this intimidation?'

Collins, on the other hand, condemned de Valera's emotive language. 'It is the language of a despot posing as a greater lover of liberty than other men — of a despot who shouted the name of liberty louder while he trampled the forms of liberty underfoot,' Collins told a rally in Wexford on 9 April. 'If we proceed to fly at each other's throats, the British will come back again to restore their Government, and they will have justified themselves in the eyes of the world. They will have made good their claim that we were unable and unfit to govern ourselves. Would not Mr de Valera, then, pause and consider where his language, if translated into action, was hurrying the nation? He had much power for good or evil. Could he not cease his incitements — for incitement they were, whatever his personal intentions? Could he not strive to create a good atmosphere, instead of a bad one?'

The Roman Catholic archbishop of Dublin, Dr Edward Byrne, invited leaders of both sides to a peace conference in Dublin on Wednesday, 12 April. Griffith and Collins were on one side and de Valera and Brugha on the other. The attendance also included the archbishop and the respective lord mayors of Dublin and Limerick, Laurence O'Neill and Stephen O'Mara. All that resulted from this meeting, however, was an agreement to meet again the following week. At least the archbishop had got the two sides talking to one another around a table, but with Easter coming up, he had to ask for a week's recess. De Valera agreed, but the real power on the Republican side had already slipped from the hands of the politicians.

In the early hours of Good Friday, 14 April, the anti-Treaty IRA, under Rory O'Connor, occupied the Four Courts and a number of other buildings in Dublin. Between three and four hundred men were estimated to be involved in the operation. There were all kinds of rumours of a *coup d'état*, but O'Connor said that they just occupied the buildings, because they did not have enough room elsewhere. He added, however, that scrapping the Treaty was the only way of avoiding civil war.

The similarity with the start of the Easter Rebellion, six years earlier, was unmistakable. Although de Valera was again assumed to be behind the takeover of the Four Courts, he had nothing to do with it. In fact, he had not even been informed, much less consulted in advance. Nevertheless he did nothing to disabuse the public misconception.

A Labour Party deputation that called on him later the same day found him particularly unreceptive to their pleas for peace. 'We spent two hours pleading with him, with a view to averting the impending calamity of civil war,' one member of the deputation later recalled.

'The majority have no right to do wrong,' de Valera told them. 'He repeated that at least a dozen times in the course of the interview,' according to one of those present. He refused to accept he had a 'duty to observe the decision of the majority until it was reversed'.

Some years later de Valera tried to justify the stand he took at this time. 'What appeared to be an obvious wrong was being justified by the idea that it was backed by the majority vote of the people,' he explained. 'I said that that did not justify wrong. That never justified wrong. If you got a unanimous vote of the people telling you to go and shoot your neighbour, you would be quite in the wrong in carrying out that majority will. You would not be right. Therefore the majority rule does not give to anybody the right to do anything wrong, and I stand by the statement.'

In a purely abstract sense he was undoubtedly correct, but he was not talking in the abstract on that Good Friday. Taking his remarks in their proper context, he was contending that the anti-Treaty IRA had a right to ignore the wishes of the majority of the Irish people. Moreover, he issued an inflammatory proclamation that weekend which ended with an emotional appeal to the youth of the country. 'Young men and young women of Ireland,' he concluded, 'the goal is at last in sight. Steady; all together; forward. Ireland is yours for the taking. Take it.' It is hard to see how such a statement could have been interpreted as other than an appeal for young people to support the anti-Treaty IRA which had just seized the Dublin buildings.

At a rally in the Theatre Royal, Dublin, on Easter Sunday de Valera said that they had been hearing wails about disunion. Although none of them wanted disunion, he warned that a certain section of the Irish people, followers of those who had died for Ireland, would go marching on. It did not matter whether they would be few or many; they were that section of the Irish nation which had been the point of Ireland's spear in the past. If people wanted to unify the nation they could do so only by uniting behind that section.

Collins spoke in Naas that day. Some of those who preceded him on the platform had raised questions about de Valera's decision not to go to London for the Treaty negotiations. 'I am not going to argue as to why de Valera stayed behind,' Collins told the crowd, 'but I know the reason, because I spent five hours with him. I can say if he had gone over you would not have got what we got in the Treaty.' The crowd cheered loudly.

'We might as well tear off the veil of sanctity of Mr de Valera,' Collins added.

'It is time,' someone in the crowd shouted.

'I am going to do it from this time forward, and I am going to tell the people where we all stand,' Collins said. 'The position is rapidly developing into a state of civil war. The condition of the country is unstable. Life is insecure. Liberty is imperilled. This state of things must be brought to an end. It is a question now between ordered Government and anarchy. The people want ordered Government. They must, and will, have it.'

When Collins talked about life being insecure he could hardly have envisioned what would happen on his return to Dublin that night. He was dropped off outside Vaughan's Hotel. As he got out of his taxi, he paused to talk with Seán Ó Muirthile and Gearóid O'Sullivan on the footpath outside the hotel. Just then a group of Republicans rushed out of No. 44 and began shooting. It was initially reported that they tried to kill Collins, but this was obviously not the case.

The affair was related to a number of incidents that had occurred in the area earlier in the evening. Some pro-Treaty soldiers who cruised the area in a car had exchanged shots with those in No. 44. During the later incident

Collins never thought they were firing at him, but he still chased one of the men into a doorway and took a pistol off him.

The garrison in the Four Courts later issued a formal statement emphasising 'definitely and emphatically that an attack on Mr Michael Collins was not in any way intended or contemplated. He happened to be in the vicinity during the incidents at Parnell Square, and thus got implicated in the matter.'

———————

When Archbishop Byrne's peace conference reconvened at the Mansion House on the following Thursday, the atmosphere was poisoned by the personality differences. At one point Brugha accused Griffith and Collins of being British agents. The archbishop demanded that the accusation be withdrawn. Brugha agreed but proceeded to explain that he considered those who did the work of the British government to be British agents.

'I suppose we are two of the ministers whose blood is to be waded through?' Collins snapped.

'Yes,' replied Brugha quite calmly. 'You are two.'

For months vile accusations had been hurled at Griffith and Collins, while de Valera stood by indifferently, depicting himself as having consistently tried to maintain the Republican position. He never denied his willingness to compromise with the British, but now he contended that there was never any possibility that this compromise would have been inconsistent with the Republican ideal.

'Was that your attitude?' Griffith asked. 'If so a penny postcard would have been sufficient to inform the British government without going to the trouble of sending us over.'

De Valera tried to explain himself, but Griffith interrupted. 'Did you not ask me to get you out of the strait-jacket of the Republic?'

'Oh, now gentlemen, this won't do any good,' the archbishop interjected.

'I would like to explain,' de Valera said, 'because there is a background of truth to the statement.' He said he was thinking of the strait-jacket of the isolated Republic when he asked Griffith to go over.

There was so much bitterness now between Griffith and Collins on one side and de Valera and Brugha on the other that the two sides had to withdraw to separate rooms while the others vainly tried to mediate. The discussions were then suspended until the following week, and the various leaders headed off for rallies around the country that weekend.

Collins headed for Kerry where the two IRA brigades had gone strongly anti-Treaty. There was a split in north Kerry within the No. 1 Brigade going back to before the truce as a result of problems between the brigadier,

Paddy J. Cahill, and the IRB man, Humphrey Murphy, but the latter went anti-Treaty anyway despite his IRB connections. Murphy and Brigadier John Joe Rice of the No. 2 Brigade both proscribed the pro-Treaty rallies planned for Collins in Killarney on Saturday and Tralee the following day.

Collins arrived by train in Killarney together with Seán Mac Eoin, Kevin O'Higgins, and Fionán Lynch, as well as a twelve-man army guard under Joe Dolan. They were met at the railway station by an anti-Treaty officer who told them that the meeting would not be allowed. Posters had already been put up around the town banning the gathering and the platform built for the occasion was burned down. The heavily armed contingent of anti-Treaty people had a Thompson sub-machine gun, but their threats were withdrawn following the intervention of a Franciscan priest. The meeting was then held in front of the Franciscan Church, where the sloping ground formed a natural platform

'"Maintain the Republic," Mr de Valera and his followers exhort us,' Collins exclaimed. 'What Republic? Do they mean the Republic we have had during the last few years with the British here — a Republic functioning incompletely, with British laws, British taxation, British stamps affixed to our cheques and agreements, paying our revenue to the British? Is that the Republic we are to maintain? A Republic during which the enemy was here hunting, imprisoning, torturing, shooting and hanging our people.'

Next day Collins and company went on to Tralee, where they met as much opposition. Special trains had been put on for the Sunday meeting, but only the Dingle train reached Tralee. Others from Killarney, Kenmare, and Newcastle West were stopped because rail lines had been taken up. Virtually every road leading to the town was also heavily obstructed. Collins and his colleagues were at morning mass when the dean of Kerry denounced the efforts to prevent the meeting.

The military escort under Dolan had been strengthened with the addition of a further twenty-four men under Commandant Dinny Galvin of Knocknagoshel. He had been told to disarm the opposition and he not only seized some of their weapons but also arrested a number of IRA men.

Humphrey Murphy protested about this to Mac Eoin, who was clearly unwilling to allow their old IRB ties to influence his attitude. He knocked Murphy down a stairs and then jumped on him and began pummelling him. Collins broke them up and pushed Mac Eoin into a closet to cool down. He then compelled him to apologise to Murphy and a kind of truce was arranged. The men arrested by Galvin were released and the gunmen from each side withdrew to different sides of the town and agreed not to disrupt the meeting.

The *Kerry Leader* newspaper had come out that Friday with a series of questions that Robert Barton had posed for Collins to answer in Tralee.

They were the kind of questions that would be asked again and again over the next fifty years. Barton asked whether Collins and Duggan had flatly refused to present the counter-proposals following their return to London on the Sunday before the Treaty was signed. They certainly had refused, but Collins responded with a disingenuous distortion in which he sought to brush aside the question by appealing to the emotions of the crowd.

'No,' Collins lied. 'We did not definitely refuse. We put it like this, and there are members of the Dáil cabinet who will bear me out on this.' Brugha had complained at the cabinet meeting about the exclusion of Barton from the talks and Collins said that he just adopted the attitude that Barton could try for himself.

'Go ahead and see what you can do,' Collins told him at the time, according to himself. 'That is the reason that I did not go, and my staying away got better proposals than we would get otherwise, because they thought that I was going to take the field against them again.' The crowd cheered loudly. This was a time when emotion had more influence than reason.

De Valera had been in Tuam and Galway over the weekend. Speaking in Galway on the Sunday, he again denounced the stepping-stone idea. If the Irish people wished to be free in future, he said, they 'could not put aside the physical force weapon'. But in Dublin next day he took a very different line as he stressed that he was a moderate. 'I am not an extreme man,' he told a meeting near Boland's Mills. 'I have always regarded moderation in everything as the highest human virtue.'

Few people realised then that de Valera was now impotent when it came to influencing hard-line Republicans. 'If de Valera were on your side,' Mary MacSwiney wrote to Richard Mulcahy, 'we should still fight on. We do not stand for men but for principles, and we could not more accept your Treaty than we could turn our backs on the Catholic Faith.'

She was in for a rude awakening a couple of days later when the Catholic hierarchy issued a blistering condemnation of the 'immoral usurpation and confiscation of the people's rights' by those in the Four Courts 'who think themselves entitled to force their views upon the nation'. According to the bishops, 'the one road to peace and ultimately to a united Ireland, is to leave it to the decision of the nation in a general election, as ordered by the existing Government, and the sooner the election is held the better for Ireland'.

The O'Connor faction was determined to prevent elections, however, and de Valera was grasping at straws. He publicly supported their opposition to the elections by contending not only that the electoral register was out of date, but also that the British were really making a mockery of the democratic process by using their threat of war to bolster support for the Treaty. He charged that Winston Churchill was deliberately exploiting 'the fear of renewed warfare' as a means of getting the Irish electorate to 'go to the polls and support the Treaty'. Hence, he argued, the Republicans were justified in preventing such an election.

His objections to the electoral register were largely spurious, and this would become particularly apparent when he refused to consider several suggestions put forward by Griffith and Collins. They even offered to arrange a referendum in which all adults could participate — whether their names were on the register or not. The people would meet at the same time in designated localities throughout the country and would vote by passing through barriers where they would be counted, but de Valera refused to consider such 'Stone Age machinery'.

He simply did not want any election at the time, and he publicly justified his refusal to co-operate on the grounds that there were 'rights which a minority may justly uphold, even by arms, against a majority'. He wanted the vote postponed for a further six months. 'Time would be secured for the present passions to subside,' he argued, 'for personalities to disappear, and the fundamental differences between the two sides to be appreciated — time during which Ireland's reputation could be vindicated, the work of national reconstruction begun, and normal conditions restored.'

'We all believe in democracy,' he told John Steele of the *Chicago Daily Tribune*, 'but we do not forget its well-known weaknesses. As a safeguard against their consequences the most democratic countries have devised checks and brakes against sudden changes of opinion and hasty, ill-considered decisions.' In America a treaty needed the approval of a two-thirds majority of the United States Senate for ratification. As the Irish system had 'not yet had an opportunity of devising constitutional checks and brakes', he intimated it was legitimate for the anti-Treaty IRA to do so. 'The Army sees in itself the only brake at the present time, and is using its strength as such,' he said.

For one who had championed the right to self-determination for years, de Valera had drifted into an untenable position in his efforts to obscure his own differences with Republican militants like O'Connor.

'We took strong actions against the *Freeman's Journal*, and we have never tried to conceal what we have done since the Army was reconstituted,' O'Connor declared publicly. 'Everything that has been done has been done openly and above board, and that is more than can be said of those who want to bring Ireland into the British Empire.'

This was obviously a reference to Collins who, for some months, had been playing a very devious role not with only the Republicans, but also the British and even his own colleagues, especially when it came to matters relating to Northern Ireland. While the partition question had not figured in the Treaty dispute, it began to develop as an issue during 1922 as the Northern situation deteriorated. The January agreement with Craig proved futile. Part of the agreement covered the release of prisoners. On 14 January ten Monaghan 'footballers' going to a football match in Derry were arrested in Tyrone. In fact, they were really planning to spring three men under sentence of death for killing a warder during an earlier escape attempt from Derry Jail.

When the men had still not been released by 26 January Collins wrote to Craig complaining that he had been led to believe that the men would be promptly released. Craig's reply was moderate and conciliatory in tone.

'If the prisoners will at once apply for bail, I will direct the Attorney General not to oppose,' Craig replied. But Collins did not want anyone recognising a Northern Ireland court. From the introduction of partition he was determined 'to keep striving in every way' to end it. 'The north-east must not be allowed to settle down in the feeling that it is a thing apart from the Irish nation,' he wrote to de Valera in January 1921. Although Craig welcomed the signing of the pact as an indication of recognition, Collins still insisted on his side that the new policy 'must be coupled with a strict campaign of "non recognition"'.

Collins was secretly encouraging Northern nationalists to refuse to co-operate with the unionist authorities. Nationalist-controlled councils were urged not to recognise the Stormont government, and the Provisional Government promised to fund their activities, as well as some three hundred Catholic schools that refused to co-operate with the North's Department of Education. In addition, in the coming weeks Collins agreed to fund a seventy-two man Republican Guard in Belfast, and he and his chief of staff, Eoin O'Duffy, arranged to supply the IRA in Northern Ireland with weapons that were handed over by the British forces to the Provisional Government. One of the men who actually delivered the guns in Northern Ireland was Seán Haughey, the father of the future Taoiseach, Charles J. Haughey.

O'Duffy notified Collins of his plan to spring the three men in Derry Jail by kidnapping 'one hundred prominent Orangemen in Counties Fermanagh and Tyrone'. The kidnappings were initially postponed because of the Collins–Craig agreement, but on 7 February, when the three con-demned men in Derry had still not been reprieved, bands of the IRA crossed the border and kidnapped forty-two unionists and held them as hostages. The aim was obviously to take more, and there were reports that up to seventy hostages had been taken, but the Northern police captured eleven of the IRA men from Leitrim and Longford. The great irony was that the death sentences of the three men had already been commuted to prison terms that day.

Andy Cope assured London that the Provisional Government 'are doing their best' in difficult circumstances. 'Collins has had great difficulty in hold-ing in certain sections of the IRA who were out for hostages,' Cope wrote.

Collins acted as if the whole thing was natural and predictable. 'Naturally the people whose feelings were outraged by the impending executions would take some action of this kind,' he declared. 'The blame lies with the people who delayed until the last moment in giving a decision as to the fate of the men in Derry Jail.'

He was acting in a dishonest, underhanded manner, as he lied shamelessly to the British and even his own colleagues, including President Griffith, who was in London for talks with the British at the time. 'The diehards here are representing what appears to me to be the taking of hostages against the execution of political prisoners in Derry as an invasion of Ulster,' Griffith warned as he asked Collins to issue an immediate repudiation and an assurance that 'every possible step will be taken to have these hostages released and to prevent the malign influence at work in England against the Treaty from scoring a success'.

'Throughout yesterday I was extremely anxious as to what might happen in view of pending executions of the three men in Derry prison,' Collins wrote to Lloyd George. 'I made special efforts to prevent acts of violence on the part of my people and as soon as I heard of reprieve last night I took steps to have information conveyed without delay to leading men on border in order to allay anxiety and to ensure against any untoward incident.'

Not only had he not tried to stop the kidnappings, but he had also sent two men, Joe Dolan and Charlie Byrne, to England to kill the two hangmen. 'Mick Collins told us to get them at all cost,' Dolan later recalled, 'but if we were captured we could not expect any help from him, as we could not identify ourselves as part of the newly formed National Army.' Fortunately for the two hangmen, they had already left for Ireland, but Dolan only learned that when he called to one of their homes and actually talked to the man's wife.

If the British were deceived about his role in the kidnapping, they were not deceived for very long. 'If your people are going to pop into Ulster and take off hostages every time the Northern Government enforces the law in a way you dislike there will be reprisals,' Churchill warned Griffith in London on 9 February. 'We will have a fortified frontier and we will have to put there Imperial troops because they would be more impartial than Northern Ireland troops.'

The British asked Collins for an assurance that he would take 'immediate steps to ensure release of prisoners and to provide against any repetition of these grave outrages'. They even credited the Provisional Government the following week with securing the release of twenty-six of the hostages. The British clearly realised that Collins was involved, but they had always been anxious to avoid a break on the Ulster issue. Hence they turned a blind eye to his behaviour.

The Provisional Government was deliberately trying to destabilise conditions in the North. Richard Mulcahy, the Minister for Defence, noted that 'the general aim underlying all operations in Carsonia is to disorganise the economic structure of the territory and to make the hostile inhabitants realise that aiding and abetting the activities of the Enemy does not pay'.

On 10 February the IRA tried to arrest a group of eighteen Northern policemen who were travelling from Belfast to Enniskillen by train. For part of the journey the route went through County Monaghan and the train even had a stop in Clones. Commander Matt Fitzpatrick of the IRA approached the train with his revolver drawn and called on the police to surrender. But they shot him in the head and he died instantly. This led to an extended gunfight in which a sergeant and three constables were killed and the others taken into custody by the IRA.

The incident prompted a horrific retaliation in Belfast, where thirty-nine people were murdered in the next three days. In Milewater Street a bomb was thrown among teenagers playing in the street, killing five of them. 'In my opinion,' Churchill wrote to Collins, 'it is the worst thing that has happened in Ireland in the last three years.' Craig had already denounced it as a 'dastardly outrage', but Collins complained that the Belfast regime could prevent such outrages if they would 'adopt a sufficiently stern attitude'.

De Valera had no involvement whatever in the kidnapping or the Clones incident, but the press mistakenly thought he was behind them. Some British advisers allowed themselves to be deluded by the press reports and their own wishful thinking that Collins was acting in a strictly honourable way. 'As has been stated in the papers these were engineered by de Valera and his party who got hold of local sections of the IRA,' Tom Jones noted. 'It is hoped that Collins is re-establishing his authority.'

Of course, the sectarian outrages were on both sides. In a three-week period during February, 138 people were killed — 96 Catholics and 42 Protestants. The principal murdering group on the unionist side was the Ulster Protestant Association, a 150-strong group based in a public house in east Belfast. There was also a police element involved, especially the notorious Inspector John W. Nixon. Those elements were as unfit for service as the worst elements of the Black and Tans had been in the South before the truce.

On the night of 24 March five policemen raided the home of a Catholic publican, Owen McMahon. He was lined up with his six sons and a barman who was lodging with the family and they were shot one by one. Only his youngest son, John, aged eleven, survived the massacre by hiding under a sofa. There murders were believed to have been a reprisal for the shooting of two policemen in the area the previous day.

Although Collins had not calculated to provoke such outrages, he persisted with his efforts at destabilising the situation and then blaming Craig's regime for what was happening. To a degree his tactics seemed to be working when Churchill chided Craig that the outrages in Belfast 'were worse than anything which has occurred in the south'.

The initial agreement between Craig and Collins had been warmly welcomed in the North with cross-community support, but it had foundered when Craig failed to keep his side of the agreement to ensure that Catholics expelled from the docks would be re-employed. 'Not one single expelled Nationalist or Catholic worker has been reinstated in his employment,' Collins wrote to Craig on 23 March 1922.

Craig did not deny this. He just pleaded an inability to keep his side of the agreement. 'No Government could compel workmen of one class or another in any industry to work with any other unless with the general approval of the workmen themselves,' Craig declared the following week. He said he had persuaded the workers to agree if employment reached its old level that they would 'allow Catholics back to the yards'.

Craig contended that the January agreement was really undermined by Collins's attitude on the Boundary Commission. In particular, Collins had kept him 'entirely in the dark' about believing 'that large territories were involved in the Commission and not merely boundary lines', Craig explained in a statement on 28 March. Ever since the signing of the Treaty, Collins had made no secret of his expectation that the Boundary Commission would transfer large areas, but it was a measure of how little the partition issue had actually figured in the Treaty dispute in the South that Craig could claim to have been unaware of this.

With the situation in Belfast becoming steadily more dangerous, representatives from the three governments met in London on 29 March. It was the first meeting of its kind ever. By the following day, the three sides had negotiated another agreement, which was signed this time by Collins, Duggan, O'Higgins, and Griffith on behalf of the Dublin government; by Craig, Lord Londonderry, and E. M. Archdale for the Stormont regime; and by Churchill, Worthington-Evans, and Sir Hamar Greenwood for the British government.

'Peace is to-day declared,' the agreement began. It outlined a reorganisation of the police in Northern Ireland. In mixed areas the police were to be made up of an equal number of Catholic and Protestant policemen, and the specials (the various police reserves) not required were to be withdrawn and were to surrender their weapons. The uniformed police were also to be dis-armed, and all searches were to be conducted 'by police forces composed half of Catholics and half of Protestants', with the military being used as an armed back-up. A joint committee, comprising an equal number of Catholics and Protestants, was to be set up to hear complaints. All IRA activity was 'to cease in the Six Counties', and it was agreed that political prisoners would be released.

Unlike the euphoric cross-community acceptance that initially welcomed the first agreement, the second one was never really accepted. The agreement was published on 31 March, but next day, after an RIC constable was shot dead, a party of policemen from Brown Square Barracks in Belfast went on a violent rampage in Arnon Street. They killed one man in each of the first two houses that they raided, used a sledgehammer to murder the occupant of a third house, and shot and fatally wounded that man's seven-year-old son.

De Valera declared in Dundalk that the Belfast murders already made the latest agreement with Craig a mere 'scrap of paper'. That would soon become apparent to all.

Craig was a particularly hard-headed and obstinate character. It used to be said that he was once kicked in the head by a horse, and that the poor horse had to be put down with a broken leg. Despite several requests from Collins to have the proposed bipartisan committee investigate the Arnon Street killings, along with the murders of two policemen, Craig refused to act. It would be 'injudicious' to go back on any of those killings 'in view of the pleasing fact that peace has reigned for over twenty-four hours', he wrote on 4 April.

'It is imperatively necessary to have inquiry into all cases, including the two constables,' Collins replied. 'We believe continuation of peace and restoration of confidence depend on the inquiry. The conditions of the Agreement must apply rigidly from date of signing; otherwise they are valueless.'

'I differ profoundly,' Craig responded. 'A few days were required to establish the peaceful conditions now prevailing. I cannot consent to rake up past cases.'

Collins was not even demanding an inquiry into the McMahon case; he was just insisting that the outrages that had occurred since the latest agreement be investigated. Those were not even a week old, yet Craig was dismissing them as 'past cases'.

The faults were not all on one side. In the following days Collins pleaded that he was unable to get Republicans to evacuate the Orange Lodge in Parnell Square, and he claimed 'a certain lawless section in the country has illegally reimposed the Belfast Boycott and undertaken the destruction of goods consigned from Belfast'. Many of the culprits, he contended, were driven out of Belfast themselves. In order words, he was suggesting that the unionists were really to blame for his inability to uphold his end of the latest agreement.

O'Duffy had announced the release of the remainder of the police specials arrested in Clones, but the Stormont regime procrastinated with the release of its prisoners. Craig argued that he had pointed out in London that the release would not apply 'to those convicted of grave civil offences'. Collins had supplied the names of 170 prisoners, but Craig contended they included 'a very large proportion of criminals convicted of murder and other serious crimes'. The Northern Minister for Home Affairs, Dawson Bates, was only prepared to recommend 'the release of persons convicted of technical offences of a so-called political character'.

Bates was a virile bigot who was determined to have no co-operation with Catholics. One of his contemporaries later recalled that Bates had 'such prejudice against Catholics that he made it clear to his Permanent Secretary that he did not want his most juvenile clerk or typist, if a Papist, assigned to his ministry'. The March agreement may never have had much chance of success, but it had absolutely none when Craig was not prepared to stand up to Bates and his ilk. As a result, dealing with Craig required an enormous amount of patience, and Collins, unfortunately, had very little patience and soon became exasperated.

The Provisional Government decided on 21 April that Collins should warn Churchill 'that unless immediate action were taken by Sir James Craig to show his good faith, the Provisional Government would be obliged to regard the agreement as broken'.

'General impression amongst our people in Belfast is that the Northern Government has no intention of abiding by the Agreement,' Collins wrote to Churchill on 25 April. 'You will I am sure agree that unless something is done at once to remove that impression no arrangement that I could make with Sir James Craig would be of any value.'

In the four weeks after the pact with Craig was signed, thirty-five people — twenty-four Catholics and eleven Protestants — were murdered in the North. Collins accused Craig of 'keeping attention off the daily practice of atrocities and murders'. But behind the scene Collins was still stirring things up himself with deliberate attacks on the stately homes and businesses of prominent unionists. 'For a good many months we did as much as we could to get property destroyed,' he acknowledged privately. 'I know they think a great deal more of property than of human life.'

Instructing his ministers to keep an eye on the Northern situation, Collins circularised each of them on 5 May to prepare schemes 'for non-co-operation in every possible way with the Northern Parliament' as well as 'a scheme towards making it impossible for them to carry on'.

Churchill had been uneasy about developments in the South for some time. On the day after the March agreement was signed, he was expressing reservations about arming the Provisional Government in Dublin. 'There can be no question of handing over further arms until we are assured that persons to whom they are entrusted will use them with fidelity to the Irish Provisional Government and will not allow them simply to pass into Republican hands,' he ordered on 31 March. But he was embarrassed a few days later when the ship *Upnor* was hijacked off the Cork coast by Republicans who captured its cargo of 381 rifles, 727 revolvers, 33 Lewis guns, and 29,000 rounds of ammunition.

'It is generally believed here that there was collusion between those responsible on your side and the raiders,' Collins complained to Churchill. 'We do not charge collusion from high responsible authorities but we are convinced there has been collusion from subordinates. It is absurd to believe that a vessel containing such quantities of arms and ammunition be left open to seizure in an area where it is notorious our opponents are well armed.'

In fact, Collins was still colluding in supplying the IRA with weapons for use in the North. Believing that Rory O'Connor's plan was 'to involve British troops by hook or by crook in hostilities with the IRA', Churchill was worried that events in Belfast were pushing Collins to the point that he was in league 'with avowed Republicans'. Collins and his former IRA colleagues were indeed trying to patch up their differences.

For weeks the tension between the two sides in the South had been growing and it had led to shootings in several areas around the country. Eight men had been killed and forty-nine wounded in clashes between the IRA factions. At the rally in Naas on Easter Sunday, Collins had said that the situation was rapidly developing into a state of civil war. Harry Boland, for his part wrote that 'Civil war is certain unless Collins and Company see the error of their ways and come to terms with their late colleagues.'

On 2 May Collins, accompanied by Mulcahy, O'Duffy, and Gearóid O'Sullivan, met with anti-Treaty officers — Dan Breen, Tom Hales, Humphrey Murphy, Seán O'Hegarty, Florrie O'Donoghue, and Seán Moylan. All accepted that the majority of the Irish people were in favour of acceptance of the Treaty, so they called for the two Sinn Féin factions to conclude an election pact from which a unified coalition government would emerge that would command the unified support of the IRA. This was promptly denounced by Rory O'Connor as 'a political dodge intended to split the Republican ranks'.

Nevertheless the officers from the two sides agreed to a truce two days later, and there were further talks, which included Liam Lynch, Rory O'Connor, and Liam Mellows on the anti-Treaty side. A ten-strong Dáil committee, with five from each side, was set up 'to explore every possibility of arriving at an agreement', much to the annoyance of Churchill, who ridiculed the idea of an agreed election.

'The Irish leaders move in a narrow world,' Churchill told the British cabinet on 16 May 1922. 'They had been men of violence and conspiracy and had hardly emerged from that atmosphere. They had been discussing an agreed election between the two factions by which was meant that so many seats would be assigned to de Valera and so many to the Free State.'

'It would not be an election in any sense of the word, but simply a farce,' Churchill wrote to Collins. 'It would be an outrage upon democratic principles and would be universally so denounced.'

'What troubled Collins was the split in the Army,' Seán Ó Muirthile wrote. 'There were men in the Army that he would go almost any distance to satisfy. He would rather, as he said to me more than once, have one of the type of Liam Lynch, Liam Deasy, Tom Hales, Rory O'Connor, or Tom Barry on his side than a dozen like de Valera.'

The thought of going to war against those old comrades was abhorrent to Collins, but he warned that the peace committee set up by the Dáil was a desperate effort to patch up an agreement. Collins outlined his views in an interview with John Steele of the *Chicago Daily Tribune*.

The interview took place in the Big Fellow's new office in the College of Science on Merrion Street. 'It is probably one of the most handsome and convenient Government buildings in the world,' Steele wrote. 'If it had been built specially for the purpose it could not have been better.' He actually suggested that it would 'probably become the permanent home of the Irish Government'. He was right, though it was nearly seventy years later that Charles J. Haughey moved into the building as head of government in 1991.

The room that Collins occupied was modest and plainly furnished. He had a table and an American roll-top desk. There was a host of secretaries, typists, and other staff in an adjoining room.

Collins told Steele that he had just returned from the country where he had spent the weekend reading an account of the American Revolution and the early years of the United States by John Marshall, the first chief justice of the US Supreme Court. He proceeded to quote an extract from Marshall's work:

> To be more exposed in the eyes of the world, and more contemptible than we already are, is hardly possible. No morn ever dawned more favourably than ours did, and no day was ever more clouded than the present. . . . We are fast verging to anarchy. Good God, who besides a Tory could have foreseen, or a Briton predicted, the disorders which have arisen in these states?

It was an apt quotation. 'It might pass for a history of the present days in Ireland,' Collins said. 'There are the same divisions, the same disorder, the same rebellious elements. America won through. So shall we.'

He confidently predicted that the pro-Treaty side would win the upcoming election. If de Valera and his followers continued their campaign of anarchy after losing the election, Collins said that he was prepared to take them on, but he added that there would not be civil war. It would simply be a police measure. His jaw stuck out, as he told Steele that the current peace initiative would be the last.

'If this peace effort fails, then there will be no other,' he emphasised. 'Every avenue of co-operation will have been explored and we shall have to take action to restore order in the country. It is not an easy problem; for a revolutionary Government, in the nature of things, must take some account of motives. There is a lot of plain looting, robbery, and violence going on. That is common criminality, and must be punished. Also, there is a certain amount of commandeering from what, after all, is a patriotic, if misguided motive. That, too, must be stopped; but it requires a different method.'

For one thing, gun control was necessary. 'There are too many guns in the country — uncontrolled guns,' he explained. 'A gun is a dangerous thing for a young man to have. Some day he may use it in a quarrel over a girl, or over a shilling, or over a word. That is one of the problems the revolutionary Government has got to solve, and is determined to solve; but it cannot be done in a day or two.'

De Valera had been saying that the people had no right to do wrong, but Collins challenged this. 'Any people has a right to go wrong if it wishes, and no one has the right to deny it that right, or to deny it the right to exercise it,' Collins emphasised. 'No man, and no army, has got the God-given right to say what a people may or may not do. Not even the Kaiser or the Tsar in the days of their greatest glory made such an extravagant claim.'

Even where there were checks on the powers of government, like the presence of a second chamber, there was no right to override the wishes of the people. No modern state existed on the army alone, Collins insisted. The strength of each government depended on the extent to which its executive and legislative branches were 'supported by a strong army, thus enabling it to carry out a virile policy'.

De Valera appeared to be more conciliatory after the publication of the Collins interview. He proffered an olive branch in the Dáil on 17 May. Having consistently refused to recognise the Provisional Government, he now declared that the Provisional Government 'could use any machinery' set up under the Treaty, provided they did not depart from fundamental principles. In short, he was ready to co-operate with the Provisional Government in matters which he thought would advance the cause of Irish freedom.

Collins, who had pleaded with him to adopt such an attitude months earlier, agreed to explore again the possibility of an agreement with him. When they met on 18 May, Collins offered a pre-election pact provided the pro-Treaty side was assured of a six to four majority and the minority gave an assurance that it would not try to wreck the Treaty. He was not 'looking for scalps or for anything that designated surrender', he said, but he needed an assurance that the people's will would not be frustrated. De Valera argued, on the other hand, that 'the disappearance of the party spirit would bring ample security'.

De Valera had still not abandoned Document No. 2, but Collins had little time for it. A fortnight earlier Seán T. O'Kelly had complained that Collins was completely indifferent to de Valera's alternative and even hostile to it 'as a thing of no advance on the Treaty'. In reply, Collins stated that he had 'no objection' to O'Kelly's conclusion. 'I certainly would not ask any Irishman to risk his own life or take the life of a brother Irishman for the difference — the difference which was described by Mr de Valera himself as "only a shadow".'

Yet de Valera was still insisting that the new constitution should be consistent with Document No. 2. Hence he refused to guarantee that the minority would not wreck the Treaty when he met Collins again next day. Collins eventually relented anyway, and they concluded an election pact on 20 May. In accordance with it, the two wings of Sinn Féin would put forward a united panel of candidates in ratio with their existing strength in the Dáil and, in the likely event that the party was successful, they would form a kind of coalition government in which there would be a President elected as usual and a Minister for Defence selected by the army as well as five other pro-Treaty ministers and four anti-Treaty ministers. In short, the Treaty would not be an election issue at all.

None of the principals seemed happy with the pact. Some saw it as a victory for de Valera, but he did not share that view. It 'is no victory', he wrote. He saw it as a possible 'slippery slope', because he did not believe Collins would insist on a republican constitution. De Valera, who had always seen himself as primarily a propagandist, was in a weak position in which he really felt powerless and overwhelmed. Only the previous week he was complaining that 'the propaganda against us is overwhelming. We haven't a single daily newspaper on our side, and but one or two weeklies. The morale of the people seems to be almost completely broken, but that was only to be expected when the leaders gave way.'

Griffith was disturbed that Collins had conceded too much, because the agreement had the effect of denying the people the right to express their views on the Treaty. 'If we were not prepared to fight and preserve the democratic rights of the ordinary people and the fruit of national victory,' Griffith complained, 'we should be looked upon as the greatest set of poltroons who had ever had the fate of Ireland in their hands.'

While some people saw the agreement as evidence of the Big Fellow's reluctance to break the strong bond that was believed to have existed between himself and de Valera, friends of Collins thought he had little time for any of the politicians. 'He had no great regret regarding the loss of de Valera's friendship, nor no great fear of the opposition he alone could offer,' Ó Muirthile noted. 'He did not worry too much either about parting company with others of his political colleagues.' This apparently included even Arthur Griffith.

Griffith was particularly cool towards the election pact. When he was asked if he would accept it, he was clearly reluctant. He spent some minutes reflecting, pulling nervously at his tie and wiping his glasses. The other ministers waited in silence for his answer for what seemed like a long time, and when he did assent he no longer addressed Collins as 'Mick', but as 'Mr Collins'.

Despite his own reservations about the pact, Griffith proposed it for ratification in the Dáil, and in the circumstances it was easily approved. There was a new air of party unity in Dublin, but there are grounds for suspecting that all this was intended to cover up a monumental blunder by Collins. He had secretly agreed to support a concerted campaign of action in the North. This explains why even Brugha seemed to be holding out the hand of co-operation to the Big Fellow on 17 May. 'I suggest to Michael Collins that he and I should retire from public life and go to the north of Ireland on a defence crusade in favour of our people there.'

The campaign in the North, which was set to begin next day, was to involve arson and destruction of commercial property in Belfast as well as RIC barracks, stately homes, and railways in different parts of the province. Collins was supposed to provide support from the South, but reneged at the last moment. He had probably agreed to the whole thing as a means of pro-moting IRA unity in the South, and having backed out he grasped at the chance of concluding the election pact with de Valera.

Fourteen people were murdered in Belfast over the weekend. Six more were killed on Monday, 22 May, including the first political assassination. William J. Twaddell, a unionist member of the Stormont parliament, was shot dead in the street by the IRA. Later that day the Northern government implemented the Special Powers Act, which authorised the Minister for Home Affairs to adopt draconian measures, like arrest without warrant and internment without trial. It also permitted prisoners to be flogged and even executed, coroners' inquests to be dispensed with, organisations to be banned, and meetings to be prohibited by ministerial order. That night the police began a sweep of Northern Ireland, backed up by the military. They arrested over three hundred and fifty suspected Republicans and interned them without trial. No loyalists were interned, even though they had been responsible for most of the murders. This, of course, further alienated the nationalist community.

The Sinn Féin Ard Fheis, which adjourned back in February, was re-convened on 23 May to approve the election pact. Collins indicated that he was endorsing the pact even if it endangered the Treaty.

'We have made an agreement which will bring stable conditions to the country, and if these stable conditions are not more valuable than any other agreement,' he said, 'well, then, we must face what these stable conditions will enable us to face.' He accused the unionists in the north-east of organ-ising a last desperate stand for ascendancy, but in reality it was more like a desperate attempt for nationalist unity on his part. It did not matter whether those present supported the Treaty, or any alternative, so long as they spoke with one national voice, he argued. Since all of them were against partition, he said, they should form a united front on the issue.

Although de Valera was hoping that there would be no contests in the election, Collins emphasised that the pact specifically allowed for all other groups to put forward their own candidates. In order to keep the spirit of party unity, de Valera asked that there be no further speeches on the pact. His reluctance to speak was probably a reflection of his own uneasiness about the pact, which was then ratified by a show of hands, with only four or five voting against ratification.

In an ensuing discussion Collins denounced Republican threats against the press, because the newspapers were not publishing everything they were being given. Authentic cases were published, he said, and journalists had been helpful in the matter, so there was no justification for the threats against the newsmen. He was obviously playing to the press gallery as he raised the spectre of the attack in which Rory O'Connor and his gang had wrecked the machinery of the *Freeman's Journal* some weeks earlier.

'If you are for that kind of freedom,' Collins said, 'I have no use for it.'

Collins was engaged in a devious game in which he was telling various people what they wished to hear. 'Unity at home was more important than any Treaty with the foreigner,' he told some anti-Treaty people. 'If unity could only be got at the expense of the Treaty — the Treaty would have to go.' Yet he was genuinely trying to reconcile the irreconcilable in seeking to draft a republican constitution that would be compatible with the Treaty.

Mary MacSwiney questioned his sincerity about seeking such a constitution. 'If he is sincere in that, why is he risking civil war on the acceptance of the Treaty?' she asked. 'Collins is undoubtedly a clever man, and I am sorry to say an unscrupulous one but do you think for an instant that he can beat L. George in the game of duplicity?'

The British were particularly upset at the news of the election pact in Dublin on top of the upsurge in violence in the North. Churchill described the pact to the cabinet as a disastrous agreement that would prevent the Irish people expressing an opinion on the Treaty and leave the Provisional Government 'in its present weak and helpless position'. Publicly, however, he adopted a more reserved attitude. 'We have not yet been able to form any final conclusion in regard to it,' he said. 'We have, therefore, invited the Irish signatories to the Treaty to come to London to discuss the matter with the British Government.' In effect, the invitation was more like a summons.

Collins told Churchill that the pact with de Valera was necessary as an election would otherwise be impossible. It was, he claimed, the only means of securing a vote on the Treaty. 'The idea was to try and get a non-party Government so as to secure tranquillity in Ireland and at a later date stage a proper election on the main issue,' he explained.

'The two parties agree to simply monopolise power,' Churchill told his colleagues. 'The one inducement offered to the public to accept the agreement is the hope of escaping from anarchy.'

Field Marshal Sir Henry Wilson, who had recently retired as chief of the imperial general staff and had been elected to Westminster for North Down, was scathing in his attitude towards the pact. 'The story of the surrender of the Government to Mr de Valera was one of the most pitiful, miserable, and cowardly stories in history,' Wilson declared. 'Now Mr de Valera had Mr Collins in his pocket, and it was another proof that, quite apart from the misery of the thing, the Government had miscalculated every single element that went to make the Irish situation.'

Wilson had been invited to advise the Stormont government on security matters in Northern Ireland. He warned that English public opinion would be manipulated by British propaganda into accepting a republic in the twenty-six counties, just as it had got accustomed to murders.

'There is no doubt that at the conferences which are now to take place there is a very grave danger that the British Cabinet will come to the view that the pact between Mr Collins and Mr de Valera does not violate the Treaty,' Wilson argued. 'Should that happen, it will be not only a direct menace to Ulster, but, by establishing an independent Republic within the Empire, it will be the beginning of Imperial disruption.'

When the Irish delegation headed by Griffith and Collins went over to London to discuss the draft constitution during the second week of June, they found the British deeply uneasy over the terms of the election pact. Hugh Kennedy, the principal constitutional adviser to the Irish side, warned that provision in the election pact for a coalition with the anti-Treaty element would be a violation of the Treaty. 'You cannot have a coalition Provisional Government consisting of pro-Treaty and anti-Treaty members,' Kennedy explained. 'Every member of the Provisional Government must accept the Treaty in writing.'

While in London, Collins put up a stout defence of his actions. When Austen Chamberlain pressed him to disavow the IRA's campaign, he replied that he would not 'hold the hands of the northern government when Catholics were being murdered'. He was 'in a most pugnacious mood', according to Tom Jones, who noted that the Big Fellow 'talked on at a great rate in a picturesque way about going back to fight with his comrades'. He accused the British of being 'bent on war', because they were doing nothing about the situation in Belfast. Jones noted that Collins went 'on and on at great length about the Ulster situation'.

Collins had 'become obsessed' with Northern Ireland, according to Lloyd George, who found himself in the unenviable position of trying to placate the volatile personalities of both the Big Fellow and Churchill. He felt there was 'a strain of lunacy' in Churchill, and he said that Collins was 'just a wild animal — a mustang'. When someone suggested that negotiating with Collins was like trying to write on water, Lloyd George interjected, 'shallow and agitated water'.

Eamonn Duggan tried privately to impress on the British that they should realise that Collins had been under enormous pressure. 'We ought to remember the life Collins had led during the last three years,' Jones noted. 'He was very highly strung, and overwrought, and sometimes left their own meetings in a rage with his colleagues.'

He had enormous ministerial duties as Chairman of the Provisional Government and Minister for Finance. He was faced with a serious deficit as revenue was expected to fall £10 million short of the £30 million that the government expected to spend, yet that was only a minor problem in comparison with the difficulties of his other functions. He was chief propagandist for the Provisional Government as he travelled to speaking rallies around the country, often under the most trying conditions. He was also the person mainly responsible for conducting the thorny, day-to-day negotiations with the British at an intergovernmental level and with both the Republican and unionist minorities in Ireland, as well as being ultimately responsible for the drafting of the new constitution, not to mention being up to his neck in a conspiracy to destabilise Northern Ireland. Any one of those functions was a full-time job, especially when it frequently involved trying to reconcile the irreconcilable. In the process he left himself open to the charge of dealing in bad faith with everyone — the Republicans, the unionists, the British, and even his own colleagues. The Big Fellow had taken on too much for any one man.

There was no doubt that the British had solid grounds for objecting to the election pact, because its full implementation would almost inevitably violate the provision stipulating that all members of the Provisional Government had to signify their acceptance of the Treaty in writing.

'Does it matter if de Valera is in charge of education?' Kevin O'Higgins asked the British. 'Are we bound to take steps which would wreck the Treaty?'

De Valera realised that the aim would be to appoint him to some innocuous post like Education, which he intended to refuse. He was hoping to be elected Minister for Defence instead.

Without the pact, Collins contended, the anti-Treaty IRA would disrupt the balloting by intimidating people and burning ballot boxes, with the result that there would be no coherent expression of the public will. While the number of visionary and fanatical Republicans was comparatively small, a larger criminal element would support them in order to generate a disorder that they could exploit for their own personal gain. The election pact afforded the opportunity of isolating the criminal elements so that they could be tackled first and a climate could then be created for a proper, free election. As things stood the Provisional Government would not be able to protect all the RIC, especially in isolated areas.

Far fewer people had been killed in the whole of the twenty-six counties since the Treaty was signed than in Belfast alone. Ten Protestant people had been murdered in Cork during late April, but the condemnation of this had been universal throughout the South. When Sir Henry Robinson, a Protestant civil servant, asked Collins for protection he was told that the Provisional Government was in no position to protect anybody; he and his family 'had much better clear out, and come back later when things had settled down a bit'.

The Provisional Government had even less chance of protecting all the people who would wish to vote in the general election. It was only by concluding the pact within Sinn Féin that it would be possible to hold an election. As already mentioned, Collins had insisted, as part of the deal, that other parties and individuals should be free to contest the election. Some of them were likely to defeat anti-Treaty Sinn Féin candidates, he predicted, with the result that there would be an even greater pro-Treaty majority. Not only would this be tantamount to endorsing the agreement but it would also undermine the existing argument that the Dáil had been elected on a platform to uphold the Irish Republic and did not therefore have the authority to implement the Treaty.

Churchill later explained the situation to the House of Commons. If the pact led to an improvement in the conditions of social order throughout the twenty-six counties and a cessation of all attacks upon Ulster as well as upon former servants of the Crown and Protestants in the South, then those advantages could 'be set off against the disadvantages of increased delay in ascertaining the free will of the Irish people in respect of the Treaty'.

'If we are wrong,' Churchill continued, 'if we are deceived, the essential strength of the Imperial position will in no wise be diminished, while the honour and the reputation of Ireland will be fatally aspersed. By doing nothing we may yet succeed. But if we fail in spite of all our efforts and forbearance, then by these efforts and that very forbearance we shall have placed ourselves upon the strongest ground, and in the strongest position, and with the largest moral resources both throughout the Empire and throughout the world, to encounter whatever events may be coming towards us.'

While Collins was in London there was trouble on the Donegal–Fermanagh border around the villages of Pettigo and Belleek. The former was in Donegal and the latter over the border in Fermanagh. A force of IRA men fired on policemen in Belleek. Collins assured Churchill that the anti-Treaty IRA was responsible. 'You told us that these forces were not your forces,' Churchill reminded him a few days later, 'you disclaimed any responsibility for them. I announced this in Parliament in your presence the same afternoon.'

Churchill forcefully defended the integrity of Griffith and Collins in that speech. 'I do not believe, as has been repeatedly suggested, that they are working hand in glove with their Republican opponents with the intent by an act of treachery to betray British confidence and Ireland's good name,' he told the House of Commons. 'I am sure they are not doing that.' After listening to Churchill's speech from the strangers' gallery of the House of Commons, Collins endorsed what had been said, but before taking his leave he seemed rather morose.

'I shall not last long,' he told Churchill. 'My life is forfeit, but I shall do my best. After I am gone it will be easier for others. You will find they will be able to do more than I can do.' Collins then left for Dublin. 'I never saw him again,' Churchill added. But he did send him a stern message shortly afterwards when he learned that Collins had lied about the troops in Belleek and Pettigo.

'It is with surprise that I received the Communiqué issued from GHQ Beggar's Bush that there were "no other Irish troops", other than "our troops", i.e. Free State Troops, "in the district now or then" and I shall be glad if you will explain the discrepancy,' Churchill wrote. Collins had essentially been caught lying, and Churchill was determined to force the issue, even though Lloyd George wished at all costs to avoid 'fighting in the swamps of Lough Erne'. Churchill insisted on having his way and even threatened to resign, if necessary.

The British army sent in heavily armed troops to clear the IRA out of Belleek. After a few shells were fired, the IRA fled and the British pushed on to Pettigo, much to the annoyance of Collins, who protested strongly about the incursion into the twenty-six counties. Despite his grave misgivings about the venture, Lloyd George was able to celebrate that night 'a famous victory' in what was called 'the great bloodless Battle of Belleek'. In fact, seven IRA men had been killed.

The Northern offensive had been a disaster for Collins. Indeed, he had already abandoned it, seeing that the Provisional Government had decided on 3 June 'that a policy of peaceful obstruction should be adopted towards the Belfast Government'. In other words, the offensive was being called off in favour of a more passive approach.

With the round-up and internment of IRA activists, reports from Belfast were extremely gloomy. 'The Military Organisation is almost destroyed,' one report warned. 'Under present circumstances,' another noted, 'it would be impossible to keep our Military Organisation alive and intact, as the morale of the men is going down day by day and the spirit of the people is practically dead.'

Meanwhile the delegation in London was abandoning the Big Fellow's hope of persuading the British to accept a constitution compatible with Document No. 2. The draft constitution excluded the Treaty oath and incorporated a clause stipulating that 'the legislative, executive, and judicial authority of Ireland shall be derived solely from the Irish people'. There was also a clause stipulating that only the Free State parliament could declare war on behalf of the country. If the British parliament ratified such a constitution for the Irish Free State, this would be tantamount to acknowledging the right to neutrality — that prized right which de Valera had contended would make 'a clean sweep' of the whole defence question during the Treaty negotiations.

The British disliked the manner in which the role of the King was played down in the draft constitution. Although the functions of the Crown were not defined in Canada, or even in Britain, Lloyd George noted that it was of 'a greater potential force' than other aspects of the everyday government of a dominion. This was what de Valera had been contending, but the British had to play the issue down as they had previously argued that the King was only of symbolic significance.

Tom Jones had feared that 'Collins might appoint a charwoman' to the post of Governor-General. 'I see no great objection if she's a good one,' Jones added, 'but others may take a different view of what is fitting.'

The British insisted on the inclusion of the Treaty oath in the constitution, because its omission could be seen as a violation of the agreement. Griffith had no intention of defending the republican symbols of the draft constitution to the point of breaking with the British. The Treaty oath was therefore incorporated into the constitution and the Treaty itself was scheduled to the document, with the stipulation that the Treaty would take precedence.

The text of the constitution was only released on the eve of the election, which had eventually been set for 16 June. As a result the Irish people did not have a chance to see it until it was published in the daily newspapers on election day. While this fulfilled the strict letter of the Ard Fheis agreement that the constitution would be published before the election, it effectively denied critics the chance of explaining the document before polling. By then, however, Collins had ridden roughshod over the spirit of the election pact.

Speaking in Cork on the eve of the election, he virtually asked voters to support others, rather than vote for anti-Treaty candidates on the Sinn Féin panel. 'I am not hampered now by being on a platform where there are coalitionists, and I can make a straight appeal to you, to the citizens of Cork, to vote for the candidates you think best of, whom the electors of Cork think will carry on best in the future the work that they want carried on,' he said. 'You understand fully what you have to do, and I will depend on you to do it.'

In Clonakilty later that night, he told the gathering that they had a duty to vote for the people that they thought would carry out their policy. There was no doubt this was a violation of the spirit of the election pact. Of course, it should be pointed out that the anti-Treaty faction had already violated the pact by engaging in some blatant intimidation to prevent pro-Treaty independents and candidates of other parties contesting the election.

That same day *The Irish Times* published a letter in which Dr Browne, the bishop of Cloyne, announced that he was subscribing to the election fund of two independent pro-Treaty deputies in his east Cork diocese. This, of course, was tantamount to asking his flock to vote for those people.

Even though Sinn Féin had deliberately avoided making the Treaty an election issue, there was no doubt about the outcome. The election count took over a week, but from very early on it was clear the electorate were in favour of the Treaty. Of the sixty-five pro-Treaty Sinn Féin candidates, fifty-eight were elected, while only thirty-six of the anti-Treaty Sinn Féin people were successful. Even that exaggerated the anti-Treaty support, because seventeen of them were returned without opposition. Where the seats were contested, forty-one of forty-nine pro-Treaty candidates were successful, while only nineteen of forty-one anti-Treaty candidates were elected.

The popular vote painted an even bleaker picture for the anti-Treaty side, which received less than 22 per cent of the first preference votes cast. No anti-Treaty candidate headed the poll in any constituency, and Sligo–Mayo East was the only constituency in the whole country where a majority of voters supported anti-Treaty candidates. Had the Labour Party, which was pro-Treaty, run more candidates it might have surpassed the anti-Treaty Sinn Féin vote, seeing that the total vote of Labour's eighteen candidates was only 1,353 votes short of the combined total of the forty-one anti-Treaty candidates who faced opposition. Labour candidates actually won seventeen of the eighteen seats that they contested. There was absolutely no doubt that the Irish electorate favoured acceptance of the Treaty, at least as a short-term measure.

In Dublin the Republicans fared dismally, winning only one of the eighteen seats in the city and county. In the city they lost four of their five seats, only Seán T. O'Kelly being re-elected; and they failed to win any seat in the remainder of County Dublin, where Patrick Pearse's mother lost out, even though she was the only anti-Treaty Republican seeking election in the six-seat constituency. The poll there was headed by Darrell Figgis, who ran as a pro-Treaty independent. Thomas Johnson, the Labour leader, came in second.

'Labour and Treaty sweep the country,' Harry Boland noted in his diary. Yet he and his colleagues had no intention of accepting the popular verdict. Two days after the election, the anti-Treaty IRA held another convention at which it was proposed to give the British government seventy-two hours, notice of their intention to terminate the truce. Although twelve of the sixteen-man executive supported the motion, it was vigorously opposed by the chief of staff, Liam Lynch, and also by Cathal Brugha. When the matter was put to a vote, the proposal was narrowly defeated by 118 to 103 votes.

Rory O'Connor and other hard-liners refused to accept the decision. They returned to the Four Courts, where they locked out those who had voted against their motion. The twelve dissident members of the executive repudiated Lynch and elected a new chief of staff of their own, Joe McKelvey.

De Valera played no part in the machinations of those in the Four Courts. He concentrated instead on political matters, denouncing the decision of the people. 'These results seem, indeed, a triumph for the Imperial methods of pacification,' he contended in a statement issued on 21 June. As far as he was concerned, the Irish people were intimidated into voting as the British desired by the threat of war. 'But their hearts and their aspirations are unchanged,' he added. 'Ireland unfree will never be at rest, or genuinely reconciled with England.'

De Valera still confidently expected to be a member of the new cabinet in line with the election pact and he was determined to oppose the ratification of the new constitution. 'It will exclude from public service and disenfranchise every honest Republican,' he contended. 'Dáil Éireann will not dishonour itself by passing it.'

The Roman Catholic hierarchy denounced conditions in the country and called upon the people to insist that the government prevent Ireland being rushed headlong into the abyss. Next day, 22 June, the political climate was further poisoned with the assassination of Sir Henry Wilson in London by two members of the IRA, Reginald Dunne and Joseph O'Sullivan, who were captured after a short chase. The murder sparked a chain of events that were to have tragic consequences for the nation.

'Documents have been found upon the murderers of Field Marshal Sir Henry Wilson which clearly connect the assassins with the Irish Republican Army, and which further reveal the existence of a definite conspiracy against the peace and order of this country,' Lloyd George complained. 'The ambiguous position of the Irish Republican Army can no longer be ignored by the British Government. Still less can Mr Rory O'Connor be permitted to remain with his followers and his arsenal in open rebellion in the heart of Dublin in possession of the Courts of Justice, organising and sending out from this centre enterprises of murder not only in the area of your Government but also in the six Northern Counties and in Great Britain.'

The British assumed the Four Courts element was behind the murder. Before the truce Dunne and O'Sullivan had reported to Rory O'Connor, who was in charge of IRA activities in England for a time. But some of those closest to Collins later stated that it was the Big Fellow himself who ordered the hit on Wilson, without telling his government colleagues. Of course, there is no more definite proof of this than there is of him ordering the Squad to kill the various detectives in 1919. History must rely on the word of people like Liam Tobin, Frank Thornton, Joe Dolan, and Joe Sweeney.

Collins actually met Joe Sweeney within hours of the killing.

'How do we stand about the shooting of Wilson?' Sweeney asked.

'It was two of our men did it,' Collins replied, looking very pleased with himself.

When Liam Tobin told Richard Mulcahy that Collins was behind the killing, Mulcahy was so annoyed that he threatened to resign. It was a reckless act that threatened to destroy everything. Collins had allowed his weakness for intrigue and his own turbulent nationalism to get the better of his judgment.

De Valera had no involvement whatever in the murder. 'I do not know who they were who shot Sir Henry Wilson, or why they shot him,' he told the press. 'I do not approve but I must not pretend to misunderstand.' Later he would contend that the killing of Wilson more than any other single happening was responsible for the breakdown of the uneasy peace, because, he claimed, it was Churchill's virtual ultimatum which prompted the Provisional Government to attack the Four Courts.

'Now [that] you are supported by the declared will of the Irish people in favour of the Treaty,' Churchill warned Collins, the British government felt that 'they have a right to expect that the necessary action will be taken by your Government without delay'. The British offered to furnish artillery for an attack on the Four Courts.

'Hitherto we have been dealing with a weak Government, and have been anxious to do nothing to compromise a clear expression of Irish opinion; but now that the Provisional Government is greatly strengthened, it is its duty to give effect to the Treaty in the letter and the spirit without delay,' Churchill told the House of Commons on 26 June. He went on to accuse those in the Four Courts of encouraging 'murderous outrages' not only in Ireland but 'also probably in Great Britain', which was an obvious reference to the murder of Wilson.

'The time has come when it is not unfairly premature, or impatient for us to make this strengthened Irish Government and new Irish Parliament a request in express terms, that this sort of thing must come to an end,' he continued to the cheers of the House. 'If it does not come to an end — if through weakness, want of courage, or some other even less creditable reason, it is not brought to an end, and a speedy end — then it is my duty to say, on behalf of His Majesty's Government, that we shall regard the Treaty as having been formally violated, that we shall take no steps to carry out or legalise its further stages, and that we shall resume full liberty of action in any direction that may seem proper.'

'Let Churchill come over and do his own dirty work,' was the Big Fellow's initial reaction.

It was Ireland's great misfortune at this time that the man at the helm of Irish affairs in Britain was someone as volatile and tempestuous as Churchill, who prided himself as a man of action, but whose judgment on Irish matters was suspect, to say the least. The British commander in Ireland, General Sir Nevil Macready, was actually ordered to attack the Four Courts, but he astutely delayed, while those in the building forced the pace of events themselves.

On 27 June they raided the premises of a Dublin car dealer and seized sixteen cars in which they planned to convoy a small force to Northern Ireland, where they planned to restart hostilities with the British. Forces of the Provisional Government managed to arrest some of the raiders, and those in the Four Courts retaliated by seizing J. J. 'Ginger' O'Connell, the deputy chief of staff of the Provisional Government's army.

At this point Collins had had enough. 'The Irregular Forces in the Four Courts continued in their mutinous attitude,' he observed in some notes drawn up during the Civil War. 'They openly defied the newly expressed will of the people. On the pretext of enforcing a boycott of British goods, they raided and looted a Dublin garage, and when the leaders of the raid were arrested by the National Forces, they retaliated by the seizure of one of the principal officers of the National Army.'

The Provisional Government had two courses open to it, Collins contended: 'either to betray its trust and surrender to the mutineers, or to fulfil its duty and carry out the work entrusted to it by the people'.

An ultimatum was sent to those in the Four Courts to withdraw by the early hours of 28 June. At the same time the Provisional Government issued a statement to the press. 'Outrages such as these must cease at once and cease for ever.' Business life had been suffering and this resulted in unemployment and distress. 'The Government is determined that the country shall no longer be held up from the pursuit of its normal life and the re-establishment of its free national institutions'.

When the time-limit on the ultimatum expired, the forces of the Provisional Government bombarded the building. In view of Churchill's comments in the House of Commons hours earlier, Republicans concluded that the attack was launched at the bidding of the British, who provided the heavy artillery. Just as the attack on Fort Sumner marked the opening of the American Civil War, the attack on the Four Courts would henceforth be considered the start of the Irish Civil War.

12

The Civil War

After three days of shelling, the Republicans in the Four Courts surrendered, but not before blowing up much of the building, which contained the Public Record Office and some irreplaceable documents. Churchill was delighted. 'If I refrain from congratulations it is only because I do not wish to embarrass you,' he wrote to Collins. 'The archives of the Four Courts may be scattered but the title-deeds of Ireland are safe.'

De Valera immediately condemned the pro-Treaty forces for attacking their former comrades in arms 'at the bidding of the English'. Those in the Four Courts 'would most loyally have obeyed the will of the Irish people freely expressed', he contended. They had shown contempt for the will of the people and de Valera had shown his own contempt for the truth in the way he supported them. He would soon come to regret his support for the undemocratic behaviour of O'Connor and his colleagues. Yet at the time de Valera asked the Irish people to rally to their assistance: 'Irish citizens, give them support! Irish soldiers, bring them aid!' He joined the Republicans occupying the Hamman Hotel on O'Connell Street.

After a couple of days, J. F. Homan, a senior member of St John's Ambulance Brigade, sought to mediate an end to the assault. 'They, and their leaders, are at liberty to march out and go to their homes unmolested,' Collins told him, 'if only they will deposit their weapons in the National Armoury, there to remain until and unless in the whirl of politics these men become a majority in the country in which case they will have control of them.' He was careful to use the words 'deposit their weapons' rather than 'surrender' them.

Homan sought out de Valera and found that 'he was anxious for an immediate peace'. But he was insisting that the Republicans should be allowed to keep their arms. 'He told me he would be prepared to recommend to the insurgents, and was confident he could get them to agree, to go home, each man carrying his weapon with him.' But Collins was insistent that they had to lay down their arms.

'There is no use negotiating with Mr Collins,' Cathal Brugha told Homan. 'What exactly did Mr de Valera propose?'

Homan told him what the former President had suggested.

'He could not carry the fighting men with him on that,' Brugha replied. 'The most they would agree to would be to leave this place with their arms and go and join our men fighting elsewhere. And, for my part, I would oppose even that. You are wasting your time. We are here to fight to the death.'

The Provisional Government was prepared to be reasonable, Collins assured the Catholic archbishop of Dublin, the lord mayor, and Cathal O'Shannon of the Labour Party. 'We don't want any humiliating surrender,' he emphasised. But it was necessary to restore order. The archbishop and lord mayor agreed with him that there would be further trouble if the Republicans were allowed to keep their weapons. O'Shannon thought, however, that they might have a change of heart.

'Had the offer been accepted,' de Valera later contended, 'the whole civil war would have ended with the Four Courts incident and terms would have been arranged before the war had properly commenced.'

The second Dáil was supposed to meet on 1 July to dissolve itself so that the new Dáil could come into existence, but the whole thing was prorogued by the Provisional Government. The Dáil was supreme, so Collins and his colleagues had no legal authority to postpone it, with the result that de Valera characterised their actions as a *coup d'état*. Of course, to Collins this was just arguing about legal niceties.

From this point on for the remainder of his short life Collins was the driving inspiration and real leader of the forces of the Provisional Government, while de Valera was a hunted man with no real military influence and very little political influence for the time being. As early as the second week in July Erskine Childers was writing that 'Dev says we should surrender while we are strong.'

De Valera and others slipped out of the Hamman Hotel and headed south for the province of Munster, which was a Republican stronghold. He joined those at the IRA headquarters in Clonmel and served as adjutant to Seán Moylan, the director of operations, but the Republican operations were in a shambles and the IRA was soon in full flight. 'The Chief is at GHQ, hale and well, the same honest, straightforward, unpurchasable man that you knew,' Harry Boland wrote to Joe McGarrity on 13 July 1922. 'All the calumny that has been heaped upon him is British inspired; they failed to bribe or intimidate him, they now try the weapon of slander.'

Even though the former President really had little influence any more, he was still held primarily responsible for the Civil War. For instance, an editorial in the pro-Treaty organ, *The Free State*, began:

Why?

Because Eamonn de Valera refused to accept a Treaty signed by Irish Plenipotentiaries.

Because Eamonn de Valera refused to accept the majority vote of his Cabinet.

Because Eamonn de Valera refused to accept the majority vote of Dáil Éireann.

Because Eamonn de Valera refused to accept the majority vote of the Irish people.

Because Eamonn de Valera incited neurotic young men and emotional young women to set aside a principle which governs the politics of every civilised country, and drove them to make war on their own people under the pretext of 'maintaining the Republic', which he himself abandoned in July 1921 . . .

Thomas Johnson, the leader of the Labour Party, protested against the proroguing of the Dáil for two weeks until 15 July. He contended that the people's representatives were being 'treated with contempt'.

'It is impossible for Parliament to meet in the present circumstances,' Griffith wrote. But the statement that the inaugural meeting of the new Dáil had been prorogued for a fortnight was issued by the Provisional Government over the names of Collins and Diarmuid O'Hegarty, who stated that 'for certain causes and considerations it is expedient that the said meeting should be postponed'. At the same meeting it was decided that attacks on Republican strongholds 'should be vigorously continued'.

'What really happened was that the executive usurped the government of the country and by a *coup d'état* established a new government,' de Valera later contended. 'It was really in consequence of that that I felt that I could consistently and constitutionally take up arms and fight for the constitution.' Of course, this argument was disingenuous, because he had already offered his services to the Republicans before the opening of the new Dáil was postponed.

While Collins may have violated the spirit of the election pact with de Valera, he had remained within the letter of the agreement prior to polling, but he made no effort to uphold his end of the pact after the election. In response to a question as to whether de Valera would be excluded from the cabinet, he told a *Daily Express* reporter that 'acceptance of the Treaty by members of the Provisional Government is a clause of the Treaty'.

'It may be well to keep open some avenue or avenues to peace,' Collins wrote to Thomas Gay. 'We don't wish for any surrender of their principles.'

Yet it was necessary to have his opponents accept the verdict of the people in favour of the Treaty. The government had shown its determination to uphold the people's rights, and it had 'answered the challenge to Governmental authority by the recovery of General O'Connell' and by clearing out the occupied buildings. 'Every constitutional way is open to them to win the people to their side, and we will meet them in every way if only they will obey the people's will and accept the authority of [the] Government of the people. That alone is our concern,' Collins wrote.

As things stood he felt that the Republicans had been taught a lesson, and while it might be necessary to teach them another one, he was confident that the Provisional Government would be in a strong position so long as the public were aware that it was prepared to be reasonable. Having gained an important advantage by the surrender of O'Connor and Mellows at the Four Courts, he was anxious not to make the mistake of building sympathy for them by taking 'resolute action beyond what is required'.

The casualties in the nine days of fighting in Dublin were 654 killed. One of those was Cathal Brugha, who was mortally wounded at the Hamman Hotel on O'Connell Street. He died on 7 July, but Collins clearly took no delight in the death of his bitterest enemy. In spite of all, he still recognised that Brugha was sincere in his beliefs. 'Many would not have forgiven — had they been in my place — Cathal Brugha's attack on me on 7 January,' Collins wrote. 'Yet I would forgive him anything. Because of his sincerity I would forgive him anything.'

'At worst he was a fanatic — [he] fought in what has been a noble cause,' he continued. 'At best I numbered him among the very few who would have given their all that this country — now torn by civil war — should have its freedom.'

Collins decided to devote all his energies to ending the Civil War by asking the cabinet to appoint him commander-in-chief of the army and relieve him of his ministerial duties until further notice. W. T. Cosgrave took over as acting Chairman of the Provisional Government. Some people later suggested that this actually amounted to a *coup d'état* in which Collins was ousted, but this was absurd, because the whole thing was done at his own request.

De Valera believed it to be a tactical move so that Collins could ingratiate himself with the soldiers who were so mistrustful of all politicians. It was a way of building up rapport with the men to prosecute the war more effectively. However, Commandant Peter Young, the army archivist, has argued that Collins's action was an astute move to bolster the army. 'Putting him in uniform, at the head of an army defending the existence of the new state, and with a press that was largely pro-Treaty, raised his stature to heroic proportions,' Young wrote. 'The army as well as the general population required a sense of identity. Without the appointment of Collins as Commander-in-Chief, it is only too likely that it would have been beset by local rivalries and animosities.'

As a leader the Big Fellow exuded a degree of authority and control that nobody else could have commanded. Collins was obviously aware of that, since he spent so much time in the following weeks visiting army units on tours of inspection.

There was no rift with Cosgrave, even though he was primarily a politician who had first been elected as a Sinn Féin candidate to Dublin Corporation in 1909. Although de Valera dismissed him as 'a ninny', and Kevin O'Higgins reportedly sneered at him as 'a Dublin corporator', Cosgrave was greatly underestimated by many of his contemporaries. Collins was reputed to have sworn in exasperation at 'the clerical susceptibility of Cosgrave's personality', but they obviously had an easy relationship with each other.

Cosgrave later recalled how Oliver St John Gogarty and the Big Fellow used to call out to his home and deliberately shock him. Collins would roar with laughter at Gogarty's more irreverent remarks, especially when he noticed Cosgrave's stunned expression. 'I often thought that pair of rascals took more delight in shocking me than in talking serious business when they came out to tea,' Cosgrave said.

Collins essentially wrote his own terms for Cosgrave to take over as Chairman of the Provisional Government. 'It would be well, I think, if the Government issued a sort of official Instruction to me nominating the War Council of Three, and appointing me to act by special order of the Government as Commander-in-chief during the period of hostilities,' he wrote to Griffith, whom he asked to issue a general address calling on him to carry on the fight for Irish freedom, this time against the armed minority who were trying to establish a dictatorship without regard to the wishes of the people.

The government promptly issued the address on the lines suggested by Collins. It was signed by Griffith and all the other members of the cabinet. This was really a propaganda document that was designed to dramatise the determination of both Collins and the government to end the fighting as quickly as possible.

'You have been entrusted with supreme command of the National Army, and with General Mulcahy and General O'Duffy you have been constituted a War Council to direct the military operations now in progress,' the address began. 'An armed minority, possessing no authority, is waging war against the people to force them to submit to a dictatorship; and the Army which has recently freed the people from foreign tyranny must now resist this domestic encroachment upon their liberties.'

'The Irish Army, therefore, is fighting for the same principle as that for which we fought the British, the right of the Irish people to be masters in their own country, to decide for themselves the way in which they shall live and the system by which they shall be governed,' it continued. 'The Irregulars' method of warfare is utterly destructive of the economic life of the nation. Sheer brigandage is a fair term to apply to it. Wherever they go they burn and wreck property, destroy roads, railways and bridges, seize food, clothing and supplies even from the poorest people, conscript men into their ranks, and use forced labour. In short they are doing their best to ruin and demoralise the country.'

Both de Valera and Collins were highly conscious of the need for effective propaganda. 'The newspapers are as usual more deadly to our cause than the machine guns,' de Valera complained the previous week. Other than Collins, however, members of the Provisional Government did not appreciate the value of propaganda and this would only become apparent to Cosgrave more than a decade later. In a technical sense Collins was firmly establishing the principle of civilian control and taking his orders from Griffith and the Provisional Government, but the reality was somewhat different.

Cosgrave informed him, for instance, that 'it was the general opinion that the Government should be kept in constant touch with the military situation throughout the country, and it was decided that the Army authorities should be asked to have reports forwarded regularly to me in my capacity as Acting Chairman, similar to those reports which were formerly supplied to you'. Yet the nature of the subsequent correspondence was more Collins informing the government about what he had decided to do, rather than seeking permission. It was Cosgrave who was consulting him, rather than the other way round.

When Collins decided to postpone the Dáil for another two weeks until the end of July, he instructed Kathleen McKenna of the Publicity Department to emphasise that he hoped the struggle would be ended in two to three weeks. 'We suggest once more that the Government would act wisely in explaining to the country the nature and extent of the resistance that remains to be overcome,' Collins advised. 'A perfectly frank statement on the subject would define the Army's goal and would secure not merely the whole-hearted, but the intelligent co-operation of the Irish people.'

When public bodies sympathetic to the Republicans, such as the Cork Harbour Commissioners, wrote complaining about the suspension of the Dáil, Collins was careful to reply openly in a reasonable manner. This was not the brash, arrogant young man who had announced back in April 1919 that they were going to initiate the War of Independence whether people wanted it or not. 'Even now it is a simple matter to end hostilities if those who are opposing the People's Will but turn from their resistance and give the People the chance they desire,' Collins replied. 'No member of the Government wishes to prolong the struggle, but equally, no member of the Government, and, I am certain, no right thinking man in the whole of Ireland can contemplate, without a shudder, the triumph of an armed minority over the People.'

Collins was still waging a somewhat reluctant war in that he was anxious for peace on moderate terms. When Thomas Gay wrote to him complaining about the hard-line approach being taken by the Provisional Government, Collins seemed to agree. 'Generally speaking, what you say represents to a very large degree my own feelings about the main situation. Anybody who is out for blood or scalps is of little use to the country.'

'I think it very necessary that our Press Organs should be very reticent in their tone about both active Irregular and Political Opponents,' Collins warned Cosgrave. 'Much of the criticism lately has been inclined towards abuse. This is not good from our point of view, and it is not the best way to tackle them.' He did not doubt that many of them deserved to be abused, but they were not 'the real driving force' on the Republican side. 'The men who are prepared to go to the extreme limit are misguided, but practically all of them are sincere,' he continued. 'Our propaganda should be on a more solid and permanent basis even if what may look to be advantages have to be sacrificed.'

On 26 July it was decided to postpone the Dáil for a third time until 12 August. Collins demonstrated himself to be amazingly perceptive. 'We are in a strong position,' he wrote to Mulcahy. 'The opponents have shown themselves entirely, without an objective.' Not only did they not have a cohesive plan for the present, but they had none for the future either. 'These leaders are waiting for something to turn up. When the Four Courts were attacked they said "the people are coming round to us" — but the people have resolutely refused to come round to them, and they must realise that without the people they have no hope.'

The war would still be going on nine months later and Liam Lynch, the Republican leader, would still be fantasising about the arrival of heavy artillery to turn the tide of battle in his favour. De Valera would be pleading with Republicans to recognise the rights of the majority, in marked contrast with his own earlier public remarks. Of course, the conflict had by then taken some dreadful turns, and the resulting recrimination would poison Irish political life for the next half-century. Had Collins lived, would it have been different?

There is no doubt that he was anxious to avoid recrimination. 'It was pointless placing blame,' he warned Mulcahy. 'What matters is not the past six months but the present position and the future six months and after that the future six months — the entire future.'

Collins was as concerned about the government's public image as about the military side of things. He agreed with Desmond FitzGerald that censorship should be kept on broad, general lines, rather than specific details. 'It should be very nominal,' he advised Mulcahy. 'We might get more good from a communication to the press giving them general lines to go on rather [than] relying on the public spirit to omit certain things.'

He was anxious that the government should take responsibility for decisions, while the cabinet seemed quite content to leave things to him. 'It was decided that the Government will support the Military Authorities in whatever steps they may consider necessary to restore order in districts where military operations have ceased, but in which outbreaks of violence still continue,' he wrote to Mulcahy. 'I am afraid it is not very helpful to us, and we shall therefore have to frame proposals to be sanctioned by Government.' In short, he was calling the shots but he was anxious to avoid the appearance of military dictatorship not just by asking the government to sanction what the army was doing, but instead by asking the government to direct the army to do so..

Collins was already looking to conditions after the Republicans had been defeated. 'When the Military effort is ended with the defeat of the hostile forces, peace can be said to have been restored. But peace will have to be maintained!' He wanted local committees to promote confidence so that the people would 'become actively interested in the new life of the Nation'. Yet after he died, the opposite would happen. The Republicans were excluded as much as possible and many were forced to emigrate to find a living abroad.

Some members of the government were so hostile to the Republicans that they had no time for efforts to persuade them to give up the bomb and the bullet, and they tended to resent the efforts of those who were still trying to negotiate, but Collins still persisted and encouraged others to do likewise. 'You need never have any fear that I will not appreciate any effort that is calculated to make things go in the right direction,' he wrote to Thomas Gay on 1 August. 'If people had a little more forbearance, and a little truer appreciation of the other people's opinion, we might never have got into this present morass.'

A few days earlier he had actually sent a note to his old friend Harry Boland: 'Harry — It has come to this! Of all things it has come to this. It is in my power to arrest and destroy you. This I cannot do. If you will think over the influence which has dominated you it should change your ideal.

'You are walking under false colours. If no word of mine will change your attitude then you are beyond all hope — my hope.'

A couple of days later Boland was shot and mortally wounded while 'trying to escape'. Collins was grief-stricken at a cabinet meeting some hours later. 'He spoke bitterly but movingly of his former comrade,' according to Ernest Blythe.

'The man who shot him must come forward and say he did it,' Collins declared. 'We are a government now and we cannot have any more of this business of shooting a man running away.'

'Last night I passed Vincent's Hospital and saw a small crowd outside. My mind went in to him lying dead there and I thought of the times together, and, whatever good there is in any wish of mine, he certainly had it. Although the gap of 8 or 9 months was not forgotten — of course no one can ever forget it — I only thought of him with the friendship of the days of 1918 and 1919.'

Boland's sister Kathleen was with him when he died. She asked who had shot him but he would not say. All he said was to bury him beside Cathal Brugha.

Collins was told that he supposedly asked Kathleen: 'Have they got Mick Collins yet?' But that was too much to take in.

'I don't believe it so far as I'm concerned and, if he did say it, there is no necessity to believe it,' Collins wrote to Kitty Kiernan. 'I'd send a wreath but I suppose they'd return it torn up.'

Kitty was obviously very upset when she replied. 'I have lost a good friend in Harry — and no matter what, I'll always believe in his genuineness, that I was the one and only. I think you have also lost a friend. I am sure you are sorry after him.'

Collins met Kitty the same day as he received that letter and they had lunch together in a private room of the Shelbourne Hotel. He was apparently not as sympathetic about Boland as he might have been, because he later wrote and asked Kitty not to misunderstand whatever he had said about him. 'You'll also appreciate my feelings about the splendid men we have lost on our side, and the losses they are and the bitterness they cause, and the anguish. There is no one who feels it all more than I do. My condemnation is all for those who would put themselves up as paragons of Irish Nationality, and all the others as being not worthy of concern.'

The People's Rights Association of Cork, another Republican front, wrote to Collins on 1 August, observing that Liam Lynch had indicated that the Republicans would lay down their arms when the Provisional Government stopped attacking them, and that his forces would have no difficulty giving allegiance to the second Dáil, or the third Dáil once it met. The association therefore wished to know:

1. Do you agree to arrange for such a cessation of hostilities as General Liam Lynch intimates he is prepared to accept?
2. Do you agree to call forthwith a meeting of the Second Dáil, to be followed by a meeting of the Third Dáil, as previously arranged, and to allow the sovereign assembly of the people to decide on the necessity or policy of a bitter and prolonged civil war?

Collins replied promptly that the address should really have been sent to the government, not to him as commander-in-chief of the army, seeing that he was just implementing government policy, which was insisting that the

Republicans should submit to the rule of the people in the form of the duly elected government. Nevertheless he proceeded to answer the question anyway.

'When the irregulars — leaders and men — see fit to obey the wishes of the people, as expressed through their elected representatives; when they will give up their arms and cease their depredations on the persons and property of Irish citizens, then there will be no longer need for hostilities,' he explained.

If they wished to end the conflict, all they had to do was stop fighting. To secure their freedom all the arrested Republicans had to do was merely sign the following statement:

> I promise that I will not use arms against the Parliament elected by the Irish people, or the Government for the time being responsible to that Parliament, and that I will not support, in any way, any such action. Nor will I interfere with the property or the persons of others.

Since most of the prisoners had refused to sign such a form, he concluded that they obviously intended to take up arms again against the government. 'If this is the spirit which animates Liam Lynch,' he continued, 'it is very little good endeavouring to talk about terms.'

'I will entreat your representatives to look facts squarely in the face,' Collins concluded. 'The time for face-saving is passed. Irregular leaders, political and military, got an opportunity of doing this over a period of seven or eight months. The issue now is very clear. The choice is definitely between the return of the British and the irregulars sending in their arms to the people's Government, to be held in trust for the people.'

The war was going well for the Provisional Government. Free State forces landed in Tralee on 2 August and the largest town in the south-west fell in an afternoon. When Collins asked for another postponement of the Dáil, this time until 24 August, his motivation seemed as much political as military. 'We would have occupied sufficient additional posts in the South to dominate entirely the positions, and would be able to indicate so definitely our ability to deal with the military problem there, that no Parliamentary criticism of any kind could seriously interfere with that ability.'

He explained that he wanted to 'confirm to the general public our determination to clean up the matter definitely' lest the southern anti-Treaty forces would conclude that the government forces were reluctant 'to face them boldly', and had merely turned to the Dáil out of weakness. Risking this could lead to a 'rise in morale of the irregulars', which could then have serious consequences.

He had decided to put the partition question on the back-burner for the duration of the Civil War in the South. He softened his public stand in relation to the North during an interview with the *Daily News*. 'My attitude towards Ulster, which is the attitude of all of us in the Government, is not understood,' he said. 'There can be no question of forcing Ulster into union with the 26 Counties. I am absolutely against coercion of that kind. If Ulster is to join us it must be voluntarily. Union is our final goal; that is all.' Ever since the failure of the May campaign things had been getting quieter in the North and the latest remarks were seen as an enunciation of a more conciliatory Northern policy.

His political and military policies in regard to Northern Ireland were obviously in disarray. On taking over as acting Chairman of the Provisional Government, Cosgrave was shocked to learn of the situation in regard to paying groups in the North not to recognise the Stormont regime. 'The question of payments in the Six-County area is in a pretty chaotic condition,' Cosgrave wrote to Collins on just his second full day in the new job. 'There was no authority to spend money raised by taxing the South in the North,' he added. 'The Northern Government may be enabled to avoid its own proper liabilities and this is done in such a manner that the Free State tax payer cannot tell that his money is being spent in this way.'

'The people were for a peace policy and for a recognition of the Northern Government,' Mulcahy wrote to Collins on 24 July. 'They are even giving information to the Specials. Our officers seem to realise there is no other policy for the North but a peace policy of some kind, but the situation for peace or war has gone beyond them, none of them feel they are able to face the policy of one kind or the other.'

'I have scarcely a moment for any business other than the urgent business of restoring peace and settled conditions to the country,' Collins wrote to Churchill next day. But he had no intention of forgetting about the partition issue. 'Believe me,' he added, 'this all-important question is never far removed from my thoughts and were it not for my new obligations and commitments I would be devoting all available time and energy towards its solution.'

'The civil war will be over in a few weeks and then we can resume in the North,' he told an IRA group from the North at Portobello Barracks on 1 August. 'You men will get intensive training.'

Collins left some notes that were drawn up around this time. 'The humiliating fact has been brought home to us that our country is now in a more lawless and chaotic state than it was during the Black and Tan regime,' he wrote. 'No one can or will wish to deny that if we can speak with a united national voice to North-East Ulster, that voice cannot be ignored. If the so-called Government in Belfast has not the power nor the will to protect its citizens, then the Irish Government must find means to protect them. But we must show that we can protect our citizens in all parts of Ireland as we can and will.'

'I am forced to the conclusion that we have yet to fight the British in the North-East,' Collins warned Cosgrave on 3 August. 'We must by forceful action make them understand that we will not tolerate this carelessness with the lives of our people.'

'At the present I think we ought to be making every possible effort to develop the Intelligence system in the North-East and with that end in view you will prepare at once draft INTELLIGENCE FORMS suitable for use in the North-Eastern area,' Collins wrote to Joe McGrath, the director of intelligence, on 7 August. 'The forms should be drafted on the basis of one Command for the entire area.'

He reaffirmed his commitment to the area in a further meeting with other Northern members of the IRA two days later. 'Many and varied views were expressed, some quite heatedly,' one of the men recalled, 'but the only statement of importance now was the final summation and decision of Michael Collins.'

'With this Civil War on my hands, I cannot give you men the help I wish to give and mean to give,' Collins emphasised. 'I now propose to call off hostilities in the North and to use the political arm against Craig so long as it is of use. If that fails the Treaty can go to hell and we will start again.'

Yet he took time to send a lengthy protest to Churchill on the gerrymandering system that the unionists were introducing in Tyrone and Fermanagh, which he said was designed to 'paint the counties of Tyrone and Fermanagh with a deep Orange tint' in anticipation of the Boundary Commission.

One consequence of his Northern policy was already preying on his mind — the need to help Dunne and O'Sullivan who were about to be executed for the murder of Sir Henry Wilson. Collins wrote to Cosgrave as acting chairman of the Provisional Government to intercede with the British government on behalf of the two men. 'I am of opinion that we must now make an official representation that mercy be extended to these men,' he wrote. 'Please let me know what is being done in the matter.'

O'Sullivan and Dunne were duly hanged. If the Big Fellow gave the order, as those close to him said, then they took their secret to the grave with them.

The Civil War meanwhile was claiming more lives. Collins and other army leaders were joined by members of the government at a funeral mass at Portobello Barracks on 8 August for nine soldiers killed in Kerry. 'The scenes at the Mass were really heartbreaking,' he wrote to Kitty Kiernan afterwards, 'The poor women weeping and almost shrieking (some of them) for their dead sons. Sisters and one wife were there too, and a few small children. It makes one feel, I tell you.'

Up to this point Collins had been stressing the necessity for moderation, but it was significant that he wrote to Joe McGrath next day that 'any man caught looting or destroying should be shot on sight'.

On 12 August the Provisional Government claimed that Cork city was firmly in the hands of its forces. Collins was in Tralee that day when he got word of the sudden death of Arthur Griffith from a brain haemorrhage in Dublin.

'There seems to be a malignant fate dogging the fortune of Ireland, for at every critical period in her story the man whom the country trusts and follows is taken from her,' Collins told reporters in Tralee. 'It was so with Thomas Davis and Parnell, and now with Arthur Griffith.'

'Only those who have worked with him know what Arthur Griffith has done for Ireland; only they can realise how he has spent himself in his country's cause,' Collins continued, adding that he had 'no shadow of doubt' that the President's untimely death had been hastened by mental anguish as a result of the Civil War.

'Is it possible that the death of Mr Arthur Griffith may unite the nation?' a reporter asked.

'At the moment I am a soldier, but I think I can promise that if those who are against us will, even now, come forward and accept the terms offered by the Government, our differences can be composed.'

'I must not be misunderstood on this point,' he continued. 'Militarily, our position warrants us in our belief that our opponents are in a hopeless position. Look at the map: see where our troops are, what they have achieved, and where the armed forces of the other side have been driven. But, even so, it is not too late for de Valera and those who are with him to honour the passing of a great patriot by now achieving what that patriot has given his life for — a united Ireland, and Irish nation.'

Collins related how Griffith likened the de Valera party to Dermot McMurrough. 'He was the man who first brought the British to Ireland,' Collins explained. De Valera and company were really trying 'to bring the British back as conquerors, and what true Irish patriot can wish for that?' he asked.

Collins was convinced the Civil War was coming to a close. 'The military situation is entirely satisfactory,' he told reporters in Limerick on his way to Dublin for Griffith's funeral. He added that the main military operations would be completed within the next fortnight. 'I can advise the Government that, as far as the military situation is concerned, the new Parliament can meet at any time,' he added. 'Whether it will be further postponed out of respect to the late President Griffith I do not know.'

At Griffith's funeral on 16 August Collins marched in uniform at the head of the headquarters staff officers, with Mulcahy by his side. It was his first public appearance in the uniform of commander-in-chief. They marched at a slow pace through the city, with the result that spectators got a good look at him. It would be the last time that most would see him.

'I marched just behind him in the ranks, and heard the murmurs of admiration which rose from people on the route,' Piaras Béaslaí wrote. 'The people looked to him with confidence as the one man who could get the nation out of the morass into which it had sunk.'

Two days later Collins was ambushed in his car near Stillorgan, County Dublin, but his own report of the incident was initially ignored. He complained to the Publicity Department that he recounted the 'incident to the Government meeting last, but apparently it was not of sufficient interest for publication'.

> The Commander-in-Chief's car was ambushed at 1 p.m. on Friday about one mile the Dublin side of Stillorgan, on its way from Greystones. Second Driver Rafter was wounded on the hip and is now in Baggot Street Hospital. One bomb and between 20 and 30 rifle shots fired. Fire was returned. Casualties of attackers unknown. Car badly damaged.

He certainly wanted people to know about the ambush. 'I find myself in far more danger since the peace came than ever I did in the war,' he told a reporter for one of the London newspapers next day, 19 August, when the Big Fellow had another narrow escape. This time the touring car in which he was travelling accidentally collided with a military tender carrying troops in Dún Laoghaire. 'The crowd which collected round the damaged vehicles recognised the General and cheered him,' according to *The Irish Times*.

That same day George Bernard Shaw gave a press interview after a two-week stay in Ireland. 'Ireland is obviously on the point of losing its temper savagely,' he explained.

> When the explosion comes, General Collins will be able to let himself go in earnest, and the difficulty of the overcrowded jail and the disbanded irregulars who take to the road again the moment the troops have passed will be solved, but there will be no prisoners; the strain will be on the cemeteries.
>
> General Collins beat Sir Hamar Greenwood at the wrecking game because he had the people with him. What chance against him has Mr de Valera without military aptitude or any of Sir Hamar Greenwood's enormous material resources? Of course he can enjoy the luxury of dying for Ireland after doing Ireland all the damage he can.
>
> 'What matter if for Ireland dear we fall' is still the idiot's battle song. The idiocy is sanctified by the memories of a time when there was really nothing to be done for Irish freedom but to die for it; but the time has now come for Irishmen to learn to live for their country.

The latter sentiments were part of the argument that Collins had put forward in favour of the Treaty. Collins had met him socially during his visit, which leads one to wonder if Shaw had detected a growing impatience on the part of the pro-Treaty leader.

'I'm going to try and bring the boys around,' Collins reportedly told Patrick Moylett that evening, 'if not, I shall have to get rough with them.' Next morning, 20 August, he set out on his fatal trip to the south. As he was about to leave, he met Joe Sweeney.

'I don't know what you're up to, but I would advise you not to go,' Sweeney said.

'Ach, nobody will shoot me in my own county,' the Big Fellow replied.

He did not attend the cabinet meeting that day, which took a momentous decision on the North. Ernest Blythe, who had been vocal in favour of a militant policy in the South prior to the arrival of the Black and Tans, warned the cabinet that the aggressive policy towards the six counties was counter-productive. He therefore advocated that the payment of Northern Catholic teachers be wound up and the pro-Treaty IRA disbanded in the North. The Provisional Government formally adopted this 'peace policy', but it is significant that it did so subject to 'the approval of the Commander-in-Chief'. It was obvious that they still looked to Collins as the man in charge.

In the eyes of the public the Civil War was still a kind of contest between Collins and de Valera, who was preoccupied with the thought of arranging peace. 'In Fermoy, Mallow, and other towns, the people looked at us sullenly, as if we had belonged to a hostile invading army,' Robert Brennan recalled. 'Dev had seen all this, as had I, and that was one of the reasons he was so desperately trying for peace while he still had some bargaining power.'

'Any chance of winning?' de Valera asked himself. 'If there was any chance, duty to hold on to secure it. If none, duty to try to get the men to quit — for the present. The people must be won to the cause before any successful fighting can be done.'

Like Collins, he appreciated the value of propaganda, but the Republicans had no newspapers on their side, and they were badly organised. Rory O'Connor had claimed that they were establishing a military dictatorship, but he and his supporters were in jail, and Lynch, who took over from them, had not agreed with those tactics. Thus the Republicans did not even claim to have a government.

De Valera was trying to persuade them to give up the fight. 'Dev passing through your area talking peace,' Liam Lynch wrote to his deputy chief of staff, Liam Deasy. 'Give him no encouragement.'

'Dev's mission is to try to bring the war to an end,' Deasy told his men, adding that they were 'on no account to give Dev any encouragement as his arguments don't stand up'.

De Valera met Deasy in Gurranereagh, County Cork, on Monday, 21 August. 'We discussed the war situation far into the night,' Deasy recalled.

'His main argument was that, having made our protest in arms and as we could not now hope to achieve a military success, the honourable course was for us to withdraw.' Deasy agreed to an extent but pointed out that the majority of the IRA 'would not agree to an unconditional cease-fire'.

It was after nine o'clock next morning when de Valera and Deasy reached the tiny village of Béalnabláth, where they were told that Collins and a small military convoy had passed through only minutes earlier. Deasy remarked that the IRA should prepare an ambush in case Collins returned by the same route later that day. One of those present remarked that Collins might not leave his native county alive.

'I know and I am sorry for it,' de Valera is reputed to have responded. 'He is a big man and might negotiate. If things fall into the hands of lesser men there is no telling what might happen.' Yet only a few days earlier he reportedly told the writer Peter Golden that his great fear was that 'the next step will be a military dictatorship set up by Mick Collins, taking his orders from England'.

The Big Fellow strode into the lobby of the Imperial Hotel in Cork late on Monday night to find the two guards on duty sleeping. He walked over and grabbed them and banged their heads together.

Next morning he set out early with a small escort convoy which consisted of Lieutenant Smith, a motorbike outrider, followed by an open Crossley tender with two officers, two machine gunners with a Lewis gun, and eight riflemen. This was followed by a Leyland Thomas touring car with Collins and Emmet Dalton in the back seat, and two drivers in front. The rear of the convoy was brought up by an armoured car.

Collins noted in his pocket diary that they departed at 6.15 a.m. He planned to go to Macroom first, where he had promised the Lewis gun to the local captain. Only a few miles outside Cork they ran into difficulties. The retreating Republicans had destroyed a number of bridges in the area. Shortly before eight o'clock they reached Macroom, where they employed a local hackney driver, Tim Kelleher, to guide them by back roads to Bandon, because a bridge on the main road had been blown up. On the way they passed through Béalnabláth at around 9 a.m.

The locality was a hive of Republican activity. Volunteers retreating from Limerick, Kilmallock, and Buttevant as well as from Cork city were all in the general area. They planned to have a staff meeting at Béalnabláth that day.

Denis Long, who was there on guard duty for the Republicans, gave Smith directions to Bandon. He noticed Collins in the convoy as it passed.

There was talk about ambushing Collins at Béalnabláth while de Valera was in the village, but he had moved on before the actual ambush.

The Republicans were determined to respond to what they considered his audacious challenge. They placed a mine in a metal tin with sticks of gelignite and buried it in the road near Béalnabláth. They then commandeered a four-wheel dray, being driven by Stephen Griffith, who was told to take his horse to a local farm and await further developments. They took one of the wheels off the dray and propped it up on boxes of bottles and then waited throughout the remainder of the day. The number lying in wait fluctuated anywhere from the twenty-five estimated by Deasy to much more, depending on who was telling the story.

Meanwhile Collins continued on his journey. On reaching Bandon, Kelleher explained that he needed to return to Macroom as he had a prior commitment.

'We won't let you walk back to Macroom and won't disappoint your friend,' Collins explained. 'We will send you back by car.'

He wrote out a military chit. 'Take that to some man like yourself and he will drive you back to Macroom.' On the way back Kelleher and his driver stopped at Long's pub in Béalnabláth for a drink and found the place packed with Republicans.

As Collins and his party went on to Clonakilty, they had a good deal of trouble with the touring car, possibly caused by dirty petrol. They had to push it on a number of occasions, especially up some of the steeper hills. Although Collins was commander-in-chief, he was always ready to lend a hand with the pushing himself.

On the way to the village of Kilmurry, Smith knocked on the doors of some houses and shouted, 'The Commander-in-Chief is coming.' The locals thought they were expected to come out to cheer, but no one appeared, except one man who raced out to usher his ducks from the road.

Collins was now in his own home territory. With the capture of Cork, he and Dalton were confident that the Civil War could not last much longer. The Republicans had been virtually routed.

'It was a beautiful August day,' Dalton recalled. 'Because there were still daily ambushes, I was in trepidation of what could happen, but Collins saw no danger.'

'It's almost over,' he said. In a sense it was a prophetic remark, because it was almost over for him.

The journey was punctuated with stops. The armoured car was inevitably lagging behind and on one occasion the convoy had to go back to find it. On another occasion they found it parked outside a public house, where the crew were having a drink. Private John O'Connell explained they had stopped because the car needed water. Collins was understanding. 'Sure the car needs a drink, why not the men?' There were other delays to clear obstacles, like felled trees on the road to Clonakilty. Collins helped with the clearing. 'Show me that axe, boy,' he said to one soldier. 'It's not the first time I have used one.'

The group stopped for a meal at Clonakilty, and Collins met some old friends. Afterwards they went on to Rosscarbery and from there to Skibbereen, where Collins and Dalton had a brief exchange with the famous writer, Edith Somerville, before heading back for Cork shortly after 4.30 p.m.

On the return journey Collins talked of his old friends on the Republican side. 'He spoke of Tom Hales with affection tinged with sadness,' Dalton recalled. 'Their broken friendship appeared to have affected him.' He had called on Hales when he visited his brother Johnny on Spike Island during the truce.

'I'd rather have Tom Hales with us than twenty others,' Collins had told a reporter some weeks earlier.

On reaching Sam's Cross, Collins stopped off at the pub of his cousin, Jeremiah Collins. The Big Fellow bought two pints of Clonakilty Wrestler for each of his crew. While there he met his brother, Johnny, and two of his daughters, along with his first cousin, Michael O'Brien. He told them that his main goal was to end the Civil War, and then he would be rededicating himself to the task of securing full national freedom. He was not about to be content with the Treaty settlement but would get further concessions from the British government once peace was restored. He seemed in good form, according to Johnny, but this was probably because his spirits were lifted in the midst of his family and friends, not to mention that he had consumed a fair bit of alcohol that day.

'I hope you are travelling in the armoured car, Mick, because there is still danger around,' Johnny said.

'Not at all, this is my bus,' the Big Fellow replied motioning towards the open touring car.

'Be careful of yourself.'

'You need have no worries about me,' he replied. 'Didn't I elude the Auxies all these years!' The Big Fellow was showing off before his own folk.

He crossed the road for a brief visit to his aunt, Michael O'Brien's mother. The convoy moved on to Bandon and from there back by the same route through Béalnabláth, where the Republicans had been waiting all day. When the convoy had not returned by 7 p.m., the Republicans assumed they either were not coming back that night, or else had taken another route. The ambush was therefore called off. Tom Hales had been reluctant to ambush Collins, but Deasy had insisted. Now Deasy concluded it was pointless waiting any longer.

'From what I know of Collins, he's not going to come back tonight,' Deasy said. 'We'll have another try in the morning.'

Seven men were left to dismantle the mine and clear the road. With the light failing around 7.15 the Free State convoy approached the ambush site.

'We had just reached a part of the road which was commanded by hills on all sides,' Dalton recalled. It was an ideal spot for an ambush. Suddenly they heard gunfire from both in front and behind and a bullet shattered the windscreen of the touring car.

'Drive like hell!' Dalton shouted, but Collins put a hand on the driver's shoulder.

'Stop!' he ordered. 'Jump out and we'll fight them.'

'We leapt from the car and took what cover we could behind a little mud bank on the left side of the road,' Dalton explained. 'We continued this fire for about twenty minutes without suffering any casualties.' There was then a lull in the enemy firing. Collins got to his feet and went over behind the armoured car and used it for cover as he fired some shots.

'Come on boys!' Collins shouted. 'There they are, running up the road.' Dalton noted that Collins left the protection of the car and moved about fifteen yards up the road. He dropped into the prone firing position and opened up on the retreating Republicans.

A few minutes elapsed when Commandant Seán O'Connell came running up the road under fire and threw himself down beside Dalton. 'They have retreated from in front of us and the obstacle is removed,' O'Connell said. 'Where is the Big Fellow?'

'He's all right,' Dalton replied. 'He's gone a few yards up the road.' They could hear Collins shooting. He was standing up on the road firing as if he was daring somebody to shoot him. It seemed an amazingly foolish thing to do. Had the drink dulled his senses, or was he incredibly naive when it came to an ambush situation?

'Next moment,' Dalton continued, 'I caught a faint cry: "Emmet I'm hit."'

Dalton and O'Connell found Collins lying on the road, still clutching his rifle. He had a large gaping wound at the base of the skull behind the right ear. 'It was quite obvious to me with the experience I had of a ricochet bullet, it could only have been a ricochet or a "dum-dum",' Dalton said later.

O'Connell dragged Collins behind the armoured car. 'I bandaged the wound and O'Connell said an "Act of Contrition" to him,' Dalton recalled. 'He was dying if not already dead.' O'Connell later said that Collins rewarded him with a slight pressure of the hand as he said the "Act of Contrition" into his ear.

The body was placed on the armoured car and moved down the road out of danger and it was then transferred to the touring car for the trip to Cork. They asked a local man, Ted Murphy, to guide them to the nearest priest. He got into the tender.

'This is a night that will be remembered,' one of the soldiers remarked.

'Why?' Murphy asked.

'The night Michael Collins was killed.'

'Between 11.00 and 11.15 p.m. there was a knock on the door of my house,' Father Timothy Murphy recalled. 'My housekeeper answered it. She called me and said I was wanted outside. A soldier and a civilian who lived locally were standing at the doorway. The soldier asked me to come outside as there was a soldier shot.'

'It was a dark night and the soldier carried in his hand an old carbide lamp which was giving a very bad light,' he continued. 'I walked out to the roadway where the convoy had stopped. There was a soldier lying flat with his head resting on the lap of a young officer. The young officer was sobbing and crying and did not speak.'

The priest could see they were looking for the last rites for their dead comrade so he turned to go back into the house for the necessaries without saying anything, but the men misinterpreted his gesture. They thought he was refusing Collins the last rites.

'One of my officers raised the rifle to shoot the priest and only that I struck up the barrel the priest would have been shot,' Dalton explained later. 'The bullet was actually discharged.' They then drove off, incensed at what they considered the unchristian behaviour of the priest. This incident left a grim impression on the minds of the entire party.

As with the assassination of President John F. Kennedy over forty years later, the question of who actually shot Michael Collins has become more complicated with the years. Only seven men initially formed the remnants of the ambush party, but they were joined by others during the shooting. At the end of the ambush Liam Deasy came running back.

'Why didn't you blow up that blasted mine?' he demanded.

'The mine was disconnected,' Timmy Sullivan snapped. 'They were your orders.'

'All right!' Deasy acknowledged.

'We got one man,' said Sonny Neill.

They retired to Bill Murray's kitchen for tea.

'Fifteen minutes earlier and the lot would have been wiped out,' one of the men remarked.

At least, Neill said, he 'dropped one man'.

When the men had finished eating, Seán O'Galvin arrived with the news that Michael Collins was shot. Anne White, the priest's housekeeper, had sent word to him.

Sonny Neill grabbed the arm of Bill Power beside him. One of the men jumped up and said 'There's another traitor gone.'

'He's dead,' said Sonny Neill, rising from the table. 'May the Lord have mercy on his soul.' With that he walked out of the house.

In the following years there would be accounts of those who arrived on the scene in the midst of the shooting. One story concerned a group of

Kerrymen, who were heading home through the fields after the defeat in Cork. They were attracted by the shooting near Béalnabláth. 'We saw an army column stopped on the road below,' Michael O'Donoghue from Glenflest recalled. 'Of course we threw ourselves down. The shooting had stopped now. There was a "Whippet" armoured-car at the end of the line and there was a big man like he was standing on top of it looking around. The fellow next to me put up his gun and fired a shot and we saw the big man fall. I hit down the gun.'

'What did you do that for?' O'Donoghue asked. 'Do you want to draw them on us!'

They then got out of the place and did not learn until the following day that the big man was the Big Fellow himself. Father Patrick J. Twohig supports this story with a somewhat contradictory piece of evidence. There was a dance that night in Ballingeary. Pádraig Greene, a teacher from Ballinalee, County Longford, was in the area to attend an Irish course. He was standing with Liam Twomey, a local Republican, when O'Donoghue and the other Kerrymen arrived in the hall.

'What the hell is Mike Donoghue doing here!' exclaimed Twomey, who went over to talk to him, while Greene stayed put.

Moments later Twomey returned with tears in his eyes. 'Michael Collins was shot this evening at Béalnabláth,' Twomey said. 'My mother isn't going to like this!'

Father Twohig further boosts the story with another account by another Kerryman, Robert (Bobs) Doherty from Glenflest. He and another Kerryman, James Sheehan from near Killarney, were making their way home together. They were not part of O'Donoghue's party. They heard the firing over a nearby hill. They each had a rifle and they raced over the hill.

'We dived for cover,' Doherty said, recalling that the grass was still wet from a recent shower. 'There were some men already in position near us, and a little distance away. I didn't know who they were. There was an armed column below us on the road and a big man started to walk away from it. Someone near us fired just then and I saw the big man fall. I heard him say — "I put two into him!" That's all I know.'

It was the early hours of the following morning before news reached army headquarters in Dublin. A telegraph operator handed the message to the adjutant general, Gearóid O'Sullivan. He then went to the bedroom of Emmet Dalton's brother, Charlie. He stood there momentarily silent. 'Charlie,' he said, 'the Big Fella is dead!' With that he broke down and wept uncontrollably.

The IRA man who told de Valera next day was pleased at the news, but the Long Fellow displayed no satisfaction. 'It's come to a very bad pass when Irish men congratulate themselves on the shooting of a man like Michael Collins,' was his reputed reaction.

Richard Mulcahy took over from Collins as commander-in-chief of the government forces. He received an extraordinary letter from Frank Aiken, who would later take over as head of the IRA under rather similar circumstances following the killing of Liam Lynch in action some months later.

'Accept my deepest sympathy for the loss of our old friend Mick,' Aiken wrote on 27 August 1922. 'God rest him! I know you'll acknowledge that I am truly sorry for him even though I have been in arms against him lately.' Aiken went on to observe that it was Collins 'who most of all was responsible for the building up of the strength of the nation'. That same day Austin Stack wrote to McGarrity that Collins 'did great work for Ireland up to the truce — no man more'.

With even his bitterest enemies prepared to acknowledge that he had contributed more to the cause than anybody else, it was probably inevitable that some would have difficulty accepting that one of his own countrymen had killed Collins without even knowing it was him. In time the finger of suspicion would be pointed at others as various conspiracy theories floated around.

Jock McPeake, a Scot, came under suspicion because the machine gun in the armoured car had jammed. Some thought in trying to free it, he might have fired a careless shot and killed Collins accidentally. Later when he defected to the Republican side in an effort to flee the country, he came under suspicion of have deliberately killed the Big Fellow.

Others, knowing that de Valera had been in Béalnabláth on the fateful day, would become suspicious of his role and the whispering began. 'Where was de Valera when Michael Collins was shot?' a Catholic priest asked publicly five years later. 'There was a scowling face at a window, looking out over that lovely valley, and de Valera can tell you who it was,' Canon Cohalan declared.

A local parish priest wrote to *The Cork Examiner* to confirm the canon's insinuations. 'De Valera's presence at Béalnabláth in the early part of the day was a notorious fact witnessed by many persons,' Father P. Treacy wrote. 'In the morning of the day of the murder he was seen superintending the arrangements and about mid-day motored back to Ballyvourney.'

There is no doubt that de Valera was some miles away from Béalnabláth when the ambush took place. He certainly took no direct part and it is most unlikely that he had any input into the ambush, because Deasy had no time for his military views.

Later the conspiracy theories would be taken further with Seán Feehan's suggestion that Emmet Dalton may have killed Collins. Dalton had served in the British army in the First World War, but like many others had joined Collins in the War of Independence. Most of those closest to Collins became disillusioned with the Free State authorities after his death. Dalton resigned from the Free State army as a major general and tried his hands in a number of different ventures in later life. During the Second World War he worked for British intelligence in MI6 and hence the conspiracy theorists jumped to the conclusion that he might have been a British agent all along and that he killed the Big Fellow.

There is no real evidence to support the conspiracy theories. In the last analysis he was probably shot by one of the Republicans who did not even recognise him. It was war and the men on both sides were shooting at the enemy.

13

De Valera Proved
Collins Right

Professor T. Desmond Williams concluded that both de Valera and Collins were partly to blame for the Civil War. 'Collins tried to do too much,' he wrote, 'de Valera too little.'

De Valera did try hard to end the conflict, but he found himself hamstrung by some of his own earlier comments. He admitted that he had been foolish to defend Rory O'Connor's patently undemocratic comments. In late 1921 de Valera was insisting on political control of the IRA, but once he lost power he reversed his position and endorsed the repudiation of the Dáil.

'Rory O'Connor's unfortunate repudiation of the Dáil, which I was so foolish as to defend, even to a straining of my own views in order to avoid the appearance of split, is now the greatest barrier that we have,' de Valera wrote in September 1922. In defending O'Connor, for instance, he said that those in the Four Courts 'would most loyally obey the will of the Irish people freely expressed', but he knew that the overwhelming majority of the people were in favour of the Treaty. Any doubts were clearly removed by the election results of June 1922, yet de Valera still supported those in the Four Courts, who were by then a minority within a minority.

When the third Dáil convened in September 1922 he decided, on grounds of 'principle and expediency', not to take his seat. 'Our presence at the meeting would only solidify all other groups against us,' he wrote. Privately he admitted that the majority of the people clearly supported the Treaty, and hence the Civil War resistance involved 'armed opposition to what is undoubtedly, as I have said, the decision of the majority of the people'. He acknowledged that the Republicans were therefore engaged in 'the repudiation of what they recognise to be the basis of all order in government and the keystone of democracy — majority rule'.

De Valera realised that this was an untenable position, but he had no chance of persuading the Republicans to lay down their arms, because Liam

Lynch refused to call a meeting of the IRA executive. The Civil War became dirtier the longer it continued. Erskine Childers was executed in November 1922 for the possession of a small pistol that Collins gave him. In retaliation the IRA announced that it was going to shoot all members of the Dáil who voted to make the possession of arms a capital offence. Mulcahy had asked the Dáil to pass such a law, because otherwise, he warned, the soldiers would essentially take the law into their own hands and begin killing prisoners.

When two Dáil members were shot on 7 December, the government responded by summarily executing the four most prominent Republican prisoners that it had been holding since the surrender of the Four Courts — Rory O'Connor, Liam Mellows, Dick Barrett, and Joe McKelvey. While there was no doubt that all had forcefully resisted the authority of the Dáil and the Provisional Government, they had never been charged, much less tried or convicted of any offence. By its actions, the government indicated that it would ignore the law and use prisoners as hostages. The military soon followed suit with its own reprisals. There was a series of horrific incidents in Kerry involving the Free State army in March 1923.

On the night of 6 March five Free State troops were killed in Knock-nagoshel. They included two former members of the Squad, Michael Dunne and Edward Stapleton. Some of their former colleagues reacted with ferocity. General Paddy O'Daly ordered that reprisals should be taken. Colonel David Neligan, the Big Fellow's former spy, selected nine Republican prisoners in the jail in Tralee, and they were taken out to Ballyseedy Cross. Captain Ned Breslin, another former member of the Squad, supervised the proceedings as the prisoners were tied together around a pile of stones in which a mine had been placed, and they watched as the men were blown to pieces. One of them was a brother of the woman Breslin would later marry.

By a freak, one prisoner was blown clear and escaped to tell the story, as did another man in a relatively similar incident near Killarney the same day. But the following week Free State troops in Cahirciveen shot each of five prisoners in both legs to make sure that they could not escape, before they were thrown on a pile of stones in which a mine had been placed. They were then blown up. In this instance, one of the Free State soldiers was so revolted by the behaviour of his colleagues that he defected and told the story. The war had degenerated to greater depths of depravity than were ever reached in the Black and Tan period.

Following the death of Liam Lynch in April 1923, de Valera managed to persuade the IRA to call off the fight and dump their arms. From hiding, de Valera issued statements to the press to get his message across to the public. He contended that the people still did not appreciate the real humiliation of the Treaty.

'But,' he declared, 'they soon will. The fate of the North-East boundary clause and the amount of Ireland's share of the Imperial burden will be determined sometime. When it is, and the boundary clause has been waived, or some new ignominious bargain has been struck to evade it, and when, in addition, the full weight of an Imperial contribution of some ten to fifteen millions annually is being pressed upon their shoulders, the people will surely wake up, become conscious of the full extent of the deception that has been practised upon them, and learn what it is that those who gave their lives to prevent the consummation of this "Treaty" hoped to save them from.'

When a general election was called for August 1923, de Valera announced his intention to stand for the Dáil and address a public rally in Ennis. He was promptly arrested at that meeting. 'We have arrested the man who called up anarchy and crime, and who did more damage than anyone could have conceived, or than was ever done by the British,' Minister for Justice Kevin O'Higgins declared. 'Through him, and at his instigation, a number of young blackguards had robbed banks, blown up bridges, and wrecked railways, and that in the name of an Irish Republic.'

The government decided to prosecute him 'with the least possible delay', but the Attorney General was only able to put together a pathetic case. The only 'real evidence' that could be found to substantiate any charge of misconduct during the Civil War was an inflammatory letter de Valera had written to the secretary of Cumann na mBan on 5 January 1923. In view of the enormity of the accusations made against him by members of the government, it would have been utterly ludicrous if he was charged only with inciting Cumann na mBan, of all organisations! Yet the government ordered he should be held indefinitely without trial as a danger to 'public safety'.

Throughout the Civil War many Republicans had looked on de Valera with deep suspicion and distrust, but this was forgotten once he was arrested. He 'was captured just in time to escape oblivion', according to one editorial. He might have faded out in ridicule, had the government treated him 'as a political curiosity', because there were deep divisions in the Republican ranks over his role in calling off the Civil War.

For six months de Valera was held in solitary confinement and only allowed to see an American lawyer in January 1924 after the Free State government sued for control of the money that de Valera had deposited in the United States in 1920. He told the lawyer that he wanted to fight the case 'wholly for propaganda' reasons. 'The vital weakness of the Free State Government was that it knew nothing of the psychology of the people,' he said. 'They are incapable of feeling the nation's pulse. They have no publicity department worth talking of. Any government that desires to hold power in Ireland should put publicity before all.' This would be the secret to how de Valera would eventually rout his political opponents.

The Cumann na nGaedheal government was maintaining that the Boundary Commission, which had been postponed as a result of the Civil

War, would transfer substantial areas of Northern Ireland to the Irish Free State, but following his release from jail in 1924 de Valera privately told his Republican colleagues that the South would get nothing. 'It was meant to fool and could be used at any time to get out of anything on the grounds that the taking away of portions of the Six Counties might be uneconomical,' he noted astutely. He did not explain this publicly because, of course, to have done so would have left himself open to the charge of undermining the Free State's case, and he was keenly aware of the danger of being made a scapegoat for the unfavourable report that he expected from the commission.

'The object of the Free State,' he warned his colleagues, 'was to make it appear that we by our opposition had smashed the possibility of the North coming in. We have to be very careful.'

Henceforth in his speeches attacking the Treaty, he would concentrate on the partition question. He said that he had refused to take his seat in the Dáil because it was a partition parliament, whereas his real reason was, in his own words at the time, 'a matter purely of tactics and expediency'.

After a general election was called in Northern Ireland in the autumn of 1924, de Valera announced Sinn Féin would put forward candidates to allow the Northern people to demonstrate 'their detestation' of partition. He defended the seat he won in South Down in May 1921, but when he went to speak in Newry, he was arrested, served with an exclusion order, and put back over the border. He ignored the order the following day and was again arrested and this time sentenced to a month in jail.

Although Lloyd George had already explained publicly that the phrase in the Treaty stipulating the Boundary Commission would transfer areas in accordance with economic and geographical conditions was included to ensure that isolated nationalist pockets of Belfast and unionist pockets of Dublin would not be transferred, the commission interpreted it differently. It concluded that transferring the contiguous nationalist areas of Northern Ireland to the Irish Free State would render Northern Ireland an unviable economic entity and would thus be contrary to the stipulation that the transfer should be in accordance with economic conditions.

Had Lloyd George deliberately deceived Collins or merely encouraged Collins to deceive himself? Shortly before Lloyd George became Prime Minister in 1916 Prime Minister H. H. Asquith had appointed him to try to settle the Ulster problem. He suggested granting Home Rule to the twenty-six counties at that time. He told John Redmond that partition would only last for the duration of the war, but he wrote to Edward Carson that partition would be permanent whether the unionists of six counties desired it or not. Thus there can be little doubt that, whether Lloyd George deliberately deceived Collins or not, he was not above engaging in such deception.

The Boundary Commission decided to transfer only a few Protestant areas of the twenty-six counties to Northern Ireland and about as much area from the six counties to the South. An agreement was hastily concluded with the British to scrap the commission's findings and leave the border as it stood. In return, the British waived some of the Free State's public debt, but de Valera ridiculed the financial concessions.

When de Valera tried to lead Sinn Féin back into the Dáil, he was blocked because a majority in the party insisted that their abstention had been a matter of principle. In March 1926, therefore, de Valera broke away from Sinn Féin and founded Fianna Fáil in May. When he and his Fianna Fáil colleagues tried to take their seats in the Dáil following the general election in June 1927, they were told they would first have to subscribe their names to a book containing the Treaty oath. They refused and afterwards issued a statement emphasising that 'under no circumstances whatever' would they subscribe to the oath.

They planned, instead, to collect the 75,000 signatures necessary to call a referendum to amend the constitution by abolishing the oath. Collins had insisted on the inclusion of that provision in the constitution as his way of ensuring that the people could get rid of the obnoxious aspects of the Treaty, but now his successors blocked de Valera from using the method. They amended the 1922 constitution by abolishing the referendum provision.

De Valera then did another about-face. Noting that Collins and his successors had described the oath as a meaningless gesture, de Valera announced in August 1927 that Fianna Fáil would put that to the test. He signed his name in the book but proclaimed he had no intention of binding himself to the oath. Once he and his Fianna Fáil colleagues signed, they were allowed to take their Dáil seats.

After the economic depression hit, governments were ousted from office around the world, and the Irish Free State was no different. Fianna Fáil came to power as a minority government, with the help of the Labour Party in 1932. De Valera promised not to victimise his Civil War opponents, or the civil servants who had loyally served the previous government, but many were naturally fearful for their jobs.

Johnny Collins, Michael's oldest brother, was particularly anxious. His first wife had died in 1921 and he married Nancy O'Brien and started a second family after Michael's death. In 1932 he was pretty desperate as he had a young family and had only a temporary civil service job. He made frantic efforts to have his appointment made permanent before the change of government, but he was unsuccessful. In desperation, his wife explained their plight to the wife of a prominent Fianna Fáil politician. A few days later, de Valera sent word that the appointment was being extended for six years and that he could keep the job as long as he was able to do it.

There was subsequently a controversy over blocking supporters of Collins from erecting a large headstone over his grave. But the real issue here was the size of the headstone, which was larger than the specifications allowed for everybody else. Maybe it was small of de Valera not to use his influence to allow the Big Fellow have a bigger headstone than the others, but then there were the families of others also to be considered.

During the 1930s de Valera systematically dismantled the Treaty and thus proved that Collins was right in his assessment that the 1921 agreement could be the stepping-stone to the desired freedom. On coming to power in 1932 de Valera admitted he had underestimated the real significance of the Treaty.

The Dáil passed legislation to abolish the Treaty oath, and the government went on to demand that the British renegotiate the financial settlement that had been postponed during the Treaty negotiations. De Valera contended that the Free State had been needlessly paying land annuities arising out of the land purchase Acts of around the turn of the century. The Government of Ireland Act 1920, which had partitioned Ireland, had specified that the land annuities would be handed over to the respective governments in Dublin and Belfast.

Article 5 of the Treaty had subsequently acknowledged that the Free State would 'assume liability for the service of the public debt of the United Kingdom', but it specified that 'any just claims on the part of Ireland' would be taken into account. The Irish side had not admitted a responsibility to pay any money but merely agreed to consider the question separately and pay, if money was owed. Article 2 of the Boundary Commission agreement of 1925 specifically released the Free State from the obligation under Article 5 of the Treaty.

When de Valera moved to revise the Treaty, however, W. T. Cosgrave and his colleagues secretly encouraged London to resist. In April 1932 Senator John McLoughlin, the leader of the Irish Senate, personally delivered a secret message from Cosgrave to J. H. Thomas, the British Dominions Secretary, encouraging the British to adopt an intransigent attitude. Cosgrave asked for 'a firm and early statement' from the British government. A couple of days later, Donal O'Sullivan, the clerk of the Senate, told Thomas that Cosgrave was anxious for the British to outline the actions they would take if the bill abolishing the oath was passed.

The requested 'firm and early' statement was drafted by the Chancellor of the Exchequer, Neville Chamberlain, approved by the government, and read to parliament by Thomas on 11 May 1932. Britain warned that there would be no further agreements negotiated with the Dublin government if it persisted with the legislation to remove the oath.

De Valera insisted, however, that the oath taken by members of the Irish parliament was strictly an internal Irish matter that was none of Britain's business. Collins had advocated the Treaty as a stepping-stone to the desired freedom, but Cumann na nGaedheal repeatedly invoked the memory of Collins to have people stand by the agreement as if it was an immutable settlement for which he and others had died.

'Those who supported the Treaty in 1922, and those of us who fought to maintain it,' the former Cumann na nGaedheal minister, Fionán Lynch, wrote to the press, 'will consider ourselves traitors — traitors to the memory of Collins and O'Higgins and of the scores of National Army men who gave their lives that the Treaty might be secured for the people of this State — when we desert the cause for which they died and go over to those who were responsible for their deaths.'

De Valera was eager to negotiate on the land annuities question, but the British were reluctant, because they realised he had a good legal case. Neville Chamberlain privately admitted to his colleagues in March 1932 that de Valera had 'an arguable point', on the grounds that the wording of the Boundary Commission agreement absolved the Dublin government 'from liability for the service of the Public Debt of the United Kingdom, and that the Irish annuities form part of the Public Debt'. As a result Chamberlain felt there was 'a certain risk that an arbitrator might hold that Mr de Valera is right from a purely legal and technical point of view, and it would seem most undesirable that we should expose ourselves to such a decision'.

De Valera offered to submit the issue to the international court in The Hague, but the British insisted on the arbitration of a Commonwealth tribunal. He agreed to an international tribunal provided its members were not restricted 'solely to citizens of the States of the British Commonwealth'. The British were unwilling to agree to this.

When the Irish government withheld the land annuities payments in July 1932, the British retaliated immediately by placing tariffs on imports from Ireland, and Dublin responded with tariffs on British imports. This marked the beginning of the Economic War, which was to continue for almost six years.

In January 1933 de Valera called a surprise general election in which Fianna Fáil secured an overall majority, the first in the history of the state. His new government used the stepping-stone approach to whittle away at the Treaty, dismantling the objectionable aspects one by one. Speaking at Arbour Hill on 23 April 1933 de Valera explained he would not willingly assent 'to any form of symbol' incongruous with the country's status as a sovereign nation. 'Let us remove these forms one by one,' he said, 'so that this State that we control may be a Republic in fact and that, when the time comes, the proclaiming of the Republic may involve no more than a ceremony, the formal confirmation of a status already attained.'

In August 1933 he introduced three separate pieces of legislation limiting the country's connections with the British Crown. The first two curtailed the powers of the Governor-General and the other bill abolished the right of appeal to the judicial committee of the Privy Council. In 1934 there were three further pieces of legislation. The Citizens Bill defined Irish citizenship, while the Aliens Bill defined British subjects as aliens in the Irish Free State, and the third bill accorded British subjects the same privileges as Irish citizens while residing in the Free State.

Any lingering confusion about the legality of the unilateral dismantling of the Treaty was eliminated by a ruling of the judicial committee of the British Privy Council. It ruled that 'the Statute of Westminster gave to the Irish Free State a power under which it could abrogate the Treaty'.

During the British abdication crisis of December 1936 when the dominions were asked to pass legislation recognising the abdication of King Edward VIII, de Valera took the opportunity to formalise the real position of the British King in Irish affairs. In addition to the requested legislation recognising the abdication, he also rushed through the External Relations Act, which, he explained, formally eliminated 'the King from all those articles of the Constitution which seem to give him functions here in our internal affairs'. The position of the Crown was being clearly defined in the Irish Free State before the new King's accession to the throne.

As long as the Free State was associated with the dominions and as long as they recognised the British King 'as the symbol of their co-operation' in matters like the appointment of diplomatic representatives, the External Relations Act authorised the Irish government to ask the British King to act on its behalf, but only on the advice of the Irish government. Some thought de Valera should have gone all the way and declared a republic, but he ruled this out for the time being. 'I do not propose to use this situation to declare a republic for the twenty-six counties,' he explained. 'Our people at any time will have their opportunity of doing that. We are putting no barrier of any sort in the way. They can do it, if they want to do it, at any time.'

In 1937 the de Valera government proposed a new constitution, which was ratified by a referendum of the people. The Irish Free State formally became Ireland. The office of Governor-General was abolished and replaced with an elected President as head of state. The country was now a republic in all but name.

Faced with the choice of accepting what had been done, or expelling Ireland from the British Commonwealth, the British announced they were 'prepared to treat the constitution as not affecting a fundamental alteration' in Ireland's position 'as a member of the British Commonwealth of Nations'. The British had in effect accepted that de Valera had remodelled the Commonwealth concept.

There were still a few issues to be resolved from the Treaty, like the ongoing financial dispute and Britain's right to Irish bases. There can be little doubt that de Valera was greatly strengthened by his own enhanced international standing during the 1930s.

Ireland was one of the few countries in Europe with a Roman Catholic majority which remained a democracy. Countries like Italy, Hungary,

Austria, Poland, Spain, and Portugal all succumbed to dictatorships during the interwar years, and the most notorious dictatorship of all, that of Hitler, had its power base in the Roman Catholic state of Bavaria.

Some Irish people genuinely feared that de Valera might try to set up a dictatorship, but it was those who had supported Collins who flirted with fascism under the hysterical leadership of Eoin O'Duffy. As police commissioner in 1932 he had tried to organise a *coup d'état* to prevent de Valera coming to power. In 1933, when de Valera's opponents came together to form Fine Gael, O'Duffy was chosen as the party's first leader, and he proudly advocated the fascist policies of Mussolini, much to the embarrassment of his own party, which quickly replaced him with Cosgrave as leader.

For many people the real proof of Ireland's independence was the way in which de Valera managed to keep the country out of the Second World War. Some have argued that this was at the cost of national self-respect, because he pursued a selfish policy that was blind to standards of international morality, but that assessment ignores the stands that he took in the run-up to the conflict.

De Valera distinguished himself as a vocal critic of international aggression in the 1930s, when he served as president of both the Council and the Assembly of the League of Nations. 'No state should be permitted to jeopardise the common interest by selfish action contrary to the Covenant,' he declared in his opening address to the Assembly in September 1932. He was alluding to Japan's recent invasion of Manchuria.

'This morning Mr de Valera made the best speech I ever heard from a President of the League,' wrote the correspondent of the London *Daily Herald*. 'That is not only my own judgment. It is the opinion of almost every League journalist with whom I have spoken.'

It was not just talk. On 6 December 1932 the Irish representative co-sponsored a resolution that would have compelled the Japanese to halt the invasion. But Britain and France resorted to the disastrous policy of appeasement.

Three years later de Valera was even more forceful in denouncing Italy's plans to invade Abyssinia. 'The final test of the League and all that it stands for has come,' he told the Assembly of the League of Nations on 16 September 1935. 'Our conduct in this crisis will determine whether it is better to let it lapse and disappear and be forgotten.' He indicated that Ireland was prepared to fight the Italians on behalf of the league, if the world body decided to confront them. 'It would be contrary to the spirit of the Covenant' to refuse to take part in any 'collective military actions to be taken by the league', de Valera declared on Radio Éireann on 4 October 1935.

His unequivocal support of the league met with a certain amount of criticism at home, even from within his own party. Kathleen Clarke contended that the government should have used its stand at the league 'for bargaining purposes' in order to extract economic concessions from the British in return for supporting their call for sanctions against Italy.

'If we want justice for ourselves, we ought to stand for justice for others,' de Valera contended. 'As long as I have the honour of representing any government here outside, I stand, on every occasion, for what I think is just and right, thinking thereby I will help the cause of Ireland, and I will not bargain that for anything.'

The British again resorted to appeasement, this time with the support of Winston Churchill and Anthony Eden, who were afraid of antagonising Mussolini. Hence the opportunity to take a proper moral stand was lost. De Valera therefore emphasised that he no longer had any confidence in the league and was determined that Ireland should remain neutral in the inevitable major conflict that would follow.

'Peace is dependent upon the will of great states,' he declared on 2 July 1936. 'All the small states can do, if the statesmen of the greater states fail in their duty, is resolutely to determine that they will not become the tools of any great power, and that they will resist with whatever strength they may possess every attempt to force them into a war against their will.'

De Valera's conduct was the logical consequence of the failure of the great powers to take a moral stand against the aggression of Japan and Italy. His statesmanship at that time stands out in magnificent contrast to that of Churchill and Eden, the men who later made their reputations in opposing the appeasement policy that they had nourished at a crucial juncture.

With the Second World War approaching, the British decided to try to resolve the ongoing difficulties with Ireland. They agreed to end the Economic War and drop their various financial claims in return for a £10 million payment. They also agreed to the complete abrogation of the defence clauses of the Treaty, which afforded the British three permanent bases and the right to any other bases they might desire in time of war. The agreement were ratified, despite the vociferous opposition of Churchill.

During the Second World War, Ireland proclaimed neutrality, but de Valera secretly gave the Allies practically all the help that Ireland could give. He did refuse to hand over bases, but he contended that those bases would be virtually useless, because the shipping lanes around the south of Ireland were too exposed to attack from occupied France. Britain's north Atlantic lifelines went around Northern Ireland, where the Allies already had bases. Eventually the British and Americans decided that bases in the south of Ireland would actually have been a liability.

An enormous amount of secret intelligence co-operation was afforded to the Allies, with de Valera even going so far as to authorise the use of Irish diplomats in Berlin, Rome, and Vichy as spies for the Office of Strategic Services, the American wartime forerunner of the Central Intelligence Agency.

Yet the Allies deliberately sought to discredit de Valera. The Americans requested him to expel the Axis diplomatic and consular representatives and later, before the end of the war, asked for permission for the Allies to seize the German legation in Dublin in order to capture German codes. Those requests were not prompted by security considerations. They were political requests, deliberately worded to provoke refusals, so that the Allies could depict de Valera as having been unhelpful during the conflict and could thereby undermine his potential to secure American public support, if he tried to make an international issue of the partition question after the war.

In 1948 all the other parties in the Dáil and some independents got together to form a national coalition to oust de Valera. One of its principal acts was to pass the Republic of Ireland Act, under which Ireland was formally proclaimed a republic in 1949. But as de Valera had predicted sixteen years earlier, this proclamation involved 'no more than a ceremony, the formal confirmation of a status already attained'.

During his final years in politics, de Valera abandoned his often demagogic approach to the Northern question and emphasised instead what he had recognised as early as 1921, that partition could not — and indeed should not — be ended by force. When the IRA resorted to violence in the 1950s, his government reintroduced internment and quickly undermined the campaign, though it would erupt again during the latter years of his presidency in the late 1960s.

Probably de Valera's greatest political achievement was in getting rid of the gun from twenty-six-county politics. Of course, some will say that he was partly responsible for introducing it in the first place, but that dubious distinction really belongs to Collins. It was he who was determined to provoke an armed conflict in 1919 while de Valera was anxious to take a political path.

De Valera made some monumental blunders in relation to the 1921 Treaty. He probably did more than anybody in the spring of 1922 to rouse the disastrous passions that led to the Civil War, but then he also deserves credit for persuading the Republicans to dump their arms and quit that conflict. He paved the way for the return to normality by refusing to victimise his former Civil War opponents after coming to power in 1932. He systematically dismantled the objectionable aspects of the Treaty and was largely responsible for the 1937 constitution, which proved to be a remarkably durable document, despite some flaws.

In the process the Long Fellow proved that Collins was right about the benefits of the Treaty, that it did provide the freedom to achieve freedom. Of course, in the process he also proved that the British would accept External Association. Would they have done so in 1921, if Collins and company had held out for External Association?

The partition issue was one aspect of the Treaty about which Collins was not right. Had he lived would things have turned out differently? There was little doubt that he was much more determined to force the partition issue than de Valera. 'Collins stands almost alone among the revolutionary leadership of 1917–22 in his genuine and consistent concern for Irish unity and the welfare of the northern nationalists,' Eamon Phoenix concluded. 'His emotional commitment to unity was in sharp contrast to the view of de Valera who by 1921 had effectively acquiesced in the right of the northern unionists to secede from the Irish state.'

After the signing of the Treaty de Valera advocated that the Dáil should accept the clauses on Northern Ireland, which he included verbatim in his own alternative, Document No. 2. But he later exploited the partition issue in a cynical way, pretending that he had opposed the Treaty because of partition. Indeed, he would later harp on the partition issue so much that he would virtually create the illusions that the Treaty was responsible for partition and that it led to the Civil War.

'Of all the major leaders of the independence movement,' Martin Mansergh concluded, 'Collins had the politically most active and militarily most aggressive approach to the North.' His non-recognition policy in education and local government was to prove counter-productive while his involvement in the assassination of Field Marshal Sir Henry Wilson, if true, was the height of recklessness.

The Big Fellow's machinations in regard to Northern Ireland in 1922 raised serious doubts about his credentials as either a statesman or a democrat, and those doubts would not have been alleviated by the subsequent actions of some of his closest colleagues as they protested their commitment to his ideals in later years. There was the barbarous behaviour during the Civil War of Paddy O'Daly and David Neligan in Kerry, where they were primarily responsible for the Ballyseedy massacre. Later Liam Tobin and others close to Collins were responsible for the infamous Army Mutiny of 1924, and Eoin O'Duffy not only toyed with the idea of staging a *coup d'état* in 1932, but later tried to take the country down the path of fascism.

It is pointless to speculate about what would have happened if Collins had lived, whether Ireland would have remained a democracy during the 1930s, or whether the country would have ended up in a sectarian civil war over Northern Ireland.

The manner in which de Valera managed to overcome his earlier mistakes was a testament to his political skills. If one assesses his achievements dispassionately, he stands out as the most accomplished Irish politician in the twentieth century. Maybe Collins would have been even greater, but he did not live long enough, and people cannot be judged by what they might have done.

All too often the struggle between Collins and de Valera is presented in absolute terms, with one being totally right and the other completely wrong. That is a gross oversimplification. There were rights and wrongs on both sides. Each made a monumental contribution in his own way, while their differences were largely the result of their power struggle.

As an unwanted child with a dubious heritage, de Valera developed a craving for position. He had a formative need to be somebody, and hence he desired power so that the position would be meaningful. He clung to office much too long. He only stepped down as President of Ireland in 1973 when he was constitutionally debarred from running for a third term; he was ninety-one years old at the time. He clung until his death in 1975 to his office as chancellor of the National University of Ireland, to which he was appointed in 1921. His fifty-four-year tenure is likely to be a record that will never be equalled, but the assessment of his contribution as chancellor is contained in a short pamphlet.

Collins was probably driven by his father's deathbed declaration that he would one day do great things for Ireland. He desired power in order to achieve goals. He did not require position to gratify any kind of craving for recognition. He worked well with Mulcahy as chief of staff of the IRA and with Griffith as acting President and later as President, and he even stepped down as Chairman of the Provisional Government in favour of Cosgrave in July 1922 in order to devote his full energies to concluding the Civil War.

The legacy of the power struggle between the Long Fellow and the Big Fellow has been the separate existence of Fianna Fáil and Fine Gael, both of which trace their beginnings to their differences over the Treaty, although both parties were founded after the Civil War. Their separate existence is a debilitating reminder of the power struggle between de Valera and Collins. There was little substance to their differences, which both characterised as merely a shadow, but that shadow has been allowed to cloud Irish politics ever since.

Bibliography

Primary Sources
Irish Army Archives, Dublin
Irish Army Records

Marquette University, Milwaukee, Wisconsin
Michael Collins Papers

National Archives, Dublin
Dáil Éireann Papers
Irish Government Papers

National Archives, Washington, D.C.
United States State Department Papers

National Library of Ireland
Joseph Brennan Papers
Daniel F. Cohalan Papers
John Devoy Papers
Frank Gallagher Papers
George Gavan Duffy Papers
John J. Hearn Papers
Thomas Johnson Papers
Patrick McCartan Papers
Joseph McGarrity Papers
Kathleen McKenna Napoli Papers
Art O'Brien Papers
William O'Brien Papers
J. J. O'Connell Papers
James O'Mara Papers
Austin Stack Papers

Private sources
Michael Collins Papers
John M. Feehan Papers
Austin Stack Papers

Public Record Office, Kew, London
British Cabinet Papers

Foreign Office Papers
Dominions Office Papers

Trinity College Dublin, Manuscripts Department
Robert Barton Papers
R. Erskine Childers Papers

University College Dublin Archives
Ernest Blythe Papers
Seán MacEntee Papers
Mary MacSwiney Papers
Richard Mulcahy Papers
Ernie O'Malley Papers
James Ryan Papers

Published Works

Andrew, Christopher, *Secret Service: The Making of the British Intelligence Community*, London, 1965

Andrews, C. S., *Dublin Made Me: An Autobiography*, Cork, 1979

Bailey, Thomas A., *Woodrow Wilson and the Great Betrayal*, New York, 1945

Barry, Tom, *Guerilla Days in Ireland*, Tralee, 1962

_____, *The Reality of the Anglo-Irish War*, Tralee, 1974

Barton, Robert, 'Why Collins Signed', *Sunday Press*, 26 September 1971

Béaslaí, Piaras, 'How it was Done — IRA Intelligence', in The Kerryman, ed., *Dublin's Fighting Story*

_____, *Michael Collins and the Making of the New Ireland*, 2 vols, Dublin, 1926

_____, 'Twenty Got Away', in The Kerryman, ed., *Sworn to be Free*

Beaverbrook, Lord, *The Decline and Fall of Lloyd George*, New York, 1963

Bennett, Richard, *The Black and Tans*, Dublin, 1959

Birkenhead, Frederick, Second Earl of, *F. E. The Life of F. E. Smith, First Earl of Birkenhead*, London, 1960

Boland, Kevin, *Up Dev*, Dublin, 1977

Bowden, Tom, 'Bloody Sunday — A Reappraisal', *European Studies Review,* January 1972

_____, 'The Irish Underground and the War of Independence, 1919–21', *Journal of Contemporary History*, 1973

Bowman, John, *De Valera and the Ulster Question, 1917–1973*, Oxford, 1982

_____, 'De Valera on Ulster, 1919–20: What he told America', *Irish Studies in International Affairs*, 1 (1979):3–18

Bowyer Bell, J., *The Secret Army*, London, 1970

Boyce, D. G., *Englishmen and Irish Troubles: British Public Opinion and the Making of Irish Policy, 1918–1922*, Cambridge, Mass., 1972

Boyle, Andrew, *The Riddle of Erskine Childers*, London, 1977

Breen, Dan, *My Fight for Irish Freedom*, Dublin, 1950

Brennan, Robert, *Allegiance*, Dublin, 1950

Brennan-Whitmore, W. J., *Dublin Burning: The Easter Rising from Behind the Barricades*, Dublin, 1996

_____, *With the Irish in Frongoch*, Dublin, 1917

Bromage, Mary C., *Churchill and Ireland*, Notre Dame, Ind., 1964

_____, *De Valera and the March of a Nation*, Dublin, 1956

Browne, Kevin J., *Eamon de Valera and the Banner County*, Dublin, 1982

Buckland, Patrick, *James Craig: Lord Craigavon*, Dublin, 1980

Buckley, John Patrick, 'The New York Irish', PhD Dissertation, New York
    University, 1974

Callwell, C. E., *Field Marshal Sir Henry Wilson: His Life and Diaries*, 2 vols, London,
    1927

Cameron, Sir Charles, *An Autobiography*, Dublin, 1920

Canning, Paul, *British Policy Towards Ireland 1921–1942*, Oxford, 1985

Carroll, Denis, *They Have Fooled You Again: Michael O'Flanagan (1876–1942),
    Priest, Republican, Social Critic*, Dublin, 1993

Carroll, Francis M., *American Opinion and the Irish Question 1910–1923*, Dublin,
    1978

Carson, William A., *Ulster and the Irish Republic*, Belfast, 1956

Carty, Xavier, *In Bloody Protest: The Tragedy of Patrick Pearse*, Dublin, 1978

Casey, Con, 'The Shooting of Divisional Commander Smyth', in The Kerryman,
    ed., *Rebel Cork's Fighting Story*

Caulfield, Max, *The Easter Rebellion*, London, 1964

Chamberlain, Austen, *Down the Years*, London, 1935

Churchill, Winston S., *The Aftermath*, London, 1929

_____, *Thoughts and Adventures*, London, 1932

Coffey, Thomas M., *Agony at Easter: The 1916 Rising*, London, 1969

Collins, Michael, *Michael Collins in His Own Words*, ed. by Francis Costello, Dublin,
    1997

_____, *The Path to Freedom*, Dublin, 1922

Collins, Stephen, *The Cosgrave Legacy*, Dublin, 1996

Colum, Pádraig, *Arthur Griffith*, Dublin, 1959

Coogan, Tim Pat, *De Valera: Long Fellow, Long Shadow*, London, 1993

_____, *The IRA*, London, 1971

_____, *Ireland Since the Rising*, London, 1966

_____, *Michael Collins: A Biography*, London, 1990

Costello, Francis, *Enduring the Most: The Life and Death of Terence MacSwiney*,
    Dingle, 1995

Cronin, Seán, *Irish Nationalism: A History of Its Roots and Ideology*, Dublin, 1980

_____, *The McGarrity Papers*, Tralee, 1972

_____, *Washington's Irish Policy, 1916–1986*, Dublin, 1987

Crozier, Frank, *Impressions and Recollections*, London, 1930

_____, *Ireland for Ever*, London, 1932

Cruise O'Brien, Conor, *States of Ireland*, London, 1972

Curran, Joseph M., *The Birth of the Irish Free State, 1921–1923*, Alabama, 1980

Dáil Éireann, *Correspondence Relating to Peace Negotiations, June–September, 1921*,
    Dublin, 1921

_____, *Official Report: Debate on the Treaty Between Great Britain and Ireland*,
    Dublin, 1922

_____, *Official Report: for periods 16 August 1921 to 26 August 1921, and 28 February
    1922 to 8 June 1922*, Dublin, n.d

Dalton, Charles, *With the Dublin Brigades, 1917–21*, London, 1929

Dangerfield, George, *The Damnable Question*, London, 1977

Darling, Sir William Y., *So It Looked To Me*, London, 1952

Deasy, Liam, *Brother Against Brother*, Cork, 1982

_____, *Towards Ireland Free: The West Cork Brigade in the War of Independence,
    1917–1921*, Cork, 1973

de Burca, Padraig and John F. Boyle, *Free State or Republic?*, Dublin, 1922

de Valera, Eamon, *The Hundred Best Sayings of Eamon de Valera*, Dublin, 1924

_____, *Ireland's Case Against Conscription*, ed. by Robert Brennan, Dublin and London, 1918

_____, *Ireland's Request to the Government of the United States of America for Recognition as a Sovereign Independent State*, Washington, D.C., 1920

_____, *Quotations from Eamon de Valera*, ed. by Prionsias Mac Aonghusa, Cork, 1983

_____, *Speeches and Statements by Eamon de Valera, 1917–1973*, ed. by Maurice Moynihan, Dublin, 1980

Doherty, Gabriel and Dermot Keogh, eds, *Michael Collins and the Making of the Irish State*, Cork, 1998

Drudy, P. J., ed., *Irish Studies 4: The Irish in America*, Cambridge, 1985

Dudley Edwards, Owen, *Eamon de Valera*, Cardiff, 1987

Dudley Edwards, Ruth, *Patrick Pearse: The Triumph of Failure*, London, 1977

Dwane, David T., *The Early Life of Eamon de Valera*, Dublin, 1922

Dwyer, T. Ryle, *Eamon de Valera*, 2nd ed, Dublin, 1998

_____, *De Valera's Darkest Hour: In the Search for National Independence, 1917–1932*, Cork, 1982

_____, *De Valera's Finest Hour: In the Search for National Independence, 1932–1959*, Cork, 1982

_____, *De Valera: The Man and the Myths*, Dublin, 1993

_____, *Irish Neutrality and the USA, 1939–47*, Dublin, 1977

_____, *Michael Collins and the Treaty*, Cork, 1981

_____, *Michael Collins: 'The Man Who Won the War'*, Cork, 1990

_____, *Strained Relations: Ireland at Peace and the USA at War, 1941–45*, Dublin, 1988

Edmonds, Sean, *The Gun Law and the Irish People*, Tralee, 1971

Ervine, St John, *Craigavon: Ulsterman*, London, 1949

Fallon, Charlotte H., *Soul of Fire: A Biography of Mary MacSwiney*, Cork, 1986

Fanning, Ronan, *The Irish Department of Finance, 1922–1958*, Dublin, 1978

Farragher, Seán P., *Dev and his Alma Mater*, Dublin, 1984

Farrell, Brian, *Chairman or Chief? The Role of the Taoiseach in Irish Government*, Dublin, 1971

Feehan, Seán, *The Shooting of Michael Collins: Murder or Accident?*, Cork, 1981

Figgis, Darrell, *Recollections of the Irish War*, London, 1927

FitzGerald, Desmond, *The Memoirs of Desmond FitzGerald*, London, 1968

_____, Review of *Peace by Ordeal*, *The Observer*, 16 June 1935

FitzGerald, William G., ed., *The Voice of Ireland*, London, 1924

Forester, Margery, *Michael Collins: The Lost Leader*, London, 1971

Gallagher, Frank, *The Anglo-Irish Treaty*, ed. by T. P. O'Neill, London, 1965

_____, *Four Glorious Years*, Dublin, 1951

Garvin, Tom, 'Dev and Mick — 1922 Split as Social Psychological Event', in Gabriel Doherty and Dermot Keogh, eds, *Michael Collins and the Making of the Irish State*, Cork, 1998

Gaughan, J. Anthony, *Austin Stack: Portrait of a Separatist*, Dublin, 1977

_____, *The Memoirs of Constable Jeremiah Mee, RIC*, Dublin, 1975

_____, *Thomas Johnson*, Dublin, 1980

Gilbert, Martin, *Winston S. Churchill, 1916–22*, London, 1975

Gleeson, James, *Bloody Sunday*, London, 1962

Golden, Peter, *Impressions of Ireland*, New York, 1923

Golding, G. M., *George Gavan Duffy, 1882–1951*, Dublin, 1982

Good, Joe, *Enchanted by Dreams: The Journal of a Revolutionary*, Dingle, 1996

Griffith, Kenneth, and Timothy E. O'Grady, eds., *Curious Journey: An Oral History of Ireland's Unfinished Revolution*, London, 1982

Gunther, John, 'Inside de Valera', *Harper's Magazine*, 176 (August 1936):310–17

Gwynn, Denis, *De Valera*, London, 1933

Hancock, W. K., *Survey of British Commonwealth Affairs: Problems of Nationality, 1918–1936*, London, 1937

Harkness, David, 'Mr de Valera's Dominion', *Journal of Commonwealth Political Studies*, 8:206–27

Harrington, Niall C., *Kerry Landing*, Dublin, 1992

Hart, Peter, *The IRA and Its Enemies: Violence and Community in Cork, 1916–1923*, Oxford University Press, 1998

Hawkins, F. M. A., 'Defence and the Role of Erskine Childers in the Treaty Negotiations of 1921', *Irish Historical Studies*, 11:250–70

Hayes, Michael, 'Dáil Éireann and the Irish Civil War', *Studies*, Spring 1969

Healy, T. M., *Letters and Leaders of My Day*, London, n.d

Holt, Edgar, *Protest in Arms: The Irish Troubles, 1916–1923*, New York, 1961

Hone, Joseph, *W. B. Yeats*, London, 1942

Hopkinson, Michael, *Green Against Green: The Irish Civil War*, Dublin, 1988

I.O., *see under* Street, C. J. C

James, Robert Rhodes, *Churchill: A Study in Failure, 1900–1939*, London, 1970

Jones, Thomas, *Lloyd George*, London, 1951

_____, *Whitehall Diary: Volume 3: Ireland, 1918–1925*, ed. by Keith Middlemas, London, 1971

Jordan, Neil, *Michael Collins: Screen Play and Film Diary*, London, 1996

Kavanagh, Seán, 'The Irish Volunteers Intelligence Organisation', *Capuchin Annual*, 1969

Kee, Robert, *Ireland: A History*, London, 1981

_____, *The Green Flag*, London, 1972

Kelly, Bill, 'Escape of de Valera', in The Kerryman, ed., *Sworn to be Free*

Keogh, Dermot, *Ireland and Europe, 1919–1948*, Dublin, 1988

_____, *The Vatican, the Bishops and Irish Politics*, Cambridge, 1986

Kerryman, The, ed., *Dublin's Fighting Story, 1916–1921*, Tralee, n.d

_____, *Rebel Cork's Fighting Story*, Tralee, n.d

_____, *Sworn to be Free: The Complete Book of IRA Jailbreaks, 1918–1921*, Tralee, 1971

Lavelle, Patricia, *James O'Mara*, Dublin, 1961

Lawlor, Sheila, *Britain and Ireland, 1914–23*, Dublin, 1983

Lee, Joseph, and Gearóid Ó Tuathaigh, *The Age of de Valera*, Dublin, 1982

Lee, J. J., *Ireland, 1912–1985*, Cambridge, 1989

Litton, Helen, *The Irish Civil War: An Illustrated History*, Dublin, 1995

Lloyd George, David, *Where Are We Going?*, New York, 1923

Lloyd George, Richard, *Lloyd George*, London, 1960

Longford, Earl of, and Thomas P. O'Neill, *Eamon de Valera*, Dublin, 1970

Longford, Lord, *Peace by Ordeal*, rev. ed., London, 1962

Lynch, Diarmuid, *The IRB and the 1916 Insurrection*, ed. by Florence O'Donoghue, Cork, 1957

Lyons, F. S. L., *Ireland Since the Famine*, rev. ed., London, 1973

Mac Aonghusa, Proinsias, *Eamon de Valera: Na Blianta Réabhlóideacha*, Dublin, 1982

Macardle, Dorothy, *The Irish Republic*, Dublin, 1937

_____, *Tragedies of Kerry, 1922–23*, Dublin, 1924

McCartan, Patrick, *With de Valera in America*, Dublin, 1932

McCartney, Donal, 'De Valera in the United States', in Art Cosgrove and Donal McCartney, eds, *Studies in Irish History Presented to R. Dudley Edwards*, Dublin 1979

_____, *The National University of Ireland and Eamon de Valera*, Dublin, 1983

McColgan, John, *British Policy and the Irish Administration, 1920–22*, London, 1983

_____, 'Implementing the 1921 Treaty: Lionel Curtis and Constitutional Procedure', *Irish Historical Studies*, March 1977

McCoole, Sinéad, *Hazel: A Life of Lady Lavery, 1880–1935*, Dublin, 1996

McCormick, Donald, *The Mask of Merlin: A Critical Study of Lloyd George*, London, 1963

MacCracken, J. L., *Representative Government in Ireland: A Study of Dáil Éireann, 1919–1948*, London, 1958

McDowell, R. B., *The Irish Convention, 1917–18*, Dublin, 1970

MacDowell, Vincent, *Michael Collins and The Brotherhood*, Dublin, 1997

Mac Eoin, Uinseann, ed., *Survivors*, Dublin, 1980

McGarry, Seán, 'Michael Collins', in The Kerryman, ed., *Dublin's Fighting Story*

McInerney, Michael, 'Gerry Boland's Story', *The Irish Times*, 8–19 October 1968

_____, 'James Ryan', *The Irish Times*, 15–17 March 1967

_____, 'Seán MacEntee', *The Irish Times*, 22–25 July 1974

Mackay, James, *Michael Collins: A Life*, Edinburgh, 1996

McKenna Napoli, Kathleen, 'In London with the Treaty Delegates', *Capuchin Annual*, 1971

McMahon, Deirdre, *Republicans and Imperialists: Anglo-Irish Relations in the 1930s*, London, 1984

_____, 'Michael Collins: His Biographers, Piaras Béaslaí and Rex Taylor', in Gabriel Doherty and Dermot Keogh, eds, *Michael Collins and the Making of the Irish State*, Cork, 1998

MacManus, M. J., *Eamon de Valera*, Dublin, 1944

Macready, General Sir Nevil, *Annals of an Active Life*, 2 vols, London, 1924

Mansergh, Martin, 'The Freedom to Achieve Freedom?', in Gabriel Doherty and Dermot Keogh, eds, *Michael Collins and the Making of the Irish State*, Cork, 1998

Mansergh, Nicholas, *The Commonweath Experience*, 2 vols, London, 1982

Martin, Francis X., ed., *Leaders and Men of the Easter Rising: Dublin 1916*, Ithaca, N.Y., 1967

Midleton, Earl of, *Ireland: Dupe or Heroine*, London, 1932

_____, *Records and Reactions, 1856–1939*, London, 1939

Mills, Michael, 'Seán Lemass Looks Back', *Irish Press*, 20 January–6 February 1969

Mitchell, Arthur, *Revolutionary Government in Ireland: Dáil Éireann 1919–22*, Dublin, 1995

Moody, T. W., ed., *Nationality and the Pursuit of National Independence*, Dublin, 1980

Morgan, Austen, *Labour and Partition: The Belfast Working Class, 1905–23*, London, 1991

Mowat, Charles L., *Britain Between the Wars, 1918–1940*, Chicago, 1955

Moynihan, Maurice, *see under* de Valera, Eamon

Mulcahy, Richard, 'Chief of Staff, 1919', *Capuchin Annual*, 1969

_____, 'Conscription and the General Headquarters Staff', *Capuchin Annual*, 1968

_____, 'The Irish Volunteer Convention, 27 October 1917', *Capuchin Annual*, 1967

Mullins, Billy, *The Memoirs of Billy Mullins*, Tralee, 1983

Murdoch, R., 'Robert Barton', *Sunday Press*, 26 September–3 October 1971

Murphy, Donie, *The Men of the South in the War of Independence*, Newmarket, Co. Cork, 1991

Neeson, Eoin, *The Civil War in Ireland, 1922–1923*, Cork, 1966

_____, *The Life and Death of Michael Collins*, Cork, 1968

Neligan, David, *The Spy in the Castle*, Dublin, 1968

Nicolson, Harold, *King George V*, London, 1952

Nunan, Seán, 'President de Valera's Mission to the USA, 1919–20', *Capuchin Annual*, 1970

O'Brien, William, *Forth the Banners Go*, Dublin, 1969

_____, *The Irish Revolution and How It Came About*, London, 1923

O'Brien, William and Desmond Ryan, *Devoy's Post Bag, 1871–1928*, Dublin, 1953

Ó Broin, León, 'Joseph Brennan, Civil Servant Extraordinary', *Studies*, Spring 1977

_____,ed., *In Great Haste: The Letters of Michael Collins and Kitty Kiernan*, Dublin, 1983

_____, *Michael Collins*, Dublin, 1980

_____, *Revolutionary Underground: The Story of the Irish Republican Brotherhood, 1858–1924*, Dublin, 1976

_____, *W. E. Wylie and the Irish Revolution*, Dublin, 1989

O'Carroll, J. P., and John A. Murphy, eds, *De Valera and His Times*, Cork, 1983

O'Connor, Batt, *With Michael Collins in the Fight for Irish Independence*, London, 1929

O'Connor, Frank, *The Big Fellow*, rev. ed., Dublin, 1979

_____, *A Book of Ireland*, London, 1959

_____, *My Father's Son*, Dublin, 1966

O'Connor, Joseph, 'Boland's Mills Area', *Capuchin Annual*, 1966

O'Connor, Ulick, *Oliver St John Gogarty*, London, 1964

_____, *A Terrible Beauty*, London, 1975

Ó Cuinneagáin, Mícheál, *On the Arm of Time: Ireland, 1916–22*, Tanatallon, Co. Donegal, 1993

Ó Dochartaigh, Tomás, *Cathal Brugha*, Dublin, 1969

O'Doherty, Katherine, *Assignment America*, New York, 1957

O'Donoghue, Florence, *No Other Law*, Dublin, 1954

_____, *Tomás MacCurtain: Soldier and Patriot*, Tralee, 1971

O'Donovan, Donal, *Kevin Barry and His Time*, Dublin, 1989

O'Faolain, Sean, *De Valera*, London, 1939

_____, *The Life Story of Eamon de Valera*, Dublin, 1933

O'Farrell, Padraic, *The Seán MacEoin Story*, Cork, 1981

_____, *The Ernie O'Malley Story*, Cork, 1983

O'Halloran, Clare, *Partition and the Limits of Irish Nationalism*, Dublin, 1987

O'Halpin, Eunan, 'British Intelligence in Ireland, 1914–21', in Christopher Andrew and David Dilke, eds, *The Missing Dimension: Governments and Intelligence Communities in the Twentieth Century*, London, 1984

_____, 'Collins and Intelligence', in Gabriel Doherty and Dermot Keogh, eds, *Michael Collins and the Making of the Irish State*, Cork, 1998

O'Hegarty, P. S., *A History of Ireland Under the Union, 1801–1923*, London, 1952

_____, *The Victory of Sinn Féin*, Dublin, 1924

O'Kelly, Seán T., 'Memoirs', *Irish Press*, July 1961

Ó Luing, Seán, *Art Ó Griofa*, Dublin, 1953

_____, *I Die in a Good Cause*, Tralee, 1970

O'Mahony, Seán, *Frongoch: University of Revolution*, Dublin, 1987

O'Malley, Ernie, *On Another Man's Wound*, Dublin, 1936
_____, *The Singing Flame*, Dublin, 1978
Ó Muirthile, Seán, 'Memoirs', MS in Mulcahy Papers
O'Neill, Marie, *From Parnell to de Valera: A Biography of Jennie Wyse Power, 1858–1941*, Dublin, 1991
Ó Néill, Tomás, and Ó Fiannachta, Pádraig, *De Valera*, 2 vols, Dublin, 1968–70
O'Neill, Thomas P., 'In Search of a Political Path: Irish Republicanism, 1922–1927', *Historical Studies*, 10:147–171
O'Reilly, Michael W., 'Prison Incidents', *Capuchin Annual*, 1967
O'Sullivan, 'The Despatch Childers Censored', *The Irish Times*, 22 June 1976
O'Sullivan, Donal, *The Irish Free State and Its Senate*, London, 1940
O'Sullivan, Michael, *Seán Lemass: A Biography*, Dublin, 1994
Owens, Frank, *Tempestuous Journey: Lloyd George — His Life and Times*, New York, 1955
Pakenham, Frank, *see under* Longford, Earl of
Pearse, Mary Brigid, *The Home Life of Patrick Pearse*, Cork, 1979
Pearse, Pádraic, *The Political Writings and Speeches of Patrick Pearse*, ed. by Desmond Ryan, Dublin, 1966
Phillips, W. Allison, *The Revolution in Ireland, 1906–1923*, London, 1926
Phoenix, Eamon, 'Michael Collins: The Northern Question, 1916–1922', in Gabriel Doherty and Dermot Keogh, eds, *Michael Collins and the Making of the Irish State*, Cork, 1998
Riddell, Lord, *Lord Riddell's Intimate Diary of the Peace Conference and After 1918–1923*, London, 1933
Robinson, Lennox, ed., *Lady Gregory's Journal*, London, 1976
Roskill, Stephen, *Hankey: Man of Secrets*, 2 vols, London, 1970–74
Rumpf, E., and A. C. Hepburn, *Nationalism and Socialism in Twentieth-Century Ireland*, Liverpool, 1977
Ryan, Desmond, *The Phoenix Flame*, London, 1937
_____, *Remembering Sion*, London, 1934
_____, *The Rising: The Complete Story of Easter Week*, Dublin, 1949
_____, *Unique Dictator: A Study of Eamon de Valera*, London, 1936
Ryan, Meda, *The Day Michael Collins was Shot*, Dublin, 1989
_____, *Michael Collins and the Women in His Life*, Cork, 1996
Salvidge, Stanley, *Salvidge of Liverpool*, London, 1934
Sceilg [J. J. O'Kelly], *The National Outlook*, Dublin, n.d
_____, *Stepping Stones*, Dublin, n.d
Scott, C. P., *The Political Diaries of C. P. Scott, 1911–1928*, ed. by Trevor Wilson, London, 1970
Severn, Bill, *Irish Statesman and Rebel: The Two Lives of Eamon de Valera*, Folkstone, 1971
Shakespeare, Sir Geoffrey, *Let Candles Be Brought In*, London, 1949
Smuts, J. C., *Selections from Smuts' Papers*, Vol. 5, ed. by Keith Hancock, London, 1973
Snoddy, Oliver, 'National Aid, 1916–1917–1918', *Capuchin Annual*, 1968
Stevenson, Frances, *Lloyd George: A Diary by Frances Stevenson*, ed. by A. J. P. Taylor, London, 1971
Stewart, A. T. Q., *Edward Carson*, Dublin, 1981
_____, ed., *Michael Collins: The Secret File*, Belfast, 1997
Street, C. J. C, *Administration in Ireland, 1920*, London, 1922
_____, *Ireland in 1921*, London, 1922

Talbot, Hayden, *Michael Collins' Own Story*, London, 1923

Tansill, Charles Callan, *America and the Fight for Irish Freedom, 1866–1922*, New York, 1957

Taylor, Rex, *Michael Collins*, London, 1958

Tierney, 'Calendar of Irlande', *Collectanea Hibernica*, Nos. 21–3

The Times, *History of The Times: The 150th Anniversary and Beyond, 1912–1948*, New York, 1952

Towey, Thomas, 'The Reaction of the British Government to the 1922 Collins– de Valera Pact', *Irish Historical Studies*, 22:65–76

Townsend, Charles, 'Bloody Sunday: Michael Collins Speaks', *European Studies Review*, 1979

_____, *The British Campaign in Ireland, 1919–21: The Development of Political and Military Policies*, London, 1975

_____, 'The Irish Republican Army and the Development of Guerilla Warfare, 1916–1921', *English Historical Review*, 94:318–45

_____, *Political Violence in Ireland*, Dublin, 1983

Twohig, Patrick J., *The Dark Shadow of Béalnabláth*, Cork, 1991

_____, *Green Tears for Hecuba*, Cork, 1994

Valiulis, Maryann Gialanella, *Portrait of a Revolutionary: General Richard Mulcahy and the Founding of the Irish Free State*, Dublin, 1992

Walsh, J. J., *Recollections of a Rebel*, Tralee, 1944

Ward, Alan J., *Ireland and Anglo-American Relations, 1899–1921*, London, 1969

West, Nigel, *MI5: British Security Service Operation, 1900–1945*, London, 1981

White, Terence de Vere, *Kevin O'Higgins*, Tralee, 1966

Whyte, J. H., *Church and State in Modern Ireland, 1922–1979*, Dublin, 1980

Williams, T. Desmond, ed., *The Irish Struggle*, London, 1966

Wilson, Trevor, *The Downfall of the Liberal Party, 1914–1936*, Ithaca, 1966

Winter, Ormonde, *Winter's Tale*, London, 1955

Young, Peter, 'Michael Collins: A Military Leader', in Gabriel Doherty and Dermot Keogh, eds, *Michael Collins and the Making of the Irish State*, Cork, 1998

Younger, Calton, *Ireland's Civil War*, London, 1968

_____, *A State of Disunion*, London, 1972

Contemporary Newspapers and Periodicals

Baltimore Sun
Blackwood's Magazine
Boston American
Boston Herald
Chicago Daily Tribune
Christian Science Monitor
The Cork Examiner
Éire
Evening Echo (Cork)
Evening Herald
Evening Telegraph
The Free State
Freeman's Journal
Gaelic American
Irish Independent
Irish Press (Philadelphia)

The Irish Times
Irish World
Kerryman
Leader (San Francisco)
The Liberator (Tralee)
Manchester Guardian
Milwaukee Journal
The Nation
New York American
New York Evening Post
New York Globe
New York Times
New York World
Nineteenth Century and After
The Observer (London)
Philadelphia Public Ledger
Poblacht na h-Éireann
San Francisco Chronicle
The Times (London)

Index